Eduard Vehse

Memoirs of the court and aristocracy of Austria

Vol. 1

Eduard Vehse

Memoirs of the court and aristocracy of Austria
Vol. 1

ISBN/EAN: 9783337104276

Printed in Europe, USA, Canada, Australia, Japan

Cover: Foto ©Andreas Hilbeck / pixelio.de

More available books at **www.hansebooks.com**

MEMOIRS
OF THE
COURT AND ARISTOCRACY
OF
AUSTRIA

Edition strictly limited to 500 copies.

Five extra copies have been printed on Japanese vellum, but are not offered for sale.

Charles V

*From the Original by Holbein in the Private
Collection of the King of the French.*

MEMOIRS

OF THE

COURT AND ARISTOCRACY

OF

AUSTRIA

BY

Dr. E. VEHSE

TRANSLATED FROM THE GERMAN
BY
FRANZ DEMMLER

IN TWO VOLUMES—VOLUME I

LONDON

H. S. NICHOLS

3 SOHO SQUARE AND 62ᴬ PICCADILLY W.

MDCCCXCVI

Printed and Published by
H. S. NICHOLS,
AT 3 SOHO SQUARE, LONDON, W.

PUBLISHER'S NOTE

THIS issue of the Court Memoir Series is the "Memoirs of the Court of Austria." The original work was written by Dr. E. Vehse, a German historian, and translated into English by Franz Demmler.

Charles Edward Vehse was born on the 18th of December, 1802, at Freiberg, and studied law at Leipzig and Göttingen; in 1825 he obtained a post in the Dresden State Archives, or Record Office; in 1838 he went to America, and the year following returned to Germany, and after other travels settled in Berlin in 1843, thence removed to Switzerland, lived from 1857-1862 in Italy, and finally in Saxony, where he died on the 18th of June, 1870. His principal work is the "History of German Courts after the Reformation" (48 vols.) He also, among many other works, wrote "Shakespeare as Protestant, Politician, Poet and Psychologist."

The translation from which this issue is reprinted was originally issued in 1856, and this edition has been considerably revised and many notes have been added.

A Supplement also has been annexed continuing the history of Austria from the death of Francis II. to the year 1888.

LONDON, *March* 30*th*, 1896.

PREFACE

The "Memoirs of the Court of Austria" are the English version of the corresponding part of the series published by Dr. E. Vehse under the title of "History of the German Courts since the Reformation." The author, in speaking of the character which he wished to impart to his work, quotes the saying of Horace Walpole : "I am no historian; I draw characters, I preserve anecdotes, which my superiors, the historians, may enchase into their weighty annals, or pass over at their pleasure." Whilst, however, protesting against the pedantry of the learned writers of history, who, notwithstanding their profound erudition, only too frequently fall into the traps of those *fables convenues* with which their path is beset on all sides, he lays claim to the merit of having studiously drawn, not from the books of theoretical historians, but from those sources which men experienced in the ways of the world and in the conduct of affairs have left to us. "Writing," he continues, " for Germans (who are so very particular concerning literary authorities) I used the caution of giving from those sources the *verba ipsissima* of contemporaneous narratives. If a writer does that, and if it is acknowledged on all sides that he has written conscientiously and impartially, he ought not to be expected to quote for every little fact the source or book from which he may have taken it. He who does not falsify history in its great features will surely not invent the lesser ones ; and he may fairly be supposed to have taken the latter from hundreds and hundreds of books which he read for his purpose, and many a one of which did not yield him more than perhaps one little item. If it were requisite to make a display of my preparatory studies (during twelve years), I might furnish a list of books, the titles of which would rather surprise even very great men of the republic of letters. I was always quite satisfied only to find some small trait; but how many were the books which I had to read without any remunerating result whatever!"

The principal authorities are mentioned occasionally throughout the book. It will not however be deemed out of place here to say a few words on three of the writers whom Dr. Vehse has most frequently quoted. The following notices are taken from various parts of the work.

Count Francis Christopher Khevenhüller, born in 1589, was since 1616, for an aggregate period of fourteen years, under three Emperors, Matthias, Ferdinand II., and Ferdinand III., ambassador ordinary and extraordinary at Madrid. There he was made a knight of the Golden Fleece. He had likewise some diplomatic missions to Florence, Turin, and Mantua; to the court of Paris; to Archduke Albert at Brussels; to the courts of the three spiritual Electors; and to Munich. Khevenhüller was one of the first gallants at court, but withal one of the most learned nobles and most able men of business in the whole monarchy. Like Sir Christopher Hatton, he was celebrated for his skill in dancing, and, moreover, for his horsemanship. Much greater fame, however, was gained for him by the records of his life so rich in experience. His *Annales Ferdinandei* are the most important of all German works of history from the Reformation down to Frederic the Great. He published them after his return from Spain, in 1640-1646, at Ratisbon, in an edition of not more than forty copies, intended for "great lords," among whom they were distributed. It is a work similar to that which De Thou wrote for France—a contemporaneous history of all the European states, in which he himself had been an important actor. The work had been calculated to fill twelve folios, of which nine only were published at the time. When his heirs wished to publish a new and complete edition, permission was refused by Leopold I.; in 1721 Charles VI. at last granted it. The Annals comprise the period from the birth of Ferdinand II., in 1578, to his death in 1637. They contain the most varied and important state papers, resolutions, despatches, relations, and such like.[1]

Elizabeth Charlotte Duchess of Orleans, born in 1652, was the daughter of Charles Louis, Elector Palatine, and granddaughter of the " Winter King " of Bohemia. Having married, in 1671, the Duke of Orleans, brother of Louis XIV., she became a widow in 1701, and died, in 1722, as the mother of the notorious Regent. Although unfortunately ugly, she kept her own at the French court by her strong sense and by her powers of mind; even Louis XIV. did not disdain to consult her, not only in affairs of the royal family, but also in those of the state. Her father lived in morganatic marriage—in his case a specious term for bigamy—with a Countess Degenfeldt. Most of the letters of the Duchess were written to a half-sister of hers by that morganatic union, and the correspondence passed to the family archives of the Counts Degenfeldt at Eibach in Würtemberg, from which it was published by Wolfgang Menzel. The collection, as far as printed until now (1853), comprises the correspondence with that half-sister Louisa, and with Caroline of Anspach, the Queen of George II. The letters are most remarkable for their plain-spoken *naïveté*, and for the unconcern with which the writer does not shrink from telling *everything*. The most hidden secrets of the German courts (and also of the court of William III. of England) are laid bare in them.

Joseph von Hormayr, born in 1782 in the Tyrol, was descended from an ancient Tyrolese family, which became extinct at his death. He was an extraordinary character from a child, and he published his first book at the age of twelve. His memory was truly wonderful, such as has been possessed only by a very few learned men, by Julius Scaliger or Pico de Mirandola. He would, for instance, repeat in order the names of a collection of 9,000 portraits in the possession of his father; he knew by heart some hundreds of dramas and ten or twelve thousand verses from the classics of all nations; he, moreover, was able to recite the first three books of the Æneid, not only straight on, but also backwards. With equal facility he

[1] Count Khevenhüller died in 1650, at Baden near Vienna, as governor of Croatia.

retained names, dates and numbers; he had a very keen eye in discerning handwritings and physiognomies, and after any length of time he would most accurately recognise and identify them again. Having entered the Austrian public service in 1797, he became, in 1803, director of the imperial family and state archives, which post he held upwards of twenty-five years. In 1828 King Louis of Bavaria called him into his service. In 1832 he became Bavarian minister at Hanover, then at Bremen; after which he returned to Munich as director of the archives and councillor of state. He lived to see the outbreak of the Revolution of 1848, in which year he died. Hormayr, besides his eminent natural talents, had the advantage of his position as keeper of the Vienna archives—perhaps the richest in the world—and moreover of his personal and intimate acquaintance with the most distinguished persons of the highest society in the imperial capital. His views of the duties of the historian he laid down when answering the reproach of indiscretion which was made to him, by quoting the saying of Cicero: " *Prima historiæ lex est, ne quid falsi dicere audeat, ne quid veri non audeat.*" Even Count Mailath, Hormayr's most bitter opponent, is obliged himself to confirm many of his statements.

F. D.

March 15th, 1856.

CONTENTS OF VOL. I

CHAPTER I

MAXIMILIAN I.—(1493-1519).

	PAGE
1.—His parentage and character—The "Felix Austria Nube"	1
2.—The Emperor Maximilian's family	24

CHAPTER II

CHARLES V.—(1519-1556).

1.—His youth and education in the Netherlands	30
2.—Accession in the Netherlands and in Spain, and election as Emperor	39
3.—The French wars—Battle of Pavia—Assault of Rome—Challenge between Charles and Francis I.—Siege of Vienna by the Turks in 1529	45
4.—The Sickingen Feud and the Peasants' War	65
5.—The Diet of Augsburg, and the French wars to the Peace of Crespy, 1544	83
6.—The Smalcalde war—Battle of Mühlberg	97
7.—Maurice's expedition against Charles	114
8.—Resignation of Charles V.—His death in Spain	147
9.—Personal notices of Charles V.	154
10.—The family of Charles V.	171

CHAPTER III

FERDINAND I.—(1556-1564).

1.—Personal notice of the Emperor	176
2.—Position of the nobility under Ferdinand I. in Austria—The first Protestant "chain of the nobles"	179
3.—Ferdinand's family—Philippina Welser and her children	186

CHAPTER IV

MAXIMILIAN II.—(1564-1576).

1.—Personal notices of the Emperor	193
2.—State of religion—The army—The Austrian nobility is made, by the matriculation of 1572, a close corporation	195
3.—The family of the Emperor Maximilian II.	201

CHAPTER V

RODOLPH II.—(1576-1612).

	PAGE
1.—His court at Prague—His antiquarian, alchemical, and magic hobbies	204
2.—The Italians at the imperial court—First beginnings of military rule—The first camarilla of clerks and valets	213
3.—Reformation and counter-reformation in Austria	220
4.—State of Hungary—The Bohemian "Royal Letter"—Rupture with Matthias—Deposition of Rodolph—Latter days and death of Rodolph II.	228
5.—Rodolph's natural children	235

CHAPTER VI

MATTHIAS—(1612-1619).

1.—Personal notices of the Emperor 237
2.—The Thirty Years' War—"Defenestratio Pragensis"—Characteristics of the actors in it 240
3.—Downfall of Cardinal Clesel—Death of Matthias . . 246

CHAPTER VII

FERDINAND II.—(1619-1637).

1.—Personal notices of the Emperor—The three *steins* (stones), the three *bergs* (mounts), and the *dorf* (thorp) . . 252
2.—Count Thurn before Vienna—"Nandy," Thonradl, and Dampierre's cuirassiers in the Hofburg—Election of Ferdinand as Emperor of the Romans, and of the Elector Palatine Frederic as King of Bohemia 260
3.—Frederic's hopeless situation at Prague—The Bohemian aristocracy, and Calvinist outrages 267
4.—The expedition of Tilly and of the Duke of Bavaria to Bohemia—The battle of the White Mountain, and the executions in the Ring at Prague 273
5.—The new Catholic aristocracy of Austria, and the great creation of Counts and Princes 292
6.—The Protestant partisans, Mansfeld, Brunswick, &c. . 294
7.—Wallenstein and his plans for the establishment of the absolute sovereignty of the Emperor 300
8.—Gustavus Adolphus of Sweden and the battles of Breitenfeld and Lützen—Wallenstein generalissimo "in absolutissimâ formâ" . 321
9.—Wallenstein's downfall—Rewards bestowed on his betrayers and murderers—Piccolomini, Aldringer, Colloredo, Butler, Leslie, &c. 352
10.—Duke Bernard of Weimar 378
11.—Death of Ferdinand II.—His family . . 385

CHAPTER VIII

FERDINAND III.—(1637-1657).

1.—Personal notices of the Emperor—The premier Maximilian von Trautmannsdorf 388
2.—The last period of the Thirty Years' War, and the last Papist generals of the Emperor, Gallas and Piccolomini—The last Protestant generals of the Emperor, Holk, Götz, and Melander—Holzapfel—Austrian plans for seducing the Hessian and Bavarian armies—Baner's and Torstensohn's campaigns . 390
3.—The peace of Westphalia and the new position of the imperial court with regard to the German princes and to the aristocracy in the Austrian dominions 408
4.—Diet of Ratisbon—Death of Ferdinand III.—His family . . 417

CHAPTER IX

LEOPOLD I.—(1657-1705).

1.—The election of the Emperor at Frankfort 420
2.—Leopold's ministers: Portia, Auersperg, Lobkowitz, Montecuculi, Sinzendorf, Lamberg, Schwartzenberg, Hocher, &c. . . . 425
3.—Wedding festivities at the marriage of Leopold I. with the Spanish Infanta, 1666—The great equestrian ballet during the carnival of 1667 440

MEMOIRS
OF
THE COURT OF AUSTRIA

CHAPTER I

MAXIMILIAN I.—(1493-1519).

1.—His parentage and character—The "Felix Austria Nube."

THE founder of the Austrian monarchy as a European power was the Emperor Maximilian I. Rodolph of Habsburg, the first of the dynasty, had laid the foundation of the family estate of the house of Austria; under Maximilian it was, by three fortunate marriages, raised to the rank of the first empire of the civilised world. Rodolph of Habsburg was possessed only of the dukedom of Austria with its capital Vienna, and of the two Alpine countries, Styria and Carniola. In the course of the fourteenth century, the third Alpine country, Carinthia, and the fourth and most important one, Tyrol, besides Austria beyond the Inn, and the possessions in Swabia and Alsace, were added. Maximilian afterwards acquired, towards the end of the fifteenth century, the rich Burgundian Netherlands, and, moreover, the vast Spanish monarchy; and, lastly, secured to his House, by the act of settlement concluded at Vienna in the year 1515, the eventual acquisition of the two crowns, the Magyaric of Hungary and the Sclavonic of Bohemia.

An organised and permanent court did not exist at Vienna under Maximilian. His immediate successor (Charles V.) mostly resided in Spain and the Netherlands, the following

Emperors alternately at Prague and Vienna. Rodolph II. remained constantly at Prague, and never once, as Emperor, entered Vienna. It was not until the Thirty Years' War, under Matthias, and especially under Ferdinand II., that Vienna became the fixed and ordinary residence of the Austrian monarchs.

Maximilian was the son of the pompous, pedantic Emperor Frederic III.,[1] who had lost a leg, and who died of a surfeit of melons in 1493, at the age of eighty-eight. His mother was the beautiful and lively Eleanor of Portugal. He was born in 1458, became Emperor at the age of thirty-five, and reigned during more than a quarter of a century, from 1493 to 1519. His mother he lost when a boy; at the time of her death she had scarcely completed her thirtieth year.

In childhood, Maximilian gave but little promise. He was five years old before he learned to speak even a few words. Until his twelfth year he was tongue-tied, so that most people considered him an idiot. After that time, however, his mind expanded with singular quickness; not, indeed, by the study of theology, medicine, and the black art, in which his father caused him to be instructed, but by the reading of knightly adventures and of the chronicles, as well as by the study of what was then called the science of mining; of war and artillery; and of architecture, painting, and music; towards which pleasanter pursuits he was drawn by the natural bent of his own disposition. He inherited the lively temperament of his mother. Even as a youth he would, like a keen sportsman, range the fields and woods, and cross over precipices and glaciers, hunting the wild goat, or in search of adventures such as the whole of his life was replete with. He became one of the boldest chamois hunters, as well as one of the most gallant lovers of the fair sex.

At the age of nineteen he hastened to the Netherlands to marry the beautiful Mary of Burgundy, the richest heiress

---

[1] Sometimes named Frederic IV., as Frederic, son of Albert I., was chosen in 1314, but was taken prisoner by the other candidate, Louis of Bavaria, and then renounced his claim.

in Europe, the only daughter of the Duke Charles the Bold, who fell in the battle of Nancy against the united hosts of the Swiss and of the Duke of Lorraine.

Mary chose Maximilian from among twelve suitors who aspired to the rich prize of her beauty and of her boundless wealth. The States of the Netherlands had, after the death of Duke Charles, wished her to marry the Dauphin, afterwards King Charles VIII. of France; but an embassy arrived from the Emperor Frederic, exhibiting a letter and a ring which Mary, with the consent of her father, had sent to Maximilian. This prince was considered the handsomest youth of his time; at all events, such was Mary's opinion of him. The repute of extraordinary manliness preceded him, and he was the son of the monarch who sat on the first throne of Christendom. Mary had either made his acquaintance at a former interview, or, as is stated by others, had only seen his likeness and ever since felt an affection for him. She therefore now declared openly and frankly that "him she had chosen in her heart, and him she would have for her spouse and no other." Mary's stepmother, Margaret of York, the third and last wife of Charles the Bold, sent to the son of Cæsar 100,000 guilders to assist his straitened finances. Maximilian thereupon made a splendid entry into Ghent, clad in silver-gilt armour, and riding on a magnificent brown charger; instead of a helmet he wore round his golden locks a precious wedding garland of pearls and costly jewels; his retinue were electors, princes, bishops, and six hundred noble lords. Having alighted at his quarters, he received a message from the Princess, who sent to welcome him and to invite him to her. After supper, therefore, Maximilian rode by torchlight to her palace, and Mary went to meet him. When they came in sight of each other, they both knelt down in the open street, and then fell into each other's arms, Mary calling out, with tears in her eyes, "Be welcome to me, thou scion of the noble German stock, whom I have so long wished to see, and whom I am now rejoiced to meet." On the third day following (19th of August, 1477) the marriage was celebrated.

But this happy union lasted no more than four years and a half. Mary had borne to her lord a son, Philip, who afterwards became the heir of the Spanish monarchy, and a daughter, Margaret. She was far advanced in pregnancy with a third child, when, being out hawking, she was thrown from her horse, which, falling upon her and crushing her against the stump of a tree, injured her most severely. From feelings of delicacy she concealed this until it was too late for medical aid, and she died (16th of March, 1482) at the age of twenty-five, in the bloom of her years. "Never, as long as I live, shall I forget this bonny wife of mine," were the words with which Maximilian parted from her corpse.

After Mary's death the whole country broke out in open rebellion. Maximilian, who in his Habsburg dominions used to respect none but the clergy and the nobles of the land, was utterly amazed at the extraordinary liberty of the Flemish burghers in their large, industrious, and wealthy cities. He had not succeeded in making himself popular with the sturdy Netherlanders, who were by no means inclined to bow down before him, and whom he, on his part, treated with genuine Austrian harshness and superciliousness. The mercenaries of Maximilian's body-guard especially had committed many acts of insolence and oppression. A rebellion broke out in Ghent. Maximilian put it down by means of executions. He then left that city to reside at Bruges. It was in vain that his jester, Conrad von der Rosen, warned him not to allow himself to be caught there. His mercenaries were one day drilling in the market-place of Bruges. On the captain's giving the German word of command "*Steht*" (Halt), the bystanders mistook it for the Flemish "*Slät*" (Slay), and the mercenaries having at the same time lowered their lances, the citizens, believing that they were going to be attacked, marched under the fifty-two banners of their several guilds to the market-place, disarmed the troops, and put Maximilian and his councillors in durance vile (5th of February, 1488). This captivity lasted four months. Conrad von der Rosen made an unsuccessful attempt to rescue his royal master.

He plunged at night with two swimming belts, one for himself and another for Maximilian, into the ditch of the castle of Bruges, where the illustrious prisoner was confined; but the swans attacked the faithful jester and drove him back with their wings. The Emperor Frederic was at last obliged to send an imperial army to liberate his captive son; after which Maximilian again had forty of the most stiff-necked burghers of Bruges put to death.

Maximilian, when a prisoner at Bruges, had been for two years the Roman King elect. He held the Regency in the Netherlands as guardian of his son Philip until 1494, when the Prince, having completed his sixteenth year, undertook the government himself. Since 1490, however, Maximilian resided principally in the Tyrol, where Sigismund, a cousin of his of a younger branch of his family, ruled. This Prince was first married to a daughter of James I. of Scotland, and afterwards to a daughter of the founder of the Albertine line of Saxony, both of which unions were without issue. He was a very weak-minded and profligate, but withal tyrannical and most eccentric, personage, and the laughing-stock of his servants, who led him at pleasure by contriving to make mysterious voices, as of ghosts, speak to him from the stoves and roofs, and other quite extraordinary places. Maximilian at last, with the consent of the States, forced him, in 1490, to resign; and the crazy old prince was confined to twelve castles which he reserved to himself, and seven of which he called by his own name, as for instance, Sigismundsburg, Sigismundskron, &c. At these castles he passed his time in the pleasures of the chase and in angling, till his death in 1496, when the Tyrol was re-united by the lucky heir Maximilian with the family possessions of the House of Habsburg.

The Tyrol became the favourite abode of Maximilian. The Habsburgers had for many years called it "the heart and the shield of their house." And, indeed, its position made it a most important political link in the dominions of Austria. It was coterminous with the powerful republic of Venice, which, like France, was one of the principal rivals of Habsburg; and, moreover, with the Swiss Republic, which had wrested its liberty from its Austrian rulers. Too heavy a yoke might have driven the Tyrolese into the arms of either of these two republics. The Tyrol besides connected Austria Proper with its outlying provinces near the Lake of Constance, in Swabia, and the Alsace. In consideration of this politically important position, it was looked upon as the most precious gem of the monarchy, where the policy of the House of Habsburg continued to respect the old liberties, rights, and customs even in the days of Ferdinand II. and Leopold I., when the popular liberties were crushed in the Archdukedom itself, and in Bohemia, and were at least attempted to be crushed in Hungary. It was also very important in a commercial point of view, being the high road for all traffic to and fro across the Alps. Much money was thus drawn into the country, whose agriculture and cattle-breeding were raised by it to a state of high prosperity. The fairs at Botzen, having been established as early as the time of Frederic Barbarossa, were then most flourishing, and became a source of great wealth to the country. Maximilian used to say of the Tyrol, "It is a coarse coat of frieze, but it keeps one warm." He liked to dress in the Tyrolese fashion, in a green short coat, with a broad-brimmed green hat on his head.

The hills and valleys of the Tyrol are full of memorials of his sporting adventures. The most famous is that which he met with on the precipice called the Martinswand, and which has been celebrated by Collins's poem. On this steep rock in the Zirler mountains, in the valley of the Upper Inn, he caused a wooden cross, forty feet high, to be erected on the brink of the giddy height in token of his wonderful escape. In 1490 an angel, or rather the Tyrolese chamois-hunter, Oswald Zips, who halloed to him, and who was therefore ennobled under the name of Hollauer von Hohenfels (High-rock), is said to have saved him there from starving, after his having remained in this perilous position for two days and two nights. At another time Maximilian, on a steep rock in the Tyrol, stood his ground against a ferocious bear. The Netherlands were likewise the scene of many of his hunting adventures. In the Brabant forest one day a stag met him in a narrow close path, and was going to leap over him, when Maximilian stabbed him with his sword through the heart, and thus flung the creature back. Being also passionately fond of hawking, he sent for hawks from the most distant countries, even from Tartary, and employed for this sport a staff of upwards of sixty persons under fifteen head falconers.

Maximilian was bold even to temerity. At Munich he once went alone into the cage of a lion, forced open its jaws and pulled out its tongue, whilst the beast quietly submitted to it. At Ulm he mounted the highest ledge of the tower of the minster, and, stepping out upon the iron bar by which the beacon lantern was suspended, balanced himself on one foot, poising the other in the air.

Maximilian inherited very little of his father's nature and disposition; in fact, he took much more after his mother and grandmother. Like the latter, the Polish Cimburga, he was of extraordinary strength, and like his mother, the lively southron, Eleanora of Portugal, full of spirit and animation. Fanciful and romantically chivalrous, he has been called "the last knight, with whom the middle ages were buried."

He was most active in war as well as in the lists. When he held his first Diet at Worms the French knight Claude de Barre, a man of gigantic strength, hung out his shield from the window of his inn, challenging all the Germans to single combat. Maximilian then had the arms of Austria and Burgundy hung by the side of the shield of the Frenchman, whom he conquered with the sword, after the lances of both had glanced from the cuirasses. Such was Maximilian's strength that he would wrench off iron bars merely with his hand. There was no one more skilful as an archer, no one more expert as a horseman, than he. He was the best shot, the best gunner and manager of the ordnance, as he was likewise the first in all field sports. Gunnery was one of his hobbies; in battle he very frequently pointed the cannon himself, shooting as if for a match with the regular artillerymen. In the Netherlands he once landed under the fire of the French guns, and took their pieces from them. The Emperor had the four largest arsenals of that time—at Vienna, at Innsbruck, at Görtz, and at Breisach. Among his famous cannons, some of what he called his sharp (saucy) wenches bore the names "the Fair Semiramis," "the Fair Helena," "the Fair Medea," "the Fair Dido," "the Fair Thisbe." Others were called "the Weckauf" (the Awakener), and "the Purlepaus." Maximilian, with the help of George of Frundsberg, his brave captain in war, organised the paid militia, which had been established since the times of the Hussite War, under the name of the German Lansquenets. He formed them in regiments, and they soon became the dread of all Europe. He knew very well how to manage them; and on one occasion when they mutinied, growling at him for their pay, he pacified them at last, with the help of his jester, by some broad jokes.

Under Maximilian the soldiery began to form a distinct class. They made war for the mere pay, without caring in the least for what object. The princes would retain these mercenaries in time of peace also, partly as body-guards and partly as garrisons in the fortified places. This caused a very material change in the political constitution of Europe. In ancient times the whole people had carried arms; in the middle ages only the feudal nobles and the burghers; yet these also now gradually left the profession of arms entirely to the soldiery. Thus the power which had formerly rested with the people, then with the nobility and the cities, was more and more exclusively transferred to the princes.

Maximilian, however, was not yet able to accomplish great things with the help of his Lansquenets. Being a bad financier, he always lacked the money to pay them. He was therefore called, in derision, "Poco denari" (the Penniless). His best treasure was always in pledge with his rich subjects, and once (see Rymer's "Fœdera," xiii. p. 234), in 1505, being in great straits for money, he even pledged to King Henry VII. of England, at that time reputed to be the richest prince in Christendom, the celebrated *fleur de lys*, the largest jewel of those times, which he had inherited from Mary of Burgundy. The money lent by the royal pawnbroker on this security amounted to 50,000 crowns, at four shillings sterling each.

Maximilian was exceedingly free and open-handed, the very opposite of his stingy, avaricious father. This generous disposition he showed even when a mere boy. His father having one day given him a dish with fruit and a purse with money, he kept the fruit and gave the money to his servants. When the father sighed, "That will be a scattergood" (*Streugütlein*), Maximilian replied, "I will not be king of the money, but of the people, and of all those who possess money."

Maximilian, in an Austrian "patriarchal" way, loved the people, who reverenced him, and he lived with them on very good terms, especially with the burghers of the free imperial cities and their fair wives and daughters. Once, in the camp before Padua, he was warned against the Italian viands of a sutler's wife; but he ate the whole of his portion, saying, "Never fear; she is an Augsburg woman, and they are very good people." Maximilian, therefore, was very popular with the German burghers; he shared in their feasts, engaged in their shooting-matches, and danced at their balls. The chronicles of Augsburg mention the magnificent dances got up in this city for him, as well as for Philip of Burgundy, his not less gallant son; in particular, how in the courtyard of the "Frohnhof," the house of the bishop, on St. John's eve, bonfires fifty feet high were lit, round which the royal guests danced the torch-dance with the daughters of the patrician houses. It was on account of the ladies that Maximilian liked Augsburg better than any other city in the world, for which reason Louis XII. of France generally used, in jest, to call him "the Burgomaster of Augsburg." He also liked a dance with the ladies, married and unmarried, of Nuremberg. On one occasion he allowed himself to be disarmed and made captive by them to dance with them a few days longer. It is even recorded that at Ratisbon he let the light of his countenance shine upon that portion of the fair sex whom, in the language of those times, we might call the "Ladies Errant." The magistracy, well knowing the imperial court and its ways, had banished the whole set of them from the precincts of the city, as long as the Diet should last. They therefore appeared supplicating in a body before the gay Emperor, as he approached the city where he was going to take in hand the grave business of the German Empire. And, indeed, his Sacred Cæsarean Majesty succeeded in smuggling them through the gate by a most extraordinary device. He smilingly ordered the frail petitioner who was standing near him to catch hold of the horse by the tail, the second to seize the gown of the first, and the third that of the second, and so on to the last. In this manner the expelled beauties made their way back into Ratisbon, and were not ungrateful.

Vienna, on the other hand, Maximilian did not like. He could never forget that, when in 1462 the people of that capital besieged his father in his palace (the Hofburg), until Podiebrad of Bohemia came to his rescue, he, at that time a boy not quite five years of age, had to suffer cruelly from hunger, the pangs of which were but scantily relieved by a small supply of game from his well-beloved court tailor, Kronberger.

Maximilian was most good-natured and affable, and very forgiving, even to those who might have done him personal wrong. The nobles of his household, taking advantage of this, cheated him right and left. One of them, otherwise a devoted servant of his, had once embezzled several thousand florins, when the Emperor asked him, "What does a thief deserve who has stolen such and such a sum?" naming the exact amount. The gentleman answered, "He deserves to be hanged;" on which the Emperor, tapping his shoulder, said, "By no means; we want your services some time longer." To the clergy he showed just as much deference as his ancestor Rodolph had done; he never allowed a priest to stand in his presence. To the fair sex he was so gallant and polite that he would not "*thou*" even the meanest woman. He was personally very unpretending, and one day said to a poet who was fulsome in his praise, "My dear fellow, I am sure you do not quite know me, nor any other prince."

Once he caused diligent inquiries to be made into his pedigree, when a wag wrote on the wall of the courtyard of his castle the well-known lines:

> "When Adam delved and Eve span,
> Who was then the gentleman?"

The Emperor wrote the answer underneath:

> "I am a man as others be,
> But that the Lord exalted me."[1]

The King of France he used to call a king of asses, because his subjects would bear any burden he imposed upon them; the King of Spain, a king of men, as they only obeyed him in what was reasonable; the King of England, a king of angels, for he commanded them but what was just and fair, whereas they, on their side, obeyed him willingly and rightly. Himself he called a king of kings, "for," said he, "they obey us when they please."

Maximilian was exceedingly jealous of his descent and imperial prerogative. He commissioned seven historiographers to find out the origin of his house—the most brilliant, but not the true one from the cradle of his house at the small castle in the Argau. About a dozen pedigrees were produced in consequence, the most learned of which went back as far as Adam. Maximilian, to use his own expression, wanted in every way to "outdo Julius Cæsar, and to be *semper e familia Caroli Magni*." This *Carolus Magnus* was, by hook or by crook, to be made his ancestor. Maximilian quartered with the arms of Spain those of Portugal and England, because his mother was a princess of Portugal, descended from the house of Lancaster. In virtue of this Lancastrian descent, he quartered also the arms of France. Besides the arms of Hungary and Bohemia, he assumed those of the Byzantine Empire, as "being only severed from the Roman Empire owing to the arrogance of the Greek Church, wherefore God had

---

[1] "Ich bin ein Mann, wie ander Mann,
Nur dass mir Gott die Ehre gann."

chastised it, and made it subject to the heathen, and King Maximilian or his descendants might hope in a short time to reconquer it." He pretended to be related to the Imperial family of the Palæologi. On his coins he called himself, like the Grand Turk, the Shahs of Persia, the Great Mogul, and the Czars of Russia, "the Ruler of all the Countries of the Orient and Occident"; or else, "The King of all Christendom and of several other Provinces."[1]

He once formed the intention, after the example of Frederic Barbarossa, to put himself, as the first warrior of Christendom, at the head of an army of crusaders, to proceed down the Danube, to free Constantinople, and to drive the Turks back into Asia. For this purpose, Pope Leo X. had already given him the consecrated sword and cap; and the Diet of Augsburg, in 1518, on which Luther also made his appearance, granted him, for this war against the infidels, the subsidy of a poll-tax. Maximilian caused himself also to be elected successor to the throne of Sweden, and even put his opponents in that kingdom under the ban and double ban of the Empire. Poland was to acknowledge his supremacy, and to absolve the order of the Teutonic knights from its allegiance, to which the latter had been subjected in the peace of Thorn; and moreover render to him the coast of the Baltic and the mouth of the Vistula.

Maximilian was the first potentate who drew the Muscovites into the family of the European States, concluding a treaty of alliance with Russia, until then an Asiatic power. He sent ambassadors, arquebusiers, gunners, gunsmiths, armourers, and miners from the Netherlands, Tyrol, and Styria, to Ivan Vasilevitch, who broke the yoke of the Tartars, and to his son Vasilij, who retook Smolensk from the Poles.

The first ambassador sent by Maximilian was the rich baron, George Schnitzenbaumer, of Carniola, who was

---

[1] By the countries of the Orient he meant Hungary, Bohemia, Croatia, and Dalmatia; by those of the Occident, the Spanish kingdoms. His title ran thus: Christianitatis ac aliorum regnorum Rex Heresque (XP. AC. A. Reg. R. HER. Q.); he also called himself Plurimum Europæ provinciarum Rex et Princeps potentissimus.

directed, *ad captandam benevolentiam*, to address the Czar as
"*Emperor and Autocrat of all the Russias.*" But the second
ambassador, the celebrated Syndic of Augsburg, Conrad
Peutinger, was obliged, in the relation which he had to
lay before the Diet in 1514, to express a doubt whether
Schnitzenbaumer had not exceeded his instructions in con-
ceding to the Czar anything that might be contrary to the
His Imperial Majesty's conscience, to the style and ordi-
nances of the Holy Roman Empire, or to the Christian
religion. In 1517, the learned Sigismund von Herberstein
went as ambassador to Russia; and his voluminous work
describing that embassy and another in 1526, published in
1549 in Vienna and 1557 in Basle, first introduced that
country to the knowledge of the people of Europe. Maximilian, and after him Charles V., continually planned
attempts at conversion, by which the Eastern and Western
Churches were to be united. Maximilian also repeatedly
entertained projects of marriage with Russia. On the
other hand, he was hostile in his policy against Poland,
which at that time extended from the Baltic to the Black
Sea, and from Posen and Cracow to Smolensk, and which
then was ruled by Sigismund Jagello, one of the greatest
kings of his age.

Maximilian, after the death of his first wife, remained a
widower for twelve years. He never as long as he lived
forgot his beloved Burgundian Mary, the mere mention of
whose name brought tears into his eyes. He once on his
knees entreated the celebrated Abbot Trittheim of Würtzburg
to conjure up before him her dear shade. The abbot undertook to do so, forbidding the Emperor at his peril to address
the vision which should appear before him. But Maximilian,
unable to control his overflowing heart, addressed the beloved
form with the most endearing words, and thus destroyed the
charm. Yet the proud ruler of Austria, who was so fond of
surrounding himself with the halo of Carolingian descent,
married in 1494, just one year after his accession, in second
wedlock, a lady "of no birth whatever"—Blanca Maria,
who, it is true, like his first wife, brought him great wealth,

being the daughter of Duke Galeazzo Sforza of Milan, a descendant of that first Sforza whom Maximilian's father, the Emperor Frederic III., had refused to invest, as the bastard of a peasant, with the duchy of Milan. In those times, however, Blanca was not the less considered for all that; as in Maximilian's reign the principle was still valid which is in force to the present day in England, that the wife shares the superior rank of her husband irrespective of her own.

After the death of his second wife, Blanca Maria, the Emperor conceived the strange plan of becoming Pope. In Maximilian's correspondence with his only daughter, Margaret of Austria, Regent of the Netherlands (published in Paris in 1839), we find a letter of the old Emperor, dated September 18th, 1512, in which he tells Margaret "that he did not think it meet to marry again, that he had even resolved upon living henceforth in perfect celibacy. He intended to send, on the day following, his beloved Matthew Lang of Wellenburg, Bishop of Gurk, to Pope Julius II., who had the ague and could not live much longer, to induce his Holiness to make him (Maximilian) his coadjutor, so that after the death of the Pontiff he might succeed to the Papal see. He would then be ordained a priest and afterwards canonised as a saint; his daughter, therefore, would after his death be obliged '*to worship him*,' whereat he should feel very much '*glorified*.' With 200,000 or 300,000 ducats he hoped to carry his point with the cardinals." He signed himself, "Your good father, Maximilian, Pope that is to be." The plan was not, however, carried out, although Maximilian had pledged his best jewels with the great banking-house of Fugger at Augsburg, to procure the large sums requisite " to refresh the parched throats of the cardinals."

Gaiety, magnificence, and pleasure reigned paramount at Maximilian's court. Whatever tends to embellish and cheer life was there to be found. Maximilian therefore cultivated science and the fine arts with the greatest assiduity. He also devoted himself eagerly to the study of astrology, just as his father had done before him. But most fondly of all did

Maximilian love history, "that noble damsel," as Fugger, the author of "The Mirror of Honour of the Archducal House of Austria," writes, "who, under his reign, was led forth again from her dark dungeon full of moths and rust to the light of day." Maximilian himself dictated to his secretary, Treizsauerwein, the history of his father and his own, under the allegorical title, "Der Weiss Kunig" (the Wise King). He also composed the plan of "Theuerdank," *i.e.*, "The Knight thinking of Adventures," a book which describes his own chivalrous deeds and dangers, and which was worked out in German verses by Melchior Pfinzing, the provost of St. Sebaldus of Nuremberg. Maximilian has written, on all sorts of subjects, no less than twenty-two books, which are still extant in the imperial library at Vienna (*Hofbibliothek*). There are also to be found there those strange questions which, in 1508, he put to Abbot Trittheim. As, for instance, "Since Christendom comprehends only a small part of the globe, should not everyone who believes in a God be saved by his own religion?" "Why is Revelation in so many points obscure and contradictory, stating what one does not care to know, and not stating what one would so much wish to know?" "Why should witches have power over the evil spirits, whilst an honest man cannot get anything from an angel?"

In Maximilian's reign lived the poetical shoemaker of Nuremberg, Hans Sachs, and the great painter and engraver, Albert Dürer, also at Nuremberg. The latter he esteemed very highly, and repeatedly had his portrait painted by him, even at his last Diet in 1518. The celebrated friend of Albert Dürer, Williebald Pirkheimer, a learned patrician and senator of Nuremberg, likewise belonged to the circle of the Emperor's friends, which comprehended, besides many others, the illustrious John Reuchlin; the famous captain, George von Frundsberg, and the bishops Hans von Dalberg of Worms, the restorer of German learning and art, and Christopher Stadion of Augsburg.

But, notwithstanding his personal amiability, which is the most interesting feature in his history—much more interesting than anything he ever performed—he was out of his place as well in the council as in the battle-field. The feats of a knight, of a hunter, of an athlete, and the achievements of a patron of art and science, are far from being deeds which are looked up to in an Emperor. Maximilian was a man of genius, restlessly active, always forming new plans; but he was not a great character as a ruler. In all his thoughts, plans, and acts he was deficient in energy and greatness, in tenacity and steadfastness of purpose, in consistent and sustained application. He was more of a *preux chevalier* than of an Emperor. He had inherited from his father, besides his good-humour, that petty spirit of detail and of trifling which wastes great energies on little matters. He by no means succeeded in outdoing Julius Cæsar; on the contrary, he was only too often himself outdone. Like his father, he never accomplished anything great. He did not take in his own hands the reform of the Church, on which all the great interests hinged that stirred up in his time the minds of the European world. He never accomplished anything of the least importance against the Turks, at that time the principal enemies of the western world. Under him Italy was lost. As early as 1494, in the second year after his accession, Charles VIII. made his great victorious campaign into that country; and at the death of Maximilian, Milan and Genoa were in French hands. *Under Maximilian, Switzerland, this important bulwark in the south, completed its separation from the German Empire by refusing to acknowledge the Imperial Court of Chancery.* The Swiss now became more and more subject to the influence of France, and their country was thenceforth the nursery of mercenaries for France in her wars of defence against the threatening supremacy of the House of Habsburg, and at a later period, under Louis XIII. and Louis XIV., in their wars of conquest at the expense of the German Empire. Maximilian never succeeded in making himself truly respected, either by his own countrymen, the Germans, nor even, in his French, Swiss, and Venetian wars, by the foreigner. He was very often the "Knight of the Rueful Countenance," and was laughed at and ridiculed. Machiavelli, the greatest political genius of his, and one of the greatest of all times, said of him, "Maximilian thinks always to act independently, and yet he follows the first impulse only; he has a rich stock of plans, but they all in the execution turn out differently from his first intention." Even his jester, Conrad von der Rosen, used to tease him about the strange devices which he often formed. One day when playing at cards with him, he said to him, "Look here, Maxey, as such a king of cards thy princes do consider thee." In very many things Maximilian did not follow the best counsel, for he always followed his own. He had for his chancellor Cyprian Sernteiner von Nordheim, of an ancient Tyrolese family, a man of sound common sense, spotless fidelity, and so simple that, for the conclusion of the treaty of Blois in 1505, he rode from Innsbruck on horseback as courier, day and night, all the way to Blois, carrying his only silk suit behind him on his horse. This chancellor wrote from Duisburg (January, 1509) to Paul von Lichtenstein, "His Majesty can never be quiet, and that's why such as we can do so little."

With Maximilian, as we have said before, the middle ages were buried. He put down the disgraceful club law (*Faustrecht*) by proclaiming at the Diet of Worms in 1495 the celebrated "General Peace of the Empire" (*Landfrieden*), with and through which a new era is ushered in. By virtue of this enactment every attempt at taking the law in one's own hand, as well as of waylaying and of levying blackmail in the Empire, was thenceforth to cease. But it was much easier to pass the law than to enforce it. A long time after the highways remained unsafe, and people could not travel without taking from one town to the other an escort of horsemen or of arquebusiers, who went in waggons. It was one of the principal objects of the "General Peace" that the feuds of the members of the Empire should no longer be settled by force of arms, but by the legal, peaceful decision of the Imperial Court of Chancery (the *Reichskammergericht*). The Empire thus entered into one general confederation, whereas formerly, for the maintenance of peace, a number of particular and provincial confederations of the princes and the nobles on the one hand, and of the towns and cities on the other, had existed. These particular and provincial federations were now to be abolished. The Imperial Court of Chancery, being the general federal tribunal, was empowered in the name of the Emperor to put the contending and refractory lieges under the ban of the Empire. The judge in chancery (*Kammerrichter*), the person who presided over this court, was appointed by the Emperor. Its fifty assessors were elected by the members of the Diet. The Imperial Court of Chancery held its first sitting on the 3rd of November, 1495, at Frankfort, presided over by the Imperial High Steward, Count Eitelfried of Zollern, to whom, as to the first judge in chancery, the Emperor delegated his sceptre as the wand of office. At first the Court of Chancery was itinerant, following Maximilian even into the Netherlands; but in 1527 it was permanently established at Spires, until, in 1693, during the French wars under Louis XIV., it was removed from the Rhine farther into the interior of Germany, to Wetzlar in Westphalia. A second imperial court, the Aulic Council (*Reichshofrath*), was established at Vienna.

This rule of the law and law courts, substituted by Maximilian for the old law of arms, seemed, however, to the members of the Empire, to the powerful princes, as well as to the great number of the smaller barons and knights, a hardship and a disgrace. They wished to remain warlike knights as before, and for a long time kicked against the new order of things; for the new judges, the councillors of the Imperial Court of Chancery, were no longer, as heretofore, the peers of those who were to be judged by them. They were some of them lawyers and doctors, and the barons only called them "the writers." They were salaried, and the barons showed a particular aversion to paying for the law. It is true that, because the lawyers were to be feed, lawsuits became more and more tedious; and as the proceedings were no longer carried on orally, but in writing—no longer publicly, but in close chambers—they became interminable. In Göthe's "Götz von Berlichingen" the antagonism of the old knights of the sword and the lance against these new knights of pen and paper is sketched with masterly skill. Sickingen's downfall only reduced the barons to obedience. The greatest misfortune, however, was that the court was utterly wanting in power to enforce its decrees against the more powerful princes of the Empire, who altogether refused to obey them. These, being neither more nor less than the first vassals of the Empire, quite systematically arrogated to themselves the sovereignty over the territories which they held as fiefs of the Empire; and, establishing, in imitation of the Imperial Court of Chancery, territorial courts of their own, they presumed henceforth to treat imperial cities which happened to lie within their territories, and counts and lords holding their fiefs from the Empire, but whose possessions were enclosed in theirs, as their own vassals. This mode of taking the law into their own hands they even continued to employ against the Emperor himself. The Smalcalde war, indeed, very nearly brought them to ruin; but the expedition of the Elector Maurice against Charles V. again made the power of the princes triumph *de facto*, until the Peace of Westphalia established it also *de jure*.

Under Maximilian the new bureaucratical element already began to make its power to be felt. The lawyers now became, like the soldiers, a particular and most influential class in the State. Everything was henceforth settled according to the Roman law, written in a language which was unintelligible to the illiterate. The differences of the Justinian codex from the old common law were made use of to raise the power of the princes to a still higher pitch. The sophistry of the lawyers became a formidable tool in the hands of the princes, and soon a traffic was carried on with the law, just as until then had been carried on by the priests with indulgences. As early as that time the Italian Patricius wrote: "The German jurists turn and twist everything according to their own pleasure. It is their greatest pride, at the Diets, to give their oracular verdicts as the councillors of the princes. They foster litigations for their own purposes, to obtain the sovereign power for their princes."

To Maximilian is owing the division of Germany into circles, which was settled at the Diet of Cologne in 1512. He formed ten circles of the Empire. These were the following:

1. The Swabian circle; comprising Würtemberg, Baden, and Alsace, all the country to the Lech, between the Neckar and the Lake of Constance, with the exception of the West-Austrian possessions in Alsace and in Swabia, which were reckoned with the Austrian circle.

2. The Bavarian circle; comprising the country from the Lech to the frontiers of Austria and Bohemia, and from the archbishopric of Salzburg to the territories of Nuremberg, Bamberg, Anspach, and Baireuth.

3. The Austrian circle; consisting of all the Austrian countries, the outlying provinces in Alsace and Swabia, as well as the Tyrol and Austria proper.

4. The Franconian circle; from the country of Henneberg, which it included, to the territories of Nuremberg, Bamberg, Anspach, and Baireuth, which it likewise included; and from the frontiers of the Saxon Vogtland to the bishopric of Würtzburg, the latter also included.

5. The Upper Saxon circle, with the electorate and the duchies of Saxony, Thuringia, Misnia, besides Anhalt, the electorate of Brandenburg, and Pomerania.

6. The Lower Saxon circle; comprising all the Brunswick possessions, the archbishopric of Magdeburg, and the duchies of Mecklenburg and Holstein.

7. The Westphalian circle; all the country from the Weser to the Rhine; the Westphalian bishoprics and the duchies of Berg, Nassau, and Oldenburg; and besides, on the left bank of the Rhine, the duchies of Juliers, Cleves, and Guelderland, and the bishoprics of Liége and Utrecht; Guelderland and Utrecht were, however, separated again under Charles V., in 1548, from the Westphalian circle, and embodied with the Netherlandish provinces.

8. The Electoral Rhenish circle; comprising the archbishopric of Cologne, with the duchy of Westphalia; the archbishopric of Mayence, with the county of Eichsfeld in

Thuringia; the archbishopric of Trèves; and, lastly, the Electoral Palatinate, with Heidelberg.

9. The Upper Rhenish circle; comprising, on the right bank of the Rhine, the Wetterau, the whole of Hesse and the bishoprics of Hersfeld and Fulda; on the left bank, the possessions of the junior branches of the Palatine houses Simmern and Zweibrücken (Deux-Ponts); the bishoprics of Worms, Spires, and Strassburg; and Lorraine.

10. The Burgundian circle; consisting of the newly acquired Netherlandish provinces of Austria, to which, in 1548, Guelderland and Utrecht were added; seventeen provinces in all.

On the other hand, there were excluded, as no longer belonging to the German Empire:

1. Switzerland.
2. Bohemia (at that time in the possession of the Jagellons, although being still enumerated in the Golden Bull as an electorate), with Moravia and Lusatia.
3. The possessions of the Teutonic knights in Prussia, on the shores of the Baltic and on the banks of the Vistula, which, in the peace of Thorn, in 1466, had become subject to the sovereignty of Poland.

Bohemia, which, since the days of Podiebrad in 1462, had sent no more representatives to the German Diet, was reintroduced into the deliberative body only in 1708.

The unity brought about by this organisation of circles was, however, only a formal one, linked together by very feeble and loose ties. What Germany most wanted in the times of Maximilian was the restoration of the old imperial rule, the establishment of a paramount central power, by which alone might have been cemented a strong and close union of the scattered members of the Germanic body. An attempt to bring this about had already been made during the last years of the reign of Frederic III., and at the beginning of Maximilian's, by the first dignitary of the Church of Germany, the Elector Primate of Mayence, Berthold, of the house of the Counts of Henneberg.

He planned a representation of the Empire by a permanent council, somewhat after the fashion of the English parliament. This representative body, according to his scheme, was to be divided into two chambers—one, the Upper House, as an assembly of the princes; the other, the House of Commons, in which the deputies of the lower nobility and gentry, and those of the cities were to sit. An imperial tax was to be levied for the maintenance of an army of the Empire, dependent on the Diet.

In this manner the principle would have been established that the high aristocracy were to look upon the peasantry as their tenants, but not as their subjects; as by imposing a direct tax the Empire claimed the *exclusive* right of sovereignty over all the lieges within its territory. The imperial tax was to be paid by all without exception; by clergy as well as laity, by high and low, by the prince and the day labourer.

Had the idea been carried out, the subsequent destructive riots of the peasantry would have been crushed in the bud; and so likewise would the new constitution, when once firmly established, have prevented the schism in the German Church by a *national* reform of the existing ecclesiastical abuses. A united Germany might have successfully made head against the Pope, who would as little have denied his assent to the accomplished fact of enacted decrees in this instance, as he did in the case of those of the Council of Basle.

No opposition was at that time to be apprehended from the princes of the Empire against Berthold's plans, which, on the other hand, would have been even supported by the representatives of the moneyed interest, the cities; and also by the peasantry, whose power was as yet unbroken. But it was Maximilian himself who in every possible way crossed the plans of Berthold and opposed the scheme of a parliamentary constitution.

All he cared for was the old policy *of increasing the family possessions of the reigning house of Austria*, and of raising it by great marriages to the rank of a European power. The constitution would have fettered Maximilian's hands; by giving it his royal assent he would have had to renounce the advantage of being able to increase the family estate by the help of the Empire. The idea of placing himself by a parliamentary German constitution at the head of the most powerful, best organised, and freest state of Europe did not enter his "Austrian patriarchal" mind. And yet the sacrifice would have been so small for the prize! And yet, the hereditary succession would not have been refused to an Emperor, had he only consented to restrain by his own accord the power of his crown!

Berthold died in 1504. He was the last great primate of the German Church, *i.e.*, German Church as correlative with the German Empire. His successors, especially the third one, Albert of Brandenburg, who lived during the Reformation, had no idea of reconstructing the Empire; on the contrary, a servile tool of the Bishop of Rome, he assisted in destroying it.

The greatest event which happened during Maximilian's reign was undoubtedly the commencement of the Reformation. The Emperor survived Luther's placarding his ninety-five theses on the palace chapel at Wittenberg somewhat more than a year. The last act of his government was the Diet of Augsburg, where Luther presented himself before the Cardinal Legate Cajetan. The aged, infirm Emperor, who had arrived there before Lent, to be able to share in the feasts of the carnival, opened this Diet on the 1st of August, 1518. He wished to bring about at it the election of his grandson Charles as King of the Romans, and then to resign his crown, to spend the remainder of his days at Naples, under whose beautiful sky his physicians had led him to hope he would recover his health. Yet the election did not come to pass, neither did the projected war against the Turks. On the contrary, it was remarked by some of the members of the Diet, that the Turk most to be feared had better be looked for in Italy. All complained to Maximilian of the scandalous sale of Romish indulgences. The Emperor himself very likely leaned towards the opinion that the immoderate pretensions of the Pope might be somewhat lowered by Luther. He said to the Elector of Saxony, Frederic the Wise, "We must save this monk for future occasions, maybe we shall want him;" and to the Saxon councillor Pfeffinger, "How is your monk? indeed, his *positiones* are by no means to be despised. He will have fine sport among the parsons." Yet Maximilian was not the man to open his mind to the momentous signs of the times. He died without in the least suspecting what a mighty future was dawning.

Maximilian left Augsburg in October with a foreboding of his approaching death. On arriving at the pillar called "the Rennsäule," in the valley of the Lech, he once more turned towards the city, crossed himself, and said, " Well, the Lord bless thee, my own fair Augsburg; we have had many a joyous day in thee, and now we shall never see thee again." He rode by way of Füssen to his country of Tyrol; first to Ehrenberg to enjoy the noble sport of hawking. From thence he went to Innsbruck, carrying with him a chest, which he had caused to be made three years before, and in which was enclosed his coffin, with all the requisite funeral fittings. At Innsbruck the townspeople refused to take in his carriages and horses, as, by the dishonesty of the imperial servants, some debts still remained unpaid from former occasions. The animals and equipages were, therefore, left during the night in the open street. Maximilian, who heard of it in the morning, was thrown into a fever by his anger at the insult. He, notwithstanding, embarked in the cold of January on the Inn for Upper Austria, on his way to Vienna. But he only reached Wels, where he died, 12th of January, 1519, in the sixtieth year of his age.

2.—*The Emperor Maximilian's Family.*

Maximilian left, by Mary of Burgundy, his first wife, one son and one daughter.

The latter, the Princess Margaret, had been chosen in 1483, when still an infant, to reconcile, by a marriage with Charles VIII. of France, the growing jealousy between the houses of Habsburg and Valois.

But Charles VIII. having married Anne, the heiress of Brittany, whom Maximilian had intended for his own second wife, Margaret was, in 1497, married at the age of seventeen, to the son of Ferdinand the Catholic, the Infant Juan, who died in the year of his marriage. She then married in 1501 Duke Philibert II. of Savoy, who died in 1504. Both marriages having proved very unhappy, Margaret did not intend to marry again; notwithstanding which, a new match was at least contemplated, from political motives, with Henry VII. of England, concerning which a remarkable correspondence is quoted in Rymer's "Fœdera," xiii. p. 173. Margaret afterwards went to the Netherlands to superintend the education of her nephew Charles V.; and after the death of her brother Philip, in 1506, she was appointed by her father Regent of the Low Countries, and died there, at the age of fifty, in 1530.

Maximilian's only son by Mary of Burgundy was Philip the Handsome, or, as he was also called, Philip of Austria, who died before his father. According to the accounts of the times, he was a remarkably good-looking man, with beautiful golden hair, but very fond of pleasure and dissipation. He was in 1496, at the age of eighteen, married to the heiress of the Spanish monarchy, the jealous and afterwards melancholy Infanta Juaña (Jane the Insane), the daughter of Ferdinand the Catholic and Isabella. The bride was at that time in her eighteenth year.

Philip the Handsome died, after being married for ten years, in 1506, at Burgos, poisoned by his own jealous wife. From the memoirs of Frederic II., Elector Palatine, written by his secretary Thomas of Liége, and published by Edward von Bulow, it appears that the gay Philip the Handsome used to go out with the equally gay Prince Palatine in search of nocturnal adventures among the fair ladies of Barcelona.

Philip left two sons, who became the founders of the two great branches of the Habsburg dynasty, the Spanish and the Austrian. They were the two Emperors Charles V. and Ferdinand I. Besides them, Philip left four daughters.

Of these, Eleanora was married in first wedlock at the age of twenty-one, in 1519, to Emmanuel, King of Portugal, who was more than double her age, and the second time to

Francis I., King of France, again with a view to reconcile the houses of Habsburg and of Valois. Having been again left a widow in 1547, she went in 1556 with her brother Charles V. to Spain, where she died in 1558. Before her being forced into the first of these two political marriages with the old and ugly King of Portugal, there had been between her and the above-mentioned Count Palatine Frederic an attachment, which was, however, abruptly broken off by her proud brother Charles. After the death of the King of Portugal in 1521, Frederic again entertained sanguine hopes of an alliance with the young royal dowager; but he had at last to content himself with marrying one of her nieces, the daughter of her sister Isabella.

This Isabella, the second daughter of Philip, was married in 1515, at the age of fourteen, to the King of Denmark, Christian II., surnamed the Bad, who was expelled his kingdom in 1523. She died in 1525.

The third Princess, Mary, married in 1521, at the age of sixteen, Louis II., King of Hungary and Bohemia, the last of the Jagellons, who was killed in 1526, in the battle of Mohacz, against the Turks. Mary, after Margaret's death in 1530, became Regent of the Netherlands, from whence she went with her brother to Spain, where she died in a convent in 1558, one month after her brother. Mary was the favourite sister of her brother Charles, and the only person in the imperial family well inclined towards Luther and the Reformation. De Thou states her to have been a rigid and even "austere moralist, of a courage far above her sex, and the most severe judge of everything like impurity. Our people," he says, "mortified by the frequent invasions which during her Regency were made in France, imputed to her, by all sorts of impertinent insinuations and licentious soldiers' ditties, a connection with M. de Brabençon (the first Prince of Aremberg), a man still in his prime, but who was even more distinguished by his bravery and loyalty than by his personal advantages. But she had such a horror of every such criminality that she obstinately refused the Emperor's entreaties to forgive one of his favourites, a young man of the highest nobility, who had brought one of her maids of honour to shame. She publicly threatened that she would have the offender executed on the spot if she should ever meet him, even if it were at the court of her own brother."

The fourth daughter of Philip the Handsome was Catharine, born in 1507, after the death of her father. She married, in 1525, John III., King of Portugal, and, after being left a widow by him in 1557, she died likewise in Spain (1578). She was the Princess whom Charles V., in 1520, before his election as Emperor, promised to the Elector Frederic the Wise for his nephew John Frederic the Magnanimous, who was afterwards outlawed by him. The match was sedulously urged on by the Emperor's brother Ferdinand and the ambassador Hannaert; but the plan failed, owing to the spread of the Lutheran doctrine in Saxony. It was, however, even at a very late period, recommended to the Emperor by the Councillor of State Breda. This match might possibly have prevented the bloody conflict of the two religions. It is rather remarkable that this marriage, which would have been most auspicious for the interests of *Germany*, was not concluded by Austria.

The gay and gallant Emperor Maximilian had a considerable number of illegitimate children of both sexes. Four sons and five daughters are known with certainty. Four sons rose in the Church; three of them, however, without attaining any great celebrity. These three were George, archbishop of Valencia, after having been from 1525 to 1539 bishop of Trent, and from 1544 to 1557 bishop of Liége; Leopold, the provost of Cordova; and Maximilian of Amberg. George is only remarkable for having been the first illegitimate scion of the house of Habsburg who bore the name "*Ab Austria.*"

The most celebrated natural son of the Emperor Maximilian was Matthew Lang von Wellenburg, the son of the fair patrician lady, Margaret Lang, of the Sulzer family of Augsburg. The Emperor ennobled him, and procured for him the bishopric of Gurk, and always treated him as a favourite and as his most confidential minister. In 1508

Lang went to Cambray, and there joined, in Maximilian's name, the alliance against Venice. In 1510 the Emperor sent him to France to Louis XII., with whom he concluded the treaty against Pope Julius II. and the Holy League. In 1511 and 1512 he was sent to Italy, and succeeded in bringing about the reconciliation of the Pope with the Emperor. In 1515, at the great Vienna meeting with the two Kings of Hungary-Bohemia and of Poland, he secured to Austria, by the well-known act of settlement, the reversion of the first-named twin crowns. At the outbreak of the Reformation he became one of its most bitter enemies. In 1519 he was appointed Archbishop of Salzburg, and the Pope gave him the cardinal's hat. Lang was an exceedingly eloquent and adroit man, yet he was just as famous for his elasticity of conscience as for cleverness. He surpassed in splendour all the cardinals and archbishops of his time, and in this respect certainly did not belie his Cæsarean descent. He died, as Cardinal Archbishop of Salzburg, in the reign of his nephew Charles V., 1540.

A striking likeness to the Emperor, and the parental affection received at his hands by Sigismund von Dietrichstein, caused the latter to be considered likewise as an illegitimate scion of Maximilian. The mother, the beautiful Countess Barbara von Thurn, married Pancras, the first baron of the name of Dietrichstein, the founder of the still existing princely house of that name. At that meeting with the Kings of Hungary and Poland in Vienna, in 1575, Maximilian had the marriage of his beloved Sigismund Dietrichstein with Barbara von Rothal, baroness of Thalberg, celebrated; and such splendour and magnificence was displayed at the wedding that all the contemporaries spoke of it with the highest admiration. Maximilian requested, even in his last will, that Sigismund should be buried at his feet at Wienerisch-Neustadt.

Count Ludwig von Helfenstein, the same whom in 1525 the rioters in the peasants' war forced to run the gauntlet through their spears, was likewise thought by some to have been a son of the "Last Knight of the Middle Ages"; but, according to other and more reliable accounts, he was the husband of one of the natural daughters of the Emperor.[1]

The number of these daughters, as we have said before, is known to have been five. Their husbands, as far as they have been ascertained, were Count John of East Friesland, married to Dorothea; and Louis von Herlemont, a Netherlandish lord, married to Anna. One of the daughters is known by her full name, Ottilia Lang von Wellenburg, a sister of the Cardinal Archbishop of Salzburg; she was wedded to the patrician of Ulm, John von Schad, to whom she brought the noble estate of Wellenburg.[2]

---

[1] The Helfensteins were a very old Swabian family. The connection of Ludwig with the Emperor Maximilian was through the lady who undoubtedly was his natural daughter. The fact is established among others by Sattler's Chronicle.—*Translator*.

[2] See Appendix A for samples of the style and courtesy used in Maximilian's diplomatic and private correspondence.

CHAPTER II

Charles V.—(1519-1556).

1.—His youth and education in the Netherlands.

MAXIMILIAN was succeeded by his grandson—the son of the King and Archduke Philip—Charles V., undoubtedly the greatest prince whom the house of Habsburg has produced. Whilst the romantic, chivalrous Maximilian entirely belonged to the middle ages, which terminated with him, Charles V. is in every sense a man of a new era, a deep politician, and a true disciple of the statecraft of Machiavelli. Maximilian was all his life restless, impetuous, and adventurous: Charles as quiet and circumspect as a man could be. Maximilian was the very type of imaginative enthusiasm, frequently overshooting its own mark; Charles, the man of calm, quietly reasoning common sense, and of most cautious political wisdom. Maximilian's form fades away in the bright evening sun of the expiring poetical middle ages: Charles meets our eye, stern and melancholy, in the dawn of a new, matured, and coolly calculating age. The greatest question of the sixteenth century, the Reformation, was looked upon by the grandfather as a mere parsons' quarrel: to the other it appeared as a dangerous rebellion; and he opposed the movement of the new religious spirit, against which the Pope had hurled the spiritual thunderbolt of his anathema, with the ban of the Empire, and with all the worldly expedients of the new system of polity. Neither Maximilian nor Charles comprehended the true importance of the religious question or recognised the necessity of placing himself at the head of the movement, to guide it, and to carry it out in a national German spirit and for the interests of Germany. Maximilian, in his gay carelessness, underrated its importance: Charles, in his melancholy scruples, overrated it. He saw in the new heresy only the great danger to the ancient political system of the German Empire, and on this ground he tried to wage a war of extermination against it. Neither of them was equal to the idea that a new system was to be introduced—a compact unity of Germany, a unity in that form which England alone of all the States of Europe has succeeded in establishing. Just as England, on the basis of the unity which was centred in its parliament, separated herself from the Pope, and made head against him, so Germany also ought to have done. But Charles aimed at sovereignty after the example of France, and his plan was to keep up the connection with the Roman Pontiff. As this plan was baffled by the Elector Maurice, the Emperor succumbed under the old aristocracy of princes. He was obliged to consent to a religious compromise. This completely altered his position, and his new position was a false one. He could no longer be looked upon as the secular protector of the Church, in which light he wished to be considered, according to the old political system of the Empire, for he had forfeited this title after having allowed another Church besides the old one to be tolerated in Germany. The very thing which he had tried to prevent was brought about, notwithstanding all his endeavours to the contrary. The old system in which Church and State, hierarchy and feudality, had been most closely interwoven, was now dissolved; a holy Roman Empire was henceforth an anachronism and a nonentity.

Napoleon took a very correct view of the position of Charles V. According to the reminiscences of Chancellor Müller of Weimar, he expressed himself, in 1813, during a ride from Weimar to Eckardsberge, to the following effect: "Charles V. would have acted wisely and well to have placed himself at the head of the Reformation. As the temper of the people then was, it would have been an easy thing for him to obtain by its means absolute rule over the whole of Germany."

The cradle of the Habsburg dynasty had been in the

mountains of Southern Germany, and near the lakes of Switzerland. Rodolph had transferred it eastward to the valley of the Danube, and there the foundation of the power of the house was laid. The meteor Charles, which shed the greatest lustre on that house, rose from the west, from the German Ocean.

Charles V. was born 24th February, 1500, at Ghent. The man, who was to become the ruler of two hemispheres, came into the world quite unexpectedly; his Spanish mother being surprised by the pangs of labour during a festivity at court.

Ann Sterel, the wife a German gentleman at Philip's court, a lady of good sense, of an excellent heart, and of great knowledge of the world, became his nurse. After the prince was weaned she remained in charge of him whilst his parents travelled to Spain. Charles's brother Ferdinand was born in 1503 in Spain. The chief governess of Charles was the Countess de Chimay. This lady was from the same Netherlandish family of Croy, to which also Charles de Croy, his governor, and William de Chièvres, his governor-in-chief and lieutenant-general of the Netherlands, belonged, whom Charles's father Philip appointed when he went to Spain.

Charles was surrounded by princely splendour even in his cradle. His father made him at his christening, 8th April, 1500, a present of the duchy of Luxemburg, from which the prince had his first title, until, in 1506, he inherited, on the death of his father, that of King of Spain. His old great-grandmother, the widow of Charles the Bold, Margaret of York, who had been a contemporary of the wars of the Roses, presented to him the figure of a child in massive silver, carrying, on a golden salver, a set of jewels. His aunt Margaret, Duchess of Savoy, the sister of his father, and afterwards regent of the Netherlands, gave him a golden plate, likewise spread with pearls and precious stones; William de Chièvres, a suit of silver armour inlaid with gold, the breastplate of which was decorated with a large phœnix; the Lord John of Berghen, a golden sword; the city of Ghent, a most ingeniously wrought ship of silver; several abbots, the Old and

New Testaments, the binding of which was of massive gold, studded with pearls and jewels. But, with all this princely magnificence, Charles's youth in the Netherlands, where he was reared, was very cheerless and gloomy. No parents' love exercised its genial influence over the tender years of his infancy and boyhood. When he was six years old his father Philip died suddenly in Spain, far away from him, after having lain on a sick bed only seven days, 26th September, 1506. His mother Joan, daughter of Ferdinand of Arragon and Isabella of Castile, likewise lived in Spain, and a deep gloom had settled on her mind. Jealousy of her husband had made her melancholy. This jealousy, indeed, was so violent that she poisoned him; a fact which has been fully ascertained from a letter written by one of Philip's generals. This account has been published by Hormayer in the "Historical Annual" for the year 1849, the last which he edited.

The writer of the letter very probably was that Count von Fürstenberg who commanded the 3,000 German soldiers with whom Philip, in the spring of 1506, embarked for Spain. Hormayer had before published in the "Austrian Plutarch" a letter of his to the Emperor Maximilian, dated 12th May, 1506, in which the following passage occurs: "The worst enemy whom my gracious lord of Castile (Philip) has besides the King of Arragon—[his father-in-law, Ferdinand, after Isabella's death, 1504, quarrelled with him about the regency of Castile]—is the Queen, his Highness's spouse. She is more wicked than I can write to your Imperial Majesty, and I have no doubt your Majesty has found that out much better than I am able to do. Her Highness will send to-morrow all the ladies, married and unmarried, back to Brabant whom the King has brought with her; she does not wish to have them about her, except one old woman, and her she keeps."

The letter of a later date by the same writer, communicated by Hormayer in the "Historical Annual" of 1849, runs thus: "The good King Philip was suspected by his Queen of an amour, and that without reason, as was afterwards discovered; but she took it so much and grievously to heart that she at last resolved to kill her lord and husband in revenge for it. As women are so easily moved and impelled, according to the old adage, 'that they have long robes but short counsels,' thus it also happened that she got so utterly beside herself as to poison her good and innocent husband, although it was to her own loss. Shortly after, she found out that she had been wrong, and that she had allowed her quick temper to get the better of her. Then she began to rue what she had done, and found no rest, tormented as she was by the furies of remorse; and, as she had her husband no more, and could not get him back, she began to love him twice as well as before, and grieved and fretted so vehemently that at last she went out of her mind altogether, and became quite childish. People did not dare at first to inform the Emperor Maximilian of this murder, nor even of the death of his son; but when he had been dead for some time accounts were sent, from one post to another, announcing his illness, and that he was getting worse and worse, until at last the whole secret was disclosed."

Having thus lost her beloved husband by her own fault, in the tenth year of their married life, grief for his death reduced her more and more to a state of insanity, as all her passionate love for him had now revived. She ordered his body to be taken from the tomb, and had him placed in her chamber, splendidly attired, and encased in a glass coffin. Here she looked at him for hours, embraced his embalmed remains, and watched day and night over him. Still possessed by her inveterate jealousy, she would not allow anyone of her own sex to enter the room. At last she was with difficulty prevailed upon to allow the body to be placed in a vault in the Charterhouse of Millaflores, near Burgos. But as soon as this was done her mind completely gave way. Her father, Ferdinand, during a former absence of her husband in the Netherlands, had shut her up as a prisoner at Medina del Campo. She now fancied that she was again a prisoner and kept away from her beloved one. Her people were at last obliged to urge her to have the vault opened once more, that she might convince herself of Philip's death. She had it done, but took the coffin now with her in her travels. She travelled at night with burning torches, the corpse of her husband being driven before her on a bier. Strange to say, a prophecy had foretold to Philip that he should travel in his kingdom longer after his death than during his life. Joan continued to console herself with a tale which a Carthusian friar had once told her, "that there had once been a king who had come to life again after fourteen years." She waited like a child for that happy day; but when it came at last, and she found herself bitterly disappointed, she fell into hopeless insanity, and had to be confined in a tower. Here she passed the remainder of her days, surrounded by cats, with which she amused herself. She survived her husband fifty years, dying about nine months before the abdication of her son Charles, who, properly speaking, during her lifetime reigned in Spain only in her name, all the royal decrees being headed by the joint names of Donna Juaña and Don Carlos.

Charles V. was likewise separated from his brother Ferdinand, who was educated in Spain. His sisters only, especially his favourite sister Mary, were brought up with him. Their education was, as has been said before, superintended by their aunt Margaret, the Duchess Dowager of Savoy, whom her father the Emperor Maximilian had, in 1506, made Regent of the Netherlands. There was appointed under her, as Lieutenant-general of the Netherlands and chief governor of Prince Charles, who was then six years old, William de Croy, baron de Chièvres and Arschott, whose nephew, Charles de Croy, acted as under-governor. William de Chièvres had, of all persons, the greatest influence upon the disposition of Charles; from his bringing up, as many lights as shades have resulted in the character of this remarkable prince, who appeared upon the world's stage at one of the most critical periods of the history of Germany.

Some very interesting letters are extant from the time of Charles's earliest boyhood. Charles de Croy wrote from Mechlin, 7th October, 1506, very shortly after Philip's death, to the old Emperor Maximilian in Germany:

"SIRE,—In order to offer you some consolation, I certify to you that your grandson and granddaughters are in very good health, and are having a pleasant time, as is natural to them. I have told them of their misfortune—at which they are grieved as children would be, and more than I thought—and amongst other things that they have still a kind parent in you, Sire, I recommend them to you, and hope that your affection for them may be increased."

On 9th April, 1507, the Emperor writes to his daughter Margaret (in French):

"I am very glad that you find our children so pretty, and that they long after me; tell them that I shall soon come, but that I am now prevented from being of any service to them. To-day I issue letters to the whole Empire, calling it to arms, and I promise help to the Pope. The King of Arragon is going to Spain immediately with his wife, whom the devil has got with child. She is about four months gone.[1] The plan is to make war against the King of Castile (Charles V.) and others, to drive them out of the country and then to take possession of it. For the Queen his daughter is and remains *fantastica*—brûlez, ma chère fille, cette lettre de votre bon père Maximilien."

On the 19th September, 1508, Chièvres writes (in French):

"Your Majesty's grandson, and the Princesses his sisters, are coming on very well indeed, and it is really astonishing how beautiful they grow up. In obedience to your Majesty's wishes, I will take care that he shall learn the Brabantian language as soon as his tongue is sufficiently pliant for it, and that he shall learn how to read it."

The principal instructor of the prince in the languages, and especially the classical ones, as also in religion, was the learned Dean of Louvain, Adrian Florentius of Utrecht, who, after the death of Leo X. was raised by his pupil to the papal chair, which he occupied from the 9th of January, 1522 to the 15th of September, 1523, as Adrian VI. Adrian had the greatest difficulty in inculcating into his pupil the rudiments of Latin. In vain he represented to the prince that the Emperor, his grandfather, insisted above everything upon his speedily acquiring this language. Charles answered, with boyish warmth, "But my grandfather has not surely ordered you to make a schoolmaster of me." This aversion, however, vanished when the mind of the prince was sufficiently matured to comprehend what treasures the language of the

---

[1] Germaine de Foix, Ferdinand's last wife, shortly afterwards miscarried, whereby Ferdinand the Catholic was baffled in his wish of excluding his grandson Charles through a son.

Romans contained. Adrian had no less difficulty in inducing the prince to get through the whole of the Bible. The boy wanted to have to do with nothing but the heroic books—Judges, Kings, and Maccabees. Thucydides, of all authors, became his greatest favourite, although he only read him in the French translation of Bishop Claude of Marseilles. He used to keep him under his pillow as Alexander did the "Iliad," and this Greek historian afterwards always accompanied him to the camp.

Even before his accession, at the age of sixteen, Charles spoke six languages with great fluency. He used to say, when still a youth, "that he learned Italian to speak with the Pope; Spanish, to speak with his mother; English, to speak with his aunt (Catharine of Arragon, Queen of Henry VIII. of England); Flemish, to speak with his friends and playfellows; French, to speak with himself; and German, in order to be qualified to become Emperor."

His two other instructors appointed by De Chièvres, besides Adrian of Utrecht, were Charles Cernio, a Netherlander, who infused into him that love of travelling which during the whole of his life remained a prominent feature of his character; and the Castilian Antonio Vacca, a learned lawyer.

The prince at an early age showed great proficiency in all manly and chivalrous sports, being in this respect a perfect counterpart of his grandsire, whom he also emulated in gallantry towards the fair sex, only that he carried on his intrigues with much greater secrecy.

William de Chièvres was an exceedingly rigorous governor, insisting with inexorable tenacity upon the prince's doing everything to acquire business habits. Charles was not once allowed to stay away from the sittings of the Council of State, where he generally had to act as secretary. Chièvres slept in the prince's room, who was obliged by him immediately to open the despatches which might arrive at any hour of the night; and, whether they were important or not, briefly to state his opinion in the margin. Whilst thus introducing Charles into the routine of business, he broke his wayward and restless disposition. The liveliness of the youth changed into gravity, and all the passions of his ardent soul became subordinate to one—the ambition of showing himself worthy of his princely calling. An instance is recorded of Charles's uncommon liveliness, which happened when his grandfather brought with him to Mechlin the celebrated painter Lucas Cranach, who was to paint for the Emperor the portrait of his grandson. The prince, at that time in his eighth year, at first baffled every endeavour of the artist to take his likeness, and would not keep quiet for one moment. At last his tutor Adrian hit upon the plan of suspending against the wall opposite a splendid set of arms by the side of the portrait of the King of France. From that moment the Prince kept his keen glance steadily fixed upon the lineaments of the hereditary enemy of the house of Burgundy and upon the arms. Charles had not yet completed his fifteenth year when he was told that the Count of Angoulême, afterwards King Francis I., had taken away by force Claude, the daughter of Louis XII. of France, to whom he was himself affianced. He merely remarked: "Well, do you think that I ought to be angry at it? On the contrary, I am very glad. Now, as I am no longer bound to the French by any tie, I may hope one day to make war against them to my heart's content."

Ambition at an early age threw Charles's mind back on its own resources. A profound reserve, a spirit entirely living within itself, independent of all but its own intrinsic energy, soon showed itself as the groundwork of his character. The gloomy sadness of his mother, which in a wonderful manner was blended in him with the levity of his gay father, grew more and more upon him the more his mind became matured. There was evidently more of the Spaniard than of the German in him. The grave business to which he was kept when still a youth, and his isolation within the cold barriers of royal pomp, with no loving parents near him to cheer his tender years, brought out even more forcibly the natural melancholy of his disposition.

Charles, at the age of scarcely eighteen, one day made his

appearance at a great tournament in Valladolid. On his blank shield only the word "*Nondum*" was written. Afterwards his motto was "*Plus ultra!*" Ludovico Murliano, who had suggested it to him, got the cardinal's hat for it. The "*Plus ultra*," with the pillars of Hercules, was placed by Charles on his coins and his seals, with the legend underneath, "*Sobrie, juste et pie.*" He also used the motto, "*I and the right moment against any two of them.*" His coat of arms was charged with two spheres. Yet all his royal splendour left him unsatisfied. The monarch whom a Persian ambassador once addressed as "the King who had the sun for his hat" passed through life joyless. This feeling of void grew so intense towards the end of his life that, having with most bitter mortification arrived at the conviction of the vanity of all human ambition, tired of the greatness of this world and of the pomp of royalty, he resigned all his lustrous crowns to retire into the devotional solitude of a small monastery of Jeromites in Spain. Charles, after being all his life a politician, ended as a hermit. He exchanged his two favourite authors, the old heathen Thucydides and the modern heathen Machiavelli, one of whose books he constantly carried about him in his pocket, for St. Augustine and St. Bernard. His ardent ambition was cooled down; but the fundamental type of his nature, melancholy, outlasted the passion which had gnawed him during the whole of his worldly career.

2.—Accession in the Netherlands and in Spain, and election as Emperor.

At the age of fifteen, in 1515, Charles undertook the government of the Netherlands, which, being the land of his birth, he all his life continued to prefer to any other. The 23rd of January, 1516, marked the death of Ferdinand the Catholic, his grandfather on the mother's side, who had until now carried on the regency of Castile. Charles now set out (12th of August, 1517) for his newly inherited kingdom—the country of the strictest Roman orthodoxy, the country of the Inquisition, whose King bore the emphatic title of "The

Catholic." He embarked at Middleburg in company with his sister Eleanora and William de Chièvres, who was now placed at the head of his court as lord chamberlain. On the 20th of September, 1517, Charles landed at Villa Viciosa in Asturia; but, on account of the plague having broken out there, he returned to Santander, from whence he went by Burgos and Valencia to Tordesillas near Valladolid to his mother, who, notwithstanding her derangement, was exceedingly rejoiced to see him.

The first governmental act of Charles in Spain was the removal of his brother the Infant Ferdinand, at that time not more than fourteen years old, and who had until then been brought up at Valladolid. He was sent to the Netherlands, because Charles had ascertained that the young prince had been egged on to intrigues against him, the King. The motives which caused him to remove his brother guided him also in the dismissal of the aged Cardinal Archbishop of Toledo and Grand Inquisitor Ximenes, who had succeeded Ferdinand the Catholic in the regency of Spain, and had reduced the Spanish grandees to obedience by a militia of 30,000 burghers. Charles, at the suggestion of Chièvres, sent word to the cardinal at Valladolid that his merits were so great that Heaven only could reward them, and that he therefore allowed him to end his days in quiet in his see. The cardinal was so chagrined at this sarcastic message that he died a few hours after having received it, 8th November, 1517, without having seen Charles. He had reached the advanced age of eighty-one years. On the 4th of January, 1518, the young King held at Valladolid his first Castilian Diet; and in May, at Saragossa, the first for Arragon. After this he remained in Spain until the spring of 1520. In the meanwhile his other grandfather, Maximilian, the German Emperor, had died. Charles was just staying at Barcelona when, in the beginning of the year 1519, he received the news of his death, on which he immediately took measures for obtaining the imperial crown of Germany, for which Francis I., the French King, was his rival competitor. Charles accordingly sent his ambassadors to Frankfort, where the election was to take place. He availed himself for this purpose of his connection with the celebrated bankers Fugger at Antwerp, who were a branch of the great Augsburg firm: his agents were ordered to do as the delegates of the French King did—they bribed the electors. The election cost 852,989 florins.[1] The German princes, who so bitterly reviled the Pope for having sent to them the hateful vendor of indulgences Tetzel, to extort money for "the Roman grace," now took money themselves. The Elector Palatine was paid 40,000 florins for his vote. Frederic the Wise of Saxony alone did not debase himself; he returned the considerable sum of money which the Spanish ambassadors sent to him. They then begged him that he would allow them to distribute part of it among his courtiers. Frederic, however, answered, "I cannot forbid them to accept what is offered to them, but whoever takes even one florin will leave my house to-morrow." Charles could not prevail upon Frederic the Wise to take anything for his vote but the promise of giving one of his own sisters to Frederic's nephew, the same who was afterwards known as John Frederic the Magnanimous, and who lost his electorate in the battle of Mühlberg. The Fuggers did then what the Rothschilds have been in the habit of doing since; they promoted as much as possible the election of Charles by protesting the French bills of exchange and honouring none but the Spanish ones.

At first the German electors had hit upon the expedient of offering the crown, not to either of the two powerful rivals, but to Frederic the Wise. He, however, declined it. He was fifty-six years of age, and, being a really wise man, he felt diffident of the sufficiency of his own strength for carrying such a heavy burden as the crown of Germany. Thereupon the King of Spain was proclaimed on the 28th of June, 1519. But the Spanish ambassadors had, for the security of the princes, to sign in the name of their master the first "Electoral Capitulation." The good-natured Germans quite

---

[1] Annual pensions to the amount of 70,400 florins, and a round sum of 504,060 florins, to be paid down at the election, had been promised by Maximilian as early as in October, 1518.—*Lanz, State Papers of Charles V.*

seriously expected to tie down by a sheet of parchment a power of such magnitude as was at the command of Charles. None of the Emperors before him had possessed those immense territorial resources which were at the disposal of the heir of the crowns of Burgundy and Spain. The "Capitulation" contained the provisions—that the Emperor should conclude no alliance with foreign powers nor declare any war without the consent of the German electors and princes; that he should introduce no foreign soldiery into Germany; that, moreover, no member of the Empire was to be put under the Emperor's ban without the assent of the princes in council and without being heard in his defence; that Charles as soon as possible should in person make his appearance in the Empire, and should reside there for the greater part of his time; that all the business of the Empire should be conducted in the German or Latin language; and lastly, that all the offices in the Empire or the court should only be filled by native Germans. *The powerful heir of the crowns of Burgundy and Spain broke every one of these stipulations.*

On the 20th of May, 1520, the newly elected Emperor left Spain with the fleet sent to him from Flanders. After paying a visit to Catharine of Arragon in England, he went to the Netherlands, landing at Flushing, and then proceeded to Bruges, where his aunt Margaret and his brother Ferdinand received him.

On the 22nd of October Charles rode into Aix la Chapelle, where, according to ancient usage, the head of the holy Roman Empire was to be crowned. He there appeared pale, grave, taciturn, and melancholy. He had, as it were, as his symbol, a hollow figure to precede him, in which a man was walking. This figure represented Charlemagne, the Prince who first established the *Roman* Empire of the *German* nation. The entry lasted from between two and three o'clock in the afternoon to eight o'clock in the evening, there being 5,000 horses and 3,000 men-at-arms in five divisions, picked troops, under the command of Francis de Castilalt. The procession was headed by the servants and the baggage; after which followed the princes, lords, counts, and barons, nearly 1,000 horses, all of them dressed, as an old account states, in the King's colours, and most of them in raiments of silk velvet, and gold brocade, and also otherwise embroidered with pearls and precious stones. They were followed in their turn by the twenty-four pages of the Emperor on horseback, dressed in parti-coloured suits; one side, crimson satin, trimmed with gold and silver brocade; and the other, gold and silver brocade trimmed with crimson satin. After them came the master of the horse, the kettle-drums, and twelve trumpets; six persons who flung silver and gold coin to the people; the herald with a silver-gilt staff surmounted by an eagle; then followed the electors, the princes, and bishops; the Earl Marshal of the Empire, Von Pappenheim, with a drawn sword; and then the Spanish King Charles, clad in a suit of armour, over which he wore a coat of gold brocade. He was mounted on a magnificent charger, beautifully caparisoned and decked out with gold brocade. He showed his horsemanship to great advantage. On his right rode the Archbishop of Cologne, and on his left the Cardinal of Mayence. After Charles came, riding alone, the ambassador of the King of Bohemia and Hungary, who represented his master also as an elector of the Empire. Then came the ambassadors of England and of Poland, the cardinals of Sitten, Salzburg, and Toledo. All these princes were surrounded by their body-guards on foot. The Emperor had a hundred Germans dressed in velvet and in the King's colours, and a hundred archers in coats of silver brocade, both of these bodies wearing halberds.

Charles took his oath on the "Capitulation." On the following day he was crowned with great pomp and magnificence. He already then began to carry matters with a very high hand; he declared that he was resolved to raise the imperial dignity to its old splendour, and that it was by no means his will and intention that there should be many masters, but one alone. He completely overawed the German princes by his proud, taciturn, Spanish *grandezza*. The old etiquette of the Empire left it optional to address the Emperor by the courtesy of "Imperial Highness," or "Imperial Grace," or "Imperial Majesty;" but he strictly insisted upon that of "Imperial Majesty."

From Aix la Chapelle Charles betook himself to Cologne, whence he summoned his first Diet to meet at Worms on the next Epiphany. All the six electors and many princes of the Empire, secular and spiritual, were present here in person. They looked somewhat poor by the side of the magnificent Netherlandish, Spanish, and Italian lords whom Charles had brought with him. The poorest of all in appearance was that humble monk of Wittenberg, who had likewise been summoned to the assembly of the great. But Luther's spirit at Worms conquered the spirit of Charles, and stamped upon the history of the world the new era which dates from that Diet.

The day appointed for the opening of the Diet was the 28th of January, 1521. Not without a meaning had the fifth Charles selected for it the fête of Charlemagne, the first Charles. Luther arrived at Worms on the 16th of April. On the 18th he delivered his celebrated declaration, which will live for ever in the annals of the world, "Concerning Holy Writ, and the public, distinct, and clear reasons and causes," &c. On the 26th of April he left Worms, and on the 8th of May Charles issued the famous Edict of Worms, in which he enhanced the papal anathema against the humble monk by the ban of the Empire, just as the Swabian Emperors had done against Arnold of Brescia and those of the house of Luxemburg against the Hussites.

On this Charles returned from the Diet to Spain, taking the same road by which he had come, through Flanders and England. At Dover, where he landed, he was received by Cardinal Wolsey. Henry VIII. entertained the Emperor with great magnificence at Greenwich, at Wolsey's palace in London, and at Windsor. At the latter place Charles was created Knight of the Garter, and a contract of marriage was concluded between Charles and Henry's daughter, then in her seventh year. The betrothal was to have been acted upon as soon as the Princess should have completed her twelfth year. This infant bride was no other than the "bloody Mary," who afterwards, at the age of thirty-eight, married the Emperor's son Don Philip, who was her junior by eleven years.

The fleet with which Charles sailed from Southampton to Spain consisted of 180 Netherlandish ships; as ally of the King of England, he very discreetly appointed the admiral of the English fleet, the Earl of Surrey, an imperial admiral.

For nine years Germany did not again see her imperial master. Charles bided his time, true to his motto, "*Nondum.*"

Charles left in Germany a regency, under his brother the Archduke Ferdinand, with whom the Elector Frederic the Wise of Saxony succeeded in acquiring great influence. Whilst the religious movement was going on in Germany, Charles thought of nothing but of carrying out his vast political plans. First of all it was requisite to reduce Spain to obedience, and then to begin the contest against his principal rival *for the object which has remained the keystone of the Habsburg policy to this very day*—THE CONQUEST OF ITALY—*which the founder of the dynasty, in order to raise the Swiss baron to the head of the Germano-Roman Empire, had in former times himself made over to the French.*

3.—*The French wars—Battle of Pavia—Assault of Rome—Challenge between Charles and Francis I.—Siege of Vienna by the Turks in* 1529.

As soon as the Emperor had gone to Germany for the coronation, a rebellion broke out in Spain, caused by the avarice of the Netherlandish councillors whom he had there appointed, and by the heavy taxes exacted by them. This rebellion Charles very adroitly availed himself of to introduce into Spain an absolute government, after the pattern of that which Francis had before him established in France. The Communeros of the Santa Junta of Castile had been conquered already, during Charles's absence, near Villalar, by the royal troops, with the help of the nobility; and the head of the Junta, Don Juan de Padilla of Toledo had been executed. Charles, on his return to Spain (1522), cut down the liberties of the Cortes to such a limit that they could no longer interfere with his absolutist tendencies. He then launched with all his might into the war against France, for which purpose he allied himself with England. Francis I. was to be forced to evacuate Milan and Genoa, and to leave Charles sole master of Italy, where Naples and Sicily already obeyed the Emperor's sway.

Charles had the good fortune of being aided by excellent commanders in war. He was one of the first modern princes who succeeded in securing for himself the services of able generals. The Spanish army was commanded by Prosper Colonna, of the ancient celebrated Ghibelline Roman house; one of whom, in the days of Philip le Bel of France, had boxed the ears of the Pope. Colonna was Viceroy of Naples. He had serving under him the man who became the first captain of his age, Fernando de Avalos, Marquis of Pescara, the husband of the beautiful Vittoria Colonna, to whom Pescara had been affianced since his third year, and who, after his early death, celebrated his memory in a spirited heroic poem. Pescara was prudent and brave, but at the same time a most stately and gallant man; in his suit of red, with a short, sleeveless black coat over it, and wearing a lansquenet's hat surmounted by large waving plumes, he made a most imposing figure at the head of his Spanish arquebusiers, whom he knew right well how to command, and whom, in fact, he had made an invincible troop. This Spanish army under Colonna and Pescara was now joined by the burly old George of Frundsberg with his German lansquenets, for whom he had caused two thousand peasants to cut a road over the roughest Alps of the Valteline. Colonna, Pescara, and Frundsberg jointly defeated, in 1522, the French and their allies, the Swiss, near Biccocca, not far from Milan. By this battle, which Charles won, and by that of Marignano, which Francis I. had won seven years before, the power of the Swiss was broken for ever. They henceforth became the mere mercenaries and prætorians of foreign princes, and the horn of Uri no longer resounded but to call the herds of cattle on the Alpine meadows. In 1523 the Constable Charles, Duke of Bourbon, Count of Montpensier, a cousin of the

King of France, was induced, by a provocation received from the latter, to go over to the Emperor; and in 1524 Charles V., with an imperial army, invaded Provence, and laid siege to Marseilles; but without result, as the English fleet did not arrive, and the Emperor's admiral, Hugo de Moncada, could not keep the sea against the French squadron, which was commanded by the celebrated Andrew Doria.

In the following year we find Francis I. in Italy, whither he had led, across Mount Cenis, a numerous French army, supported by 8,000 Swiss and 5,000 German lansquenets, the so-called Black Guard, which dated from the times of Matthias Corvinus. After the conquest of Milan by Francis, the two armies encountered on the banks of the Ticino, near Pavia, which town was garrisoned by imperial troops under Antonio de Leyva. The King of France had taken a strong position in the park of Pavia. Here he was attacked by Pescara, Frundsberg, Bourbon, and Charles de Lannoy (Viceroy of Naples since the death of Prosper Colonna, and ancestor of the present Princes of Rheina-Wolbek in Prussia). Frundsberg gathered his twenty troops of lansquenets round him and spoke to them: "My dear brothers and sons, we have a proud enemy before us, but we have always beaten his men and captains; and now also, with the help of God, you will do your duty as honest Germans!" Upon this all the men and officers cheerfully raised their hands and called out that he was a father to all of them, and that they would willingly lay down their lives for him.

In the night of the 23rd of February, 1525, Pescara ordered the wall of the park to be battered. The morning dawned before the breach was yet made. It was the Emperor's birthday. The breach being opened, Pescara marched against the small palace of Mirabella, which his nephew, the Marquis del Vorsto, speedily took by a spirited assault. The balance of the victory, however, remained long undecided, until at last Pescara threw out, as skirmishers, his Spanish arquebusiers, with their matchlocks, which were still rested on forks. Not one of them missed his man; and the French cavalry—the gendarmes of the King—were thrown into confusion, which grew worse when the imperial garrison of Pavia came out and took them in the rear. All now fled, even the Swiss, quite contrary to their usual custom; and also the Black Guard, which Frundsberg caused to be cut down nearly to the last man, as a chastisement for their having, as Germans, enlisted under the French king. In that forest-garden of Pavia the flower of the French chivalry fell round their chivalrous King Fràncis, who, conspicuous by his glittering shirt of silver mail and his waving plume, made a desperate resistance. All pressed round him to protect him; four marshals fell by his side, and after them his grand equerry, St. Severin, whose duty it was to ward off the strokes which were aimed at the King. The crowd was so close that there was no room for shooting. Francis, still in his saddle, was as if wedged in by a wall of corpses. He was just going to cross a bridge, when his horse, struck by a shot, fell, and rolled over him. The Spaniards and Germans now began to quarrel as to which of the two nations should have him for a prisoner. But Francis, although bleeding in his forehead, his hands, and his legs, continued to fight on foot, striking down two more of his foes. Nicholas, Count of Salm, who had attacked him with his cuirassiers, and wounded him in the right hand, was stabbed through the thigh. All now called upon the King to surrender, when Pompérant, a knight of the Constable of Bourbon, came up, and, although Francis was disfigured by blood and dust, recognised the King of France from his chivalrous defence. Falling on his knees before Francis, he adjured him to surrender to Bourbon. The King, however, called out, "I know of no Duke of Bourbon but myself; I'll rather die than surrender to the traitor Bourbon; let the Viceroy of Naples be summoned."

As Lannoy made his appearance the King pledged himself to him as his prisoner, offering in token the gauntlet of his right hand. After this, Lannoy on his knees received the bloody sword of Francis, to whom he returned his own, with the words, "It is unseemly that such a great King should stand without arms before a subject of the Emperor."

Francis was now led to the neighbouring Carthusian convent at Pavia, where he wished to pray. The first thing that met his eyes on entering the chapel was an inscription on a side altar taken from the Psalms: "It is good for me that I have been afflicted; that I might learn thy statutes." Francis, smiling, pointed out the words to Lannoy. He then was led to a tent, from whence he wrote to his mother those famous words, "*Madame, tout est perdu, sauf l'honneur.*" His person was entrusted to the safe keeping of the Spanish Colonel Alarçon, and he was taken to the fortress of Pizzighetone.

The Emperor Charles was in Spain, in his palace at Madrid. There he received, through the commander De Peñalosa, who was sent as a courier, the news of the great victory of Pavia, of the captivity of the King, and of the complete conquest of Italy. A fortnight after the day of Pavia not a Frenchman was to be seen in Italy. Charles, after having heard the news, and received the sword of Francis, remained speechless for some moments; after which he was heard saying to himself, "The King in my power, the battle won for me." Then, going to an adjoining room, he knelt down in prayer before an image of the Virgin. The Emperor wrote to Lannoy:

> "What you have now to be most diligent in is to collect money, because it is always useful; I will do the same in this direction, &c. I do not know where to employ myself, unless it be against the infidels; I have always been desirous of so doing, and at this hour not less. Assist to well arrange affairs, so that before I become much older I may do that by which God may be served, and that I may not be to blame. I call myself old, for in this case the time which is past seems to me long and the future far."

Henry VIII. of England, the Emperor's ally, demanded neither more nor less than that Francis should be deposed and himself crowned King of France. On the other hand, all that had been alienated from the territory of the German Empire, and especially the old Duchy of Burgundy, was to be ceded to the Emperor. But Charles would not enter upon such a treaty of partition, and England separated from this alliance and sided with France, whereupon the projected marriage between Charles and Mary Tudor was given up.

The Pope now, after England, became Charles's worst enemy. The Bishop of Rome, remembering the time of the Hohenstaufen, was more afraid than anyone of the excessive power of the Emperor. The Holy Father therefore allied himself with all the Italian powers against Charles in the so-called Holy League of Cognac. Clement VII. even tried to gain over Charles's best general, the Marchese Pescara, by the offer of the crowns of Naples and Sicily. But Pescara remained true to his master, and soon after died, being not more than thirty-six years of age, on the 29th of November, 1525, and was succeeded in the chief command of the Emperor's army by the Constable of Bourbon.

Francis had requested to be conducted to Spain, where he hoped in person to receive better conditions from Charles. During the passage, the ships having sailed from Genoa in June, 1525, Doria with his galleys met the squadron in the Gulf of Lyons. But the Viceroy of Naples, who escorted the King, called out to Doria that it would be death to the King if he dared to make an attack. Upon this the Spanish squadron proceeded on its way, and reached the coast of Spain without any further molestation. Francis landed at Valencia, and he hoped now to have an interview with Charles. But Charles came not. Francis then wrote to him the two following letters, which have been lately communicated in the "Papiers d'Etat du Cardinal de Granvelle":

I.

"If my cousin, the Viceroy of Naples, had given me my liberty sooner, I should ere this have made my submission. Having no other comfort in my misfortune than my faith in your clemency, and the hope that you will generously use the fruits of your victory, I beg you to deal with me tenderly, knowing that your rule has always been marked by honour and magnanimity. And if you be pleased to deal with me truly and pitifully, and with treatment befitting a King of France, who would become your friend and not die of despair, you would gain a friend instead of a useless prisoner, and make a King your slave for ever. Therefore, not to weary you any further by this sorrowful letter, I will end by submitting myself to your clemency, who have no other wish than to be called by another name than prisoner.

"Your good brother and friend,

"FRANCIS."

II.

"Seeing that since the letter that I have written you it has pleased you to send me M. de Reux, who returns to you, I have thought to write you this letter so that it may please you to recognise the duty in which I wish to place myself, having sent to Madame my mother [Louise the Regent of France] the decision I ought to come to with regard to my deliverance, begging you to be so kind as to receive it and judge it as an emperor would who desires rather to do honour to himself than hurt to the one who hopes so much mercy and kindness of you, and who will be, instead of your slave, ever your good brother, friend, and grateful

"FRANCIS.'

To this Charles made answer as follows:

"I have received your two letters, &c., and everything is understood; they abound with good words, as one would expect from as virtuous a prince as you are. But neither on your part nor on that of Madame la Régente, to whom, you write me, you have referred, has any answer been given to the proposals I advanced; neither have any other overtures been made to me. That is not the way to arrive at peace, which I desire should be general and durable, for the sake of God and also of Christianity, guarding my honour without staining yours, conserving my friends and also desiring to see you delivered, when you will recognise the goodwill I have to be and remain your true brother and friend,

"CHARLES."

Charles for a long time made no preparation whatever to see his illustrious prisoner, although he had him brought, in the month of August, to the neighbourhood of Madrid for better security. Francis, in September, fell sick with vexation. His sister Margaret, Duchess of Alençon, the poetess, and friend of Calvin, came to see him, and paved the way for negotiations. At last Charles came and tried to console the captive King by courteously holding out to him a prospect of a speedy arrangement. Francis recovered his health, but not his liberty; at least not for some time, as his captivity lasted upwards of a year.

In Charles's council opinions differed as to what should be done with the royal prisoner. One party, to which the Chancellor Gattinara belonged, advised the Emperor to treat Francis with generosity, which very likely might destroy for ever the seeds of dissension. The other party, comprising Lannoy, the Duke of Alva, Count Henry of Nassau (uncle of William of Orange), and the Emperor's most influential confessor, the Dominican Garcia de Loaysa, wished to turn the occasion as much as possible to advantage. The Emperor steered a middle course. As Francis ostentatiously professed his readiness to resign the crown of France, Charles decided upon releasing the King, but with the condition of his renouncing for ever Burgundy, Flanders, Artois, and Italy.

The wily disciple of Machiavelli, for once overshooting his mark, forgot that it was his own policy to let might go for right, and that therefore Francis, when he had once recovered his might, would take very good care to recover his right also. Francis was to become Charles's brother-in-law by marrying his sister Eleanor, the Queen Dowager of Portugal. Francis, only to escape from the captivity which had become well-nigh intolerable to him, agreed to anything and everything, and thus the peace of Madrid was concluded, which Francis signed on the 14th of January. But, with the assent of the Pope, who absolved him from the oath which he was going to take, he had already before recorded a solemn protest against the validity of the treaty, which, it is true, had been exacted from him by force. Yet he took the oath at a solemn high mass, laying his hand on the Gospel. From thence he went to Illescas, half-way between Madrid and Toledo, to be affianced to Eleanor. After this the Emperor and the King frequently met, were carried in the same litter, and called each other brothers. As they took leave of each other near a crucifix which had been set up a little way from Illescas, the Emperor said, " Remember, my brother, what you have promised me ; *tell me truly*, will you keep the articles?" Francis made such an answer as he thought it right to make. The Emperor then parted from him with the words, "There is one thing I beg of you, if you do anyhow deceive me, let it not be concerning your affianced bride—*she would not be able to revenge herself.*"

Francis now, accompanied by Lannoy, Alarçon, and a troop of gendarmes, rode to the frontier, the Pyrenees. As the cavalcade reached the river Bidassoa, Marshal de Lautrec presented himself on the opposite bank with an escort of French horsemen. In the middle of the Bidassoa, where the two parties met in the ferry-boats, the King was exchanged for his two sons, who were to be taken to Spain as his hostages. "Sire," said Lannoy, "your Highness is free; be pleased now to fulfil what you have promised." Francis hastily answered, "All shall be fulfilled." Then, after embracing his two sons, to whom he addressed the parting wish, "May God protect you, my children," he jumped into the French ferry-boat. On reaching the land, where the *might* was his, he mounted a Turkish charger which had been kept in readiness for him, and exclaimed, "*Je suis le roi, le roi!*" After this he started at a gallop to St. Jean de Luz, and from thence to Bayonne, where his family and the court expected him. This happened on the 18th of March, 1526.

Scarcely had the King of France *reached his own country in safety* when he sent his excuses to the Emperor, that he should not be able to keep the treaty, *because the States of the realm refused to give their consent to the cession of Burgundy.* He therefore offered to the Emperor a large sum of money for the restoration of his sons.

In the same fortunate year (1526) the twin crowns of Bohemia and Hungary devolved on the House of Habsburg. Louis II., the last Jagellon king of those realms, husband of Mary, the sister of Charles V. and Ferdinand, died at the age of twenty-one, after the battle of Mohacz in 1526, without leaving any children; when, according to the provisions of the Treaty of Vienna, concluded by Maximilian in 1515, the Archduke Ferdinand, husband of Ann Jagellon, and brother-in-law of Louis, succeeded. This was the third of the three great marriages with heiresses, the other two being the Burgundian Mary and the Spanish Jane, which have raised the power of Habsburg-Austria to the first rank in Europe. But it was much easier to acquire than to maintain Hungary. Germany had thenceforth to combat there her principal foe, the Grand Turk, the terrible Sultan Soleyman.[1] The ruler of the Moslems allied himself with the monarch of France, the most Christian king—whose other ally was the Pope—against the Emperor, whose exorbitant power certainly all Europe had now to fear. There was really every reason to believe

[1] Born 1495; died 1566.

that Charles would restore the Germano-Roman Empire as a universal monarchy after the pattern of Charlemagne. The fear of the accomplishment of such a plan, of which the young ambitious Emperor was perhaps not unjustly suspected, was one of the principal causes by which the schism in the German Church has been nurtured.

Immediately after taking leave of Francis, Charles V. married, in Seville (15th of March), Isabella, daughter of Emanuel the Great of Portugal—a princess who was considered one of the most beautiful women of her time.[1] He remained in Spain, whilst his army accomplished in Italy one of the boldest feats against the man whom the Emperor in public revered as the Holy Father, but against whom he was in his heart greatly incensed as against an ally of France who had attempted to induce Francis to break the peace of Madrid, and who had tried to seduce Pescara from his duty by promising him the viceroyalty of Naples. Charles, after having been apprised of the league of the Pope with France, had, by way of reprisals against him, suspended in Germany the Edict of Worms, thus allowing the German princes to reform their churches after Luther's doctrine as their consciences might dictate to them. He had asked them also for help against the Turks, expressing his belief that they would easily guess *what Turks he meant*.

Bourbon was still stationed with the Spaniards in Milan, whither George of Frundsberg, who was a friend of Luther, led to him 16,000 lansquenets, most of them likewise Lutherans. The Venetians having closed the narrow Veronese passes, Frundsberg marched across the most rugged mountains, passing the Sarke hills by a road, which in fact was only a footpath, along the edge of the steepest precipices. The old captain walked along the most dangerous spots by the lances of his men, as along a railing. He joined Bourbon on the 31st of January, 1527. The imperial army in Italy, Germans as well as Spaniards and Italians, were left without any pay, the consequence of which was that they rebelled. Bourbon applied to the Pope for money; the Holy Father

---

[1] The nuptial solemnities will be related in another place.

refused it. Frundsberg, whom the lansquenets called their father, and the enemies the "Devourer of the People," waited in vain for letters or messages from Germany, and, always showing a cheerful face and trusting in God's help, promised the lansquenets that he would not leave them until they were paid. The mutiny broke out at last; it went on from the 13th of March, in the evening, to the 15th at noon. On the 16th Frundsberg addressed his men near Bologna; but his eloquence would not avail this time, the angry children shouted, "Money! money!" and lowered their lances against their father. The old man, deprived of speech by his towering rage, raised his hands; the big tears stood in his eyes; he tried to open his lips, but sank swooning on a drum. An attack of paralysis had struck him. On this the lansquenets became silent, and quietly dispersed. On the fourth day only Frundsberg recovered his speech, but never again his strength, and he was obliged to stop at Ferrara. He recrossed the Alps in the following year, and died at his estate of Mindelheim, in Swabia, which afterwards became the property of the Fuggers, and at last of the crown of Bavaria. It is the same lordship from which, in the war of the Spanish succession, the Duke of Marlborough took his title as Prince of the Empire. Frundsberg used to say, "Three things ought to deter a nation from war: the misery into which the people are plunged; the wicked life of the soldiery; and the ingratitude of the princes, with whom the faithless are sure to rise in favour, and the well-deserving servants remain unrewarded." On the death of Frundsberg his estates were found to be mortgaged to merchants, as he had never in his life received any gratuity for his faithful services. He died on the 20th of August, 1528. Bourbon, whose tent the lansquenets had invaded, whose coat had been torn from his back, and who, amid the fury and the threats of the men, had only saved his life by flight, and by hiding himself under the straw in Frundsberg's stables, now took the chief command of the whole army, the Germans included. The soldiery, instead of pressing for their arrears, demanded speedily to be marched to Rome, where they said there would be no lack of pay, as all the money of Christendom had gathered there for centuries. Bourbon was not in a condition to oppose their request.

On the 5th of May, 1527, at sunset, the Constable with his army of 25,000 men appeared before the walls of the Eternal City. Pointing out to his troops the shining domes and pinnacles of its churches and palaces, he promised them the plunder of the place. Everything was at once put in readiness for the assault. A thick fog in the morning concealed from the Romans the approach of the hostile army. The ladders were planted without delay, and the escalade began. Bourbon was repulsed several times, the Swiss making a stout defence for the Pope, who, with his cardinals, had taken refuge in the castle of St. Angelo. At last Bourbon, being conspicuous to friend and foe by a white cloak which he wore over his suit of armour, snatched a ladder from the hands of a Spanish soldier, and began scaling it. But he had only climbed a few steps when a shot from an arquebuse struck him down. The Imperialists now entered Rome; the Swiss gradually gave way; and before evening set in the capital of the world was conquered.

The soldiery, no longer restrained by the control of a commander, continued to sack the city for ten days. The hordes of his Catholic Majesty committed atrocities equal to any which have been recorded of the Goths and Vandals. Sebastian Schärtlin of Burtembach, one of the captains, writes in his autobiography: "On the 6th of May, 1527, we took Rome by assault. We slew 6,000 men in it; sacked the whole town; took away whatever we could find in the churches or above ground; burnt down the greater part of the city; and there were all sorts of strange doings. In the castle of St. Angelo we found Pope Clement with twelve cardinals in a narrow stable, and took him prisoner, and made him sign the articles which the clerk read out to him. There was great sorrow among them; they wept very much, but we all of us grew rich." Reisner, in his quaint "Life of Frundsberg," states: "The German lansquenets put the cardinals' hats on their heads, donned the long scarlet robes, and rode on donkeys about the city. William von Sandizell (a Bavarian captain of Frundsberg's) often used to make his appearance before the castle of St. Angelo dressed up as the Pope of Rome, with the triple crown; and his men, in the cardinals' robes, bowed before him. Then the mock pontiff, with a glass of wine, officiated; and the mock cardinals drank his health after him, calling out that they were now going to make right good popes and cardinals, who would be obedient to the Emperor, and not cause rebellion, war, and bloodshed as the others had done. At last they shouted aloud, '*Let us make Luther Pope of Rome!*' whereupon all raised their hands, shouting, '*Luther a Pope! Luther a Pope!*'"

This game was carried on before the castle of St. Angelo in derision of the real Pope, who was shut up in it, first when besieged and then as a prisoner. A German lansquenet, Grünewald, especially distinguished himself in mortifying and frightening the Pope. He publicly called up to the castle, "that he would be only too happy to tear a piece from the Pope's body and take it to Luther, because the Pope had until now so vehemently opposed the Word of God." Clement VII., a scion of the celebrated house of Medici, had to pay 400,000 scudi as his ransom, and give up to the imperial troops his fortified places around Rome and in Lombardy. Until the stipulated sum was paid he was to go as prisoner to Naples, under the guard of the same Colonel Alarçon to whom Francis I. had been entrusted.

The Constable of Bourbon, because he died excommunicated, was not buried, but kept in a box in the castle of Gaëta. The Bavarian Baron von Lerchenfeld-Aham, during his journey in 1728, still saw the body. It was standing upright, in a Spanish dress, with a hat and peruke, holding a cane in its hand and wearing a sword at its side.

The Emperor, who did not care to make the world believe that the assault of Rome had happened with his knowledge and by his orders, sent letters of excuse to all the Christian princes. Whilst his soldiery, who, it is true, could no longer be restrained after having lost their commanders Bourbon and Frundsberg, kept the Pope prisoner, first in the castle of St. Angelo, then in Naples, Charles had public prayers offered for the delivery of the Holy Father in all the churches of his empire. The Pope made his escape on the eve of the 10th of December, 1527, the day on which he was to have been liberated and sent back to Rome. Lest he should a second time be exposed to the insults of the soldiers in Rome, he went, very likely with the knowledge of his gaolers, to the camp of the Holy League at Orvieto. The imperial army left Rome only after a stay of ten months, having, in retribution of the horrors committed by them, dwindled by disease to 25,000 men. It marched to Naples, which the French under Lautrec had invaded with great success. Charles was in a very critical position.

Diplomacy now came to the rescue. Charles, who was always successful on that field, executed a master stroke. He brought the celebrated Genoese naval hero, Andrew Doria, over to his side. Doria, who had been elected Doge of Genoa, now sailed with his fleet to the relief of Naples, and forced the French to raise the siege of that city. With this, fortune again turned in favour of the Emperor.

Whilst this was going on in Italy, there had been between Charles and France a new declaration of war, and, moreover, that remarkable challenge for single combat concerning which the "Papiers d'État du Cardinal de Granvelle," lately published from the public library of Besançon, have communicated the documentary evidence.

The declaration of war was made in the ancient mediæval style by two kings-at-arms of the allied monarchs of France and England, the heralds appearing in person at the court of Charles V. at Burgos, 22nd of January, 1528. On the 28th of March, 1528, Nicolaus Perrenot de Granvella had his farewell audience with Francis I. in Paris. The King wished to commit to his care the challenge to Charles bearing the same date. Granvella declined to take it; it was therefore delivered to Charles on the 7th of June of the same year, at Monçon, in Arragon, by Guyenne, *Roi d'Armes de France*, and was to this effect:

"We Francis, by the grace of God King of France, lord of Gennes (Genoa), &c. To you Charles, by the same grace elected Emperor of the

Romans, King of Spain, cause to be known, that we being warned that in some answers that you have made to our ambassadors and heralds sent you for the sake of peace, you have said that against our faith and promise we have released ourselves from your hands and power. In order to defend our honour—the which in this case is accused contrary to truth—we have wished to send you this challenge, wishing that each should have satisfaction, and also our own honour—the which we wish to defend and will defend, if God pleases, until death—we give you to understand that if you have charged us, or wish to charge us, not only in our said faith and speech, but that we have ever done anything that a gentleman loving his honour ought not to do, we say that you have lied in your throat, and as many times as you do say it you will lie, being determined to defend our said honour until the end of our life. Henceforth we shall not write anything, but will bear arms against you, protesting that, if after this declaration, in any place you write or say anything against our honour the shame of the delay of the combat will be yours, seeing that our meeting must be the end of our correspondence.

"Done in our town and city of Paris the 28th of March, 1527.

"(Signed) FRANCIS.

"(And above is put a seal of vermilion wax.)"

The challenge was provoked by the following statement, which Charles had made in a written communication to the French ambassador, Jean de Calvymont, dated 18th of March, 1528.

"Substance of the words written by his Majesty to the President and Ambassador of France, who pretended not to remember what the Emperor had previously said to him at Grenada.

"I have told you that the King your master had acted cowardly and wickedly in violating the word that he had given me at the treaty of Madrid, and that if he pretended the contrary, I would sustain it against him man to man.

"These are the very terms of which I have made use concerning the King your master at Madrid, telling him that I would hold him for a coward and evil-doer if he went from his word which he had given me; and in so qualifying him, I hold more faithfully to my promises than he to his.

"Given at Madrid, March 18th."

Charles sent to the challenge of Francis an answer to the following effect:

"I Charles, by divine mercy, Emperor of the Romans, King of the Germans, of the Spaniards, &c., to you, Francis, by the grace of God, King of France, make known, &c.

"And to this effect and more prompt expediency, I name to you now the place of the said combat upon the river which passes between Fontarabye and Andaya in such a position and in such a manner as will be mutually considered most sure and most convenient; and it seems to me that reasonably you cannot refuse, nor say you were not informed, since you were there released on giving your children as hostages and by means of your word henceforth, to be guarantee of your return; and seeing also that upon the same river were trusted your own person and that of your children, you can well trust yourself alone, since I will put myself there, and, notwithstanding the situation, will take care that neither one nor the other has the advantage. And to the effect as above, and to settle upon the choice of arms—which I consider is for me and not for you—and in order that there may no longer be any delay, we will send to the said place gentlemen from each side with sufficient power to advise and conclude all arrangements with regard to arms and any other matter touching this combat.

"And if in forty days after receipt of this you do not respond nor advise me of your intention, it will be plainly seen that the delay of combat will be yours, and that you can be accused of not having accomplished what you promised at Madrid.

"And as for your protestation that, if after your declaration I should say or write words in other places that may be against your honour, the shame of the delay of the combat will be mine, your said protestation is easily excused; for it is not for you to hinder me from speaking the truth, much as it may grieve you; and I am quite sure that I cannot reasonably take the blame of delaying the combat, since everybody can recognise the desire that I have to see the result of it.

"Given at Monson in my kingdom of Arragon the 24th day of the said month of June, 1528.

"CHARLES.

"(And sealed with his private seal.)"

Bourgogne, the king-at-arms of Charles, delivered his letter to Francis on the 10th of September, 1528. But the affair did not go any further. No duel was fought; Cardinal Wolsey having in the meanwhile, on the 15th of June, brought about a peace. Yet even as late as on the 9th of November Charles wrote to his chamberlain, William de Montfort, his ambassador in the Netherlands:

"As regarding the challenge .... do not forget to inquire in every place if I am still bound to do anything further to satisfy my honour, for I would not fail therein."

Both parties now longed for peace, which was at last concluded in 1529, at Cambray, by two ladies, Louise of Savoy, the mother of Francis; and Margaret, aunt of Charles, and Regent of the Netherlands; and which, therefore, was called the "The Ladies' Peace." The King of France paid two million crowns for the liberation of his two sons, who were still kept prisoners in Spain. Eleanor, Charles's sister, whom Francis now married, brought the young Princes back to him. Francis also renounced his claims to Italy; whereas Charles, on the other hand, did not press for the immediate cession of Burgundy, reserving, however, his claims to it. Charles likewise concluded peace at Barcelona with the now humbled Pope, Clement VII., and installed another Medici as hereditary Duke of Florence, to whom he afterwards gave his natural daughter Margaret in marriage; the duchy of Milan he restored to Francesco Sforza. Genoa remained a Republic under the Doge Andrew Doria.

Charles then left Spain, and betook himself to Italy, where he had never been before. He went there to be crowned by the Pope as Roman Emperor. On the 12th of August, 1529, he landed at Genoa, surrounded by a splendid retinue of Spanish grandees. From Genoa he went to Bologna. Here he met the Pope, kissed, according to ancient usage, on his knees the foot of the Holy Father, and was by him crowned King of Lombardy and Roman Emperor. The coronation took place on the 24th of February, 1530, the anniversary of the victory of Pavia, and at the same time his thirtieth birthday. *It was the last coronation of an Emperor performed by a Pope until the time of Napoleon.*

Great splendour and profusion were displayed on that occasion. Gold and silver coins were flung to the people on the first day by a herald, during the procession from the church after the coronation; and, on the second day, for two whole hours from the balcony and the corner windows of the palace. At the coronation banquet all the gold and silver plate and other costly vessels of the table were, after every course, likewise thrown out of the window to the people. The Spanish Charles had not one prince of the German Empire with him. This was a new fashion; no Germano-Roman Emperor had been crowned in this way before. But, on the other hand, as a faithful son of the Church, he stayed with the Pope for five months under the same roof at Bologna.

The Emperor had now his hands unfettered against the Turks, and also against the German Protestants, of whom he had very cleverly made use as bugbears to frighten the Pope. He therefore now resolved upon going to Germany, where he had summoned the princes of the Empire to Augsburg. It was the celebrated Diet at which the confession of the Protestants was brought forth, the Diet of the year 1530.

Even before having crossed the Alps, Charles received the joyful news of the departure of the Grand Turk, who had made his appearance before Vienna whilst the Emperor was engaged in settling the affairs of Italy. Never before had the Turks advanced so far westward. They had reached the height of their power under Soleyman; having become a naval power, they had conquered Rhodes, from whence the Knights of St. John were then obliged to remove to the Island of Malta, of which Charles V. made them a grant in 1530.

The Turks had invaded Hungary since 1521, after having conquered Belgrade, the key of that kingdom. In 1526, as mentioned before, Louis II., the last Jagellon of Hungary and Bohemia, was killed in the battle of Mohacz, after which the Hungarians elected John Zapolya, Count of Zips (John Zapol Scæpius). An opposition party elected the brother of Charles V., Ferdinand, Archduke of Austria, who, however, was not able to maintain himself in possession of what he considered his hereditary kingdom. Charles allied himself with the Shah of Persia, Ishmael Sophi, to have the Turks attacked in the East; his ambassador to the Shah was the Knight of St. John De Balbi. His instructions, dated from Toledo, 18th of February, 1529, have lately been communicated by Lanz.

Soleyman overran the whole of Hungary, and laid siege to Vienna for twenty-one days in autumn, 1529. His army was estimated at 250,000 men, the baggage being carried by 22,000 camels, which animals had never been seen before in those parts. The tents of the Moslems spread along the whole valley of the Danube, Soleyman's own gorgeous pavilion being pitched near Sömmering, where, dressed in silk, gold, and purple, he might be seen issuing his commands. Ferdinand, with his court, fled to Linz. Vienna was indifferently fortified, having only a single wall and a dry ditch, and it was garrisoned by not more than five regiments; but from the times of the old Emperor Maximilian, who had had a particular fancy for heavy ordnance, there were so many cannons in the town that all the wall and even the roofs of the houses could be armed with them. There were, moreover, Tyrolese miners in the city, who foiled the mines of the Turks by counter-mines; and thus all their attacks were successfully repelled.

The departure of the Grand Turk took place, after an unsuccessful general assault, on the 14th of October, 1529.[1] Soleyman left in order to escape from the cold of winter and to return at his own convenience. He took with him an immense number of captives; the kidnapped Christian children were to recruit the ranks of his Janissaries.

Hungary had to be left to the "highly favoured Turkish Emperor Soleyman," as the celebrated Sigismund von Herberstein calls him, who afterwards was sent to him as ambassador. With great difficulty Hans Katzianer,[2] Herberstein's nephew, preserved the very small part which remained to Ferdinand.

The house of Habsburg was more successful in the other kingdom (Bohemia) which Ferdinand had acquired by his marriage with Ann Jagellon. At first, in addressing the Bohemian Parliament, he spoke of the inherited claims of his wife to the crown; but this allusion very nearly cost him all his expectations, and he was forced to acknowledge by a special document that he owed the kingdom to election. He now obtained the crown from the representatives of the nation by means of the old-established electioneering expedient of bribing the voters. Yet he confined himself to promises, of which he was most lavish, especially towards the great nobles. But he took very good care to leave his promises unfulfilled. To give one example: the old Count Palatine (*Oberstburggraf*) of Bohemia, Zdenko Leo of Rozmital, brother of the queen of King George Podiebrad, had been promised 50,000 ducats, of which, after long waiting, he received a very small sum on

---

[1] Soleyman suffered a loss of about 100,000 men.
[2] Katzianer received the wolf, which had formerly belonged to the coat of arms of Zapolya, for his own. The family of Katzianer was raised to the dignity of counts in 1665.

account. When, however, in 1541, the *very welcome* fire in the archives of the parliament of Prague had *accidentally destroyed all the old documents*, Ferdinand declared, in his testament of the year 1543, "that he had given those pledges only in ignorance of the real facts of the case, and that he had since ascertained from the Golden Bull of the Emperor Charles IV., his predecessor in the kingdom, that by all means in the realm of Bohemia, after the extinction of the royal male line, the females were entitled to the succession"; moreover, he had by negotiation prevailed upon the parliament to return to him the acknowledgment which he had signed. The fate of Bohemia was accomplished only after the battle of Mühlberg, in 1547, and after the battle of the White Mountain, in 1621, in the "Altstätter Ring" at Prague, of which more hereafter in its proper place.

Charles, from the coronation at Bologna, went, in the spring of the year 1530, across the Alps, to attend at the Diet which he had summoned to Augsburg. During the nine years of his absence from Germany important changes had taken place, which might not a little aid his ambitious plans for the establishment of absolute rule, which he entertained with regard to Germany as well as to Spain.

Of the four great estates of the German Empire—*the electors and princes*, who constituted the high aristocracy; *the free cities*, which still appeared at the Diet, but made no great figure there; and, lastly, *the knights* (smaller nobility and gentry) of the empire, and *the peasantry* (yeomen), who were not represented at the Diet at all—the two latter had been crushed by the storms which the religious movement had conjured up. The German Reformers, being very well-meaning but exceedingly unpractical men, with but a very slight knowledge of the world, expected to keep their work clear of every admixture of political elements. But the worldly and political element forced its alliance upon the cause, owing to that close connection between moral and material interests which had linked together Church and State during the whole of the middle ages, and by which the two will be linked together as long as man is not a spiritualised nonentity, without human wants and human desires. The two estates which wished to derive political results from the religious movement were the lower nobility (gentry) of the empire and the peasantry. Their field of action was the *Sickingen Feud and the Peasants' War.*

4.—*The Sickingen Feud and the Peasants' War.*

The numerous nobility (gentry), vassals *in capite* of the Empire (*reichsunmittelbar*), on the banks of the Rhine, in Swabia and Franconia, wished to avail themselves of the Reformation to appropriate large estates belonging to the Church, in order thereby to be able to form a counterpoise against the princes, and to break the thraldom which they had sometimes to endure from them. A host of pamphlets were published, in which it was set forth that the authority of the imperial prerogative should be restored, the property of the Church turned to account for improving the position of the common people, of the burghers, and of the lower nobility, and the political power of the princes and prelates be crushed for ever. Francis von Sickingen had for a long time been the secret leader of the lower nobility. He was born in 1488, at his family seat of Sickingen, in the Palatinate. He was of small stature but of large mind, and of an iron will, which he brought to bear upon the most lofty aspirations. Being the possessor of a great many castles on the left bank of the Rhine, in the retired forests of Kreuznach and Kaiserslautern, to the west of Mayence and Worms, he was constantly at feud with the neighbouring princes, secular and spiritual, with the Bishops of Mayence and Worms, and with the Dukes of Lorraine. When Charles V. began the contest with France for the possession of Italy, he entrusted Sickingen, as his privy councillor and general, with the chief command on the Rhine. Sickingen there fought against Bayard. He was the idol of the soldiers; when he rode through the camp, everyone had a smile for him. The lansquenets pressed round his horse, patted it, and would also sometimes shake the hand of the knight, with whom they used to make so free that one day they snatched from his helmet the crape which he wore as mourning for his deceased wife, and fixed it to the pennons of their troops. But when, in the hour of the fray, he shouted with his voice of thunder his "At them!" he well knew he might reckon upon his men.

It was during the French war on the Rhine that Sickingen, although being the Emperor's general, began to negotiate with Francis I. His friend, the celebrated Ulrich von Hutten, had given him the far wiser and more patriotic advice to league himself with the German towns and the peasantry. Pamphlets written by Hutten, and printed at his castle of Ebernburg, near Kreuznach, or at that of Steckelberg, belonging to Sickingen, were already circulated in the villages; and they told among the people. Three years after copies of them were found among the papers of the ringleaders of the great peasants' riots. But Sickingen either would not wait for the assistance of the common people, or, in his aristocratic pride, disdained covering with his baronial shield the cause of "pepper bags and smock-frocks." He therefore allied himself with the foreigner, with whose help he hoped to carry out his far-aiming plans.

He summoned in 1522 all the imperial (*reichsunmittelbar*) nobility of the banks of the Rhine, Swabia, and Franconia to a great meeting at Landau. He was appointed captain of the League; and his enemies already began to call him the Anti-Emperor, as they did Luther the Anti-Pope. Having assembled the considerable force of 12,000 mercenaries, he invaded with them in the middle of summer the spiritual Electorate of Trèves. After having conquered the Elector, he intended to turn his arms against the other members of the high princely aristocracy. The princes were seized with terror. Men who were intimately acquainted with the general temper of the times saw very clearly the magnitude of the danger. France, however, left Sickingen in the lurch; upon which the nobility, just as happened afterwards to the peasantry, were reduced one by one by the neighbouring princes, the Elector Palatine and the Landgrave Philip of Hesse, who came to the rescue of Trèves. The three Princes of the Palatinate, of Hesse, and of Trèves, invested Sickingen in 1523 in his stronghold Landstuhl, near Kaiserslautern. The artillery of the princes knocked down the walls of the knight's castle, and a splinter from a rafter struck by a cannon ball inflicted a fatal wound on Sickingen. The three princes entered by the breach into the castle, and stood before the dying man. When the Elector of Trèves began to chide him, Sickingen only replied, "I have now to do with a greater Master than you are." Immediately after he expired. Ulrich von Hutten fled to Switzerland, where he died on the soil of freedom as the guest of the burghers of Zurich, on the island of Ufnau, in their lake, in 1525.

Thus were the German imperial nobility conquered, owing to their isolating themselves in their aristocratic pride; and never since Sickingen's defeat have they been able to recover their old importance and independent position. They had now to bow before the princes, at whose courts, at a later period, their reduced ambition was content to disport itself in diminished proportions. In a similar manner the German peasantry wrought its own ruin by plebeian stiffneckedness. Their rising was as isolated as that of the nobility; and thus they were conquered, singly, in divided hosts. It was 300 years ago just as we have seen it in our own times.[1] The energetic exertions of the armed opposition, as they were made singly, without distinct consciousness of their ultimate object, although not without great valour, could not but end in smoke.

In the most ancient patriarchal era, when the whole nation in times of war was one vast host, the German peasants had been independent freemen. Their position grew worse and worse during the feudal ages, when, partly from want of protection, and partly by force, they were driven into a state of vassalage and even serfdom. In this position, however, the services which they had to render to the lords of the noble houses were regulated by fair laws and contracts, and the protection received in exchange was an important equivalent for them. As early as the fourteenth century, in

---

[1] Written after the 1848 rebellion.

the days of Louis of Bavaria, and in those of the Emperor Charles IV., the peasantry had their riots of "poor Claus" (Nicolas) and of Hans Behem the drummer. In the Netherlands, especially in the province of Holland, the rebellious peasants were called "the Käsebrodter," from the bread and cheese on their banners. Yet their position became quite intolerable only as late as the reign of the Emperor Frederic III., when they were reduced to abject servitude and dependence. The German lords began to imitate the luxury which had been generated in the Burgundian court; and since the proud Spanish Charles had displayed his pomp and magnificence in their Diets, they did not wish to cut a less figure than the stately Netherlandish, Spanish, and Italian nobles in the suite of the Emperor. The increased expense they charged upon the peasants, by adding to their feudal burdens. This state of things was further aggravated by the extortions of the newly established lansquenets, whom the princes now kept as standing troops, and who lived principally on the peasantry. But as this soldiery was generally raised from the country population, the peasants were thereby again practised in the use of arms, and able to wield the sword and battle-axe for the recovery of those ancient rights which their oppressors had wrested from them. At the Diet of 1517 already, the Committee of the States had given it as their opinion that "the ferocity which had for some time been traceable in the peasantry, and their readiness for rebellion, were merely owing to the fact that the lansquenets, who had served in foreign wars, were dismissed to their homes again."

Another source of evil for the peasantry was the introduction of the Roman law, which gave rise to a most harassing system of tedious lawsuits, as the delays of justice became the interest of the learned lawyers, who thus were enabled to enrich themselves at the cost of their unfortunate clients. The nobles in some instances also treated the peasants with the most overbearing insolence. Thus the peasants of the Wetterau, in the Electorate of Trèves, and in Lorraine, were bound to perform the strange service of flogging, during the summer nights, the water in the moats of the seignorial castles, in order that the frogs might not annoy the lords by their croaking. The towns and cities did not care to help the peasants. They likewise looked down upon them with disdain; and on their own territories, which sometimes were very considerable, they, instead of trying to raise the condition of the country people, made it their endeavour to keep them under as much as possible. Owing to this contemptuous treatment of the peasantry, the towns and cities afterwards in their turn came to ruin. They too fell singly before the power of the princes; and, although they were the last to fall, yet fall they did.

The peasants felt the shoe pinch them, and for that reason they adopted it as their emblem on their banners. The "Bundschuh"[1] is for the first time mentioned as having been raised in 1439, at Strassburg, in Alsace. Upwards of eighty years after, in 1522, it turned up again in Southern Germany, where the sight of the neighbouring free and, owing to their freedom, wealthy Swiss, excited the anger of the German peasants, when they compared this prosperity with their own miserable condition. In the Hegau, a district of Swabia, belonging to the Duchy of Würtemberg, the peasants rose, bearing a golden shoe on their banner, with the motto:

"He who wishes to be free, may follow this sunshine."

The peasants wished the Christian freedom which Luther preached to be understood as political freedom. It appeared to them very unchristian that their lords should thus cruelly oppress them. The peasants of the Hegau were overcome; but after the autumn of 1524 the agitation spread through the whole of Upper Swabia; and when the peasants in the county of Stühlingen were commanded by their overbearing countess to gather snails for her, that her servants might wind yarn on the shells, they refused, and rose under a black, red, and white standard. During the winter of that year, King Ferdinand, the Emperor's brother, who in his absence was regent of the

---

[1] Either the "Shoe of the League," or the peasants' laced shoe. Both interpretations have been given; the latter is the more likely.—*Translator.*

Empire, appointed as general of the Swabian league against the peasants, Truchsess[1] George of Waldburg, or, as the peasants called him, *Bauernjörg* (peasants' Georgy). He was a scion of that Swabian house whose ancestor accompanied the last Hohenstaufen to the scaffold, and who there received from the hands of the unfortunate Conradin his gauntlet and his signet, to take it to Peter of Arragon; in memory of which event, the Waldburgs to this day quarter the three Hohenstaufen lions with their own arms. Truchsess was ordered to arrest the rebel peasants, and to question them on the rack as to who were their leaders; after which all should be slain who could be got hold of, their lands devastated, their houses burnt, and their wives and children expelled without any forbearance or mercy.

In 1525 the rebellion broke out in every direction. The first were the peasants of the Abbot of Kempten; they were followed by those of the Bishop of Augsburg. The peasants of Truchsess himself joined the insurrection, as did also those of the imperial city of Ulm; the most numerous host of them, however, was formed by the peasants of the neighbourhood of the Lake of Constance. The latter hemmed in Truchsess near the monastery of Weingarten, and he had to make concessions on the basis of the so-called "twelve articles" of the peasants. This summary of their demands was rapidly circulated by them throughout Germany. The peasants would agree to submit their grievances to the arbitration of a committee of umpires, which they in their simplicity wished to be composed of King Ferdinand, the Elector of Saxony, Luther, Melanchthon, and some pastors. It was just as in 1848, when also the entire salvation of Germany was expected to proceed from Frankfort alone, from those learned professors who made such fine speeches in St. Paul's church.

The twelve articles demanded that the peasants should be at liberty to choose their ministers themselves, who were to preach the pure word of God; that they should not pay more than the tithe, out of which the parish minister was to be paid, and, with the remainder, the parish expenses and those

---

[1] This title, grown into a name, corresponds to the Scotch of "Stewart."

for the support of the poor, were to be defrayed; bondage should be abolished; the socage burdens and the rate of interest be reduced. Moreover, the articles stipulated that the chase, fishery, birdcatching, and forests and woods should be free, and the property of everyone; and justice be administered by judicious men of the nobility and from the towns, not by the doctors of law, who only perverted the law and made it expensive.

The princes were far from accepting these articles, and Luther also opposed them. It was an abomination to him that the religious movement should be turned into a political one. His own inborn rustic humility could not brook the idea of allowing the great lords to be harassed by the common mass. To him doctrine and discipline appeared the only thing needful in the community; he was convinced that everything would be subverted unless the secular power were left at the helm of the State. He knew very well that the root of the evil lay with the great lords, and he wrote, "We have no one to thank for this mischief and rebellion but you princes and lords, who do nothing but grind the faces of the poor, to carry on your pomp and vanity, until the common man cannot, and will not, any longer bear it." But he stood firm to the dogma of passive obedience. To this we must add that he was afraid, and justly so, lest a mob rule should be even worse than the tyranny of the princes. After the peasant riots were put down, he said, "I certainly apprehended that if the peasants got the mastery, the devil would be abbot; but that if the princes got it, his mother would be abbess." He had to bear the reproach that the rebellion had been *his* work. There was one thing which weighed with him more than any other, and that was, not to allow the pure gospel to be compromised by the excesses of the peasantry. Their conduct, indeed, justified his fears: their demands were just and fair enough, but their untutored bands were soon carried away by their own wild passions; the complainants became the self-constituted judges of their own cause, and—a melancholy fact, which occurs over and over again—they now practised the same iniquities under which they themselves had groaned. It did not strike Luther that the best way for him would have been to go in person to the peasants, to take the lead of the movement out of their hands, and to act as mediator. The peasants set fire to the seignorial manors and to the monasteries. In those times most of the feudal donjons were destroyed; among others the magnificent castle of Hohenstaufen, the ancient hereditary seat of the Swabian Emperors. The bands of the peasants rapidly increased; in Franconia one host gathered under a black banner in the Odenwald; and another, from the valley of the Neckar, assembled under gay colours. A war of extermination was carried on against the nobles, with the cry, "*The idlers have no right to live!*" At Weinsberg, celebrated for its true-hearted women,[1] Count Louis of Helfenstein, the husband of a natural daughter of the Emperor Maximilian, had, with seventy other nobles, to run the gauntlet through their lances, whilst a piper was playing "to the dance." His wife, having her little son Maximilian with her, entreated the murderers to spare the life of her husband; but she was not listened to. The peasants wounded her boy, an infant of two years, in her arms; and, after having despoiled her of all her jewels and trinkets, sent her, together with another lady, on a dung-cart to Heilbronn. The peasants told the Council of Nuremberg in plain words "that they did not intend to rest as long as there was a house in the country better than a peasant's cabin."

Luther, being apprised of it, wrote his book against the "rapacious and murderous bands of the peasants," in which he called upon everybody "to smash, to strangle, and to stab the peasants in public and in private, just as you kill a mad

---

[1] Weinsberg castle had to surrender, after a siege, to the Hohenstaufen Emperor, Conrad III. The conqueror having given permission to the women, and especially to the noble ladies, to take away with them as much as they were able to carry, they were seen issuing from the gates with their husbands on their backs, declaring them to be their most precious possessions. The Emperor, however, allowed them to take all their clothes and jewels likewise. It was at this siege (1140) that "Guelph" (Welf) and "Ghibelin" were first heard as war-cries. The ruins of the castle, called from that incident *Weibertreu* (woman's truth), are still standing. Gold rings, with a peculiar sort of pebble which is found on its hillside, used, some sixty years ago, to be given as love-tokens.—*Translator*.

dog." "The mob needs to be ruled by force; the ass must be cudgelled. If there are any innocent among them, God will preserve and save them, just as he did Lot and Jeremiah. If He do not, they certainly are not innocent, but have at least connived at the crimes of the others by their silence."

The whole passionate, choleric temperament of Luther vented itself in these words, which remind one of the speech of Arnold, abbot of Citeaux, when, in the war of the Albigenses, he with the Count of Montfort took Bezières by assault. "Slay them all," Arnold said; "the Lord knows his own!" Luther by that pamphlet severed himself entirely from the peasants, and left them to their fate. Two circumstances had, it is true, much to do with his resolution. Carlstadt, "the heavenly prophet," had taken part with them, and the Swiss, who were particularly odious to Luther, on account of their anti-sacramentarian principles, stood in connection with them. Caspar Schwenkfeld, the notorious Silesian divine, at that time said something for which Luther never forgave him, and for which the Wittenberg reformers set him down as a visionary: "Luther has led the people from Egypt (from Popery) through the Red Sea (through the bloody Peasants' War); but he has left them in the lurch in the wilderness."

The peasants were headed by able men: by Götz (Godfrey) von Berlichingen, the well-known robber-knight with the "Iron Hand," whose castle lay on the Kocher, in Franconia, and whom they had compelled to take the chief command; and also by Wendel Hippler, chancellor of a Prince of Hohenlohe, who had voluntarily engaged in their cause. Hippler advised the peasants to take into their pay the many lansquenets who were friendly to their cause, inured to war, and ready to join them; and especially he tried to persuade them to unite themselves with the lower nobility (gentry). But the peasants were too stingy; they presumed on their own great numbers, by which they thought they would be able to make up for their want of military experience. Besides Berlichingen, however, we find other noblemen, such as the Counts of Wertheim and Henneberg, and Florian

Geyer, as captains of the peasants. They were the Mirabeaus of those days. Wendel Hippler conceived comprehensive plans for the thorough reform of the Empire. He held on the 12th of May, 1525, a high parliament of the peasantry at Heilbronn on the Neckar, their head-quarters. At this assembly the ideas which afterwards became those of the French Revolution of 1789 were for the first time proclaimed in their full bearing. It was proposed "to abolish the feudal burdens and to indemnify the princes and barons for their loss from the ecclesiastical estates, which were to be secularised; both the Church and the administration of the law were to be radically reformed; free trade to be established by abolishing the tolls and customs; a decennial tax for the Emperor to be levied; and uniform measures and weights to be introduced. The peasants were to be represented at the Diet of the Empire as a separate estate, by the side of the clergy, the princes, the barons, and the towns."

But the Lutheran peasants, unlike the Bohemian Hussites, did not obey their leaders. The peasant, it was said, wanted to be master himself. Götz von Berlichingen having secretly left them, they in their turn were defeated and destroyed singly. Truchsess von Waldburg took a terrible revenge. Würtzburg, which the peasants had taken, and where they besieged the bishop in the castle, had to be given up to Waldburg, after which he inflicted most awful chastisement on the rebels. The other princes did the same, the spiritual ones showing themselves not the least bloodthirsty. The Elector of Trèves and the Bishop of Würtzburg made a progress through their countries, accompanied by an executioner, to have the culprits put to death before their own eyes: he of Trèves is even said to have cut off heads with his own hands. As if to show the common people the ingenuity of persons of exalted birth in inventing the greatest possible variety of tortures and excruciating punishments—fingers, noses, and ears were cut off, eyes scooped out, the culprits broken on the wheel, lacerated with red-hot pincers, flayed alive, impaled, and roasted by slow fires. All were, however, surpassed in cruelty by Anthony, Duke of Lorraine, the brother of the founder of the celebrated house of Guise, and of the Cardinal of Lorraine. He caused at Saverne, in Alsace, a band of as many as 18,000 peasants to be put to the sword, an atrocity the more revolting as he had previously pardoned them.

Besides these disturbances near the Rhine, the Maine, the Neckar, and the Lake of Constance, there were other peasants' riots in Thuringia during the first four months of the year 1525. This insurrection was headed by Thomas Münzer; but here the rising had a religious character. Münzer had distinguished himself before in the religious troubles at Wittenberg, got up by him in conjunction with Dr. Carlstadt, which, however, were crushed by Luther in their very outbreak. Now Münzer came forth as a heavenly prophet, pretending to have spoken face to face with God, as Moses did. He inveighed very vehemently against Dr. Luther, whom, in a pamphlet published in 1524, under the title "Against the Spiritless Soft-living Flesh at Wittenberg," he called Dr. Lügner (liar), and he charged him with having made the Reformation an affair of the princes, whereas he himself would carry it out as an affair of the people. Münzer then already preached the principles of communism, which have turned up again in our days. He said: "The princes take all God's creatures for their property, even the fish in the water and the birds of the air. On the other hand, they say to the poor, 'It is God's commandment, Thou shalt not steal.' They themselves grind and fleece all; but as soon as a poor man lays hold even of the least that is not his he is hung, and Dr. Liar says Amen to all this. The Lord has given the earth to the faithful as their inheritance; all government ought to be carried on only according to the Bible and to Divine revelation; princes, nobles, and priests are not wanted. In the kingdom of God all men ought to be equal; *all men also ought to live in a community of goods, for all are brethren.*"

Thomas Münzer established himself in the small imperial town of Mühlhausen, where, with the help of the common people, he ousted the magistrates, and made himself the preacher and master of the town. In a printed manifesto he called himself "Thomas Münzer, with the hammer"; proclaiming in plain words that all princes were to be banished or killed. From Mühlhausen he overran the whole of Thuringia, where his peasants, like those of Southern Germany, began to destroy the castles and monasteries. At the suggestion of Luther, the Elector John, called the Constant, of Saxony—the brother of Frederic the Wise, who had just died in his quiet chamber at Lochau, in the Wittenberg district, after having strongly urged his brother to deal kindly and cautiously with the peasants—allied himself with Philip the Magnanimous, Landgrave of Hesse, and with the Duke Henry of Brunswick. Part of their united troops, under the command of Philip of Hesse, encountered the hosts of the peasants near Frankenhausen, in Thuringia, at the foot of the Kyffhäuser Mountain, on the 15th of May, 1525.

Münzer fought to the last with the greatest courage, announcing to his men certain victory against the army of the princes, and assuring them that he would catch all the bullets of the enemy in his sleeves, and that hosts of angels would come down from heaven to fight by their side. Just as the battle began, a beautiful rainbow appeared in the sky. "Look! look!" said Münzer, "here is a token of the Lord's mercy and favour." A gentleman who came from the landgrave to negotiate was, without further ado, stabbed by Münzer's orders. The peasants, having barricaded themselves behind their waggons, prepared for the stoutest resistance. But the battle was decided in a few moments. The artillery of the princes did the work, just as it had done at Landstuhl against Sickingen. Five thousand of the peasants were shot or cut down, whilst, with their hands folded in prayer, they were waiting for the Lord to fight their battle. Münzer fled to Frankenhausen, where he concealed himself in the hayloft of a house. A soldier, who happened for some purpose or other to go there, found his pocket-book by mere chance; after which the prophet was dragged forth from his hiding-place, first tortured, and then beheaded.

After the battle of Frankenhausen the most cruel executions were enacted, by which, according to a rough calculation, nearly 350,000 peasants in all parts of Germany perished. The worst consequence of all for the survivors was, that their bondage became even more oppressive than before. Then, for the first time, the game laws gave the nobles an exclusive right of chase, not merely over their own property, but also over the lands of their vassals. In some parts only, where the peasants were not put down by force of arms, better conditions were obtained; as for instance in the Breisgau and in Upper Austria. The Tyrolese also succeeded in maintaining their ancient liberties: they remained the freest of all German peasants; as likewise did the Salzburgers, whose peace was made in 1526 by George von Frundsberg. Luther asserted that bondage was allowed by Holy Scripture. He declared to Hildebrand von Einsiedel, who entertained some scruples about the hard servitude of the peasantry, "The common man must be heavily laden, otherwise he grows wanton. Where there are good poor people your honour will know how to deal leniently with them." But he was honest enough to allow himself to be taught by experience. He wrote, some time after: "I would lay a wager that, if the peasants' riots had not occurred, there would have been a rising of the nobility against the princes, and perhaps a rising of the princes against the Emperor. *So critically did the fate of Germany tremble in the balance.* Now, however, as the peasants have fallen, they alone are the black sheep, and the nobles and princes come out clear, and look as if they had never intended any harm. Yet that will not deceive the Lord. He has thereby given them a warning likewise to be faithful on their part to their own master (the Emperor)."

After the great defeat which the nobles had suffered by the downfall of Sickingen in 1523, and the peasants in the battle of Frankenhausen in 1525,—after these two heavy thunderstorms which had followed the dawn of the Reformation, the character of the movement underwent a considerable change. Until then it had been a popular movement. Now the princes came forth to place themselves at its head, and

Luther attached himself more and more closely to them. He who had hitherto maintained his independent position, who had refused to make common cause with the nobles, with Hutten and Sickingen, and who had completely kept the peasants at bay, did now join the princes, into whose hands, it cannot be denied, he delivered the new Church. In 1524, the Margrave Albert of Brandenburg, Grand Master of the Teutonic Order, came to him at Wittenberg. Luther advised him to secularise the province of Prussia, which was the property of that order. This seed fell on good ground, and yielded a luxuriant crop. As early as towards the end of 1524, a state paper was written, very likely in Saxony, and at any rate by a Lutheran pen, in which the principle was laid down that all the ecclesiastical estates of the Empire should be confiscated and employed for secular purposes. Luther was convinced that the princes alone were able to keep discipline in the new Church: it is true that he looked upon them only as bishops to make shift with for the present, out of sheer necessity, conferring on them the episcopal power *de facto* only. But this was again a most impolitic step, for this possession *de facto* was soon changed into one *de jure*, might standing in place of right. In 1523, Luther had still vindicated the right of self-government for the Church in his letter to the Bohemians: " Proof and argument from the Scriptures, that a Christian congregation has power to judge all doctrine and to institute and depose its preachers." Even as late as 1526, the Landgrave of Hesse tried, with the help of a Frenchman, Lambert of Avignon, to rebuild the Church on a democratical foundation, as it had been among the first Christians. But this constitution did not gain ground in the Lutheran Church: it only became the corner-stone of the Reformed (Calvinist) Church, which, however, was completely and widely separated from the Lutheran, on account of the quarrel about the Eucharist. The reformed German, Swiss, French, Dutch, and Scotch Churches, as also the American Protestants, have stuck to the principle that the power in the Church rested with the whole congregation : in the Lutheran Church it fell entirely into the hands of the princes. The Calvinist Church adopted a republican, the Lutheran a monarchical, constitution. With this immense difference in the organisation of both, the first great split arose between the seceders from Popery. Luther went so far in his aversion to the republicanised Calvinists in Switzerland and in the free imperial cities of South Germany, Strassburg, Basle, Frankfort-on-the-Maine, which were afterwards joined by the Netherlands, that he expressly declared that he "*would seven times rather unite with the Roman Catholics than with the Calvinists!*"

When, at the Diet of Spires, in 1526, Charles V.—having since the victory of Pavia been at enmity with the Pope—issued the decree that "every member of the Empire, until a general council, was, in matters of religion, to follow that line which he should deem best, and as he thought to be able to answer for in the face of God and the Emperor," the sanction of imperial law was stamped on the principle of the autonomy of the princes in the Churches of their territories, and thus the Reformation was entirely left to their pleasure. This was the origin of the separate Churches according to the divisions of the different territories, which were organised and managed at will by the different princes and magistrates of the free cities. Thus the Lutheran Church became but an aggregate of separate territorial establishments, loosely linked together; the unity which had ceased in the State ceased also in the Church, where, likewise, diversity and "particularism" was acknowledged as the leading principle. *The Reformers sought, for the illegitimate reform of the Church, a support in the secular legitimacy of the princes. They therefore now also proclaimed the principle of the absolute political supremacy of the powers that be, and of the duty of passive obedience in the subject. They not only withdrew from every political opposition, but decidedly declared against it. Thus the exclusion of the people from political life now became an article of faith; the natural consequence of which was that the masses lost every interest in public affairs.*

Together with absolute political power and spiritual supremacy, the *church property* also fell to the princes. All the conventual institutions were abolished. Their revenues ought to have been employed in endowing parish livings, and, as

Luther most earnestly urged, in establishing schools for educating the brutalised German peasantry, whose ignorance and degraded position he so frequently deplores in his writings. But the least part of the confiscated church property went to the parish ministers; somewhat more to the schools, yet only to the classical ones and to the universities. The common Lutheran clergyman received less than what sufficed for the indispensable necessaries of life. *The Lutheran Church has been ruined by its poverty, as the Roman by its wealth.* The village schools, which Luther so earnestly recommended to be established from the conventual property, and for the benefit of which he, in 1529, published his "Small Catechism for Children," were miserably neglected; and long after the Reformation the old brutality and ignorance were rife among the country people. The princely exchequers, on the other hand, enriched themselves with the capitular and conventual revenues, and the nobles were by no means bashful in helping themselves. Luther complains most bitterly of this wickedness, which prevailed in Saxony and in Hesse also, where, as the landgrave himself wrote to Luther, there was much "scrambling" about the property of the convents. The landgrave set the example. He gave to the son of his guardian, Count Philip of Waldeck, at his christening, as a sponsor's gift, the rich convent of Arolsen. Melanchthon, in his letters written to his most confidential friends, calls these patrons of the Evangelical Church, the Landgrave of Hesse, the Elector of Saxony, and others, without any circumlocution, "Centaurs, tyrants, and despisers of God." He says that they care only for worldly interests, and mourns over the abolition of the old constitution, the princely bishops having now been replaced by episcopal princes.

When at last the princes came to settle with the new Protestant clergy, the princes kept the power and the money for themselves, and to the clergy they left—the most profound respect of the poor people.

In Saxony, at a later period, in 1550, the Elector Maurice established with some of the conventual property the three "princely schools" (*Fürstenschulen*) at Pforta, Grimma, and Meissen. In Hesse, some of the proceeds of the confiscations were spent on the Free College of the University of Marburg; in Brunswick, on the Gymnasia. Most of all was done in Würtemberg, where there were scarcely any nobles holding their fiefs under the duke, and where the honest and energetic Duke Christopher reigned. Under his auspices the large theological college at Tübingen, called the Stift, and a number of cloister schools at Maulbronn, Bebenhausen, Blaubeuren, and Hirsau, afterwards Denkendorf,[1] were established. In Lüneburg and Mecklenburg the nobles compelled the government to change the convents into secular chapters, with canonries for the younger sons and the daughters of the nobility.

The princes, as may well be imagined, had their power vastly increased by the secularisation of the ecclesiastical property; yet the free towns and cities at that time still formed a very compact power in the Empire by their side. All the commerce was in the hands of the cities, and there were even then in Germany banking firms, whose heads, like the Florentine Medicis, became princes from merchants, as, for instance, the Eggenbergs of Grätz and the Fuggers of Augsburg. Citizens like these were a power in the State, of whose importance Charles V. was perfectly aware. The Fuggers, as has been mentioned before, had played a very prominent part in his election as Roman Emperor. Before the discovery of America, and of a shorter road by sea to India, whence the principal riches at that time were derived, the cities of Southern Germany, as well as those forming the Hanseatic League in the north, were possessed of very

---

[1] These four cloister schools (lower seminaries) are now Maulbronn, Urach, Blaubeuren, and Schönthal. The Stift, the theological seminary at the University of Tübingen, is likewise still in existence, and furnishes the majority of the candidates for the clerical offices of the Protestant Church in Würtemberg. The Church property, however, was confiscated during the reign of the late King,[*] when, supported by Napoleon, he overthrew the constitution of the country; and the expenses of those establishments, like all the rest, are now borne by the State.—*Translator*.

[*] Duke Frederic, who, in 1806, in accordance with a decree of Napoleon, took the title of King. He afterwards joined the Allies.

considerable wealth and a corresponding amount of power. No wonder that the free cities with the most determined zeal embraced the new, freer principles of the Reformation; in those of Southern Germany the bankers alone stuck to the old papal faith. The cities and princes of Northern Germany, being thorough-going partisans of Luther, became Charles's most dangerous opponents.

The Catholics, especially in Southern Germany, the secular princes no less than the princes of the Church, the bishops, had at an early stage prepared themselves to take the field against the party of the Reformers. As early as the year 1524 Archduke Ferdinand of Austria, Duke William of Bavaria, and a number of South German bishops had united in a league at Ratisbon. Against them the northern princes, John the Constant, elector of Saxony, and Philip the Magnanimous, landgrave of Hesse, concluded in 1526 the league of Torgau, which was joined by the Dukes of Brunswick-Lüneburg, the Duke of Mecklenburg, the Prince of Anhalt, two Counts of Mansfeldt, and by the most important free city of Northern Germany, Magdeburg. The firmness of the Elector of Saxony brought about in the same year the Decree of Spires, by which the Reformation was henceforth to be left to the conscience of the princes. But at a new Diet at Spires in 1529 the Catholic princes of the Empire again openly opposed the Reformation, which until then had been tolerated; and they caused a decree to be passed that everything should remain *in statu quo*, and no further extension of the reform be admitted. It was against this decree that the Lutheran members of the Diet entered their celebrated protest, from which they received the name of Protestants. It was registered on the 19th of April, 1529, and on the same day a deputation was despatched to carry it to the Emperor in Italy. The deputies met his Majesty at Placentia.

Charles, the Catholic King of Spain, having secured himself against his rival Francis I. by a tolerable peace; against the Grand Turk, the ally of the Most Christian King, by money; and against the Pope by family arrangements in Italy; gave the messengers of his protesting lieges but a very cold reception. His reply was that they should expect to be severely chastised, unless they consented at once to drop the protest. He now travelled by short stages through the Tyrol by way of Munich to Augsburg, attended by his Spanish, Italian, and Netherlandish lords and councillors. He was also met by the delegates of the Catholic German princes, who wished to bring him over to their interest; but with true Spanish *grandezza* he wrapped all his thoughts in impenetrable secrecy, referring everything to Augsburg. Three zealous Papists, the Dukes William of Bavaria and George of Saxe-Dresden and the Elector Joachim of Brandenburg, rode to meet him as far as Innsbruck. After the death of the chancellor Gattinara, who stood high in the Emperor's favour, and who in the imperial cabinet had even to the last advocated forbearance and moderation, Charles had for his principal adviser the new chancellor, Nicholas Perrenot Granvella, the celebrated father of the equally celebrated Cardinal Granvella. Nicholas accompanied the Emperor to Augsburg, and, in direct violation of the "Capitulation," became, although a foreigner, the Keeper of the Imperial Seal of Germany. He was perfectly qualified to conduct the business of the general European policy; but he was also what we should now call an ultra-absolutist, and a most zealous Papist. Some time before the Diet he was heard to say, "The Lutherans will fly in all directions, like pigeons before the hawk."

5.—*The Diet of Augsburg, and the French wars to the Peace of Crespy,* 1544.

Charles now appeared in Germany as quite a different man from what he had been nine years before at his coronation at Aix-la-Chapelle and at the Diet of Worms. He was now in the prime of life, being thirty years old. During the eight years (from 1521 to 1529) which he passed in Spain he had quietly gone through his apprenticeship as a ruler, from which he came out an accomplished politician and a worthy disciple of the Spanish priesthood. The teacher who had "boiled him hard" and put his iron stamp upon him was no other than his confessor, the Dominican Garcia de Loaysa, afterwards Cardinal and Bishop of Osma, subsequently of Siguenza, and at last Archbishop of Seville and Grand Inquisitor. He accompanied Charles in 1529 to Bologna, after which he became his ambassador at Rome. From that time he kept up a correspondence with his imperial pupil. His letters from the year 1530 to 1532, during which Charles stayed in Germany, were some years ago published from the archives of Simancas, by G. Heine. They are a remarkable monument of Spanish priestly policy, to which every tender feeling of humanity is completely unknown. Garcia de Loaysa did his utmost to force upon the young Emperor his own point of view, that with regard to the heretics, "*those dogs, there should be no question whatever of the fancy of converting souls to God; it was quite sufficient to compel bodies to obedience.*" He wrote once to Charles the following spiritual recipe: "If you are determined to bring back Germany, I see no better means than to induce, by gifts and flatteries, those who take the lead in the learned world and in the State to return to our faith, which being done, you are first to issue for the common people your imperial edicts and Christian exhortations, and if they will not obey them, then *the true rhubarb to heal them is force*.[1] Such were the insinuations under the guidance of which Charles took his measures in Germany. He now stood on the acme of his political power. His most mighty enemies were partly humbled and partly pacified; one half of Europe obeyed him, and just then one of his subjects, the Spaniard Francis Pizarro, had laid Peru at his feet—the land of gold, where the precious metal was found in such abundance as had never been known before.

This powerful ruler, not without intention, made his appearance at Augsburg on the eve of Corpus Christi, the highest festival of the Roman Church, there to hold his second Diet. Quarters were prepared for him at the palace of the "Frohnhof," the mansion of the Bishop of Augsburg;

[1] In a letter written from Rome, dated the 18th of June, 1530, shortly after the presentation of the Augsburg Confession.

but as it was full six months before he left that city, he removed to the house of his banker, Fugger.

When Charles rode into Augsburg, 15th of June, 1530, he did not at once retire to his quarters, but, after having alighted, he was, according to the then usage, led to the cathedral, with his brother, King Ferdinand of Hungary, and all the electors, cardinals, and other bishops and princes who had gone out on horseback to meet him. The following account is given by an eye-witness from the household of the Elector of Mayence:

"It was late, and the cathedral nearly dark: a great many lighted torches were therefore brought; directions also were given not to admit the people, in order to prevent a crowd. His Majesty was first led up through the middle of the nave, at the upper end of which there were three priedieus, his Majesty kneeling down on the centre one, the King of Hungary on the right, and the legate Campeggio on the left; but their chairs were not as high as the Emperor's. The Bishop of Augsburg, with his suffragans and the Abbot of St. Ulrich, all wearing their mitres, stood opposite. The Emperor and the cardinals and the electors—the Elector John of Saxony carrying the sword of the Empire—and the other bishops, princes, and lords, besides the rest of the clergy, were standing around him. The Bishop of Augsburg, with his suffragans, then began to sing, '*Et ne nos inducas in tentationem, &c.; Domine salvum fac Imperatorem, &c.; esto eis turris fortitudinis, &c.*' And then followed some fine collects *super Imperatorem*. After these ceremonies his Imperial Majesty, his Highness of Hungary, and the legate were conducted by the light of many torches, one of which I carried, to the high altar, where they knelt down; whilst the Bishop of Augsburg, with his suffragans and the abbot, stepped out before the altar, and again began to chant '*Et ne nos inducas, &c.*,' to which the choir responded, '*Amen.*' Then the *legatus apostolicus* rose, made the sign of the cross on the altar, kissed it, and gave the *benedictio apostolica;* in return, his Imperial Majesty and his Highness of Hungary bowed very low, as did also the other electors, princes, bishops, and lords: but the Landgrave of Hesse *smiled, and crouched behind a large candelabrum*. After the benediction, they began to sing the *Te Deum laudamus*, when his Imperial Majesty and the King rose, and conversed with my most gracious master of Mayence about the procession which was to be held on the following day, being the festival of Corpus Christi. Of all the electors, princes, bishops, and lords, the Elector of Saxony and the Landgrave of Hesse alone remained standing. The Lutheran Margrave George of Anspach at first knelt down likewise; but when he saw that the Elector of Saxony did not kneel, he rose to his feet."

Charles sent invitations to all the princes to join in the Corpus Christi procession. The Protestant princes were included in this summons, which in their case was coupled with a prohibition to have sermons of their own on that day. They, however, early in the following morning, rode to the Emperor's quarters, and frankly told him that they would not join the procession, but abide by their own faith. The Margrave George of Anspach and Prince Wolfgang of Anhalt expressed themselves to this effect, that rather than swerve from the word of God, they would at once kneel down to have their heads cut off. Charles then tried to soothe them, saying, in his Brabant dialect, "*Löven Fürsten nit Kopp ab, nit Kopp ab!*" ("Dear princes, not heads off, not heads off!") It being the duty of the Elector of Saxony, as Marshal of the Empire, to bear the sword before the Emperor, he was induced to join in the procession by the representations of his divines, who pointed out to him "*that the man of God, Elisha, had allowed Naaman, captain of the host of the king of Syria, to bow himself in the house of Rimmon, when his master went to worship there, and leaned on his hand.*" When, however, the host was elevated, he and Philip the Magnanimous did not bow.

Nine days after, on the 25th of June, 1530, at three o'clock in the afternoon, the Emperor Charles had the celebrated Augsburg Confession, in which the doctrine of the Protestants was embodied, presented to him in his quarters. It was signed by the five princes of Saxony, Hesse, Lüneburg, Anspach, and Anhalt, and the two imperial towns of Nuremberg and Reutlingen; the Saxon chancellor, Dr. Brück, read it out in German: the demand of the Emperor to have it read out in Latin having been met by the remark of the Elector of of Saxony, that as they were on German soil, his Imperial Majesty would allow the German tongue to be used.

Charles was highly incensed against the Elector of Saxony, the head of the German Protestants. John the Constant had sued for a sister of the Emperor as wife for his son, the Electoral Prince (afterwards the Elector John Frederic), in fulfilment of the promise which Charles, at his election as Emperor, had made to Frederic the Wise. This match having been broken off, John and John Frederic felt it most keenly as the greatest insult. Charles had also until now withheld from John the usual investiture of the electoral dignity, and he now threatened to deprive him of it altogether, unless he dropped the protestation. This was not a mere empty menace; for Charles had really entertained the plan of making Duke George of Misnia, a zealous Papist, Elector in his stead. But John remained constant. The Emperor now caused the confession of the Protestants to be replied to in a very weak "Confutation;" condemned Luther's doctrine anew; and put the Edict of Worms again in force. He then closed the Diet, which had lasted five months. The Protestants, on their side, protested; the imperial city of Augsburg, to the great mortification of the Emperor, protesting under his very eyes.

Charles went from Augsburg to Cologne, where, on the 5th of January, 1531, he caused his brother, King Ferdinand of Hungary, to be elected King of the Romans. But this election was not only protested against by Protestant Saxony, but also by Papist Bavaria. The aspect of affairs became more and more threatening. Charles went to Brussels as early as on the 27th of February, 1531. The Protestants concluded their defensive and offensive alliance at Smalcalde; the contracting parties being Saxony, Hesse, Lüneburg, Anhalt, Mansfeld, and the three Hanseatic towns of Lübeck, Bremen, and Magdeburg, besides Strassburg and seven other South German cities. In the following year an alliance was concluded even with France, at Scheyern, on the 26th of May, 1532, which was joined on the side of the German Protestants by Saxony and Hesse, and, moreover, by the Catholic Elector of Bavaria.

But war was not yet declared for the present. Charles, following the advice of his Spanish confessor, went on temporising and dissembling, only rarely allowing some chance word to escape him, from which his real and ulterior intention might be guessed. The Protestant princes themselves met him without the least guile. The Elector of Saxony especially, on the suggestion of Luther, approached him with the most hearty confidence. Luther, that excellent divine but very bad politician, was completely mistaken in the thorough-bred Spaniard Charles, who, taking much more after his mother than after his father, had been entirely converted by the training of his confessor into a Castilian, so that of the German element of his nature very little remained in him. Luther in his letters calls the Emperor, over and over again, "a quite godly and kind heart, but surrounded by many devils." He always held to it that the Emperor was not his own master, and that one ought to pray to God for him. Even so late as 1541, after the last useless attempt which was made at the colloquy at Ratisbon to bring about a union with the Papists, he wrote that, "not Charles, but the devil at Mayence, the Elector Albert, was Emperor." The good-natured Luther little suspected the Spanish leading strings in which the Emperor was kept. Luther, moreover, was thoroughly averse to a league with foreign kings, as he firmly believed that there was no faith and truth among them, and that by a league with such as these the German Empire would be torn in pieces, and given up to the Turks. Charles, again, showed himself peacefully inclined, the danger from the Turks having once more modified his policy. Soleyman, after having spent three years in preparations, broke forth anew with formidable power in 1532. He had a magnificent new imperial crown made for the occasion, which he carried with him, to put it on his head in Germany, as "Caliph of Roum," *i.e.*, as Roman Emperor.

Amid these circumstances which forced Charles to bide his time, the first religious peace was concluded, in the year 1532, at Nuremberg, in which Charles promised to leave the *status quo*, but only until a general council should be convoked. The Protestants (Lutherans), on the other hand, were obliged expressly to sever themselves from the Reformed (Calvinists); thus completing that first split among the seceders from Popery which was to bear its most unhallowed fruits for Germany in the Thirty Years' War. Shortly after the first religious peace, the German Protestants lost their head in the Elector John, whose successor, John Frederic, surnamed the Magnanimous, was far from enjoying the same respect which the noble conduct of his father had forced from the Emperor.

Soleyman, when he saw the active preparations for defence in the Austrian countries, and especially when he convinced himself that Charles had concluded peace with Martin Luther, turned suddenly round with all his forces to the East, where he began a great war with the Persians; on which Charles, towards the end of the year 1532, went to Italy to arrange matters with the Pope concerning a general council. Charles intended, after the example of Constantine the Great, to preside over this council, as the head of Christendom, and to direct it. This was not, however, at all what the Pope intended, who therefore did his utmost to evade the demands of the Emperor. The latter set out, in 1533, for Spain. There he prepared a great naval expedition to put down the intolerable piracy of the Turks. At that period the pirate States of Barbary had been formed under the protection of the Turkish Sultan. The pirate Hayradin Barbarossa, one of the boldest and most extraordinary of men, had made himself master of the Spanish castle on the island off the coast of Algiers, and founded a kingdom there; and, having likewise seized Tunis, he was invested by Soleyman with the dignity of Capitan Pasha, High Admiral of Turkey. He infested with his galleys the coasts of Italy and Spain, plundering and kidnapping Christians, spreading terror over the whole of the Mediterranean, and inflicting immense losses by seizing the merchant vessels. In vain had Doria, with eight large men-of-war and forty-four galleys, made his appearance before the Dardanelles. Although he had succeeded in taking the Asiatic castle, all his attempts against the European failed. He, however, seized Coron in the Morea.

Charles sailed on the 16th of June from Cagliari, in Sardinia, with his fleet, which was commanded by Doria as admiral, and which contained 30,000 men, to the conquest of Tunis. Whilst he attacked the walls from without, the great numbers of Christian slaves within the town set themselves free; and thus, returning as conqueror, he entered Naples at the head of 20,000 of those liberated captives. This first expedition having, however, failed to put a stop to the piracies of Barbarossa—which the latter, after the conquest of Tunis, carried on from Algiers—Charles undertook, in 1541, another expedition against that port, notwithstanding the advice of Doria to the contrary. The expedition, sailing from Majorca, was overtaken by a hurricane, which in one hour destroyed 14 large and 114 smaller ships of war, with 8,000 men. The enterprise, therefore, proved a complete failure; and the Emperor, having landed in Algiers on the 22nd of October, was, on the 22nd of November, back again in Majorca.

In 1535 the last Sforza died, who had until then been the possessor of Milan. Immediately the King of France again put forth his claims to that dukedom, asking the Emperor for investiture. Charles sent to Francis the ambiguous yet very significant answer, "What my brother the King of France wishes, I wish too." Francis on this occasion proposed an offensive alliance, offering to guarantee to Charles the hereditary possession of the German Imperial Crown, with absolute sway, if he would cede to him Milan, Asti, and Genoa. Charles did not enter upon it; and Milan became ultimately (in 1538) a province of Spain.

The third war between Spain and France now broke out. Francis I. and Henry VIII. of England sent their ambassadors to Smalcalde; and the Protestant princes renewed their alliance in 1536. Francis took Savoy. Charles, not taking any warning from the first invasion of Southern

France by the Constable of Bourbon, invaded it again, and was again unable to reduce Marseilles. He had to return, but not before he had lost his brave General Leyva. The Pope negotiated between the belligerents a ten years' truce at Nice, 1538. At Aiguesmortes, at the mouth of the Rhone, Charles and Francis had an interview, at which the Pope also was present. As Charles arrived in the harbour, Francis rowed to his ship to receive him, and conducted him on shore. Here a feast was prepared, at which the two monarchs remained until late at night. In the morning the Dauphin handed to the Emperor the water for washing, and the napkin, both rulers vying with each other in mutual demonstrations of respect and goodwill. The city of Ghent, in the Netherlands, having, on account of a new tax, rebelled against Queen Mary of Hungary, regent of the Netherlands, Francis proposed to Charles that he should take the shortest road through France to the Low Countries. Charles accepted the proposal. His jester, indeed, warned him, saying, " Charles's entering France would be a folly ; but Francis's allowing him to leave it again would be a still greater one." Charles replied, " Just because we know that he is more foolish than we are, we'll pass through his country." And pass he did. Charles, accompanied by Alba, was everywhere in France received with the greatest honours ; all the towns through which his road led him brought him their keys. At Fontainebleau, where Francis held his court, the most splendid fêtes were given to the Emperor for a fortnight. From Fontainebleau Charles made his solemn entry into Paris, on the 1st of January, 1540, and here also he was entertained with royal magnificence for a whole week. Francis introduced to him the Duchess of Estampes, his mistress, saying, " Look here, my brother, this fair lady advises me not to allow you to depart until you have revoked the treaty of Madrid." Startled at first, but speedily regaining his composure, Charles replied, " If the advice is good, it ought to be acted upon." On the following day the Emperor, as if by chance, dropped a diamond ring of great value into the hand-basin which the duchess held for him. As she offered to return it to him, he said, "It is in too fair hands; please to keep it in remembrance of me." This completely won the heart of the duchess, and he safely reached the Low Countries by way of Valenciennes. The rebellion in Ghent was soon quelled; the city, the place of his birth, surrendered on the day which had always been a lucky one to him, his birthday, the 24th of February, 1540. Charles secured its obedience by a citadel which he caused to be built there.

Francis, however, did not get over the loss of the Duchy of Milan. Charles having suffered his great loss on his second expedition to Africa, he commenced the fourth war in 1542. Charles now conferred upon his son Philip, at that time in his sixteenth year, the regency of Spain, and he left that kingdom never to see it again as Emperor and King. He went, by way of Genoa to the Rhine, to Germany. There he showed himself kinder than ever to the Protestants. The new Elector of Saxony, John Frederic the Magnanimous, was again made to hope that his son would be married to a daughter of the King of the Romans; the upshot of all of which was that the Smalcalde League lent Charles its arms against France, the Elector himself being entrusted with the chief command. The flower of Charles's army consisted of 30,000 Germans, who took St. Dizier, in Champagne. At Châlons the two armies stood opposite each other, with only the river Marne between them, the Imperialists being only two days' march from Paris, whence the inhabitants were already flying to Rouen and Orleans. No German army since the time of the Saxon Emperors had advanced so far into France. Under these circumstances Francis made proposals of peace. Charles accepted them; and on the 24th of September, 1544, peace, the last which Charles negotiated with Francis, was concluded at Crespy. France remained excluded from Italy, renounced her alliance with the Turks, and left the German Protestants at the mercy of the Emperor. In this way Charles had his hands unfettered in Germany.

The apparent kindness of Charles to the Protestants had only been an artifice of statecraft, just as in 1532, when there was danger from the Turks. The Smalcalde League allowed themselves to be outwitted by this policy. The Emperor now took in hand his old plan of carrying out the reform within the Catholic Church itself. He compelled the Pontiff actually to open the council which had been so long talked of. The Pope himself did not care much about it; to use the expression of Garcia de Loaysa, given in a letter to the Emperor, "he only swallowed it like a purge." The Emperor ordered that the Protestants should submit to the decrees of this council; but they refused to acknowledge a general council at which the Pope presided, who had already condemned them as heretics, so that no just decision could be expected. What they asked was a just council of the German nation, presided over by the Elector of Saxony. Then the Emperor resolved upon striking the decisive blow, for which the most favourable moment appeared now to have arrived. He declared that "if the Protestants refused to acknowledge the general council, he would treat them as refractory members of the Empire, setting himself, not against their religion, but against their disobedience." He also secured himself from danger in the East by leaving the Turks in possession of the greater part of Hungary, including Buda, which they had occupied since 1541; paying them besides a yearly tribute of 30,000 ducats for the smaller part of it, which he was allowed to keep. *This sacrifice he made to be enabled to put down the heretics in Germany. It was the beginning of the Spanish policy, which was afterwards continued by Ferdinand II. and Leopold I.* A Turkish pasha resided for more than 150 years at Buda, like a thorn in the side of the archducal house of Austria. The boundary was formed by the river Gran, Austrian Hungary being composed at that time of only a small part of Upper Hungary; whilst the lower provinces, as also Sclavonia and Croatia, were in the power of the Moslems. Transylvania was ruled by the family of the Zapolyas, which became extinct in the year 1571; and afterwards by Bathory and other elective princes. Charles concluded with the Turks, in 1545, a truce for five years, after which he leagued himself with the Pope for the extermination of the Protestants, and caused Spanish and Italian troops to be levied—both of which steps were in direct contradiction to the "Capitulation" which he had sworn to at his election.

In this he was guided by no religious motive, but merely by reasons of policy. Charles had never brought himself to believe that in the Reformation a great and general want of the German people was involved. He who looked upon himself as the master of the world, and who certainly ruled over peoples of the most different nationalities, was not able to place himself on a German point of view; he was and remained a stranger—a Spanish king, not a German emperor. The interests of his foreign policy weighed far more with him than the care for the home affairs of Germany.

The state of things at Cologne, however, was the most powerful incentive for the Emperor to bring matters to a point by force of arms. All the three secular Electors (of Saxony, the Palatinate, and Brandenburg; the Bohemian electorate being almost in abeyance) were devoted to the new faith; their ranks were now joined by one of the spiritual electors, the venerable Archbishop Hermann of Cologne, of the family of the Counts of Wied. He declared for the Reformation, and began to introduce it in his archbishopric. This made the Emperor apprehensive for his favourite country, the Netherlands, where he was just then staying, and it was this fear which hurried him to a decision. Charles therefore, in February, 1546, set out from the Low Countries for the Empire, and on the 5th of June opened the Diet at Ratisbon. The Protestants had neither sent delegates to the Council of Trent, which began its sittings in the December of the preceding year, nor did they now make their appearance at the Diet. Charles, without any further delay, resolved upon war to punish this twofold disobedience; and the Chancellor Granvella began secretly to negotiate with Cardinal Farnese, the papal legate.

Charles, through this channel, intimated to the Pope that he was now resolved upon exterminating the Lutheran heresy. In his public decrees and proclamations, on the other hand, he took the utmost care to represent his armament as a mere secular measure for the punishment of some princes who, by a breach of the public peace, had set the imperial authority at defiance. But, crafty as Charles was, he had to deal with one even craftier than himself; and the Pope outwitted him. The Emperor, after having broken the political ascendency of the Smalcalde League, might still have used the cause of the Reformation as a convenient tool for keeping the Pope in check. The Holy Father, to render the German princes for ever the enemies of the Emperor, quietly made known in Germany the terms of the agreement which Charles, in direct violation of the "Capitulation," had concluded with him. Pope Paul III. Farnese, the pontiff who presided over the establishment of the order of the Jesuits, followed the same line of conduct as Cardinal Richelieu did during the Thirty Years' War. Twice the German Emperors were thus duped by their own allies and fellow religionists: his Holiness the Pope and the Most Christian King, who sowed enmity between them and the Protestants, to prevent his Cæsarean Majesty from carrying out his plan of a universal monarchy.

The Protestants indeed could no longer have any doubts as to what he intended against them. But it was now too late. Even before the war began, Charles had conquered them at Ratisbon by political manœuvring. The net which he had spread for the Protestants now narrowed on all sides. The Pope had promised an auxiliary force of 12,000 Italian infantry and 4,500 light cavalry, whom his Holiness engaged to keep for six months at his own expense; besides which, he furnished 200,000 crowns for the war, and allowed Charles to appropriate half the revenues of the current year from all the ecclesiastical property in Spain, and to sell Spanish conventual property to the value of 50,000 scudi. Count Maximilian of Egmont and Büren,[1] who commanded in the Low Countries, received orders to bring up the troops stationed there. The most effective stroke, however, which Charles dealt his foes was his sowing division among the Protestants; secretly coming to an understanding with the Elector Joachim II. of Brandenburg and Duke Maurice of Saxony, whom he took

---

[1] Uncle of the celebrated and unfortunate Count Egmont.

into his own service, appointing him besides, on the 19th of June, 1546, Protector of the archbishopric of Magdeburg and the bishopric of Halberstadt. He even gave him, whilst still at Ratisbon, the eventual promise of the Saxon electorate if he would assist King Ferdinand in carrying out the ban of the Empire against his cousin, the actual Elector. Mocenigo, the Venetian ambassador, states: "Granvella told me one day that he had been the first to advise this step; at first the Emperor and others had laughed at it, as it seemed to them an affair of which no result could reasonably have been expected, considering that Maurice was an arch-Lutheran (*Lutheranissimo*), that he revered the landgrave as a father, and even more, that he had been reared by John Frederic, to whom, according to many, he owed the very possession of his country. Yet, notwithstanding all these considerations, Maurice entered into a treaty with the Emperor against his religion, his father-in-law, and his uncle."

The Protestants, who, even at the Diet of Ratisbon, had not yet been roused from their dreams of security, were at last frightened by the spreading reports of the armaments of the Emperor, which foreboded a storm gathering over their heads. They put the question to him, what he meant by his warlike preparations. Charles ordered his Vice-chancellor Naves to answer them that "all those who were obedient to him should find in him a gracious and fatherly Emperor; those, however, who set themselves against him might expect that he would make them feel his imperial authority." Soon after, when the messenger had arrived with the ratification of the Pope (24th of February, 1546), he sent word to the members of the Diet by his councillor, Dr. Viglius, that, as in so many Diets no propitious result had been effected, they should wait in patience for his ultimate gracious decision on the point of religion.

On this message the Protestant members quitted the Diet at Ratisbon without taking leave. The princes of Saxony and Hesse, the South German towns, and the Duke of Würtemberg began to arm; and the Lutheran preachers exhorted the people from the pulpits to stake their lives and their property for the defence of the pure doctrine. Luther was incessantly engaged in providing ministers and schoolmasters for his "wild, untutored German people," as he so often calls it. From want of preachers he sometimes caused journeymen printers to be ordained, who at least were able to read to the people his sermons from his Homilies. Now, as his life drew towards its close, he often sighed at the political turn which the Reformation had taken, and owing to which the Church had fallen so completely into the hands of the princes. Nor was he any longer mistaken in Charles V. In one of the letters written by him to the zealous Lutheran, Baron Jörger, of Herrnals, in Austria, he says, "I would fain have seen that servant of the devil, together with the Pope, slain." Charles's brother Ferdinand he calls "the man of wrath," and compares him to Ahab and to all the bloodstained tyrants of the Old Testament.

6.—*The Smalcalde war—Battle of Mühlberg.*

It was five months after Luther's death when the Smalcalde war broke out in July, 1546.

The forces of the South German cities of Augsburg, Ulm, and others took the field first. They were commanded by a celebrated and dreaded captain, the bold and determined knight of the Empire, Sebastian Schärtlin von Burtenbach, whose family castle lay within the territory of the free city of Augsburg. He had fought against the Turks and the French, had shared in the battle of Pavia, and been present at the taking of Rome. The Emperor Charles had in 1534 ennobled him by a diploma dated at Toledo, and had in 1546, at the Diet of Ratisbon, dubbed him an *eques auratus*. He was learned in classical lore, and very well versed in all the arts of war. He never was for half measures, but always laid it down as the first principle in war to "annihilate the enemy." His plan, therefore, was in the present instance to crush the forces of the Emperor whilst he was still gathering them; to cut him off from Bavaria and Franconia; and to compel him to fly to Austria.

Charles had not yet left Ratisbon, where he had with him only 8,000 infantry and 700 horse, German troops, whom he had in a hurry withdrawn from Hungary, besides 2,000 Spaniards. But he employed the money which he had received from the Pope and from Spain in causing levies to be made at Füssen on the Lech, in Swabia, on the frontier of Bavaria. These battalions were just going to join him at Ratisbon when Schärtlin fell in with them in the evening. The burly knight, as he tells us, intended to serenade them next morning with "his songstresses"—his cannon; but during the night the Imperialists entered the territory of the Duke of Bavaria, which Schärtlin had just been enjoined by a messenger from Augsburg not to violate, as the duke had not yet declared war. Schärtlin, therefore, devised a different plan. The papal auxiliaries, to join the Emperor at Ratisbon, had to march through the Tyrol, by Innsbruck, and the so-called Ehrenberger Klause, a strong castle commanding the whole of that mountain pass. Thither Schärtlin set out in forced marches; and after having, on the 16th of June, taken the Klause, he marched to Innsbruck, and now wished to give himself the treat of surprising the Fathers of the Church assembled in council at Trent. Then again a messenger arrived from Augsburg, with orders that Schärtlin was not to violate the Tyrolese territory, as King Ferdinand had not yet declared war. On this he angrily retired to Günzburg, on the Danube, near Ulm, where he was joined by the army of the Duke Ulrich, of Würtemberg, under the command of the brave general Hans von Heydeck. He now proposed, as a third plan, to surprise the Emperor at Ratisbon, as, owing to the reinforcements of the Imperial army having not yet arrived from Italy and the Low Countries, his Majesty had not yet more than 18,000 men with him. But this proposal also was rejected, although there was every chance that the Emperor would have had to fly, in which case all the south of Germany was lost for him. Schärtlin says that Hannibal could not have left Italy with a sadder heart than he did Bavaria.

In the meantime the Elector of Saxony and the Landgrave

of Hesse likewise appeared in the field. They had sent to the Emperor a letter, dated 4th of July, setting forth that they were not conscious of having committed any act of disobedience; but if they were guilty of any offence, it was only fair that they should be heard in their own defence, and it might then easily be proved that the Emperor was waging war only at the instigation of the Pope, to suppress the doctrine of the gospel and the liberties of the German Empire. The Emperor, in reply, on the 20th of July, at Ratisbon, put the Elector and the Landgrave under the ban and double ban of the Empire. Calling them rebels, perjurers, and traitors, he charged them with a plan of depriving him for their own benefit of his crown and sceptre; so that they might afterwards subject everyone to their own tyranny. On the 1st of August he issued mandates to the Duke Maurice, to his brother Augustus, and to the representative States of his country, to assist him with all their power in carrying out the ban against John Frederic; urging very strongly that by this means only Maurice would be able to make good his claims as nearest agnate, whereas otherwise the country of the outlawed Elector would remain in the possession of anyone who might once have succeeded in occupying it.

In the month of August the Saxo-Hessian army united near Donauwerth with the forces of the South German free cities and of the Duke of Würtemberg, which, commanded by Schärtlin of Burtenbach, amounted now to about 50,000 men. The Emperor, to meet the troops expected from Italy, and to be nearer the centre of Bavaria, removed his camp from Ratisbon to Landshut. We are informed by the "Relations" of the Venetian ambassador that Charles, with wily policy, had forbidden the Duke of Bavaria (who, on the 4th of July, married the daughter of his brother Ferdinand) to come to a rupture with the Protestants: the Emperor, whilst putting him forward as mediator, used him as a channel by which he gathered information about the movements of the Smalcalde allies; he also drew from Bavaria the supplies for his army, and caused troops to be levied in that country. The duke, as well as the Archbishop of Salzburg, the duke's brother, secretly supported him with money. Once more Schärtlin was for surprising the Emperor at Landshut with all the combined forces of the allies.

People, again, could not agree; not only were the princes jealous of the cities, but also the Elector and the Landgrave fell out about the command and the operations to be carried on. The allies, therefore, contented themselves for the present with sending letters to Charles to renounce their allegiance. The Emperor, however, without accepting the messages, sent word to the bearers by the Duke of Alba that, if they dared to come a second time, they would be hanged for their pains. In this way much precious time was wasted. Charles was joined during the period from the 14th to the 18th of August by 18,000 men—fresh troops, partly raised in Germany, partly Spaniards and Neapolitans from his Italian countries, and partly the auxiliaries promised by the Pope. These last were commanded by Ottavio Farnese, duke of Castro, the husband of Margaret, the illegitimate daughter of Charles.

With these forces Charles now advanced from Landshut to Ingolstadt on the Danube, where he arrived on the evening of the 26th of August; and, with the river and the town in his rear, entrenched himself under its cannon. Then at last the Smalcalde allies determined to make their attack by bombarding the camp of the Emperor, which at first was only surrounded by a simple ditch. And now took place the great cannonade of Ingolstadt, beginning on the 30th of August and lasting for three days—a cannonade such as had never been heard of until then, 2,000 shots being fired from 100 large guns against the imperial camp. Yet its result, like that of the Prussian cannonade of Valmy, in the French revolutionary war, was just the opposite of what had been intended. It only raised the courage of the imperial army, and the princes could not come to the determination of fighting a battle. When, on the 1st of December, the Smalcalde army marched out, and occupied a commanding eminence, Schärtlin, who had just before, with his twelve "Great Apostles," as he called his culverins, driven back the Spanish arquebusiers into the imperial camp, received from all the captains the assurance that they would willingly lay down their life for him if he would only venture an assault against the camp. But the Landgrave rode by, and, vehemently opposing the movement, called out that Schärtlin should not lead the troops astray by his rashness and folly; he and the Elector had more important considerations to take—*they had their country and their people to lose.* "*And I have Burtenbach to lose,*" replied Schärtlin, with generous indignation. The assault, which, as everybody then said, would have cost the Emperor either his liberty or his life, was not made; and Charles gained time to complete his camp. Schärtlin writes: "I saw nowhere any earnestness for an honest war." Nay, to his great astonishment, the allies—after having sent off, on the 2nd of September, the famous letter to "*Charles of Ghent, who calls himself the Roman Emperor,*" in which they renounced their allegiance to him— broke up their camp only two days after, with a view to intercept Count Maximilian of Egmont and Büren, who brought to the Emperor 15,000 men from the Netherlands. Büren, however, having on the 21st of August crossed the Rhine near Bingen and Mayence, evaded them; and marching by Frankfort and Nuremberg, reached, on the 15th of September, the Emperor near Ingolstadt, without having encountered a Protestant, as the Saxons and Hessians, seized by a panic at his approach, fled from their position near Frankfort.

Charles had now concentrated the whole of his power, which, as well as that of the allies, amounted to about 50,000 men. The badge of the imperial army was scarlet, that of the Smalcalde leaguers yellow.

The Emperor now was evidently the stronger of the two. Terror and fright went before his soldiers, especially his Spaniards, for the most part weather-beaten veterans, many of whom had fought with him in Africa, and who knew no fear. The generalissimo of the imperial army was the dreaded Duke of Alba.

The Emperor, to show his enemies that he was not afraid, always encamped near them; yet the result proved that he did so without any intention of fighting them. His object was to wear them out by protracting the war, and he hoped that, owing to their league being composed of so many and such very different constituents, of princes, great and small, and burghers of the free cities, they would disagree among themselves. He wished to gain the victory without a pitched battle, "as behoved an emperor who was carrying on war against his vassals." Advancing from Ingolstadt, he took in succession the towns of Neuburg, Donauwerth, and Lauingen on the Danube, by which means he made himself master of that river. Augsburg being threatened likewise, the citizens recalled their general Schärtlin for their own special protection. In the Smalcalde army all were disheartened; the cities—groaning under the burden of having almost entirely to maintain the armies which lay idle in the field—were greatly incensed against the princes. "The Landgrave Philip," Schärtlin writes, "was considered before all the world as a great traitor to the cause of the gospel and of the German Empire."

The letters also of the Nuremberg patrician Imhoff, published by Hormayr, imputed to the Landgrave of Hesse the guilt of treachery. The following passage occurs there: "At Halle the Count of Fürstenberg gave a great banquet, where it was said that the war had been commenced by the Landgrave *with the secret knowledge and connivance of the Emperor*, in order that his Majesty might see who would join in it, and also that the free cities might be made to suffer loss and injury, and so lose their power and glory. *Thus all has been only a sham fight, whereby to bring the cities and the German nation to harm, as is evident;* I therefore do but pity the poor Elector, whom may God comfort!" The letter containing this passage dates from the time when the Landgrave received at Halle his judgment from the Emperor, being written on the 21st of June, 1547.

The two armies marched and countermarched for two months in the face of each other, without any decisive action being fought.

Winter approached, white frosts and severe cold already began, and it rained nearly every day. Famine, disease, and mortality spread, especially in the army of the Emperor;

but, although greatly harassed, he gave orders that no one should dare to speak of winter quarters. He wished to show the enemy that it was his firm determination to keep the field. In the beginning of November news arrived of the successful progress which King Ferdinand and Duke Maurice had made in the country of John Frederic. The Smalcalde princes sent on the 13th of November a letter to the Emperor suing for peace. Charles contented himself with causing this epistle to be read out before the whole army, but gave no answer to it; only when, two days after, another letter arrived he sent word back to the petitioners by the Margrave John of Brandenburg-Cüstrin, that he did not know of any way of bringing about a peace except that the Elector and the Landgrave *should surrender at discretion*.

On receiving this answer the Smalcalde princes left their camp at Giengen, near the Danube, in the neighbourhood of Ulm, and returned to their several countries on the 22nd and 23rd of November, 1546. The Emperor set out in pursuit of them in the evening with the whole army.

It was high time for the Elector John Frederic to return to his country, whither 20,000 men followed him from South Germany. Duke Maurice, whom, with his own brother Ferdinand, as King-Elector of Bohemia, Charles had charged with the execution of the outlawry against the Elector, had seized the whole of the Electorate, with the exception of the fortresses of Wittenberg and Gotha. But when John Frederic returned in December to Thuringia he easily recovered possession. Maurice's own country, Misnia, with the exception of Dresden and Leipzig, was taken by the Elector, and Maurice himself was obliged to fly to the Bohemian frontier. The Elector then occupied Joachimsthal in Bohemia; here a deputation of the Protestant states of Bohemia appeared in the camp, and very little was wanting to cause an actual rebellion to break out in the latter country against Ferdinand. Anne Jagellon, Ferdinand's queen, having died 27th of January, 1547, the Bohemians, on the 15th of February, concluded at Prague a treaty for the protection of their constitution and their religious liberty.

They assembled an army and blocked up the high roads by barricades in order, as they said, to protect the country against the invasion of the unchristian Spanish and Italian soldiery. The cities of Magdeburg, Hamburg, Bremen, Hildesheim, Brunswick, Goslar, Lüneburg, and Hanover, likewise sided with the Elector. In Lusatia and Silesia the sympathies of the people were for him. At Rochlitz the Emperor's general, Margrave Albert of Brandenburg-Culmbach, whom Charles had sent to the support of Maurice, was arrested and kept a prisoner.

In the meanwhile the Emperor had brought the South German towns to submission. They scarcely offered any resistance, being completely overawed by the dread of Charles and his Spaniards. "Within eight days," says the Venetian ambassador, Mocenigo, "the affairs which until then seemed to be settled only by guns and artillery, by blood and bloody fights, were altogether put in the way of negotiation, and were most admirably managed by Granvella, who, by the Emperor's order, went from Lauingen to Nördlingen *without the foreign ambassadors being allowed to follow him;* the Emperor, to his own greatest honour and advantage, concluding new compromises every day, and Granvella telling the princes and towns, even if it was not true, that the Emperor was on the point of settling with this and that prince or town, and that they who settled matters first would have much better terms than any of those who were later." Thus Rothenburg, Dinkelsbühl, Nördlingen, and Bopfingen made their submission; the powerful city of Ulm likewise sent its delegates, who, most humbly kneeling before the Emperor in the open field, even went so far as to address him in Spanish. Ulm had to pay 100,000 guilders; Frankfort paid 80,000: Memmingen 50,000, and the smaller ones in proportion. In Augsburg, the first city of Southern Germany, the brave Schärtlin made a plan of defence. The city had strong walls, 200 pieces of artillery, and a numerous population of warlike citizens; but the rich patrician houses of the town secretly negotiated with the Emperor. Anton Fugger, the Rothschild of the then Europe, who wished at any price to keep up the connection with the

Spanish court and the Italian countries, went out by stealth into the camp of the Emperor, and brought back the conditions that the city was to pay 150,000 guilders, to receive a garrison of Spanish soldiers, and to banish the brave Schärtlin. The stout-hearted knight called the Augsburgers "craven cowards," and held to his contract, according to the terms of which he could not be dismissed. They then with tears begged him to go, and, as Charles demanded his being given up, he at last departed for Constance and from thence went into Switzerland.

In all these South German cities Charles put down the old guilds, establishing the absolute rule of the patrician houses which had remained faithful to the Romish Church. The cities were merely promised that they should receive the same religious rights as would be granted to Duke Maurice and the house of Brandenburg.

The South German princes who had taken part in the war—Duke Ulrich of Würtemberg and Frederic, the Elector Palatine—likewise submitted to the victorious Emperor. Duke Ulrich was so sadly broken in health, that at Ulm he had to be carried in a chair by four men into the presence of the Emperor, who, in consideration of his enfeebled state, dispensed him from asking pardon on his knees. All his councillors, however, had to kneel by his side; and he had to pay 300,000 guilders, to give up three fortresses, to surrender all his artillery, and to bind himself to assist the Emperor in carrying out the outlawry against Saxony and Hesse. The Elector Palatine Frederic II., formerly the suitor of the Emperor's sister Eleanora, had, at Halle, bowed low before the gouty Emperor, who was sitting in his chair, and who at once granted him his pardon, because, as it was expressed, he had brought not more than 900 men into the field, "in virtue of certain treaties with Würtemberg."

About that time Francis I. of France wrote to his ambassador at Cassel: "It is quite incredible that people who are in their senses, and have so much power, should rather sacrifice their money to become slaves than to purchase their liberty."

Thus the Smalcalde League in South Germany was

crushed. Charles now intended to march to Frankfort, when news came from his brother Ferdinand and from Maurice of the success of John Frederic, on which the Emperor suddenly resolved to set out for Saxony. On the 24th of March, 1547, he left Nördlingen, where he had last encamped, for Nuremberg, where his army assembled next; and from thence he went to Eger, which had been selected as another rallying point for his army. Having arrived there on the 5th of April, he was joined on the following day by his brother Ferdinand and Duke Maurice, who came from Zwickau. At Eger, Easter day was celebrated, mass being read by the younger Granvella, bishop of Arras, who, in the absence of his father, transacted the business of the Emperor. From Eger Charles then marched through the Vogtland against the Elector.

After having defeated and taken prisoner the Margrave Albert of Brandenburg-Culmbach, near Rochlitz, John Frederic had not ventured, in the month of March, to attack Maurice and Ferdinand at Dresden, although they had there only a small force. Nor did he venture to hem them in, and to advance in person to Bohemia, "which," as the Venetian ambassador Navagiero, in a despatch of 1547, says, "would have made him King of Bohemia." The plan of operation adopted by John Frederic was to hold Gotha and Wittenberg, and to take a position in Magdeburg. Unfortunately for him, he scattered his army to garrison the fortresses, as he was relying on the Bohemians. Another part of his forces, under William von Thumbshirn, he had sent to the Erzgebirge and to Bohemia, and they had already crossed the mountains. With the remainder of the troops the Elector stationed himself in Maurice's country at the Middle Elbe, near Meissen.[1]

The Emperor had 17,000 infantry and 10,000 cavalry; the Elector, whose forces had been weakened in the manner just mentioned, had not more than 4,000 infantry and 2,000 or 3,000 cavalry—only a fourth of Charles's army.

---

[1] Meissen is the German name both of the country and of the town. We have, for the sake of clearness, called the country by the usual translated term of Misnia, and the town by the untranslated name of Meissen.

On the 13th of April the Emperor arrived in the Vogtland. After passing the first night at Adorf, and the second at Plauen, he proceeded through the territory of the lords of Schönburg, down along the river Mulde to Colditz and Leisnig. From the camp near the latter town he despatched, on the 22nd of April, an ambassador extraordinary to Paris to condole with his sister on the death of Francis I., her husband. On the 23rd, a Saturday, Charles rested at a manor called Zum Hof, between Oschatz and Meissen, on the little river Jahna, and belonging to the Schleinitz family. Here he heard that the Elector had broken up his camp near Meissen, from whence, after having burned the bridge, he had marched to Mühlberg and Wittenberg. The Elector refused to believe that Charles was marching against him; he still supposed him at Eger. There was even a report that Charles was dead; and Thumbshirn left John Frederic without news from Bohemia.

On the very evening of the 23rd of April the waggons of the Emperor, with the pontoons, went down the left bank of the Elbe; the troops of the Elector marching almost by their side along the right bank.[1] Thus they went on until they arrived opposite the little town of Mühlberg, where the Elector halted. On the morning of the following day, 24th of April, 1547, a Sunday and St. George's day, the whole imperial camp was astir. A thick fog covered the country. The Emperor, King Ferdinand, Duke Maurice and his brother Augustus, and the Duke of Alba mounted their horses. The Emperor looked right stately in his martial pomp, riding an Andalusian charger decked with red silk and gold-fringed housings. He was clad in a full suit of glittering armour, with gilt helmet and cuirass, and adorned with the red gold-striped Burgundian badge; in his right hand he held a lance. He was quite grey from the tortures of gout, which had sorely harassed him, even when still at Nördlingen; his limbs were as if paralysed, his face pale as death, and his voice scarcely audible. The Protestants had for some time considered him

---

[1] See Appendix B., which contains a detailed account of the forces of the belligerents of the Smalcalde war.

as a dead man. "Like a mummy, like a spectre," says Ranke, "he advanced against them." Charles trembled every time he put on his armour, but no sooner was it buckled on than his weak, enfeebled body seemed at once braced up again by the most chivalrous courage. Thus it happened once more at the battle of Mühlberg.

Duke Maurice and the Duke of Alba were the first to reach the right bank opposite Mühlberg. They were informed by a countryman, who ferried them over, that John Frederic was attending divine service at the town church of Mühlberg; that he had sent his infantry in advance to Wittenberg; and that he intended, after the service, to follow with the cavalry. On the other bank the Elector's people were just about to undo their bridge of boats, under the protection of some arquebusiers. Maurice and Alba at once gave orders to some of the Spanish infantry of the vanguard to swim across; and the men, stripping themselves and taking their swords between their teeth, gained the other side, where they seized the bridge, which the Elector's people had in vain tried to set on fire. Now some hussars also crossed the river. The Elector's horsemen, having already set out, returned once more, but their master, after having heard the sermon and taken his breakfast, entered a carriage, as, with his bulky frame, riding on horseback was too inconvenient to him. They had, however, orders to follow him, as the people who had crossed the river were still thought only to be the escort of Duke Maurice, and were therefore not much minded.

The Emperor had complained before of the thick fog which lay over the river and over the whole country. Now, about midday it slowly cleared. Charles saw the Elbe. The sun came forth, but it was said to have been the whole day quite red, like red-hot iron, and the day seemed to pass so slowly that the people would have it that the sun stood still. When, on a later occasion, Henry II. of France asked Alba whether the story of Joshua had really occurred again in this battle, the duke replied, "Sire, I had too much to do on earth to notice what was going on in the heavens." Quite unexpectedly the Emperor was informed, by a miller of the name of Strauch, of the existence of a ford. The Elector's soldiers had carried away two horses belonging to the miller; Maurice, whose subject he was, therefore promised to replace them, besides a gift of a hundred crowns and of the manor of Borschitz, if he would lead the army over. The ford had a very firm footing; seven horses could cross abreast, the water reaching only to the saddles. Charles, without delay, resolved upon fording with his cavalry. "It was," says Mocenigo, "considered as a piece of great courage by every-one that the Emperor would thus, in his own person, wade through a rapid river 300 yards broad." Eighteen Spaniards and hussars were the first to venture through; then the princes and the army followed. The lead was taken by Duke Maurice and his brother and by the Duke of Alba; after them came the Hungarian cavalry and the other light horse, in number about 4,000, with 500 arquebusiers, whom the horsemen had taken up behind them on their horses; then King Ferdinand; and, last of all, the Emperor, the miller leading his horse by the bridle. Thus they reached the other side. The Duke Maurice now sent one of his officers with a trumpeter to the Elector, his cousin, to summon him to surrender to the Emperor. John Frederic, who had not the least notion that there could be any truth in Maurice's message, refused to comply, sending back the answer that these "were words to amuse an invalid with." The bridge of boats was now restored under the eyes of the Emperor, and the heavy cavalry, as also the infantry, crossed the Elbe by it. In the meanwhile Maurice and Alba pressed on in pursuit of the retiring Elector. The Hungarian hussars were then for the first time known in Middle Germany; they wore variegated, pointed shields, and very long lances. They and the light Neapolitan horse rode on for three hours at a gallop, without stopping, before they fell in with the Elector's cavalry.

John Frederic had been advised to advance alone with the cavalry and artillery to Wittenberg, which might be reached by horsemen that very evening. But the honest, open-hearted lord said, "What will then become of my faithful infantry?"

He thus proceeded slowly in company with the latter. He did not think that there was so much danger; his cautious soul could never believe that a whole army would wade through the Elbe. The attacks of the imperial army now became more and more serious, and it was several times necessary to turn round upon it. It soon became evident that they would have to do not with Duke Maurice alone; but people had not the least idea that it could be the whole host of the Emperor.

Three German miles from the spot, near Cossdorf, where the imperial troops had forded the Elbe, those of the Elector were at last obliged to halt. The attack became more and more perilous. Now at once the Elector felt weighing on his heart, like a heavy burden, the thought of the great responsibility of having risen against the supreme head of the Empire, who was set over him by God. He therefore went on his knees in sight of his army, raised his eyes and hands to heaven, and prayed, "O Lord, if my undertaking against the Emperor be unjust, wreak thy vengeance on me, and not on my people!"

The small army was now placed in battle array on the outskirts of a wood, on the heath of Lochau, which is now called Annaburg Heath. The infantry was covered by the wood, some artillery was placed in the centre, and the cavalry on both flanks.

The Elector had mounted a heavy dark brown Frisian horse; he wore a suit of black armour with white stripes, and underneath a shirt of close mail.

It was four o'clock in the afternoon. The vanguard of the imperial army formed in close column for a main attack; there were, besides, the horse of Duke Maurice, the Neapolitan cavalry, and the hussars. They rushed forth with the war cries "Hispania!" and "The Empire!" and the Elector's troops received them with a volley; but the latter in this moment descried at some distance the main body of the Emperor's army in full march against them, and thus they saw themselves attacked on two sides at the same time.

The bearing of the Elector had not been calculated to inspire the small Saxon army with an heroic confidence in their leader and in themselves. When therefore, in the moment of peril, he now called upon them to stand faithfully by him, as he would by them, it was too late to check the confusion which became general among the men, and something worse happened. A report by the patrician Imhoff of Nuremberg, who was serving under the Emperor's standard, sets forth: "It is very strange to hear how the Elector's councillors, and the *big talkers* whom he had about him, have dealt with him. When the battle began, the Elector called out to his people that he would on this day shed his blood and give his life for them, and he expected that they also would keep honestly to him. But when fighting commenced in good earnest, the aforesaid councillors and big talkers, on whom he relied, called out, 'Fly! fly!' and even cut down and stabbed his own people, and broke the order of his battle array. I heard this at Torgau from some of the Emperor's people, and I also saw myself in the field of battle *that everything had been done by treachery.*"[1]

The army was scattered in all directions, and first of all, in spite of all the earnest exhortations of John Frederic, the cavalry; the infantry, seeing the cavalry—the knights—fly, likewise threw down their guns and pikes, and sought safety in flight. The knights escaped; but the fate of the infantry, whom the honest Elector had wished to preserve from harm, was terrible. Notwithstanding their having thrown away their arms and asked for quarter, they were cut down to a man, in obedience to an express command from Charles. Two thousand dead were left on the field, and eight hundred prisoners were taken; among them several knights, Count Beichlingen, Count Gleichen, and others, besides several princes, as, for instance, Duke Ernest of Brunswick; and last, not least, the poor Elector of Saxony himself.

John Frederic, deserted by all his mounted companions,

---

[1] Melanchthon, who had fled from Wittenberg, showed those who visited him at Zerbst some lines on the detestable treason, in which the names of Ponikau, Carlowitz, and three others were mentioned. Hans von Ponikau was the favourite of the Elector and his chamberlain. The privy councillor Christopher von Carlowitz, and the celebrated diplomatist and chancellor, Dr. Türk, were the principal advisers of Duke Maurice.

suddenly found himself quite alone in the wood, which was strewed with corpses. Being surrounded by hussars, he made a stout defence. The blood ran down his face, over his black and white cuirass, from a wound in his left cheek, which had been cleft by a Hungarian. Yet he refused to surrender to the hussars, and likewise to the Neapolitan horsemen, who hemmed him in on all sides.

At last Thilo von Trotha, a gentleman of the household of Duke Maurice, rode up, and called out to him in German to accept quarter. To this German, John Frederic surrendered, giving in pledge a ring, which he wore underneath his gauntlet. The arms of the Saxon Elector, his sword and dagger, became the booty of the Hungarians.

The "Magnanimous" was deeply moved; the hour of misfortune had now arrived. At the same moment a thunderstorm began to rage. Then John Frederic, for once a true son of his "Constant" father, rallied and called out, "Yes, yes, thou Almighty Lord; thou hast led me here, and thou art still living; thou wilt surely bring it to pass!"

Thilo von Trotha conducted the captive Elector, under an escort of Neapolitan horse, to the Duke of Alba, the generalissimo. The latter immediately made his report to the Emperor. Charles wanted to see his noble captive at once. Three times did the Duke of Alba, otherwise so ready to obey the commands of his Emperor, refuse to lead the Elector into the presence of his Majesty, being justly afraid lest his master, in the first ebullition of his anger, would treat the prisoner too harshly. But the Emperor insisted upon having his will; he stopped on horseback on the heath expecting his humbled enemy.

When John Frederic, still bleeding from his wound, first descried "Charles of Ghent, who calls himself the Roman Emperor," as he had styled him after the great cannonade of Ingolstadt, he heaved a deep sigh, again raised his eyes to heaven, and called out, "*Miserere mei, Domine, nos sumus jam hic!*"

The Emperor recognised his captive by his Frisian charger, the same which John Frederic, three years before, had ridden at the Diet of Spires. The Elector, supported by Alba, alighted from his horse, and was at first, in the Spanish fashion, going to kneel; but, recollecting himself, drew off his gauntlet, to shake hands in the German manner, as Elector, with the chief of the Empire.

Charles declined both the humble homage and the cordial greeting. He looked very stern, and turned aside. The Elector at last broke the silence by the usual style of allocution which the Electors employed in their official communications to the emperors: "Most potent, most gracious Emperor."

Charles replied, "Ah! so am I now your gracious Emperor? It's a long time since you called me so."

The Elector continued, "I am this day your poor prisoner, and beg for princely treatment during my captivity. May it please your Imperial Majesty to behave towards me as to a born prince as I am."

The Emperor angrily retorted, "Yes, just as you have deserved; I will behave towards you as you have behaved towards me. Take him away! we know very well how to behave!"

The Emperor's brother, Ferdinand, who, as King-Elector of Bohemia, was in fact neither more nor less than the colleague of the Elector of Saxony, addressed him even more sharply, "You have wanted to expel and beggar me and my children; a nice man you are!"

John Frederic was now delivered over to the Maestro del Campo, General Giovanni Batista Gastaldo, Count of Platina, second in command to the Duke of Alba; who ordered the Spanish colonel, Alphonso Vives, to be in attendance on the prisoner, to whom the other princely captive, Ernest of Brunswick, was left as a companion. The Elector was conveyed in his own carriage to the village of Ausig, in the vicinity of the imperial camp. Spanish arquebusiers guarded the prisoners; John Frederic was, however, allowed to send for some of his people from Wittenberg as his personal attendants.

Duke Maurice returned only late at night from the pursuit of the enemy's cavalry, which the bright moonlight had favoured. He had been in the saddle for more than twenty hours on that day, which it is true was the most important one of his short earthly career. Even then he had well-nigh met with the fate which afterwards befell him at Sievershausen. An electoral trooper suddenly turned his horse round, and was going to discharge his pistol at him, but it missed fire. From another trooper he was saved by a knight of his escort, who cut the man down.

As a set-off to all these dangers, he found, on his return, his cousin a prisoner; and the electoral dignity of Saxony, which Charles had promised him, was now secured to him by the battle of Mühlberg.

The imperialists had lost less than a hundred men; the whole of the Saxon artillery, the baggage of the Elector, his carriages, his plate, and his papers fell into the hands of the conquerors.

7.—*Maurice's expedition against Charles.*

The 24th of April, 1547, the day of the battle of Mühlberg, of which Charles, with a Christianised version of Cæsar's *dictum*, wrote, "I came, I saw, and *God* conquered"—the day which had delivered into his hands the chief of the Protestants, just as the day of Pavia had the King of France —this lucky day sealed his own ruin.

Nothing seemed any more to stand in the way of his supremacy in Germany, the less so as King Henry VIII. of England and Francis I. of France had died in the beginning of that same year. But, just as the captivity of Francis did not spare Charles from the necessity of three subsequent wars with him, so John Frederic's captivity, of more than five years' duration, plunged the Emperor into the war with Maurice.

Maurice was even a more crafty politician than Charles himself; and by his policy Charles was worsted. The time was fast approaching when statecraft alone, and not the laws of morality and justice, ruled in the council of princes. The Pope had taken the lead in this policy, and Charles V., following his example, violated quite coolly, on political grounds, all the stipulations which he had solemnly sworn to on his election. How could Maurice have scrupled to overthrow the grey-headed chief who in reality had only used him as his tool for the ruin of the Smalcalde League? who indeed had given him as his reward the electoral dignity of Saxony, but upon whom he by no means looked as his benefactor, but as a common enemy, when once he had clearly convinced himself that it was Charles's intention, as soon as with the help of some of the princes he had acquired the ascendency, to keep all of them in the subjection of the imperial sway. After the battle of Mühlberg, Charles, faithful to his second motto, *plus ultra*, undoubtedly did his utmost to make Germany Spanish, or, as Maurice expressed it, "to lead from the Empire, crushed by continued extortions and by the burden of a foreign army, all the water to one mill." Everything in Germany was to have been laid at the feet of the priests and of the Spaniards. It is certainly owing to Maurice alone that Germany was not made Spanish. On high principles of justice and morality the conduct of Maurice against the Emperor certainly is never to be justified, and still less to be approved. He did the same thing against the Emperor as his unfortunate cousin had done, and yet he retained possession of the electoral dignity, which the latter, likewise his benefactor, had been made to forfeit for ever. His boldly concealed and boldly executed resistance has become a blessing to Germany, inasmuch as the free Protestantism of the north of the Empire was rendered possible by it alone. Had Charles been victorious this Protestant liberty and concomitant intellectual development undoubtedly would have been altogether stifled in the bud, and the whole of Germany would now very likely exhibit the same physiognomy which stamps Austria and Bavaria with a mark of social and intellectual inferiority. On the other hand, the unity of the German Empire, which it is true had already been dissolved by the Reformation, was now permanently broken up by Maurice; the schism of the Church became also the rending of the State, and the Empire henceforth remained divided into two camps.

The Elector Maurice was the son of Duke Henry the Pious, a brother of that well-known enemy of Luther, Duke

George of Saxe Dresden. Henry was favourably inclined towards the cause of the Reformation, and for this reason, George had intended to make over his country to the house of Austria. It was only owing to the intercession of the Elector John Frederic that, on the death of George in 1539, his possessions went to Henry, and that, on Henry's death in 1541, all the estates of the latter passed undivided to Maurice. The protection thus shown to Maurice gave John Frederic an advantage of position which Maurice was made to feel.

Maurice was born on the 21st of March, 1521, at Freiberg. At the time of the battle of Mühlberg he was twenty-six years of age. He was a powerful man, of great agility, and his swarthy features bore the stamp of the hero. His eyes were bright and sparkling, and his glance so keen and searching, that no one on whom it suddenly fell could meet it. His education was based on strange elements. His father, Henry, whom his subjects called the Pious, because they liked him for his good-nature, seems, with all his piety, to have been a man of a very peculiar stamp. As Freydiger states, in his "Secret History," he had a strange fancy for everything gaudy, and for cannon. On the latter he liked to have all sorts of hideous monsters depicted, for which Lucas Cranach the painter had to furnish the designs. He also bought all the obscene pictures which he could procure, to have them copied on his artillery; and, although he had never any use for it, yet nothing gave him greater pleasure than to hear that the Emperor Charles had spoken of his cannon. From the court of his father, Maurice came to that of the Elector of Mayence, Cardinal Albert of Brandenburg, the well-known violent opponent of the Reformation. There he saw all the luxury and wantonness of the court of an ecclesiastical prince. From thence Maurice was sent to his cousin, the Magnanimous John Frederic, where he was made acquainted with the religious monotony of a Protestant court of that time. John Frederic had his very weak points, which the clever youth easily detected. Maurice indeed soon took a dislike to his cousin, whom he used to call "The Fat Pride."

At a very early age, in 1541, even before he had completed his twentieth year, Maurice was married to Agnes, daughter of the Landgrave Philip of Hesse; and that contrary to the wishes of his father, who was so unhappy about it, that it was feared that grief shortened his days. Yet, notwithstanding this loving haste, his wife had afterwards to complain of his caring much more for hunting the wild boar than for her company. Maurice, having succeeded his father, who died seven months after his son's wedding, held his court at Dresden.

Maurice, like his father, professed the Lutheran faith; but although his cousin the Elector, and likewise the Landgrave his father-in-law, repeatedly urged him to do so, he did not enter the Smalcalde League. He was far from regarding, like John Frederic, the new creed as a panacea for all the ills of the times, from centring in its cause all his activity, and from assuming the part of a champion of the gospel. He refused to ally himself against the Emperor; nay, on the contrary, the more widely the allies separated from Charles, the more closely he attached himself to him. "He did not wish," as Melanchthon writes to Camerarius, "to be the satellite of *such* allies;" he found his most certain and immediate advantage with the Emperor. He therefore caused his trusty Christopher von Carlowitz to negotiate with Granvella; after which he came in person to meet the Emperor at the Diet of Ratisbon (May, 1546). Here he entered the service of Charles. The Emperor, on his part, not only appointed him, on the 19th of June, "conservator, executor, and protector" of the two important bishoprics of Magdeburg and Halberstadt, the possession of which he had long coveted; but he also, on the 20th of June, by word of mouth—and four months after, on the 27th of October, in the camp at Sontheim, near Heilbronn, in writing—promised him the Saxon electorate, in the actual possession of which he was placed by the battle of Mühlberg. It did not signify to Maurice that his cousin was plunged by that battle into the most bitter misery, nor that his father-in-law was drawn into the same ruin. Luther had been right in the answer which he gave to John Frederic, who once at table asked him his opinion of Maurice. The doctor warned the Elector that he should take care, or he might rear in Maurice " a young lion."

From the battlefield of Mühlberg Charles marched against Wittenberg, the fortified capital of the captive Elector. On the 4th of May the town was invested, the Emperor establishing his camp at Pisteritz, a village belonging to the university, where he remained for thirty-four days. The university had dispersed already during the previous winter. Again, as at Augsburg, at the presentation of the Confession, where Luther alone manfully and even heroically stood his ground, Melanchthon was seized with a panic, in which he wandered from one neighbouring town to the other. The citizens of Wittenberg, on the other hand, wanted to hold out to the last man; and the Elector refused to order the town to surrender, as his Electress, Sibylla of Cleves, and his family were there. Then Charles caused sentence to be passed on the unfortunate Elector, "that the aforesaid John Frederic the outlaw, as a well-deserved punishment to himself and an example to others, should be put to death by the sword; and that this sentence should be carried into effect at the place of execution appointed on the field for that purpose." The Elector had been judged, not as the Emperor's sworn " Capitulation " prescribed, with the assent of the German princes, but simply by a Spanish court-martial.

The Elector, who, when fortune still smiled on him, had been so sorely deficient in energy, showed in adversity all the heroism of the faith with which his honest and simple mind was thoroughly imbued. The sentence of death was read to him on the 10th of May while he was playing at chess with Duke Francis of Brunswick, his fellow prisoner. He quietly replied: "I cannot believe that the Emperor will thus deal with me. But, if his Majesty has fully made up his mind to it, I request to be positively informed, in order that I may settle all that concerns my wife and children."

Charles kept the dread of death for nine days hanging over his prisoner. Sastrow states that King Ferdinand especially had urged his brother to let the sentence be carried into effect. The Bishop of Arras also was for dealing with the Elector of Saxony "as with Juan de Padilla;" such was the supercilious disdain with which these Spaniards regarded the princes of the German Empire. The Elector Joachim of Brandenburg, and the Duke of Cleves, the brother of the Electress, succeeded in averting the calamity. On the 19th of May the "Wittenberg Capitulation" was concluded. John Frederic had to renounce for himself and his issue all claims to the electoral dignity of Saxony, which was transferred to Maurice—from the Ernestine to the Albertine line. The fortresses of Wittenberg and Gotha were surrendered. The ex-elector himself was to remain a prisoner at the Emperor's pleasure. The Emperor was even to have the power to send him to Spain, to be guarded there by the Infant Don Philip. For the maintenance of John Frederic and his family, part of Thuringia, the cantons of Weimar and Gotha, Eisenach and Jena, with a yearly income of 50,000 florins, were assigned. This part of Thuringia formed the nucleus of the territory, which was afterwards increased and extended by the Ernestine line. There being an article in the "Capitulation" that John Frederic should accept everything that the council assembled at Trent, or the Emperor, in virtue of his prerogative, was to order in matters of religion, the Elector stoutly refused to consent to it; whereupon Charles struck it out with his own hand.

On the 23rd of May, the Monday before Whitsuntide, the electoral garrison marched out of Wittenberg; after which, agreeably to the wishes of the burghers, the town was occupied by four troops of Germans under the Italian Madruzzi, who spoke German, and who showed himself very kind. The unfortunate Electress Sybilla, with her children, came on the 25th of May in deep mourning from the town to the camp of the Emperor, conducted by the sons of the King of the Romans. When she knelt before the Emperor to entreat for her husband, Charles immediately raised her with great urbanity, but refused her request to be allowed to keep her husband with her in Saxony. She might, however, follow him if she liked. He gave permission for the Elector to spend eight days with his family at Wittenberg Castle, and to celebrate Whitsuntide with them. On the following day the Emperor himself went into Wittenberg to look at the town, and to return the visit of the Electress. On the eve of Whitsunday the Elector entered the town, according to the beforementioned letters of Imhoff, "riveted to a waggon, under an escort of 1,000 Spanish arquebusiers, who mounted guard at the castle by day and by night." As some more Spaniards, besides these arquebusiers, wanted to enter the town, the Wittenbergers, empowered to do so by the Emperor's warrant, repelled them; "whereat," says Dr. Bugenhagen, the town pastor, in his "History of the Things that happened at Wittenberg," "several young Spaniards fell from the walls into the ditches, and so were soused like cats to the great laughter of the gentlemen and burghers. The Elector was brisk all through the town; but in the castle-yard he became pale, and the tears rolled down his cheeks. All the ladies at the windows wept piteously. There were sitting with him in the waggon, his eldest son, and his brother Duke Ernest of Coburg. The people of the town also were full of sorrow." On the 3rd of June the deposed Elector returned to the imperial camp, and his wife and children went to Thuringia, to the new home assigned to them.

Charles was heard to say, during his stay in Wittenberg: "Everything forsooth is very different in the Evangelical countries from what we imagined." As he heard that the Protestant service had been put down he exclaimed, "Who has done that for us? We have not changed anything in the Upper (South) German countries in matters of religion, and why should we do so here?" He went to see the church at the castle when those about him—Alba, and the younger Granvella, Bishop of Arras, are especially mentioned—advised him to have the "arch-heretic" Luther exhumed and burnt. Charles replied, "Let him rest; he has found his Judge already. I make war against the living, not against the dead." From this we may see that the Emperor no longer remembered his alliance with the Pope.

On the 4th of June the Emperor invested Maurice, on the

great meadow near Blesern, in sight of the whole army, with the vacant electorate of Saxony; two days after, the imperial troops marched out from Wittenberg to make room for those of the new Elector. The burghers received the new garrison with manifest sorrow. Maurice rode, " quite angry, straightway to the castle, without looking into the face of anybody." But when the burgomaster and town councillors afterwards came to wait on him, he said to them, " You have been faithful to my cousin your prince; I will ever remember that in kindness."

Charles on the 7th of June left Wittenberg for Halle, where he arrived on the 10th. The captive Elector accompanied him. Lucas Cranach, the celebrated painter and burgomaster of Wittenberg, who, as a young man of twenty-three years, had accompanied Frederic the Wise to Jerusalem, followed John Frederic, his patron and friend, into captivity. The Emperor's march to Halle was intended against the second head of the Smalcalde League, the Landgrave of Hesse, Maurice's father-in-law.

Philip " the Magnanimous " had shown himself so pusillanimous ever since the departure of the Smalcalde army from Southern Germany, that he repeatedly made proposals to the Emperor, and even on the 6th of March, 1547, offered to him a body of auxiliary troops. The fear of losing everything— which had harassed him ever since his marriage with his second wife Margaret von der Saal, in addition to, and in the lifetime of his first, Christine of Saxe-Dresden; and still more since his war in Southern Germany, when Schärtlin in plain words called him a traitor—now assailed him with double force, when he was informed of the fate of the Elector of Saxony. He negotiated with the Emperor through the Elector Maurice and the Elector Joachim of Brandenburg —the former his son, and the latter his brother-in-law—both of whom were still about the person of Charles. Philip made his submission, surrendering at discretion, offering to beg the Emperor's pardon on his knees, to pay him 150,000 guilders, to demolish all his fortresses except Cassel and Ziegenhayn, and to give up his cannon.

On the other hand, the two Electors, on the 4th of June, in a bond drawn up by Granvella, bishop of Arras, guaranteed to the Landgrave that the Emperor would not deprive him of his country, nor inflict capital punishment, nor even condemn him to "some" imprisonment, the German expression being "*einigem Gefängniss*." They likewise sent to him on the same day their safeguard. The two mediators in this bond pledged themselves to the Landgrave with their word of honour; they even vowed that, if the Emperor would not liberate him, they would surrender themselves as prisoners to the sons of Philip at Cassel.

Trusting to the Electors, Philip agreed to the conditions. When Philip's daughter, the wife of Maurice, on the 7th of June, fell on her knees before the Emperor to entreat him for her father's pardon, Charles would not give any further answer than that "Philip had to surrender at discretion." On the following day the latter arrived at Halle, where the Emperor was staying, and he supped on that evening with his son-in-law Maurice and the Elector of Brandenburg. On the next morning all the three princes breakfasted with Granvella. Here they signed that momentous document; but the word "einigem" had been changed to "ewigem"; *i.e.*, "some" into "everlasting" (perpetual) imprisonment.

In the afternoon, at four o'clock, the Landgrave had to go through the ceremony of begging the Emperor's pardon. At the so-called "residence" where the Emperor lodged, Charles was sitting on a throne under a gilded canopy, surrounded by his German, Spanish, Italian, and Netherlandish lords. Philip, dressed in a suit of black velvet, with a red scarf, knelt down, dejected and sad, on the carpet before the throne; behind him his faithful chancellor, Tileman von Günderode,[1] read out the document by which his master made honourable amends to the head of the Empire. As he did so with doleful tone and gesture, a smile flashed over the features of the Landgrave, which, perhaps, was but the involuntary protest of his natural light-heartedness against the

---

[1] Günderode followed his master to his captivity and died there.

feeling of the humiliating position in which he stood. But the grave and solemn Emperor threateningly raised his finger and said, in his Brabant dialect, "*Wart, ik wöll Der laken ler!*" ("Wait a bit, I'll teach you to laugh!")

After the vice-chancellor of the Empire, Dr. Seld, had read the answer of the Emperor, and Günderode politely thanked in reply, the Landgrave waited for a sign from the Emperor to rise. But, the sign not being given, Philip rose of his own accord, and was going to offer his hand to the Emperor; "His Majesty, however, looked sour," and kept back his own; instead of which Alba seized Philip's hand, and invited the whole company to take supper at his house. During the bustle of breaking up, the Emperor gave the verbal declaration, which, however, passed unnoticed in the din, that he would not punish the Landgrave with "perpetual imprisonment" (*ewigem Gefängniss*). Philip withdrew, and, in company with Maurice and the Elector of Brandenburg, took supper at the Duke of Alba's, who was quartered at the castle called Moritzburg. After supper the Landgrave sat down to play at backgammon with one of the Saxon councillors, Franz Kramer. It was past ten o'clock when Alba at once announced to Philip that he was his prisoner; at the same time 100 Spanish arquebusiers entered the apartment. Alba arrested the Landgrave in exactly the same manner as, on a later occasion, he did Counts Egmont and Horn. The two Electors who had pledged themselves for Philip's liberty were quite dumbfounded; Joachim drew his sword, and was going to cleave Alba's skull, calling out repeatedly, "This is the trick of a knave!" Maurice, who was deeply distressed, remained with his father-in-law during the whole night. The two Electors assured the Landgrave that on the following day they would themselves speak with the Emperor. This was done, and negotiations went on for three days about the matter; but Charles insisted upon it that the Landgrave had surrendered at discretion, and that, after the apology, he had only given him the verbal promise that he would not inflict perpetual (*ewiges*), not, however, that he would not condemn him, at least to some (*einiges*) imprisonment. This also agreed with the tenor of the bond, which the Electors, without looking closely at it, had signed in the morning.

The Landgravine Christine of Hesse and Mary Queen of Hungary in vain entreated the Emperor on their knees to liberate the Landgrave. Charles abode by his first resolution, and Maurice was not in a position to give any effective aid for the present. He was afraid, on the one hand, lest Charles might fulfil his expressed threat to have the Landgrave removed to Spain, and, on the other, lest it might occur to his Cæsarean Majesty to liberate likewise the Elector John Frederic. Thus was Maurice fairly caught in a trap. Yet, although he was obliged to bide his time, he retaliated in due season the trick which Charles had played upon him.

The Landgrave, who had often said that he was far more afraid of captivity than of death, had now to submit to being the Emperor's captive; and his fate was much worse than the one which he had thought of, and which his princely fellow-prisoner was suffering, who certainly was an infinitely more noble character. John Frederic inspired even the Spaniards with respect, nay, veneration. He also enjoyed the distinction of being allowed to remain with Charles at Augsburg during the Diet; Philip, on the contrary, was treated very severely, and was sent to Donauwerth. His Spanish guards kept up a constant noise in his quarters day and night; and the Landgrave complained bitterly of their visiting him at night "to see whether he had not escaped by a chink or a mouse-hole." He was only rarely taken out for a drive in a waggon, "as a lion in a show." Very likely he gave sufficient vent to his passionate temper, and he can hardly be supposed to have gratified the Spaniards by an excess of civility on his side.

Charles left Halle about the end of June to hold at Augsburg a Diet "for the purpose of religious union, as master and lord, and as conqueror." The journey was by Naumburg, where the new Elector of Saxony and Joachim of Brandenburg took leave of his Imperial Majesty. Maurice several times told Alba that the Diet would be short, and that things there would be managed rather by orders than by deliberation. He gave very plainly to understand that he considered this as a matter of course; for even then he already began to play his part of dissembling. Charles went by Bamberg and Nuremberg. The captured artillery, numbering 442 pieces, was for the present carried to Bamberg, to be sent afterwards as booty, and as a substantial token of the victory, partly to Spain and partly to Milan and Naples. At Nuremberg, Charles received the submission of the towns of Hamburg and Lübeck. The delegates of Hamburg, which, in the times of the German Empire, always showed great obsequiousness to the house of Habsburg, made their submission in the Spanish fashion, on their knees. As to Lübeck, the head of the Hanseatic League, it is only stated that it paid 200,000 guilders. The captive princes were generally led one day's journey ahead of the Emperor; Alba and the Spanish infantry were with them. Charles reached Augsburg on the 23rd of July, the Diet being appointed for the 3rd of September.

This Diet, held to bring about a compromise of the religious differences, was, as Sleidanus says, "a cuirassed Diet"; the Spanish and German troops of the Emperor being posted partly within the city itself, and partly in the neighbourhood. Charles, as Sastrow states, "was on good terms with his prisoner John Frederic. The latter lived in the mansion of the Welser family, only two houses from the Emperor's quarters, who again had put up at the hotel of the Fuggers in the wine market. The Emperor had caused a passage to be broken through the walls, and a little bridge to be laid across the intervening lane, so that one might go from the lodgings of the Emperor into those of the Elector. The Duke of Alba and other great lords of the imperial court frequently called on him and kept him company. He had a tilt-yard behind his house, and was at liberty to ride out in the town, and to the gardens of the patricians and burghers; but his Spanish soldiers escorted him everywhere. He was also allowed to read any books that he liked."

It was rather remarkable that here at Augsburg, when

Charles seemed to have arrived at the acme of his power in Germany, a serious danger should have threatened him from the very people who had been his tools in gaining the victories which had established his supremacy. The conduct of the imperial army had been outrageous already on the march from Saxony to Swabia, although the Emperor every evening at the halting-places caused a gallows to be erected. At Augsburg they broke out into a mutiny, their pay being in arrear for several months. It was the German lansquenets under Madruzzi who first raised the standard of insubordination. Not only were they exasperated at the captive princes being entrusted to the guard of the Spaniards, but they said that *enough money* had been paid by the conquered princes and cities, and that the Duke of Alba gambled it away, &c. One day they drew up, in closed ranks and with standards flying, in the wine market. A Spaniard who attempted to wrest the standard from one of the ensigns was cleft asunder "like a turnip." The Spaniards now occupied all the streets which led to the wine market, and John Frederic was taken to the Emperor's quarters, lest he might be rescued by force. There was great fear of the city being plundered, especially among the merchants and dealers, who, on account of the Diet, had laid in a great stock of valuable goods, silver and gold plate, silks, precious stones, and pearls. The inhabitants assembled in crowds, or kept themselves within their dwellings with their cuirasses on, and armed with arquebuses and hand-matchlocks. The Emperor now sent to the German lansquenets to know what they wanted. They, supporting their arquebuses on their left arm, and keeping with their right hand the slow-matches near the touch-hole, answered, "Money, or blood." The Emperor was obliged to send back word that they might rest assured they should be paid on the next day; he besides granted them a free pardon for having presented themselves before him in such a way. On the following morning they were paid and dismissed. Some of the ringleaders, however, were arrested on their way, and hanged at Augsburg for having cursed and abused "Charles of Ghent."

On the 15th of May, 1548, the Emperor communicated

to the Diet at Augsburg his imperial decision in the matter of religion. He published the "Interim," an attempt at compromise between the old and the new creed. Of the latter there were admitted the marriage of the clergy, and the Eucharist under both forms to the laity, *but only until the council should have decided on these points.* Of the ancient creed, the supremacy of the Pope, the mass, the seven sacraments, and saint-worship remained as articles of faith. This document being read out on the 15th of May to the assembled Diet by Dr. Seld, vice-chancellor of the Empire, a short deliberation of the Estates followed, which, however, led to no result. The Elector of Mayence then rose to thank the Emperor for his trouble, his diligence, and activity, and for his "*love of the fatherland.*" As no one ventured to raise any objection, the Emperor took the assent of the Estates for granted, and the "Interim" of Augsburg was promulgated as a law of the Empire. Already did the younger Granvella triumphantly call out, "*In this country everything is possible.*" But the Emperor was able to enforce his "Interim"—of which the people said that "it had the rogue behind it"—in Southern Germany only, where the towns were garrisoned by his Spanish soldiers. And yet 400 ministers emigrated from Augsburg, Ulm, Ratisbon, Nuremberg, and Frankfort on the Maine. The North of Germany, on the other hand, pronounced against it—Magdeburg especially, which received all those who fled on account of their religion within its walls, thus constituting itself the centre of the Protestant opposition. Of the princes of Southern Germany it was only accepted by the Elector Palatine Frederic and Duke Ulrich of Würtemberg, as also by the frightened Landgrave of Hesse; in Northern Germany by the lukewarm Elector Joachim II. of Brandenburg, led by his court preacher, the bland and pliant Agricola, who had himself been engaged in drawing it up with two Papist divines. The captive Elector of Saxony stoutly refused to accept it; and Maurice, now the most important of all the German princes, likewise pronounced against it, and caused another, the so-called "Leipzig Interim," to be written by his friend Melanchthon.

The Emperor was assailed on all sides with protestations

against the "Interim"; but the foremost in condemning it were the Papists. "And if Charles had published the gospel itself it would have been inexcusable in him, a layman," was the saying of an eminent prelate. Pope Paul III. Farnese, and the council assembled at Trent, of course opposed it just as strenuously. But the Emperor was resolved to try how far he might intimidate all the princes and towns by means of his Spaniards. To the Prince Palatine Wolfgang, of the Upper (Bavarian) Palatinate, he sent a message that he should soon see a couple of thousand Spaniards in his country. To the delegates of Frankfort, who pleaded scruples of conscience, the imperial councillor Hase replied, "Your consciences are like the sleeves of the Capuchins, which swallow whole monasteries. The Emperor wants the "Interim" to be maintained, even if it should cost him a kingdom. Only learn the old way again, or we shall send you people who will teach it you. You shall learn Spanish before we have done with you."

Even before the opening of this remarkable cuirassed Diet Ferdinand I. had sat in judgment on Bohemia. This was the first day of retribution which the house of Habsburg held in this country. The same was repeated afterwards in an aggravated form at the outset of the Thirty Years' War by the second Ferdinand.

In July, 1547, the first Ferdinand held at Prague his "Bloody Diet." The heads of the League of Prague were condemned to death—in particular the pretender to the crown, Caspar Pflugk von Rabenstein, who, however, saved himself by flight, and died unmolested at Magdeburg, the great asylum of the Protestants. The towns and cities which had joined that league lost their rights and privileges, were subjected to the jurisdiction of the Crown, and had to pay heavy fines. All the old Hussites of the Taborite party, the so-called Bohemian Brethren, had to leave the country of Bohemia for ever. They emigrated in three bodies, each upwards of 1,000 men, to Prussia.

Ferdinand now declared Bohemia an hereditary and absolute kingdom. The temper of the Bohemians was most hostile to the Germans, as may be gathered from a passage in Imhoff's Letters: "The King cannot trust the Bohemians; they do not like the Germans; call us dogs, and wish us no good." But the weight of the paramount power of Charles kept down any outbreak.

During the two years succeeding the Diet of Augsburg Charles resided in the Netherlands, whither the captive princes followed him. The Elector was kept at the imperial court at Brussels; the Landgrave was confined at Oudenard; but after the "insolence of an attempt at flight," shortly before Christmas, 1550, removed to Mechlin, to a small chamber in the imperial palace, not ten feet in length, with the windows nailed up.

On the 26th of July, 1550, Charles, with his son Philip, came to hold another Diet at Augsburg, at which the Elector Maurice was charged with carrying out the ban of the Empire against Magdeburg, the determined opponent of the "Interim." From this Diet the Emperor, in the beginning of November, 1551, set out for Innsbruck, for the avowed reason of enjoying there the fine mild air, and to be nearer the Council of Trent. The secret motive, however, for this journey, as communicated in a letter of his to his sister Mary, dated the 7th of March, 1552, was his inability to pay the German mercenaries at Augsburg and the Spanish troops in the duchy of Nuremberg.

Maurice commenced the siege of Magdeburg. Everyone in Germany dreaded lest the Emperor might be only waiting for the decrees of the council to enforce them forthwith in the Empire as religious laws, just as he had done the "Interim" of Augsburg, and lest he might for this purpose avail himself of his Spanish soldiery. All the Protestants were waiting in anxious suspense for what was to come next, and public opinion freely accused Maurice as the principal cause of all this misfortune.

The obstinacy with which the Emperor refused the liberation of the Landgrave of Hesse had completely satisfied Maurice that force alone could ensure compliance. He had, therefore, long familiarised himself with the thought of striking a great blow against Charles, of preparing it well, and of executing it suddenly and with the utmost energy, in such a way that it could not miscarry. Everything now depended on keeping the Emperor deceived as long as possible.

It may fairly be doubted whether Maurice has ever had his equal in the art of dissembling. Even the Emperor, his teacher, had not such complete control over himself. Charles sometimes spoke out very bluntly. At the Diet at Augsburg, 1530, he called the princes of Saxony heretics in plain terms. As a Protestant prince (the son of the Duke of Saxony) was about to take a seat at the imperial table, Charles exclaimed, "Catholic princes alone sit here; there is no room here for heretics." This story is told with evident relish by his own father-confessor, Garcia de Loaysa. At that time Charles thought himself safe. But he also uttered unguarded speeches whilst he was not yet prepared, and whilst it was still his wish to dissemble. At the Diet of Ratisbon, very shortly before the beginning of the Smalcalde war, he betrayed himself to the Protestants by a smile, when they presented to him a memorial in which they protested against the Council of Trent. Maurice, on the other hand, never betrayed himself. He was as thoroughly inscrutable as Cromwell himself. Not a soul in Germany, not even his most intimate confidant, Christopher von Carlowitz, had the least idea of what were really his plans. For more than two years did he keep all shut up within himself, and the Emperor, who had once deceived him, was now in his turn deceived by him so completely that undeniably it was the greatest masterpiece of political dissimulation that any German prince has ever perpetrated.

Anyone who had judged him merely from his daily habits of life would have believed that pleasure and amusements alone had charms for Maurice. At home, at his own court, he was almost constantly engaged in the pleasures of the chase; he was fond of banquets, chivalrous sports, and the revels of the carnival; and likewise in foreign courts and at the Diets he seemed only bent upon the pursuits of gaiety, and was particularly assiduous in paying his court to beautiful ladies and maidens. As to the liberation of his father-in-law, he seemed not to have it much at heart. Philip wrote to him on the 13th of November, 1547, "If your Highness were as active in my behalf as in banqueting, revelling, and gambling, my affairs would long ago have been in a better way." In the following December Maurice drove to Munich in a sledge to look after the ladies there; and this was just on the day preceding that on which Charles had promised to give an answer concerning the Landgrave, and although Carlowitz had made the most energetic representations to him about his frivolous conduct.

No wonder, then, that the Emperor believed that those had the greatest power over Maurice who abetted him in his pleasures. But the cautious and far-sighted Charles did not see through Maurice, who was even more cautious and saw further than he did. And just as little did the Venetians, those most accomplished masters of diplomacy in their day, see through him. The Venetian ambassador Navagiero, in his "Relation" of 1547, after the battle of Mühlberg, calls Maurice brave and valorous, but *precipitous* (impulsive). In the same way Mocenigo expressed himself in his "Relation" of 1547. "Maurice," he writes, "has much courage, but, it is believed, not much judgment; besides which, he is a very flighty gentleman (*non di molto consiglio, anzi leggiero*)." "From him," he said, "Charles has little to fear."

Yet it was Maurice who eventually brought about the ruin of the Emperor. He was just as circumspect and bold as he was inscrutable. After having cautiously prepared everything for the execution of his great plan, he fell upon Charles like a thunderbolt. And with true relish did he enter upon the enterprise against "this goat" Charles, as he once calls him in a confidential letter to Margrave John of Cüstrin, the brother of the Elector Joachim II. of Brandenburg.

Long before the great blow was struck he had succeeded in procuring the necessary money. As far back as 1547 he sent for the plate and valuables of the chapter of Meissen. There were some very rare and rich pieces among them; as, for instance, a silver statue of St. Benno, studded with precious stones, holding in one hand a crosier and in the other a book, the whole weighing 73 marks; a silver statue of St. Donatus, weighing 52 marks; the head of St. Briccius, with a gilt mitre; besides 140 chalices; altogether amounting in value to 150,000 guilders. No one afterwards knew what had become of all these precious objects. Maurice very likely had secretly put them in the melting-pot. In addition to this, he had borrowed considerable sums; his brother Augustus had no less than two million florins to pay for him after his death.

As early as in the summer of 1550 the beginnings of a closer alliance of Maurice with France may be traced. It was with the help of this power that he intended to humble Charles. In the following November, after the last Diet of the Emperor at Augsburg, he undertook the siege of Magdeburg, with which Charles had charged him. In February and May of the year 1551 he had at Dresden and Torgau several meetings with John of Brandenburg-Cüstrin, the brother of the Elector, with his own brother-in-law William of Hesse, and with John Albert of Mecklenburg. After this Frederic von Reiffenberg was sent as ambassador to France. About the end of September, 1551, Maurice met at Lochau, not far from the battlefield of Mühlberg, with the French envoy, Jean de Bresse, bishop of Bayonne, with whom a definitive alliance with France was concluded on the 5th of October, 1551, at Friedewalde in Hesse. It was looked upon as a remarkable omen that, whilst they were settling the treaty, all at once a flash of lightning ran through the room where the delegates were sitting.

On the 9th of November, 1551, Magdeburg surrendered to Maurice. On the 15th of January, 1552, Henry II. of France took his oath at Chambord on the Friedewalde Treaty with Maurice and the German princes. The latter were represented on this occasion by the Margrave Albert of Brandenburg-Culmbach, who had repaired *incognito* thither with Schärtlin. To the French king a prospect was held out of the imperial crown of Germany; and for the present the three bishoprics of Metz, Toul, and Verdun, "as not belonging to the German tongue," were made over to him; he was to possess them as *vicarius imperii*, as a fief of the Empire, under which title Arelat had before passed to the French crown.

Maurice did not disband the army employed before Magdeburg; on the contrary, he increased it to 25,000 men. He engaged officers who had served in the Smalcalde war against the Emperor, as, for instance, the Würtemberger Hans von Heydeck. To disguise the strength of his steadily increasing army, he employed the stratagem of dividing it and making the separate bodies frequently change their quarters at the villages. The Emperor indeed had his spies in the camp of Maurice, where Lazarus Schwendi stayed as imperial commissioner. Maurice, however, deceived all of them. Charles secretly paid pensions to two of the secretaries at the Saxon court. Maurice was quite aware of it; but he dissembled, and continued to call them in at every deliberation of the council, where he took good care always to boast of his fidelity to his Majesty; and thus the corrupt scribes unwittingly sent to Charles nothing but false reports.

The Venetians had already, in 1550, ferreted out something about the alliance between Maurice and France. Towards the end of 1551 the report of its existence was pretty general. Charles received at Innsbruck warnings from his ambassador in France and from his brother Ferdinand, who, in a letter from Vienna dated 5th of November, 1551, expressed to him his apprehensions, and advised him to liberate the Landgrave Philip. Frightened by these reports, the three spiritual Electors wanted even to leave suddenly the Council of Trent. Charles, however, had no misgivings; he could never divest himself of his expressed conviction that these "wild roystering Germans" had no capacity for such intrigues. As late as on the 28th of February, 1552, he wrote to the Elector Joachim of Brandenburg that he "expected from Maurice every obedience."

Charles was not, however, as has always been believed, taken aback by Maurice at Innsbruck. He was very well aware of his approach, although informed of it only very late. This is evident from a letter of the Emperor to his brother, dated 4th of April, 1552, which Buchholz and Hormayr have communicated. Charles writes, that he knew that Maurice had put off meeting Ferdinand at Linz, to settle accounts with him (Charles) for the grievances of the German nation. He had positive information that Maurice was on his way to Augsburg. He knew he must not tarry any longer at Innsbruck, lest he *might one fine morning be seized in his bed*. He was determined to set out that very night to Flanders, where he possessed the most power to resist his enemy. He was obliged to leave Germany *because he had no one who would declare for him, because so many took part against him, and because he no longer possessed any means of raising money*. He was placed in the alternative of either submitting to great indignity or risking a great danger. He would rather choose the latter, because he was then in the hands of God, who might help him. If Maurice were apprised of his flight, and came to Ferdinand to enter into negotiations at an advantage, Ferdinand should show every goodwill, *but take care not to settle anything definitively*.

Maurice left Dresden in the month of March for Thuringia. His army stood near Erfurt and Mühlhausen. On the 25th of March, 1552, he joined at Schweinfurt his brother-in-law William of Hesse, with whom was likewise the Bishop of Bayonne, the French envoy. They now marched in all haste by Donauwerth to Augsburg. Here Maurice arrived on the 1st of April; thus placing himself, as he expresses it, "*before the den of the fox*" at Innsbruck.

Charles had until now repeatedly given the most supercilious and defiant answers to the applications about Philip; "he would have the body of the Landgrave cut in two pieces, and send one to each of the parties who wished to force him." Notwithstanding this high tone, he had given directions to his sister Mary, the regent of the Netherlands, to enter into negotiations with the prisoner. A very important protocol, relating to one of these transactions, conducted by the President Viglius, is dated 18th of April, 1552. *The liberation of the Landgrave was to procure for Charles the consent of the two Electors of Saxony and Brandenburg to a great scheme which the Emperor was then aiming at.* He had for this very purpose invited Maurice to an interview at Innsbruck. It seemed, therefore, quite natural when one of the councillors of the latter made his appearance at that city, and quietly bespoke quarters for his master, who, he said, would immediately follow him. The Privy Councillor Carlowitz, and the Chancellor Mordeisen, the electoral Lord High Steward, as also the servants, had gone before to Landshut. Melanchthon and other divines were likewise on their way to Trent, the Emperor having ordered them to send delegates to the council; everything, in fact, was apparently done as the Emperor wished it.

On the 27th of March, 1552, Maurice, in a letter from Schweinfurt, repeated for the last time the request to the Emperor to liberate his father-in-law, as otherwise he himself stood pledged to surrender himself a prisoner to Philip's children. Charles privately sent to him to Augsburg his chamberlain and keeper of the privy purse, Hans Walter von Hirnheim. The latter had been present at Augsburg when Maurice took that city on the 1st of April, and had dined several times with him. According to what Charles writes to his brother Ferdinand, he sent Hirnheim back to Maurice, in order not to leave anything undone by which he might meet his wishes as far as possible; and he adds, that he had selected this messenger because Maurice had allowed himself to be rather influenced by people who drank with him than by persons of more judgment. Hirnheim's commission was to this effect: to induce Maurice to go to Ferdinand and negotiate with him; for which purpose Ferdinand had appointed to meet him on the 4th of April at Linz.

The Emperor's situation was desperate: he had neither troops nor money; his brother had written to him that he wanted all his forces in Hungary. The spiritual Electors, then staying at Trent, to whom he had applied; and likewise the Duke of Bavaria, wrote evasively, declaring that they wished to keep neutral. The great banking-houses in Italy and in the Netherlands, and the Fuggers at Augsburg, had refused to accommodate him, although he offered the most advantageous terms. He had lost all credit with those who had until then negotiated his loans. He did the worst thing that can be done with financial people : he broke faith. Like Prince Metternich a few decades since, he made loan after loan in the midst of peace, and then forced upon his creditors the system of permanent annuities, converting the loan into an unfunded debt, with perpetual interest — a proceeding which arrayed the whole moneyed world against him.

Yet Charles lost his credit, not only in the commercial world, but in his own family. That great scheme which he had hatched in his cabinet was neither more nor less than a combination by which the imperial dignity was to be made hereditary in his house. His brother Ferdinand had for some time been King elect of the Romans; he was to succeed to the imperial crown. Philip, the son of Charles, was to be King of the Romans, and so was Ferdinand's son Maximilian; but the latter only as "second coadjutor," as Charles expressed it. Emperor Charles was to be succeeded by Emperor Ferdinand; Emperor Ferdinand by Emperor Philip; and Emperor Philip only by Emperor Maximilian, Ferdinand's son. The imperial dignity was thus to alternate in hereditary succession in both lines. In the instructions [1] for the envoys who were sent for this purpose to the Electors, discretionary power is granted them to use every means to attain their object. "*Leur offrant*," it is said, in the instruction to Councillor Gienger, who was to have gained over the Electors of Saxony and Brandenburg, "*leur offrant la recognoissance selon leur desir, fust en honneur, promocion ou prouffit.*" To the Elector Maurice a "*declaration de la prison perpetuelle*" of his cousin John Frederic was promised, as the reward of his own consent and that of the Elector of Brandenburg to the election of Philip as King of the Romans; besides which the Landgrave was to be liberated.

This Spanish project alarmed everybody. The Emperor's own family rose against him. The secret instruction of Charles to J. de Rye, dated 3rd of March, 1552, proves that Charles suspected Ferdinand and his son Maximilian

[1] Published by Lanz, from the archives at Brussels.

of siding, neither more nor less, with his adversaries against him.

The wily monarch had been caught in his own snare. He was threatened with desertion on all sides. Ferdinand was well aware that, if Don Philip was admitted to the imperial crown, he would do his utmost to secure the succession for his own descendants; and that the Vienna branch was to be be ousted to make room for Philip and his line.

The real clue to the mystery of this general desertion is given in the State papers brought to light, which afford undeniable evidence *that it was the Pope who, to ward off the danger of a universal monarchy of the Emperor, secretly abetted Maurice and his confederates against Charles.*

The attempted flight of Charles to Flanders failed. The fox could not get out of his den, although he twice made a start. According to a letter of the Emperor to his sister Mary, he set out with the most profound secrecy, between eleven and twelve in the night of the 6th of April, notwithstanding the feeble state of his health and the tortures of gout, which scarcely ever left him. It was his intention to push on through the mountain pass of Ehrenberg to the Lake of Constance, and from thence to go by Alsace and Lorraine to the Low Countries. He was accompanied only by two of his gentlemen, his first equerry D'Andelot, and Albert von Rosenberg, besides his faithful barber Van der Fé, and two servants. Rosenberg knew the roads. Van der Fé with one of the servants went before to keep a sharp look-out, lest the Emperor should meet any troops who might recognise him. Riding along through the woods and mountains, the party reached Nassereit at eight in the morning of the 7th of April. Here the Emperor remained until two in the afternoon, and then rode on to Bachelbach, one league from the so-called Ehrenberger Klause. There he put up for the night, being too tired to proceed. Van der Fé was sent to Ehrenberg castle to get information from the commandant. This officer reported that Maurice had already set out from Augsburg, and was going on that very day (7th of April) to occupy Füssen; moreover, that the Saxon cavalry, who were foraging thereabouts, made the road by Kempten very unsafe. On receiving this intelligence, the Emperor determined on returning to Innsbruck with the same profound secrecy. Not a soul knew anything of the journey.

A second attempt at flight was likewise unsuccessful. He disguised himself as an old woman, intending to escape in a carrier's covered waggon by Ehrwald to Hohenschwangau, and from thence, through Würtemberg, by Spires to the Netherlands. His companion, Albert von Vestenberg, was ordered to answer to any inquiries, that he was conducting an old lady to the warm springs of Wildbad in the Black Forest. This journey also was kept a secret; so much so, that the Emperor's valet Dubois had to lie in his master's bed, and in the kitchen the meals were cooked just as if his Majesty were present. Two short day journeys were completed by the newly built mountain-road of the Fern. As Charles alighted in the village of Lermos to take some refreshment, a girl who had only seen his portrait cried out, "Oh! how like this old lady is to the Emperor!" Thereupon his Majesty in a fright returned home again.

In the meanwhile the negotiations between King Ferdinand and Maurice went on, contrary to the expectation of the Emperor, but not to that of Ferdinand, and sorely against the wish of his brother-in-law William of Hesse and of the French ambassador. Maurice arrived on Easter Monday in person at Linz to meet Ferdinand. He was accompanied by the Duke of Bavaria and the Bishop of Passau. All of them supped with the King and his children; and after supper it was agreed between the King and Maurice, that the next morning between six and seven they would begin to transact business.

On the 28th of April, 1552, Ferdinand and Maurice arranged that there should be a truce, in order that an assembly might be summoned to Passau to devise the means for remedying the grievances of the German nation. The truce was to commence on the 26th of May, and to last until the 8th of June. Ferdinand then set out to join his brother at Innsbruck, where he arrived with his children on the 7th of May. On the

8th Maurice was again with his confederates at the Upper Danube, where the army was stationed.

Charles had at last succeeded in raising some money: troops gathered under his banner near Frankfort on the Maine, and near Ulm; the principal force mustering at Reitti, near the Ehrenberger Klause.

Maurice had only the intervening time from then to the beginning of the truce to carry out his design. On the 18th of May, just eight days before the beginning of the armistice, he first took the field, dispersing the camp of Reitti. On the following day, Ehrenberg castle was taken, after a feeble resistance; and now the way to the Emperor lay open. Maurice forthwith deliberated with his brother-in-law and the other allied princes, whether they should proceed "to draw the fox out of his den;" and the question was decided in the affirmative. Then suddenly an event happened which brought relief to the old Emperor. The infantry of Maurice broke out in a very dangerous mutiny, the regiment of Reiffenberg claiming the usual gratuity of double pay for having taken Ehrenberg castle by storm. This riot caused a delay of two days and a half; and things were in such a critical state, that Maurice had to fly for his life and conceal himself. By this means Charles gained a respite, which enabled him to leave Innsbruck; on which step he determined as soon as he had, on the 19th of May, received the intelligence of the surrender of Ehrenberg castle.

On the same day, in the afternoon, he summoned the captive Elector John Frederic of Saxony, to meet him in the palace-garden. According to the State papers published by Lanz, he had received from him, as early as the 14th of May, a declaration in answer to the question, "What help and assistance may John Frederic expect from his relations and friends, if the transactions at Passau do not lead to any result, *and if the Emperor pronounce outlawry against Maurice.*" John Frederic had sent an envoy to Passau, and Maurice had offered to negotiate. But the final resolution of the single-minded old ex-Elector was to the effect that, if the dispute between his Majesty and Duke Maurice could not be settled, the Duke (John Frederic) could not accept from the enemies and adversaries of his Majesty any appointment and so separate himself from his said Majesty. Charles conversed with John Frederic for half an hour in the summer-house of the palace-garden; and of his own accord offered him his liberty, under the sole condition that he should voluntarily for a short time follow his court. Charles was temporising again. After having dismissed John Frederic, he gave orders that the most important papers and jewels should be placed in safety at the strong castle of Rodenegg. This being arranged, he set out with his brother Ferdinand, at nine o'clock in the evening, with the intention of passing across the Brenner, through the Puster Valley, to Carinthia.

Thus the master of two hemispheres was obliged, in a cold spring night, in a pouring rain, agonised by the tortures of gout, to make a precipitous flight. He was carried in a litter; and his servants, bearing torches, lighted him through the narrow passes of the Tyrolese Alps. All the bridges were destroyed after he had crossed them; Spanish soldiers were also placed at all the mountain passes. On the following morning the illustrious fugitive reached Sterzing, and at nightfall Brunecken, a castle in the Puster Valley belonging to the Cardinal of Trent.

In the suite of the Emperor followed the captive Elector with his friend Lucas Cranach. For the first time for five years the old prince saw no Spanish guard about him; which so gladdened his heart that he began to sing in the waggon a hymn of praise and thanksgiving. In Brunecken he delivered into the hands of the Emperor a second declaration, dated 23rd of May, and likewise referring to the execution of outlawry against Maurice, and to the war against France. He advised the Emperor to raise a German army; not to employ any Spaniards and Italians; to seize Augsburg; and to make over the country of Maurice to him and to Maurice's brother Augustus.[1]

---

[1] This latter point of the declaration is worded thus: "Touchant le point, comme l'on pourroit recouvrir les pays du *Duc Mauritz et mettre dissension entre les frères*, qu'il semble au dict seigneur duc et supplie tres

The Emperor wished to make people believe that he intended to go to Linz; but he stopped at Villach in Carinthia until the end of July. The magistrates of this town, in reward of their kind reception of the Emperor, were ennobled by him. His brother went to Passau. On the other side of the Alps, the Council of Trent had dispersed in all directions about the end of April. The partisans of the Emperor alone remained behind there, until news of the taking of Ehrenberg castle by Maurice arrived; on which the inhabitants, as well as the prelates, all fled to the mountains, to the woods, and to the lakes.

On the 23rd of May, between one and two o'clock in the afternoon, Maurice made his entry into Innsbruck, at the head of his cavalry and infantry; the French envoys also were with him. All the personal property of the Spaniards, of the Emperor, and of the Cardinal Bishop of Augsburg, Maurice left as booty to his lansquenets, who were then seen strutting about in the gorgeous Spanish dresses, with Portuguese gold coins glittering on their hats; they also used to enhance their new-blown magnificence by calling each other "Dons." *King Ferdinand's property was spared.* To Zasius, the councillor whom the latter had left behind at Innsbruck, Maurice excused his advance to that place by stating that the French envoys had so earnestly urged it, that it could not have been helped; and that he was sure to make his appearance at the conference at Passau.

Danger was threatening in a different quarter, from Henry II. of France, the ally of Maurice. He was moving to and fro in Alsace, at the same time issuing manifestoes, in which, as in those of Maurice, much was said about German liberty. In the French manifestoes, dated Fontainebleau, 5th of February, 1552, there was even a cap of liberty, with two daggers, and the word "*Libertas*" emblazoned on the top. Yet the first act by which the "Liberator of Germany"

humblement à sa dicte Majesté qu'estant publié le ban et le dict duc privé de son estat honneur et préeminence, sa dict Majesté ne donne ou permette de prendre ses pays et terres a aultre quelconque que à soy, ses frères et enfans, comme aux vrays agnats . . . . toutes fois le *Duc Auguste* assistera à ex[ecuter le] ban."—*Lanz, State Papers*, pp. 510—518.

showed his goodwill was his laying hold on the bishoprics of Toul, Metz, and Verdun, which until then had always belonged to the German Empire.

From Innsbruck Maurice started, on the 25th of May, to Hall on the Inn, and thence went by water to Passau, to be present at the assembly appointed for the 26th of May, on which day the truce began. The army retired from the Tyrol to Eichstadt. The Emperor had left the negotiations to his brother Ferdinand, and they began on the 1st of June. There were present, besides Maurice and Ferdinand, the Duke of Bavaria and the Bishops of Passau, Eichstadt, and Salzburg; the other electors and princes being represented by their delegates. The princes, both Catholic and Protestant, were unanimous in the opinion that no war should be permitted in Germany. The negotiations lasted for two months. The Emperor was decidedly against admitting the French envoy, and repeatedly advised Ferdinand to arrest him. The Frenchman left Passau on the 9th of June. As Charles refused to ratify the articles which had been agreed upon, Ferdinand had to go himself to Villach to his brother, where he wrested from Charles his assent. This happened on the 6th of July; on the 16th the treaty was signed in the Emperor's name at Passau.

At this assembly also Maurice behaved with extraordinary prudence and cunning; so much so as even to puzzle his own brother-in-law William of Hesse, who in those days wrote to the Margrave Albert of Culmbach that he received bad news from Passau. Perhaps the whole was only a sham.

Maurice had returned to Eichstadt to rejoin his army, with which he marched towards the Rhine. He wanted to reduce Frankfort, which, like Nuremberg, had remained faithful to the Emperor. When he challenged the town to surrender, he was answered that he should first become an honest Christian, and lay aside his Judas appearance. Here, again, his brother-in-law conceived mistrust, as Maurice held a secret deliberation with the magistrates of Frankfort. William, in an altercation with him, called him a traitor. At last, in the camp at Rödelheim, near Frankfort, on the 2nd of

August, 1552, he and the Landgrave William of Hesse signed the treaty of Passau—the treaty which again guaranteed to the Protestants their religious liberty.

Peace being concluded, Maurice, to support Ferdinand, marched eastward against the Turks, and Charles westward against the French; whilst the liberated captive princes of Saxony and Hesse returned to their countries.

The Emperor Charles V. repaired, on the 1st of August, from Villach to Innsbruck; thence he went to Hall and Schwetz, on the Inn; then left the Tyrol, and went by Munich to Augsburg, which he reached on the 20th of August. On the 1st of September, 1552, he there dismissed John Frederic, not without marks of regard and emotion. The ex-Elector obtained no better conditions than those of the "Wittenberg Capitulation," and at once started for his own country. Wherever he passed, he was received by the Protestants as a saint and a martyr. At Nuremberg, the delegates of the magistracy came out with forty horses to meet him. At Coburg he found his wife waiting for him. She had never cast off her mourning attire during all the five years of their separation, and she fainted when she saw her beloved lord again. In every town of Saxony, the councilmen came to meet him in their black robes of office; the burghers, either clad in armour or in their holiday suits, lined the roads; the clergy waited in the market-places, with the boys on one side, and on the other the oldest men and the young girls, wearing the Saxon garland of rue[1] in their flowing locks; the boys singing the *Te Deum* in Latin, and the girls responding with the German "Herr Gott dich loben wir." The prince passed along through their ranks bareheaded, attributing his return to the effect of their prayers. In Jena, where his sons, to make up for the loss of Wittenberg, had established a university, he was particularly pleased to see professors and students once more. By his side on the waggon sat his eldest son and his faithful friend who had shared his captivity—his beloved Lucas Cranach.

The Landgrave of Hesse returned from his confinement

[1] The Saxon coat-of-arms bears a garland of rue.

at Mechlin to Cassel. He had obstinately refused to believe in Maurice's undertaking anything against the Emperor, saying, "How shall a sparrow attack the hawk? and, besides, Maurice has himself destroyed the other birds, whereat foreign nations cannot help laughing." In Trevueren, on the 14th of September, 1552, he took leave of Queen Mary of Hungary, the then regent of the Netherlands, and went on to Cassel.

Maurice was doomed not long to survive his triumph over the Emperor. He lived only one year after the peace of Passau. On his return from the Turkish war in Hungary, he held, in the carnival of 1553, a great tournament at Dresden; after which he took the field once more against his former friend and ally, the wild Margrave Albert of Brandenburg-Culmbach. This princely freebooter had been pleased to continue the war on his own account, thus keeping up the old state of club law in Germany. No wonder that he was universally dreaded. He maintained that the treaty of Passau was good for nothing, and that "the parsons were to be thoroughly humbled." By the way, he also was always ready to pluck the "pepper bags," as he called the merchants of the cities. Having about him a few thousand cut-throats, he marched through Middle Germany to devastate the Franconian and Saxon bishoprics, all "in the name of the gospel." After this he turned against the King of France. And now the clever Charles did one of the most foolish things he had ever done in his life. Near Metz, which the imperial troops at that time were besieging, he caused Alba and Granvella to conclude with the wild Margrave the unhallowed compact, by which he took him into his service. From that time the authority of Charles in Germany completely declined. The Imperial Chamber pronounced outlawry against Albert, and the princes bound themselves, without the Emperor, to defend the peace of the country against its disturber, publicly protected and abetted as he was by the head of the Empire.

Near Sievershausen, on the Lüneberg heath, where Albert was just engaged in plundering, the Elector of Saxony fell in with him. In this encounter Maurice fell fatally wounded. Proudly seated on his charger, his breast crossed by his red scarf striped with white, his colours, he had chivalrously rushed to the combat, when a silver ball hit him through the cuirass in the back, and passed right through the body. William von Grumbach, a Franconian knight, who afterwards was quartered, in 1567, for other delinquencies, is said to have been his murderer. The wounded Maurice, in a tent which they pitched for him by the side of a hedge, received the captured standards, and also the papers of the Margrave, which he examined with eager curiosity. He likewise then and there caused Christopher von Carlowitz to draw up his will, which was sent to his brother Augustus, at that time on a visit to his father-in-law in Denmark. Two days after, Maurice died, 11th July, 1553. His last words were, "God will come"; the rest was unintelligible. Maurice had only reached his thirty-second year. He was buried in the cathedral of Freiberg, in the Erzgebirge, where his monument may be seen to this day. He left but one child, Anna, who was married in 1561, at Leipzig, to Prince William of Orange, the liberator of the Netherlands. His brother Augustus succeeded him as Elector of Saxony. Charles V. loved Maurice so dearly that, on receiving the news of his death, at Brussels, he mourned for him in the words of David over his son, "O Absalom! my son! my son! Would to God I had died for thee!" But his chancellor, Granvella, rejoiced, being of the same opinion as Antony Fugger, who was thoroughly versed in the ways of the world, and who said to him at Augsburg, "that Maurice was well out of the way, and that his death had profited no one more than his Imperial Majesty, whom he had tried to deceive and rob of his sceptre to intrude himself into his place. It had been the plan of Maurice to make himself king of Saxony, and after the defeat of the Margrave to attack his Majesty in the Netherlands, in conjunction with France." Charles expressly writes to J. de Rye and to his brother Ferdinand that he had heard of this.

The state of the times was still very critical. In a letter of Henry of Brunswick—who at Sievershausen had lost his two eldest sons—to Philip of Hesse, the following passage occurs: "As soon as the Emperor's affairs are in a better train, Germany will be in great danger. *The Emperor only wants to set the princes against each other.* It is true he used Albert as one of his hounds for the purpose; but he would be greatly pleased *if a wheel went over his leg.*" King Ferdinand, the Elector Augustus of Saxony, and other princes, having at last concluded at Eger a league against Albert of Brandenburg, Charles, frightened by the general commotion in Germany, was obliged, on the 18th of May, 1554, to confirm the outlawry. The wild Margrave had now to fly to France, but returned afterwards to Germany. He died in great misery, at the early age of thirty-five, in 1557, at Pforzheim, where he had been received by the Margrave of Baden.

In the treaty of Passau it had been agreed upon that a Diet should be summoned for the complete and ultimate settlement of the religious grievances. This was held at Augsburg, in 1555. Charles again left everything to his brother. The treaty of Augsburg, which was then concluded, secured liberty of religion to all the princes and knights, and to the senates of the free cities; that is to say, to about 20,000 privileged persons; not, however, to the twenty millions of the German people. These *might* be Protestants, but if they lived in a Catholic country the prince had the right to command them to emigrate. The principle was laid down "*Cujus regio, ejus religio*"; in other words, whatever faith the ruler of the country professed the people had to profess likewise, or to leave the country. According to the "spiritual clause," ecclesiastical princes might become Protestants in their own persons, but if bishops and abbots wished to change their religion they forfeited their sees and prebends. The countries of Catholic ecclesiastical princes must needs, therefore, remain Catholic. Of Protestants, the Lutherans alone were tolerated; the Calvinists were not included in the peace.

This treaty, or, as it is called, "Peace of Religion," was the sad ending of the Reformation. The movement, which had begun as a popular cause, terminated as a political compromise of the princes.

8.—*Resignation of Charles V.—His death in Spain.*

Since the terrible days of ignominious flight, when the proud heart of the master of two hemispheres was humbled in the loneliness of his mountain journey, amidst the excruciating tortures of disease, Charles seems to have conceived the plan of at once casting off all that pomp which had until now surrounded but not satisfied him. He had once more tried the fortune of war against France; but he was not even able to reconquer Metz. And yet he had for this very purpose had recourse to the expedient which completely destroyed his credit in Germany—that of taking the brutal Albert of Brandenburg into his service. We may gather with what feelings he did so from a letter of his to his sister Mary, to whom he wrote on the 13th of November: "Dieu scayt ce que je sens, me veoyr en termes de fayre ce que je fays avec le dit marquis, mais necessité n'a point de loy." The hand of every man was raised against him; he could not trust his own relations. The most potent and invincible Charles had indeed been brought very low, as he had to bear with the most bitter home truths from very small princes of the Empire before he confirmed the outlawry against the wild Margrave; and yet he still adhered to his principal plan of procuring the crown of the Germano-Roman Empire for his son Philip.

The old Emperor suffered more and more both in mind and body. The sharper the twinges of gout, the more his melancholy increased. He sat often for days moodily brooding, and sometimes breaking out into a flood of tears without speaking a word. Many years before, when his Portuguese wife was alive, he had entertained the plan that each should retire into a convent. In 1549, at the death of Paul III., the proposal had been made to him to become Pope, as his grandfather Maximilian had once intended to do. His physicians had long urged him to live in a warmer climate.

On the 26th of October, 1555, Charles performed the act of resigning the Netherlands to Philip, whom he sent for from England, where the Infant had lived ever since his marriage with "Bloody Mary" in 1553. The ceremony took place at

Brussels, in the same hall in which forty years before he had entered upon his reign. The gouty and melancholy Emperor rose with difficulty from his chair, his right hand resting on a staff, and his left on the shoulder of the Prince William of Orange. His speech, which he delivered in French, drew tears of the deepest emotion from the whole of that large assembly. He set forth "that since his seventeenth year all his thoughts had been bent upon the glorious government of his Empire; that he had tried to see everything with his own eyes; and that therefore his reign had been one continuous pilgrimage. He had visited Germany nine, Spain six, France four, Italy seven, and the Netherlands ten times. He had been twice in England, and as often in Africa; and had, on the whole, made eleven voyages by sea—eight on the Mediterranean and three on the Atlantic. Now, however, he was reminded, by his failing strength, to retire from the turmoil of worldly business, and to lay the burden on younger shoulders. If in all his endeavours and exertions he had neglected or mismanaged anything of importance, he from all his heart begged the pardon of all those who had been wronged by it. He would himself affectionately remember his faithful Netherlanders to the day of his death, and would never cease to pray to God for their welfare." Upon this, turning to his son, who went down on his knees before him and kissed his hand, he exhorted him, in the most impressive manner, "to do his utmost to make his reign glorious." At last he fell back breathless into his chair.

On the 15th of January, 1556, Charles resigned, in the same solemn manner, at the house of Count de Oropeza at Brussels, the kingdoms of Spain, with all their dependencies in the old and new worlds, to Don Philip; and in August, the government of Germany into the hands of the envoys of his brother Ferdinand.

Philip remained at Brussels until 1559. Charles, on the other hand, prepared to sail to Spain as soon as possible, and only waited at Flushing for a fair wind. Dr. Seld, the vice-chancellor of the Empire, his brother's envoy, was still with him. One evening he conversed with him until a late hour.

He then rang the bell, but none of the servants came. Charles thereupon took the candle himself, and lighted the doctor downstairs, saying, "Take this for ever as a remembrance of the Emperor Charles, who, after having in times bygone been surrounded by so many warriors and guards, is now deserted by everyone, even by his own servants; whom you have served so long, and who now has served you in his turn, wishing thereby to honour your virtue and ability."

On the 17th of September, 1556, Charles embarked with his two sisters Mary Queen-dowager of Hungary, and Eleanor Queen-dowager of France, on the coast of Zealand, and landed in Spain at Laredo, on the coast of Biscay. On touching the land he kissed the ground, with the words, "Naked came I out of my mother's womb, and naked shall I return thither." He kept his sisters with him as far as Valladolid, where he dismissed them. From thence he went to Estramadura, where a small house was being built for him near the Jeromite convent of Yuste. Don Philip, as a complimentary present, sent to his father, on his return to Spain, a heart of gold studded with precious stones; on receiving which Charles called out with melancholy foreboding, "God grant that his heart may not become as hard as these stones."

Philip, immediately after the Emperor's abdication at the house of Count de Oropeza, had made him wait several weeks for his stipulated annual revenue, so that Charles had not been able to pay his servants. The son afterwards even reduced the pension of his father to one-half of the amount.

The Jeromite monastery of Yuste, founded in 1410, was situate in a mountainous district, famous for its beauty and its salubrious air, and frequented even to this day, in the hot season, by the Spanish nobility and gentry. This was that most delightful valley, twelve Spanish miles long and three broad, called the orchard of Placentia, in the midst of gardens and plantations, enlivened by a profusion of cool springs and mountain torrents. Ten years before, this country had so pleased Charles, that he exclaimed, "Here is a place of rest for a second Diocletian!" He was not able to enter his new abode until February, 1557, as the building was not completed.

The house inhabited by Charles lay close to the church of the monastery. When he was ill, he might hear the mass and the chanting from his bedroom. In this bedroom was hung the celebrated "Glory" by Titian, his favourite painter, who had long travelled in his suite. The eight rooms of his mansion overlooked his own garden and those of the monastery. All was very still and lonely. Charles lived at Yuste not quite two years. During this time he only saw his sisters twice, but his son Philip never again. When the state of his health permitted, he would walk out to a small hermitage in the neighbourhood, under the shadow of some noble old chestnut trees; sometimes he would ride on a sumpter horse, but at last was unable even to do that. Having a taste for music, he loved to be present at the chanting in the church, and the superiors of the monastery took good care to assemble all the finest voices for their choir.

He had with him the afterwards so famous Don Juan d'Austria, at that time in his tenth year, who seems to have been just as mischievous as other boys, to judge at least from the fact of the peasants of the neighbourhood being obliged frequently to drive him away from their cherry-trees by pelting him with stones. Charles kept up an uninterrupted correspondence with his son Philip, and by this means took at least an indirect part in the government. On receiving the news of the victory of St. Quentin, in 1557, he asked, "Is my son in Paris?" Being answered in the negative, he gnashed his teeth with rage. The time left to him by his religious exercises he employed in gardening; he also amused himself with clocks, of which he had a great number, and which he endeavoured to make all go together; and when he could not succeed in making two to go alike for any time, he would exclaim, "Clocks are like men!"

On the day when he caused his own obsequies to be solemnised by the friars (the 31st August, 1558), he caught a cold, by which the deadly fever already in him was brought to its fatal height. He knelt several days with his eyes streaming before a large crucifix, fervently clasping it in his embrace. The learned Dominican Bartholomew de Carranza, archbishop of Toledo, administered extreme unction to the dying monarch.[1] One of his last sayings was: "*In manus tuas, Domine, commendo spiritum meum; redemisti nos, Domine, Deus veritatis:*" words which he frequently repeated during his last illness. He died on the 21st of September, 1558, in his fifty-ninth year.

Bakhuizen van der Brink, a Dutch *savant*, has published[2] some very curious details of the last days of the life of the Emperor Charles V. from the manuscript of a friar of the convent of Yuste, found in the archives in the old heralds' office at Brussels.

"On the 28th of September, 1556, Charles landed at Laredo. On the 11th of November he retired to the small town of Xarandilla, at a distance of one (Spanish) mile from the monastery of Yuste, there to wait until the house should be completed which was then building for him at the latter place. He anxiously wished to remove as soon as possible to his new residence. But although he, on the 25th of November, went himself to Yuste to inspect as much as was finished, and to urge the workmen to greater speed, the house was not made thoroughly habitable until February, 1557. It contained eight rooms, all of the same size—twenty feet broad by twenty-five feet long. Four apartments on the ground-floor were intended for the summer months; and four on the second story, with large chimneys, for winter. A wide corridor ran along the whole building on each story. The south front of the house was on each side flanked by a turret, with a fountain playing in the centre, in the basin of which trout were kept, for which the Emperor had a great fancy. On the right the building bordered on a secluded garden, richly laid out with trees and flowers of his own choosing, and likewise cooled by a jet of water. The left

---

[1] This is a mistake; the prelate only arrived after the ceremony had been performed, as the critical state of the Emperor made it advisable not to delay it any longer.—*Translator*.

[2] The German original of this volume of the present Memoirs was published in 1852, *before* Mr. Stirling's most interesting "Cloister Life." The very slight discrepancies between the accounts of the two monks are an additional proof of the *general* authenticity of both.—*Translator*.

angle joined a large courtyard adorned with a magnificent fountain, which was cut from a single block of marble; and with a sun-dial, a masterpiece of its kind, by the celebrated mechanician Gianello Torreano. By the church of the convent, which lay higher by twenty feet than the imperial villa, it was sheltered from the blasts of the north. A covered staircase like a gallery afforded to the Emperor, who was sorely troubled with the gout, an easy access to the church and gardens of the convent. The apartments were lighted by many large windows, through which the sweet balmy air poured in from the lemon and orange trees of the garden, and from which the eye might roam over the noble verdure of dark woods to the neighbouring ridges of hills, glimmering with the golden tints of their luxuriant vineyards. Although the imperial mansion was but a plain wooden structure of very humble aspect from without, yet its interior was furnished with every elegance and comfort that could make it a delightful residence.

"When Charles settled at Yuste he dismissed part only of his household, retaining in his service upwards of fifty persons, Spaniards, Netherlanders, Burgundians; the only German among them was the assistant baker. The lower officers of his court who could not be accommodated in the outbuildings of the convent, were lodged in the neighbouring little village of Quacos. Those who held the first rank among his gentlemen never left their master. His familiar circle comprised, besides his major-domo and favourite Quixada, two Flemings of Bruges—William de Male, who frequently acted as his secretary, and Henry Matthys, his physician.

"Although Charles still kept up a regular correspondence with his son Philip II., who was then in the Netherlands, and with his daughter Juaña, the regent of the kingdom of Spain, yet he withdrew his thoughts from the stormy stage which he had left for ever. Many petitioners applied for an audience, but he refused to admit them, simply referring them to those in whose favour he had abdicated. He only reluctantly consented to receive some great lords who wished to pay him their respects. On such occasions the major-domo would take the utmost care that in the presence of Charles the same etiquette should be observed as in the times when he was Emperor of Germany, King of Spain and Naples.

"The plan of his daily life was as follows: Every morning the clockmaker (mechanician) Gianello was the first to enter the room of the Emperor. He was succeeded by the friar Juan Regala, his confessor, who read prayers. After him came the surgeons and the physician. At ten, dinner was served for those officers who were to attend afterwards at the table of the Emperor; after their repast, at which the gentleman on duty presided, they followed the Emperor to mass. Divine service being concluded, the Emperor sat down to his own dinner, listening with pleasure to the discourse of Dr. Matthys and William de Male, which generally bore upon subjects of history or of military science. Sometimes the confessor was ordered to read to the Emperor during his repast a chapter from St. Bernard or any other good writer, until His Majesty fell into a nap or rose from the table to be present at a sermon or a reading of the Holy Scriptures held before the assembled friars. Charles attended mass in a raised stall set apart for him, and confessed and took the sacrament at all the great festivals; yet the Pope had dispensed him from fasting before the communion, as he was too weak and infirm to stand it."

This was the whole extent of the religious exercises of the Emperor at the monastery at Yuste. The MS. does not make the slightest mention of the discipline, in virtue of which, according to Robertson's statements, Charles had flagellated himself till the blood flowed. The Emperor, suffering severely from the gout, was scarcely able to move; he always had two of his gentlemen to accompany him, on whom he would lean when he tried to walk, or even when he was carried in a sedan-chair.

Once only did the Emperor dine with the friars in their refectory; yet, although a separate table had been dressed for him, and the cooks of the convent had done their very best duly to honour their illustrious guest, he was so little edified with the conventual bill of fare that he never repeated his visit to that dining-hall. According to the friar to whose MS. we owe our information, Charles never intended to enter their order, nor did he ever wear their dress. But it is a fact that he had his obsequies solemnised in his lifetime.

One day, when he felt particularly free from pain, he ordered mass for the souls of his ancestors and of his late Empress. On the evening of the same day he had a conversation with his confessor, and ordered for the next morning his own obsequies. It was on the 31st of August, 1558. The catafalque was erected in the large chapel of the church. Charles attended with the whole of his little court in deep mourning. The ceremony lasted the greater part of the day. When it was over Charles, in a state of great exhaustion, caused himself to be set down in the courtyard of his house, his face turned towards the east. He remained there sitting a good while, with his eyes fixed on Gianello's sun-dial. Then, rousing himself from his silent reverie, he had a likeness of his late wife brought to him, which he looked at for some time. After this he asked for a picture representing Christ in the Garden of Gethsemane, and lastly, for a third picture, a representation of the Last Judgment. All at once a shudder ran through him, when, turning to his physician, he said, "I feel unwell, doctor." This gentleman carried him to his bed, which he left no more. He died on the 21st of September, after having passed in the peaceful solitude of Yuste only one year and eight months all but nine days.

Charles in his last will directed that he should not be embalmed; but when, in 1656, his remains were transferred to the Pantheon of the Escurial, on which occasion his coffin was opened, his body was found to be quite uncorrupted.[1]

9.—*Personal notices of Charles V.*

Charles, in his younger days, and before he was tormented by asthma and gout, had been a very fine man. He was of ordinary size, rather tall than short, inclined to stoutness, but had thin legs. His complexion in the prime of life was as

---

[1] According to Mr. Stirling's account, it was embalmed on the very day of the Emperor's death.—*Translator.*

white as milk; his hands also were equally white. His hair was light, with a bright auburn tinge; since his Italian journey in 1529 he wore it cut short, on account of a tendency to nervous headache. About the same period, living much in Germany, he began to have his beard trimmed after the then existing German fashion. His first grey hairs he accidentally discovered, when not more than thirty-six years old, at Naples, whilst he was dressing for a ball, where, as he himself confesses, he " wished to please the ladies." He had them plucked out, but they grew again. His eyes were of a bluish-grey; his forehead broad and ample. His long, pale face would decidedly not have been called handsome, disfigured as it was by his large and somewhat open mouth, with the hanging under-lip of the Habsburg race, and by his protruding lower jaw, covered with a short, curly beard. His nose was very long, and strongly aquiline. Moreover he had, in his later years, but few and bad teeth left. His eyes lacked lustre. His constitution was very feeble, and his nerves were weak and irritable. He always looked grave and serious, only on very rare occasions allowing a smile to light up his pale, gloomy countenance. His melancholy temperament and his Spanish gravity showed themselves in everything. There are still in existence many of his portraits by Titian, to whom he used to pay a thousand ducats for each; Charles wished to be painted by no other artist, just as Alexander only by Apelles.

In his younger days Charles, like his brother Ferdinand, had been obliging, affable, and easy with everyone; but his principal adviser for Spain, the Grand Commander Covos, had entreated him to change this Netherlandish manner, urging that whoever wished to keep the Spaniards in their place should show himself grave and stern, as they were naturally very proud. Charles afterwards introduced the strict and solemn Spanish etiquette also in Germany; even his brother, the King of the Romans, never spoke to him but with his hat off and with a profusion of bows. At the age of twenty-six Charles married the beauteous and graceful Isabel of Portugal, then in her twenty-third year. Three

French and two English princesses had been before thought of for him—two daughters of Louis XII. and one of Francis I. of France, one daughter of Henry VII. and one of Henry VIII. of England; the last of these, the Princess, afterwards Queen Mary, became in 1554, at the age of thirty-eight, the wife of his son Don Philip, her junior by eleven years.

The marriage of Charles and Isabel was celebrated at Seville on the 10th of March, 1526. The following account is from an old contemporary pamphlet:

"The princess arrived at Seville by ship eight days before the wedding. On the 10th of March Charles came from Madrid just after having taken leave at Illescas of Francis I., until then his prisoner of war. The royal bridegroom was attended by the papal legate, Cardinal Salviati, and a great number of prelates and grandees. Before the city he was received by the Governor Philip, duke of Arschot, of the house of Croy, and by twenty-four members of the Council of Seville, who were admitted to kiss the Emperor's hand. They were followed by the Archbishop of Seville, to whom the Emperor took his oath that he would preserve the liberties of the Spanish nation. Charles wore a dress of plain white silk embroidered with gold; he was mounted on a beautiful white horse, and held in his right hand an olive branch. With a gorgeous canopy borne over him, he was led through seven triumphal arches to the cathedral, whence, after having performed his devotions, he repaired to the royal palace."

"In the third hour of the night the Emperor and the princess met in the royal hall, which was most splendidly decorated. They had scarcely saluted each other when the cardinal legate made his appearance to perform the marriage ceremony. At midnight the Archbishop of Toledo read mass, at which, after having confessed, the Emperor and the princess received the sacrament. After the blessing of the archbishop they, in a holy and Christian spirit, entered the nuptial chamber."

Charles lost his beautiful wife Isabel in 1539, after a union of thirteen years, at the birth of her fourth child, when she refused to call in a surgeon-accoucheur. After her death the

Emperor was again seized with epileptic fits, from which he had been free ever since his marriage. Charles had lived very happily with Isabel. His temper was completely changed, and he had adopted a different diet and different manners. His grief at her loss was unbounded. He sat for several days in silent despair beside her corpse, inaccessible to every thought of public business; like a madman he flew with a drawn dagger at those who dared to intrude upon the solitude of his sacred sorrow. The Duke of Borghia, the celebrated Jesuit, had to admonish him, at first gently and kindly, but at last very roughly, not to forget the living, as the dead could not come to life again. Then only Charles rallied, and allowed the beloved remains to be interred.

After Isabel's death Charles would not hear of a second marriage, although the Marquis del Vasto proposed to him Margaret, the youngest daughter of Francis I., who afterwards married Emanuel Philibert of Savoy. Not yielding in gallantry to his royal brothers Francis I. and Henry VIII., Charles again engaged in amorous intrigues, just as he had done before marriage; and when his health was repeatedly impaired by his excesses, he used the maddest cures. De Thou expressly states, that in all his love affairs he observed the greatest secrecy. But his confessor Garcia de Loaysa was very well aware of his profligacy, and again and again wrote to him during the years 1530—1532, even before the death of his wife, that he should not allow himself to be carried away by this insidious sensuality, lest on the couch of luxury and sloth he might miss the sacred purpose of his existence.

One of his natural sons was the celebrated Don Juan d'Austria, the conqueror of the Turks at Lepanto. He was supposed to be the son of Barbara Blomberg, the fair daughter of a burgher at Ratisbon, who during the Diet of 1544 had soothed the melancholy of the Emperor by her sweet singing. According to another statement — that of Girolamo Lippomani, Don Juan's envoy at Naples in 1575 — his mother was a noble lady of Flanders, Madama di Plombes, who was then still living at Antwerp, and to whom Charles had given a husband with a yearly income of 10,000 ducats. A princess of the first rank was suspected to be the real mother; but it was never known with certainty. Don Juan d'Austria was born on the 25th of February, 1545, and was in 1550, at Brussels, entrusted by Adrian, the valet of Charles, to the care of Francisco Massi and his wife Anna de Medina; a hundred crowns a year being paid for his board. He afterwards accompanied his father to Yuste, and was in Spain also kept in the most complete ignorance as to his descent. After the death of Charles he was told who he was. In 1561 Philip II. acknowledged him at a hunting party as his brother, and took him to his court. His father had in his last will expressed a wish that he should devote himself to a monastic life; but, in case he should not feel any inclination to do so, a yearly pension of from 20,000 to 30,000 ducats was settled on him, to be paid from the revenues of the kingdom of Naples.

Charles was a very proud lord, and knew better than anyone how to make himself regarded and looked up to as long as he lived. His person and character forced even his enemies to respect him; none of his contemporaries have spoken meanly of him. It was not merely the adventitious fact of his exalted position, but innate majesty and greatness which commanded the homage of the world. He showed singular power of self-control, and was anxious on every occasion to prove himself the first, not only in rank, but in fortitude and high-souled conduct.

The rule which, in this respect, he imposed upon himself he wished to be observed also by others. In several instances he opposed great sternness to the pride of the Spanish grandees, who tried to treat with contempt those whom Charles, on account of their merit, had raised to the rank which the others had been born to. His brave captain Antonio de Leyva was hated by the Spanish nobility because he was the son of a shoemaker of Navarre, and because Charles had made him a duke; he was hated by the Spanish clergy because he helped himself to their silver when he could not pay his troops in any other way; he was hated by the ladies because he did not pay his court to them; and, lastly, he was hated by the people because he lived as if the world were only made for the soldiers. There were none who loved Leyva but his men and the Emperor, who made him Prince of Ascoli and appointed him Governor of Milan. When Charles, in 1530, came to Bologna to be crowned, old Leyva caused himself to be carried in a litter to Piacenza to meet his sovereign. On this occasion, Charles, as Frederic the Great afterwards in the case of General Ziethen, made Leyva to sit down in an arm-chair and cover himself. Charles then uttered the remarkable words: "The grandees of Spain cover themselves near my throne, and should the old man of seventy years, who has been in sixty battles for me, stand bareheaded before his master, who is only thirty? I cannot, forsooth, do less than grant to personal merit the same distinction as to that which is only hereditary." In the procession, on entering Bologna, Leyva, by order of Charles, rode by the side of Andrew Doria, before the archbishops and bishops, two noblemen leading his horse. Leyva died in 1536, in the third campaign against the French.

At a festivity of the court in Madrid, when the nobility held a carousal, the courtiers agreed to exclude a certain officer who had only shortly before been ennobled, and whose name was on the list. Charles, having been informed of it, drily said to the chief equerry, on entering the arena, "Let no one take this nobleman from me; I have selected him for my own quadrille." A proud Castilian lady and an equally proud fair Neapolitan were once quarrelling about precedence at the door of the palace chapel in Brussels, when Charles promptly settled their squabble with the words, "Let the most foolish go in first."

The Cavaliere Ridolfi, in his "Vite de' Pittori Veneti," states that one day, Titian happening to drop his brush whilst being at work, the Emperor picked it up and handed it to the artist. As he saw his courtiers surprised and displeased at his condescension, he remarked, "I have always people about me who bow before me, but I have not always a Titian."

Another proof of the greatness of mind in Charles was his hatred of flattery. His son-in-law, Alexander of Medici, once recommended his *protégé*, the well-known historian Paul Jovius of Como (Bishop of Nocera, died in 1552), for a pension, with the remark, that Paul was engaged in writing the history of all the great men of his age, and that he intended to write among the others that of the Emperor. Charles replied, "Just because he intends to write my life I should be ashamed to bribe him by a pension; let him relate to us the history of bygone times, and I will read and reward him." Of this Italian Jovius, and the German Sleidanus, professor and orator of Strassburg (died 1566), Charles used to say, "What a couple of liars! the one praises and the other censures me more than I deserve." Concerning Sleidanus, Charles is stated to have expressed himself thus: "The rogue has certainly known much, but not all; he has either been in our privy council, or our councillors have been traitors." To a third biographer, a Spaniard, Sepulveda (canon of Salamanca, died 1574), Charles himself related remarkable incidents of his life, and, to use his own words, "as candidly as in the confessional." But Sepulveda was never allowed to read to him even one line of what he had written.

Charles's court was very quiet, owing to his strong dislike to noisy amusements. He did not even give banquets; nay, he always dined alone. Being fond of secrecy in everything, he had also a particular fancy for the occult arts, and occupied himself, like several of his ancestors, with the course of the planets round the sun. He had for his teacher in astronomy Peter Bienewiz, or, according to the fashion of that time of Latinising names, Petrus Apianus, a native of Leisnig in Saxony, and a professor at the university of Ingolstadt, where he died in 1552, ennobled by Charles V., who gave him for his coat-of-arms the double-headed eagle hovering in the clouds. Petrus Apianus dedicated to the Emperor his large cosmography, his "Opus Cæsareum," the Emperor paying the cost of printing; besides which, he made to his teacher an additional present of 3,000 ducats. Charles often conversed for half a day together with the far-famed astronomer, who, in 1541, at the Diet of Ratisbon, presented him with an orrery of pure gold, at the construction of which he had worked for ten years. Apianus was the best astronomical instrument maker of his time, and also had at Ingolstadt one of the earliest collection of maps, which was celebrated throughout Europe. The Emperor's favourite pursuit, besides astronomy, was the science of mechanics and mechanical works: his fancy for time-pieces was very remarkable; he had a hundred of them, and among them one in his seal ring, which struck the hour. The clever mechanician Gianello Torreano was still with him at Yuste. Among his body physicians there was the celebrated Andrew Vesali, a native of Brussels, who before that had been first professor of anatomy at Padua, and had there published a celebrated work on anatomy, with drawings from nature, in which Titian helped him. Besides the study of physical science, Charles was fond of the chase, which he often followed with but a small suite of not more than eight or ten horses, and with only a fowling-piece in his hand. The whole sport consisted in firing his musket at a bird, such as a crow or a raven, or some beast of the forest, a stag or a wild boar. "These hunts," says a Venetian ambassador, "don't cost the Emperor a hundred scudi a year." Besides this, Charles took very little exercise. In his earlier years he used to tilt in the lists, or in the open field, to run at a quintain, take part in the bull-fights, and engage in all the sports of the *manège* or of fencing. Moreover, Charles in his leisure hours amused himself, according to the fashion of the time, with his dwarfs. The Venetian ambassador, Bernardo Navagiero states in 1546, that the King of Poland had made him a present of one who was well made and very intelligent. He also found much diversion in the conversation of his jester Perico, a Spaniard, at whose jokes he had many a hearty laugh.

Charles, who in his later years had but little sleep, liked to rise late in the morning. He then first attended a private mass for the soul of the Empress, and immediately afterwards gave audience to his ministers, to which he also admitted his son Philip as soon as the Infant had emerged from boyhood. Audience being over, Charles heard a second mass for his own soul; at the conclusion of which he went directly to dinner, the rule being proverbial at the court of the Emperor "*della messa alla mensa.*" He generally dined in state, but alone at his table, at one in the afternoon. He ate much, and was fond of good cheer, preferring highly seasoned dishes, which were the cause of frequent bilious attacks. His physicians pretended that moisture and cold prevailed in his constitution; for which reason he was always craving for warmth, being fond of travelling in the heat of summer, and of living in hot rooms in winter. This may also account for his liking all those things that would drive the blood to the head and stimulate the nervous system, especially hot spices. He indulged very freely in wine; during the years 1530 to 1532 his former confessor, Garcia de Loaysa, wrote to him, "that it would be better for the general good if he would leave off drinking in the middle of the day;" and the same warning was repeated more than once. The Venetian ambassador Mocenigo writes, as late as 1547, "The Emperor ate and drank so much that everybody was amazed." The physicians, who were always present in the room during his dinner, would sometimes remind him that some dish disagreed with him. His confessor also wrote to him to "abstain from fish, as being injurious to his health." But abstain from such things he would not; on the contrary, he rather preferred the heavier meats, such as were the most injurious to his constitution, red-herrings and other salt fish, and salt dishes. "Worst of all," says Mocenigo, "he would not properly masticate his food, but he devoured it; which was in a great measure owing to the decayed condition of his teeth."

Sastrow, who saw the Emperor at the Diet of Augsburg in 1546, states, in his Pomeranian Chronicle: "I have often seen the Emperor dine at several Diets, at Spires, Worms, at Spires again, at Augsburg, and also at Brussels, when his brother King Ferdinand was present likewise, whom, however, he never allowed to sit down with him. And although his sister (Mary of Burgundy), his sister's daughter (the widow of Duke Francis of Lorraine), his brother, with his daughter the Duchess of Bavaria, all the Electors, and so many princes were there, he never gave a banquet nor kept them to dinner. When they were waiting for his coming from church, and accompanied him to the hall where he was going to dine, he shook hands with them one after the other, left them, and sat down alone without speaking. The dinner was served by young princes and counts, four courses always, of six dishes each. The dishes being placed before him on the table, the covers were removed, and he shook his head at those of which he did not wish to partake; but if he fancied one he nodded, and drew it towards him. Goodly pasties, venison, and savoury made-dishes were sometimes taken away, while he kept back a sucking pig, calf's head, or such-like. He had no one to carve for him, nor did he use the knife much himself; but he first cut his bread in small pieces, a mouthful each, then stuck his knife into the joint just where he fancied a piece, scooped it out, or otherwise tore it with his fingers, drew the plate under his chin, and thus ate in a very unaffected but neat and cleanly manner, so that it was pleasant to look at him. When he wished to drink—he only drank three times at a meal—he beckoned to his physicians, who were standing in front of the table; they went to the buffet, on which stood two silver flasks and a crystal tankard, which held as much as one pint and a half; they then filled the glass from both flasks; after which he drained it to the last drop, even if he had to draw his breath two or three times before he took it from his mouth. He seldom, however, spoke one word; his jesters would stand behind him, cutting their jokes, but he did not much mind them; sometimes, when they said something particularly ridiculous, a half-smile played round his mouth. He had fine vocal and instrumental music, though it would have sounded better in church than it did in the room. The dinner lasted not quite an hour; after which everything pertaining to it was removed, the table and chair folded up and carried out of the room, so that only the four walls remained; but they were everywhere hung with the most costly tapestry. Grace being said, a little quill was handed to him, with which he picked his teeth; he then washed and placed himself in a corner of the room near the window, where everyone might approach him to present petitions or state their case by word of mouth."

The private audiences of the Emperor used to last two or three hours; he then rested himself for one hour on an easy chair, and sent again for the ministers. After they had again withdrawn, he read or sat down to write letters. At seven in the evening, Charles took a slight collation only of sweetmeats and preserved fruits. This arrangement had been kept up ever since his twenty-fifth year. At nine o'clock he retired to bed, as did the whole of his court.

The Emperor's melancholy disposition, which he proved among other things by carrying his coffin with him in all his journeys, his excess in eating and drinking, his taking little exercise, besides his naturally chilly constitution, caused him to be nearly always ailing. In later years only, he kept stricter diet and used much medicine. "The Emperor," says the Venetian ambassador Cavalli in 1550, "would have been dead long since, if he had not done so." He was constantly tormented by gout and by spasms in the chest. He was particularly liable to catarrhal affections, and often suffered so severely from asthma that he dared not lie down in the evening to sleep, but was obliged to stand upright and keep awake, supporting himself on a table. These asthmatic sufferings only gave way to the attacks of gout which, ever since his forty-first year, returned every winter regularly, and would also harass him at other times. This broke his strength; so that he could no longer mount his horse nor follow the chase, and in his journeys he had to be carried in a litter. In 1549, the year when the papal crown was offered to him, he is described as creeping through his room, supported by his staff, with bent back, snow-white hair, deadly pale, and with beardless lips. Yet he would himself smile at his infirm appearance, saying that he was not quite so weak as he looked. He used to say of the gout, "Patience and a little screaming is a good remedy against it." Cavalli states, in 1550: "The gout sometimes rises to his head, and threatens some day to kill him suddenly." In his own apartments he often trembled at the least noise. Mocenigo writes of him: "The Emperor, which perhaps will hardly be believed, is, according to the statements of his household, naturally so nervous that he is often frightened when perchance a spider comes near him, and even trembles as on the day when the army of the Protestants drew up opposite to him at Ingolstadt. Yet, notwithstanding this, his reason had such power over his natural instinct that on many important occasions, and in the greatest dangers, he showed himself as brave and intrepid as ever prince did; and especially on that day near Ingolstadt he was seen, after the first emotion, in which even the wisest cannot altogether get the mastery over nature, at once to rouse himself and put on his armour; and, whilst the enemy kept up a galling fire upon us from their heavy guns, he rode to and fro, arraying his army in order of battle, and making every arrangement for defence. Charles remained with his troops the whole day, and did so the three following days, without showing the least fear. Granvella, who had remained behind in the town on account of indisposition, sent word to his Majesty by the confessor that an Emperor needed greater prudence, but less bravery; but Charles answered that *no King or Emperor had ever been killed by a cannon ball. If he was to be the first, it would be better for him to die than to live.*"

The Venetian ambassador, in the same report, extols the Emperor's kindness and forbearance in times of peace, but remarks that in war he had shown himself very cruel. He mentions that Charles, at the revolt of Ghent, caused a great number of the principal citizens to be executed; and that also in the battle of Mühlberg the Saxon soldiers were by his order put to the sword, even after having thrown away their arms and entreated for their lives.

Sastrow, in his "Chronicle," relates a fact which does not speak much for the kindness of Charles. The Emperor caused cannon which had been cast at Augsburg and Ulm to be driven by Swabian carriers to the Netherlands. This was in the year 1543, when he made war against the Duke of Juliers and Cleves for the possession of the country of Guelders. The roads being bad, the carriers were not able to proceed very quickly, and the Emperor was in a great hurry to fall in with the enemy. He therefore rode up to one of the drivers to urge him to speed; and when the man, not knowing the Emperor, looked cross and disregarded the order, Charles struck him with a stick on the nape of his neck. The carrier at once retorted on his Cæsarean Majesty by giving him a cut of his whip over his head, and by a curse, "May God's element confound you, you Spanish ruffian." The Emperor gave the order to take him away at once and hang him to the nearest tree. The officers, however, put off the execution until the first heat of his anger was over; and when Charles thought the order had long been carried out, they implored pardon for the man on their knees. On this the Emperor mitigated the punishment of the carrier to the effect that he should only have his nose cut off, in token of his having sworn at the Emperor of the Romans and struck him. The poor carrier even expressed his thanks for the punishment. The "Carolina," the criminal code which Charles gave to the German Empire in 1533, is likewise a very indifferent monument of his forbearance. Cutting out the tongue, cutting off ears, and tearing the flesh with hot pincers are mentioned in its notorious 198th article as mere *additions* of punishment.

For the slanderers at his court Charles devised a punishment of truly Tartar character. They had to muster every morning and for several hours to crawl on all fours and bark like dogs. This, however, lasted only a short time, as his councillors represented that the noise of the barking drove every serious thought out of their heads for the greater part of the forenoon, so that it was impossible for them to get on with their hard work.

"In money matters his Majesty is exceedingly careful; and, although he cheerfully consents to any, even the heaviest expense, where it is necessary, yet he cannot bear that one ducat of his money should be spent uselessly. He keeps a very small court, considering his being such a great Emperor. The usual service of his person and of his table do not cost him more than 120,000 scudi.[1] Contrary to his former custom, he very rarely now has new suits made for his pages, so that their clothes are nearly always torn; and even on his own dress the Emperor spends less than any nobleman of high rank would do. He says 'that one must be a fool to pay more than 200 scudi for a lining of fur.' He remembers even his smallest article of dress, and notices if one of his shirts or a handkerchief is missing. He also sometimes has his clothes mended. He is said to act in this way not for the purpose of keeping down his own expenditure, but in order that his courtiers, who are always prone to imitate him, may not have occasion to run into extravagance; for this reason the Emperor in the German wars wore suits of fustian which were not worth a scudo, and a woollen hat which did not cost more than a marcello; all the great lords of his court then dressed like him."

All these statements of the Venetian ambassador concerning the frugality of Charles with regard to dress are founded on fact; it is even recorded that once, at a review near Naumburg in 1547, when it began to rain, the Emperor took off his velvet cap and put it under his cloak.

An eye-witness who saw Charles on that occasion at Naumburg describes his appearance as follows:[2] "I had pictured to myself this great Emperor very differently. At his entry into Naumburg (21st of June, 1547), scarcely anyone was able, for the number of captains who pressed round his Majesty, to get a sight of him; but when he alighted at his quarters I saw him—a tall, somewhat stout, grave personage. He wore a black velvet cap and a red Spanish cloak coming down to the knees, yellow hose, half-boots, and a blue doublet, long moustaches, and beard on the chin. He looked cautiously round him before he went in. The Duke Maurice, who fol-

---

[1] About £24,000. Scudo (pl. scudi), about 4s.
[2] Report of the Clerk of Canals, Schirmer, in the "Materials for Saxon History." Altenburg, 1791, No. i., p. 34.

lowed him, was a tall and spare man, with keen, sparkling eyes; the Emperor's, on the contrary, were languid." On the 22nd of June the Emperor visited Alba's camp outside the town. "This time he wore a black doublet and a large white Spanish ruff. His jerkin and hose were likewise black; his head was covered with a round plumed hat, on account of the heat of the sun; he was mounted on a very fine black charger, with rich black velvet housings embroidered with gold; and was surrounded by many princes, counts, and lords, several hundreds in number." On the 23rd of June, the army marched out from Naumburg; which lasted from half-past five in the morning to one o'clock in the afternoon: "The Emperor was on horseback, dressed as on the day before, except that he wore no hat, but again his new black velvet cap, and a Spanish cloak. As it began to rain a little, Charles took off his velvet cap and put it under his cloak; so that the rain fell on his bare head, the hair of which was of a chestnut brown; whereat everyone was very much astonished. Poor Emperor! who had done such great deeds in the world, who had made war on Africa, and was the possessor of so many tons of gold, and who let the rain fall on his uncovered head!"

There was evidently in this most potent Emperor a drop left of the blood of his ancestor, Rodolph of Habsburg, who mended his clothes with his own hands. Yet it is just as true that Charles did not know how to manage finances on a large scale. The Venetian, Marino Cavalli, writes in 1550: "There is a saying that, up to ten scudi, no one in the world spends money better than the Emperor; but as to large expenses, matters go on at his court just in the same way as with other princes." He was nearly always in straits and obliged to contract debts. He was far from being displeased when, in 1530, his host, Anthony Fugger, at Augsburg, rekindled the fire which was getting low by feeding it with the old bonds of the Emperor; and yet twenty-two years afterwards the credit of Charles was at such a low ebb that no Augsburg firm, not even Anthony Fugger, whom he had so much honoured, would lend him money any longer.

In political affairs the Emperor was, among the many wise

and clever people at his court, the wisest and most clever. All business was carried on in his writing, and every argument for and against duly weighed. The ministers put questions to the Emperor, who, on his side, ruminated over them cautiously and deliberately in the quietude of his cabinet, and then gave his decision, with "Yes" or "No," and sometimes with remarks written on the margin. As a rule, everything was treated in writing. In some cases Charles would call in parties for personal conferences. The written marginal remarks were very laconic, bearing the stamp of the monarch, who wrote them or caused them to be written, and who was always most chary of his words. In the State papers of the Emperor, published by Dr. Lanz, from the archives of Brussels, such brief rescripts occur generally in forms like the following: "Bien!" "Que fait très bien." "Qui se face (fasse)." "Fiat." "En soit escript." "L'Empereur y advisera." "Sa Maj. l'a à plasir." "Cela ira bien." The signature of Charles was very different from that of his grandfather; that of Maximilian being small and cramped, that of Charles with large and tall perpendicular letters, although with some similarity to the proud slanting characters used by the French Bourbons after him. The signatures of Charles V. and Henri IV. are the largest of all those of the princes of the sixteenth and seventeenth centuries. Charles, when in Germany, always signed "Carolus."

Charles won over the Flemings and Burgundians by his affability and condescension, the Spaniards by grandeur and gravity, and the Italians by cleverness and ingenuity; yet he, the German Emperor, seems to have been least able to understand the German way of feeling and thinking. He is also well known to have loathed the German language. He called it "the language of horses." After being deserted by Maurice of Saxony, whom of all Germans he had esteemed most, he hated to have anything to do with German affairs, and left them entirely to his brother Ferdinand. It is true that, on the whole, he had a great aversion to any sort of work during the last six years of his reign, which he passed in the Netherlands. He would still give audiences, but only as it were by way of recreation for some hours after dinner. The Bishop of Arras, Granvella, who then completely ruled him, gave the decision. At last Charles retired entirely from the affairs of government, and would not sometimes for months see anybody. No one was admitted to him but those whom he expressly sent for. He was averse even to signing his name. Once they had to wait nine months for his signature, and the mere opening of a letter caused him pain in his hands. Alone in his room, which was hung with black and lighted by seven tapers, he remained for hours on his knees. After the death of his mother in 1555, he sometimes fancied he heard her voice calling to him to follow her.

Charles spoke every one of the languages of his several European kingdoms. He used to say, "As many languages as a man understands, so many times is he a man." French was the one in which he generally wrote and negotiated. It became under him the language of the court, because in it the many strangers who met there were best able to carry on their conversation. Since Charles a medley of tongues began in Germany, by which the native idiom was interlarded with French flourishes and Hispano-Italian bombast.

In the conduct of business Charles was deliberate and cautious, calm and patient in the most eminent degree. He spoke little. When he did so, he generally looked fixedly before him, or cast his eyes upwards. Long speeches always annoyed him. His usual remark was, "Cut it short," and his usual answer, "We'll consider about it." Obstinate he was too. The pressing entreaties with which the Electors Maurice and Joachim, at Halle, urged Charles to liberate the Landgrave Philip, had the very contrary effect of making the Emperor keep him a prisoner longer than he had perhaps at first intended. Charles once said to the Venetian ambassador Contarini, "It is my nature to insist obstinately upon my own opinions." The ambassador replied, "Sire, to insist on good opinions is firmness, not obstinacy." Charles then concluded the conversation with the characteristic words, "*Qualche fiate io sono fermo in le cattive*" ("I sometimes also insist upon bad ones").

Charles was excessively scrupulous; he made everything a case of conscience. His confessor therefore played a very important part. Cardinal Granvella complained that if one thought one had arrived at a result with him, the hydra of religious scruples would always start new heads. The settlement of religious differences, at the last Diet at Augsburg, 1555, Charles left to his brother, merely because he had himself strong scruples against it. Within twelve days of his death he most strongly advised his son Philip, by a codicil appended to his last will, to crush heresy in its bud.

Charles V., "The Lord," as he was called in his own court, was the last German Emperor who understood how to assert the European supremacy of the imperial dignity. His successors, with perhaps the sole exception of Ferdinand II., were far inferior to him in political greatness; they partook more of the character of territorial rulers, lords of Austria.

"A complete history of the life and reign of Charles has not yet been written, and is exceedingly difficult *to* write. The preliminary studies and the collecting of materials alone must occupy more than twenty years. It would be necessary personally to examine the documents at Vienna, at Brussels, at Mechlin, at Milan, at Naples, and Madrid—if possible, also in Rome. Many a man who with sincere earnestness entered upon this preliminary task, was paralysed by it, *crushed by the avalanche of the materials.*" It is Hormayr who says this. He spent twenty years, from 1807 to 1827, in collecting the materials for a work which he intended to call, "Maximilian I. and Charles V.; their Heroes and their Times"; but it was beyond his power to complete it.

10.—*The family of Charles V.*

Charles had an only son, Don Philip. He loved him most affectionately; it was for his sake alone that at last he entangled himself in the ruinous net from which he saw no honourable escape but by his abdication. The attempts of Charles to procure for Philip the succession in Germany estranged all hearts from the old Emperor, and even arrayed his own family against him. And yet he had to experience the most galling ingratitude from his beloved Philip.

To pave his way for his marriage with Mary of England, Charles ceded to him the independent rule of the two Sicilies. This resignation was scarcely effected when Philip, dismissing the faithful servants of the Emperor, appointed his own creatures in their places. To meet his designs on Sienna, the Emperor nominated him his vicar in Italy. Philip did not even assume the title. Charles thereupon summoned him to Brussels to concert with him important measures against France. Philip then despatched the Portuguese Ruy Gomez, Count de Silva, his favourite, with whose witty sallies he used to beguile his time. The message to his father was to the purport that he, Don Philip, as the autocrat of powerful kingdoms, could not come to him until it was clearly settled what etiquette the Emperor would observe with regard to him, and how in general he intended to treat him.

As Charles would now have been obliged to give to his enemies the welcome spectacle of a domestic quarrel by coming to a public rupture with his ungrateful son, he preferred to lay the crowns which had long been a burden to him in the hands which were so eager to grasp them.

Even more dearly than his ungrateful son, Charles loved his grandson Carlos, who at that time gave the fairest promise, but who at an early age already showed occasionally that fierce obstinacy which afterwards brought his life to such a tragic termination.

Young Carlos continually urged his grandfather to send him arms, but at once gave signs of impatience when the Emperor made him stand before him somewhat longer than usual with his cap in his hand. Being informed that in his father's marriage-contract with the English Queen, the Netherlands were eventually settled on a son of Philip by her, Carlos declared to the Emperor that, if this were true, he would not allow it, but rather take up arms against his father. He would never call Philip "Father," but reserved this name for the Emperor alone. Those of the grandees for whom he had a liking he caused to take an oath that they would follow him in all his wars. Onorato Giovanni, the tutor of Carlos, collected all his ingenious and witty sayings in a little volume, which he dedicated to the Emperor. Yet it was scarcely a judicious measure to keep the boy to a constant study of Cicero's book, "De Officiis," in order to subdue his fiery temper.

On the 12th of April, 1555, the mother of Charles, the melancholy Doña Juaña, died at Tordesillas. This death matured his determination to abdicate. During the autumn of the same year Philip came from England to Brussels by invitation of the Emperor, who, from the love which he bore to his grandson Carlos, forgot his grudge against his son Philip, and was ready to resign to him the crowns of the Netherlands and of Spain. It was about this time that the Emperor, previous to his abdication, related to Don Carlos, then a boy of twelve years, the history of his whole life, never wearying of answering the numberless questions of the prince. When the Emperor came to speak of his flight from Innsbruck, Carlos called out, "For shame! I would not have fled." The Emperor once more described to him the entire want of every means of resistance; but Carlos stuck to it, "I would not have fled." "And if," the Emperor said, with a smile, "the whole of your pages conspired to surprise you, and make you prisoner?" The Infant angrily replied, "What are you talking about? I would never fly under any circumstances."

Besides Don Philip Charles left by his wife Isabella of Portugal two princesses. One, Joanna, was married in 1553 to the Infant John of Portugal, who died in the following year. Her son was the unfortunate King Sebastian, who in 1578 was killed near Alcassar in the expedition against Morocco. Joanna became regent in Spain until the arrival of Philip in 1559, and died in the same year as her son, 1578. The second princess was Maria, married in 1548, at the age of twenty, to her cousin, who was afterwards Maximilian II., Emperor of Germany. She was the favourite child of her father, and the most pious lady of her time.

Of the natural children of Charles V., I have before mentioned the brave, ingenious, and agreeable Don Juan d'Austria. He died of poison in 1578, not having completed his thirty-third year. His heart was found to be quite dried up and his skin as if singed with fire. His brother Philip had been informed that he was in correspondence with the captive Mary Stuart, and that he plotted with the Guises to secure for himself the independent rule of some kingdom or other. His motto was, " He who does not try to go forward goes backward."

Charles had also a natural daughter by a Flemish lady, Margaret Vomgeest, who afterwards married John Vandendick. This was the masculine, shrewd Margaret of Parma, who, at the age of thirteen, in 1535, was married to Alexander Medicis, duke of Florence, and in 1538, one year after his murder, to Ottavio Farnese, duke of Parma, to whom she bore a son, afterwards the great General Alexander Farnese. From 1559 to 1567 she was, as regent of the Low Countries, at Brussels; after which she received from her brother King Philip the beautifully situated lordship of Aquila in Naples, and died in retirement at the age of sixty-four, in 1586, at Artona a Mare, an estate of the Farneses at Naples. This lady was remarkable for four qualities, which are generally considered as attributes of the stronger sex. In the first place, her masculine power of judgment; secondly, the gout; thirdly, her fondness for hunting; and fourthly, the very unladylike ornament of a moustache.

The court of Charles V. was the most numerous and brilliant which had ever been seen in Western Christendom. The flower of four great, rich, and powerful countries, of Burgundy and the Netherlands, of Spain, Italy, and Germany, combined to form it. The young Emperor arrived at the Diet of Worms in 1521 with a retinue of not less than 2,700 horses; yet, when the laurels of a succession of the most brilliant victories were heaped upon him, he began to contract his household.

It is one of the principal characteristics of great men that they know how to assemble other men of genius around them.

As the iron follows the magnet, thus great captains and statesmen will crowd about really great princes. Charles was no exception to that rule. A number of the most able generals served him in the field, and the most accomplished diplomatists in his cabinet and at foreign courts.

Diplomacy already played a very important part under Charles V. The Granvellas formed a nursery of diplomatists who were equal to the celebrated Venetian politicians. Charles knew as well as anyone the secret, which has almost become a truism, that prudence carries the day against bravery; only he was too prudent. As far as foreign policy went, he conducted his business in a most masterly style, and attained nearly all his objects; but he was caught in his own snares, in his family policy—it was his own house which brought him down.[1]

[1] Appendix C contains samples of the style and courtesy of the Emperor's private and diplomatic correspondence, and of his State papers.

CHAPTER III

FERDINAND I.—(1556-1564).

1.—Personal notice of the Emperor.

AFTER the resignation of the German crown by Charles V., his brother Ferdinand I. was acknowledged as Emperor. He was born at Alcala de Henarez, in Spain, in 1503, and remained until his eighteenth year in that country, at the court of his grandfather, Ferdinand the Catholic, who, according to the custom of that time, frequently changed his residence from one town to another. Two Spaniards, Don Pedro Nunnez de Guzman, king-at-arms of the Order of Alcantara, and Osorio, bishop of Asturias, superintended Ferdinand's education, according to the directions of the celebrated Erasmus of Rotterdam. When Charles in 1515 came as king to Spain, he sent his brother to Brussels, and Ferdinand never saw Spain again.

In 1521 Ferdinand married Anne Jagellon at Linz, both being in their nineteenth year. In 1526 he obtained the two Jagellon crowns of Hungary and Bohemia. In 1530 Charles also gave up to him the archduchy of Austria and the other family possessions of Habsburg. In 1531 he became King of the Romans. After the abdication of his brother, he styled himself Roman Emperor Elect; for, as the Pope would not acknowledge the validity of the abdication, "*because the Roman see had not been asked for its consent,*" Ferdinand did not cause himself to be crowned; nor has any German Emperor since Charles V. allowed himself to be crowned by the Pope.

Ferdinand was a Spaniard, like his brother, and yet he was very different from him; in many respects his very opposite. Charles was grave, taciturn, sedate, and always ailing; Ferdinand was ardent as the sun of Castile, gay, exceedingly communicative, disdaining neither the pleasures of conviviality nor the relaxation of music and dancing, and he enjoyed the most robust health. We have a "Relation" of the Venetian ambassador, Navagiero, of the year 1547, which must be received with circumspection, to be understood as it is meant:

"The King Ferdinand is at present in his forty-fifth year. His figure is rather small; his face thin; his hair, which is standing out, inclines to red; his forehead is of middling height; his eyebrows thick and arched; his eyes not very dark, but fine and sparkling; his nose large, somewhat aquiline; his lips thick and protruding. Since the death of the Queen he has allowed his beard to grow, which is now long and reddish, like the hair of his head. He also wears large whiskers, which are of a somewhat lighter colour. His neck is long and thick, but the rest of his body is rather thin. Examined individually, all his features are ungainly (*brutti*); but whoever approaches the King is, on the whole, impressed with his kingly appearance, and, from the spirited expression of his eyes and the energy of his mind and language, recognises in him a man who is worth looking at. He never had an illness of any consequence. For many years he has lived most regularly and methodically. He keeps open table only four times a week, in the evening, and always rises early; so that whoever, in winter, wants to accompany his Majesty to mass (as I always did on holidays) had to make his appearance at the palace at least one hour before daybreak. He is indefatigable in taking exercise. From rising in the morning to going to bed in the evening he only sits down to take his meals. All the rest of the time he is on his legs, either standing or walking, in business, in promenades, and in the chase. He seems likely to be destined for long life. Queen Anne was of distinguished beauty in mind and body. She loved the King as dearly as he did her in return; so that all the twenty-six years which they spent together (she died in childbed on the 27th of January, 1547, at Prague) their marriage was the very model of a happy union. She bore to the King fifteen children, of whom twelve are alive—three sons and nine daughters—all of them very handsome.

"The court of his Majesty would be very royal and numerous if all the servants whom the King pays were assembled in one establishment. But the King has his own servants; so has his eldest son, Maximilian" (afterwards Emperor), "and his second son, Ferdinand, and likewise the other princes and princesses who are at Innsbruck. For several years past the King has kept court together with only one of his sons; and since the death of his Queen he has reduced his household still more.

"The King," continues Navagiero, "is of sound and penetrating judgment; he also speaks the Spanish, French, German, Italian, and Latin languages very fairly." "In Latin," the learned scholar Busbeck says, "Ferdinand sometimes sins against Priscian," of which ample proofs are afforded by the letters of his which have been preserved. According to Dolce, he was fond of reading Roman and Greek history, especially Cæsar's Commentaries. He often urged his brother to give him a command in the Italian wars, and "not to allow him to dawdle about the stoves (firesides) of Germany." But Charles remained deaf to his requests. "The King," writes Navagiero, "is an excellent man of business (*gran negociante*), doing everything himself. No ambassador or anyone else can transact business except with his Majesty himself; and if a citizen wishes to present a petition it is his Majesty's pleasure always to receive it himself; and if a poor man wants to address him whilst he is going to mass or to table, the King stops, listens to him, and then disposes of his cause according as he thinks best. Yet this meddling with everything in most cases occasions great delay. His Majesty is very religious; attends mass every day, and on great holidays hears one or two sermons; he receives the sacrament, two, three, or four times a year. He is very temperate, and it is believed of him that he was ever faithful to his wife, and that his life both before marriage and after the death of his wife was perfectly chaste. He is liberal; which is sufficiently proved by the condition of his servants, who are most of them rich, whilst he is poor. Magnanimous I do not think him to be, one of the principal characteristics of that virtue being the forgetting of received injuries; but if any prince offends his Majesty he never forgets it, and it is my firm belief he would revenge it." The truth of this last feature is evidenced by the fact alluded to before, of Ferdinand's having so earnestly urged the carrying out of the sentence of death on the Elector of Saxony in the camp before Wittenberg; and also by the cruel instructions given by him in the Peasants' War to Truchsess of Waldburg.

Sastrow saw King Ferdinand at the same period from which this Venetian report dates; that is to say, at the Diet of Augsburg, in 1547 and 1548, which he attended as one of the delegates of Pomerania. He says, in his quaint chronicle, "This was not only a cuirassed, but also a very magnificent and pompous Diet, there being so many royal and princely ladies in the place. There were Italian and German dances nearly every evening. King Ferdinand especially was rarely without guests, who were always splendidly treated, and had all sorts of amusements and magnificent dances. There was most stately and well-got up *musica non solum instrumentalis, verum etiam vocalis;* besides other devices. There always stood behind the King one of his jesters, with whom he used to bandy laughable talk, and to put him down with ease. He generally had royal and princely persons (*utriusque sexus*) sitting with him at table, with whom without intermission he would keep up a pleasant conversation, *for his tongue never rested.*"

2.—*Position of the nobility under Ferdinand I. in Austria—The first Protestant "chain of the nobles."*

According to the original documents pertaining to the government of Charles V., which have been brought to light from the different archives, there can be no doubt left but that the persons who enjoyed the confidence of Ferdinand were hostile to Charles. The latter indeed had, after the Pope, no worse secret enemy than his brother, who, especially at the catastrophe in the Tyrol, worked hand in hand with Maurice. Concerning the existence of that spirit of opposition at Ferdinand's court long before that catastrophe, irrefutable evidence may be adduced from the despatches of the ambassadors of those times. The Archbishop of Lund, one of the most able diplomatists of the Emperor Charles, reports to his master, as far back as the 17th of November, 1534, from Vienna:

"As in duty bound, and according to the true state of affairs, I would point out to your Majesty that the whole government rests with the privy councillors of his royal Majesty, John Hoffman, Baron von Roggendorf, and Leonard von Fels; the latter a relation of the Cardinal of Trent (Bernhard von Glöss); and that, to call the thing by its right name, they lead the King just where they please. I see that these councillors are not very favourable to the interest of your Majesty; and I have found that, on the contrary, *they are very strongly disposed against it, and that they even express themselves hostile to it.*"

The families of the three lords mentioned in this despatch, who formed the council of King Ferdinand, the Hoffmans, Colonna-Fels, and Roggendorfs, formed also the nucleus of the Protestant band or "chain of nobles" in Austria, and maintained themselves in power for the whole of a century. After the outbreak of the Bohemian rebellion, at the beginning of the Thirty Years' War, they joined the Palatine King; and after his downfall were obliged, with the loss of all their offices, honours, and estates, to take refuge in Silesia. A fourth family belonging to this Austrian "*Fronde*" was that of the Dietrichsteins, who had been raised to such a high place by Maximilian I. They, however, remained, in the Thirty Years' War, true to the house of Habsburg; and with the Liechtensteins, who had returned to the old creed, placed themselves, in the seventeenth century, at the head of the second Catholic "chain of nobles."

Immediately after the death of Maximilian I., a strong movement arose in the Austrian hereditary countries for reforms in the constitution and administration. The regency appointed by Maximilian in his last will was set aside, and the public treasury and the arsenal laid hold of by some members of the nobility, the university, and the municipality. Sigismund von Herberstein, who was sent by the Estates of Styria as one of their delegates to Charles V. in Spain, and had an audience with him at Molino del Rè, near Barcelona, easily guessed, from the answer of Charles, that he was "very little pleased with the things which had happened in Austria and at Vienna." Ferdinand caused, in December, 1522, two noblemen, Buchheim and Eytzing, and six citizens, to be executed. This, however, did by no means crush the factious spirit of the nobility.

Concerning this spirit at the court of King Ferdinand and throughout Austria Proper, remarkable disclosures are contained in a memoir published by Dr. Lanz in the State Papers of the Emperor Charles, from the archives at Brussels. It is written in the year 1542, four years before the outbreak of the Smalcalde war. Its author, Messire Corneille Scepperus, Baron d'Eck, Chevalier Conseiller et Maistre aux Requestes de l'Empereur, was a diplomatist employed by Charles on many occasions as ambassador to the German Empire and to the Sublime Porte. It is the most remarkable document which has come under my notice among those of the earlier Austrian history anterior to the Thirty Years' War. It affords irrefragable evidence of the existence of that organised league among the nobility which has been designated the "chain of nobles"—a term which is expressly made use of in it. Some passages from it may be in their place here.

"I was, in the year 1532 and in the beginning of 1533, at the court of King Ferdinand, as well at Innsbruck and Linz as at Vienna. There I every day heard most of the ministers and grandees, as the lords Von Roggendorf, Von Fels, Von Dietrichstein, and others, abusing the Emperor. They called him the most ungrateful prince who trod the earth, and such-like expressions; indeed, they spoke so disrespectfully of his Majesty, that it was shocking, and utterly disregarding that I was the ambassador of his Imperial Majesty at the court of the King. I could not suppose *but that their object was to lower his Imperial Majesty in the estimation of his brother, of the nobility, and of all the people in the countries of the King.* They publicly asserted that the Emperor was the cause of all the misery that had befallen Germany.

"In the year 1534, on my return from Turkey, I heard it said at Nuremberg, Mayence, and Cologne, that the councillors of the King would by no means be pleased to see their master great; that, on the contrary, they endeavoured to keep him in their subjection; and those well-minded persons pitied the good King for allowing himself to be governed by people like Count Salamanca, Sigismund von Dietrichstein, and Hans Hoffman, whose object it was to get all the good places of the Austrian countries into their own hands. They, moreover, said that these people increased their party more and more every day by marriages and alliances among themselves, and especially with those who held commands within the country and in the borders. . . . . The before-mentioned Salamanca and Dietrichstein had agreed between them to ruin the King, and to buy for a ridiculously low price the Church lands which the Pope had left to the King. *With these estates they had enriched themselves.*

"I was informed repeatedly that *all the lords of Austria were leagued together for such purposes*, dropping all former enmity for the advantage which they derived from these purchases; and that, in fine, they managed matters very well between them, *and that this league they called the* CHAIN."

From this it may be seen that in Austria, as everywhere in Germany, the nobles turned the Reformation to their own advantage. Not only did they appropriate the ecclesiastical and conventual estates, but they also used the ignorant single-minded common people as the tools of their opposition against their ruler.

When Ferdinand assumed the government there were, according to the statement of a Venetian ambassador, *nine-tenths of Germany professing the new creed;* in the hereditary Habsburg dominions also by far the greater number were Lutherans. The whole nobility of Austria at that time went to study at Wittenberg. Three young men belonging to the Protestant peerage of Austria were in succession elected (honorary) rectors of the university of Luther. It is a very significant fact that the authority of the Pope at that time was generally despised, and that the two parties, the followers of the old and new creed, *lived with each other in perfect peace—the establishment of the order of Jesuits afterwards lighted the torch of discord in the Empire*. The Venetian ambassador Micheli writes, in 1564: "People have agreed to tolerate each other; in mixed communities the question is seldom asked whether anyone is Catholic or Protestant. The families also are mixed in like manner. There are houses where the elder generation belongs to one and the younger to the other creed. Brothers follow different religions, and Catholics and Protestants intermarry without any one being scandalised by it or even heeding it."

Ferdinand on his side was a Catholic with all his heart. In his last will he most earnestly warned all his sons, and especially Maximilian the eldest, against following a religious party which, being divided in itself as to doctrine, could not hold the truth. "I would rather see you dead than that you should join the new sects," he wrote in his codicil of 1555. He was an active patron of the Jesuits, having for his confessor Bobadilla, one of the founders of the order. The fathers of the Society of Jesus quietly and cautiously gained under Ferdinand a footing at Vienna. At first they were quartered with the Dominicans, gave private instruction, and tried in the distressed times of the plague to be everything to everybody; just as afterwards in China they made their way as mechanicians, mathematicians, and compilers of almanacks. Thus in Vienna they acted as physicians, effecting cures by means of Peruvian bark, which was therefore long called "the Jesuits' powder." In 1551, the first Jesuits' college which Germany has had was founded in the capital of the Habsburgs. It occupied the locality of the present Ministry of War at Vienna, and contained the secret chancellery of the Austrian province of the order. It was inhabited by eleven fathers, sent by Ferdinand's wish, and at the command of Pope Julius III., by the then still living chief founder Don Ignatio Loyola, who died at Rome in 1556. In 1552 Petrus Canisius, the compiler of the celebrated catechism, arrived. He remained until 1556, and then went to Bavaria. In 1556 Jesuit colleges were established at Ingolstadt and Cologne, in addition to the one at Vienna. From these three centres the "Spanish priests," as they were first called in Germany, spread over Austria, Bavaria, the Tyrol, Franconia, Swabia, a great part of the Rhenish provinces, and also to some extent in Bohemia.

While Ferdinand through his confessor, Bobadilla, intimately allied himself with the Pope, the Elector of Saxony, Augustus, the brother and successor of Maurice, assembled the heads of the Protestants at Naumburg in 1551. The Emperor was favourable to a union, and even the Pope, Pius IV., of the house of Medici, sent his nuncio in the person of the very clever Commendone. The right moment for a reconciliation seemed to have arrived; the great men of the reformers were dead, and the generation succeeding them were sobered down or split into different hostile parties. The gentle, timid Melanchthon, he who had given such great offence to the zealous Lutherans by his leaning towards the tenets of Calvin, especially in his "Apologia Variata" of the Augsburg Confession, died 19th of April, 1560, at Wittenberg. A few days previous to his death he had written on a sheet of paper, as in soliloquy: "Thou wilt see the light; thou wilt see God; thou wilt behold Jesus Christ; thou wilt understand those wonderful mysteries which thou didst not understand in this life—why we have been made as we are, and what is the union of the two natures in Christ; thou wilt leave off sinning; thou wilt be delivered from all evil, and *from the wrath of the theologians.*" For, although Papists and Protestants lived in peace with each other as far as the affairs of this world went, yet there were very sharp controversies everywhere about the most abstruse points of doctrine among the Protestants themselves; and it was not Melanchthon alone who complained of the clergy as the principal instigators of these constant squabbles. Commendone, the Pope's nuncio, intimated to the Protestants at Naumburg: "How much dissension is among you concerning Luther's doctrine! There is no town, no house in Germany free from theological squabbles. Men dispute with men, and children with their parents, about the meaning of the Scriptures. In company, in taverns, at drinking parties, at the gambling-tables, the most holy truths are discussed, and women take it upon themselves to decide on them. But you will never unite, because as sure as true tenets do agree, false tenets do not. The further you sail into the ocean of error, the darker are its waves."

The convention of Naumburg did not succeed in bringing about a union of the divided religious parties. As, since the downfall of the Hohenstaufen, the Empire had dissolved into innumerable small political disunited dominions, so the Church since the Reformation split into a number of particular churches, which again divided into sects. In the religious as well as in the political world, there was war of all against all. The Elector Augustus of Saxony tried, in 1580, to unite the Lutherans by a fixed symbolic form—the Formula Concordiæ, but many Lutheran princes and cities refused to accept it; nay, it soon became a Formula Discordiæ, as two of the principal persons who had sworn to it, the Electors Palatine and of Brandenburg, embraced Calvinism. The Calvinists at last split into no less than five large parties. These were, a German "Reformed Church," with the Heidelberg Catechism; a Belgian, with the decrees of the Synod of Dort; a Swiss, with the Helvetic; a French, with the Gallican Confession; and, lastly, the Church of England, with the Thirty-nine Articles.[1] The Lutheran and Calvinist preachers attacked each other with the most hateful

---

[1] Dr. Vehse here follows a prejudice which is very common in Germany. Non-theologians there generally look upon the Church of England as Calvinist, on account of bread being used in the Eucharist instead of the wafer, as in the Lutheran Church. But the very use by the earliest English reformers of the term *Protestant*, which is the historical name of the Lutherans, whilst on the Continent the Calvinists always call themselves "the Reformed Church," points to an affinity of the Church of England rather with the Lutherans than with the Calvinists, who in this country evidently have borrowed that name from the originally

bitterness, wrangling about tenets, about the meaning of a passage of Scripture, an idea, a word. Passions became heated to the highest point in these petty quarrels. Abuse stood for argument, and the upshot generally was, that each consigned his antagonist to the lowest depths of hell. The subtle, versatile Jesuits by this means gained more and more ground at the courts against the bluff, unmannered Protestant divines. The reverend fathers only bided their time for taking the offensive as soon as the disunion of their foes among themselves should be completed.

3.—*Ferdinand's family—Philippina Welser and her children.*

The Emperor Ferdinand died in 1564 of a slow fever in Vienna, at the age of sixty-one, and was buried at Prague by the side of his wife, Ann Jagellon, who had preceded him in death by seventeen years. Of fifteen fine children whom he had by her, three only survived him: Maximilian, his successor; Ferdinand, who received the Tyrol; and Charles, who received Styria. Maximilian's line became extinct with his sons; Ferdinand of Tyrol left no children entitled to the royal succession; and thus the Austrian branch of the house of Habsburg was continued by the youngest brother, Charles of Styria, the devotee, who became the father of Ferdinand II., known as Ferdinand of Grätz.

Archduke Ferdinand of the Tyrol has become famous for his morganatic marriage with Philippina Welser, who was considered the most beautiful woman of her time. She was the daughter of the Augsburg patrician Francis Welser, who did money business with the Emperor. Ferdinand made her acquaintance at the Diet of Augsburg, at which his uncle Charles V. published the "Interim," and which he himself attended on his return from the battle of Mühlberg, where

---

Lutheran reformers. This affinity is even more strongly evidenced by the unmistakeable fact of a very considerable part of the Thirty-nine Articles being taken almost literally from the Confession of Augsburg. Nor does the letter and spirit of the rubric lean more towards Calvin than towards Luther; and it would certainly be a very bold assertion that episcopacy *in its full bearing* is more at home at Geneva than at Wittenberg.—*Translator.*

he had fought in the first line at the head of the Bohemian troops. Philippina was at that time in her nineteenth year. Ferdinand had fallen most violently in love with her at first sight on meeting her in the street. He was one year older than the lady; in his features rather resembling his father, only that he was handsomer and his hair lighter. Ferdinand, the chivalrous, enthusiastic, light-hearted, and jovial swain, could not forget the beautiful Philippina. He married her privately on the 24th of April, 1548; and, notwithstanding the strong aversion of his father, had, in January, 1557, the ceremony repeated according to the rites of the Council of Trent, with the strictest secrecy, only the priest and the dowager Catherine von Loxan being present as witnesses. From 1549 to 1567 Ferdinand was his father's viceroy in Bohemia, with residence at Prague. Philippina lived in complete retirement at the castle of Bürglitz, a few leagues from the Bohemian capital. At last Philippina herself brought about a reconciliation with her father-in-law, whom she gained over by her angelic beauty. She was so fair and lovely that those who knew her were untiring in her praises. Her skin is said to have been of such transparency that when she drank red wine the dark fluid was seen through her delicate neck.[1] Philippina, in the year 1561, came *incognito* to the court of the Emperor at Prague. She threw herself at the feet of the Emperor, and told him under a feigned name the misery which the harsh father of her husband inflicted upon her. The Emperor, moved by her tale of woe, raised her, and promised to intercede with the cruel father, that he would no longer repudiate such a lovely daughter-in-law. On this Philippina made herself known. The Emperor now acknowledged their union as a morganatic marriage; their children, however, were to succeed, to the German possessions of the house of Habsburg when the whole Austrian male line of the family was extinct. But the Emperor insisted upon the marriage being strictly kept a

[1] A portrait of Philippina, representing this remarkable feature, is still extant at Nuremberg, at the old family mansion of the patrician house of Pöller, which intermarried with the Welsers.—*Translator*.

secret, a few persons of the court and the midwife being alone informed of it under a solemn oath not to divulge it. From this vow the initiated were dispensed only twelve years after the Emperor's death. Since 1567, when Ferdinand undertook the government of Tyrol, he lived with Philippina at the castle of Ambras, near Innsbruck, where he collected the celebrated gallery of portraits and armour of distinguished princes and heroes to the number of a hundred and twenty-five, which is still shown at Vienna. At Castle Ambras, an old baronial seat of the extinct illustrious family of Andechs, the fair Philippina died, on the anniversary of her wedding day, in 1580. According to Johannes Müller, at one time custos of the imperial library at Vienna, there are still extant there five folio volumes of domestic cookery and medicinal recipes which belonged to her, two of them in her own handwriting; from which we may gather that she was a right good housewife.

She left to Ferdinand two sons, who were called D'Austria. The elder, Andrew, born in 1558, became, in 1597, Cardinal of Austria, bishop of Brixen and Constance; in 1579 and 1599, he was governor of the Netherlands; and he died in 1600, during the jubilee in Rome, in the arms of Pope Clement VIII. The younger son, Charles, after having served in the Netherlands with the Spaniards and in Hungary against the Turks, got with great difficulty, in 1609, the marquisate of Burgau in Swabia. He married, in 1601, a princess of Juliers, who was already in her forty-fifth year; and he died at Günzburg, his residence, in 1618, without leaving any legitimate issue. But he had by Clara of Ferery, before his marriage, two sons and a daughter, who bore the name Von Hohenberg. The lords Von Hohenberg inherited considerable landed property from their father. Their descendants were raised, in 1677, by the Emperor Leopold I., to the dignity of Freiherren[1] von Hohenberg and Weitingen, and married into the noble houses of the Swabian peerage.

Charles Joseph von Hohenberg, the last of his line, met in 1728, on his thirty-second birthday, with a sudden and

---

[1] Corresponding to the English viscount.—*Translator*.

violent death in a very remarkable manner. He was a small, somewhat hunchbacked, jovial man, of rather sarcastic turn, but who always boasted of having the gift of "second sight." How this came true in his own case is related by Hormayr, from the report of an eye-witness, who is averse, even hostile, to everything like a belief in visions.

"Baron Hohenberg had invited for his birthday all his relations, friends, and boon companions of the neighbourhood. Ladies were not seen at his board. The first arrival was Baron von H., the lord-lieutenant of the county. The noble host received him in his usual jovial manner, led him up the staircase, and opened for him the door of the large hall; but immediately started back horrified, covering his face with both hands and trembling from head to foot. As his visitor in amazement asked what was the matter, the host in great agitation pointed towards the middle of the hall, being unable to utter anything beyond 'There! there!' The lord-lieutenant replied that he saw nothing but the large banqueting-table ready spread. Baron Hohenberg, however, exclaimed, 'There! there! don't you see that the hall is all hung with black, and also the many funeral tapers? and lo! yonder I am myself laid out on the state-bed; and oh! the nasty smell of the tapers, and the oil, and perhaps of the corpse itself!'

"The lord-lieutenant had great difficulty in inducing his host to enter the room in order that he might convince himself by touch that there was really nothing but the banqueting-table. As the guests arrived by degrees the agitation of the baron gave way to his usual joviality. He now told them that just a year before, when out hunting, a gipsy fortune-teller, after looking at his hand, had told him that he should always pass his birthday quite alone, in serious thought and prayer, secluded from the world, and even from his own people, for his birthday would also be the day of his death, and that he would lose his life by a fool.

"The guests now sat down to table, when merry toasts were proposed, wishing to the giver of the feast long life, much happiness, and a speedy marriage. After dinner the company went into the open air to amuse themselves with different rural sports. All at once some one called out, 'But where is our merryandrew, Master Michael Ganskragen (goose-neck)? Since we rose from table he has made himself scarce; he is sure to be lying dead drunk either in the kitchen or in the cellar.' The poor fellow, who used to be baited by everyone, and, especially in the games, was most liberally treated to kicks and cuffs innumerable, had taken refuge in a closet at the top of the house, known to but a few of the inmates, and which was only approached by a narrow and very steep staircase. The roysterous guests, after having searched the whole castle in vain, returned vexed and angry to the skittle-ground. Baron Hohenberg, however, told them with a laugh that he could at once bring down the jester. All followed the host, who was not long in discovering the deserter in his hiding-place; but the jester refused to open the door. In vain the master of the house tried to kick it in, until at last he remembered an old forgotten rope by which it might be opened. He pulled with all his might; but the rotten line snapped, and Baron Hohenberg, falling backwards down the staircase, broke his neck.

"When, on the following day, the lord-lieutenant, with his officials, entered the hall where the banquet had been on the day before, a shudder seized him: the corpse lay exactly in the same place, and the whole hall was fitted up as Baron Hohenberg had described it from his vision of second sight. 'Hohenberg! Hohenberg! and never Hohenberg any more!' it was then said, as is the custom wherever the shield and helmet are laid on the coffin of the last of his race."

Archduke Ferdinand of Tyrol married in 1582, two years after Philippina's death, a Mantuan princess. Anna, one of his daughters by this second marriage, became the wife of the Emperor Matthias; the other went into a convent at Innsbrück. Tyrol reverted to the imperial house.

The youngest son of Ferdinand, Archduke Charles, became the founder of the line of Styria (Grätz), which in the sequel ascended the imperial throne. Charles was twice very nearly being married to an English princess—to Queen Mary, and, after her death, to Queen Elizabeth. A despatch in the

State Papers of Cardinal Granvella (vol. iv., p. 100) shows that the former marriage was agreeable to the wishes of the councillors of Mary, who would rather have had her married to Charles than to Don Philip. The latter marriage was not effected because of their religion, and because Ferdinand would not send his son to pay a previous visit in England. Charles of Styria afterwards, in 1570, at the age of thirty, married Mary of Bavaria, who became the mother of the Emperor Ferdinand II.

Concerning the match with Elizabeth the Emperor Maximilian once wrote (29th of August, 1567) from Vienna to his brother Duke Albert of Bavaria: "Your Highness is no doubt aware that an English embassy is here; but it brings no better offers than the former ones, and it looks rather as if the whole affair would split *in negotio religionis*; for the pith of it is that they wish my lord my brother to accommodate himself to their religion *in publicis*, which my brother does not intend to do, for they will not allow him to attend mass either; and thus it looks rather as if nothing would come out of it." A second reason, based on the character of Elizabeth, Maximilian had before pointed out in a letter of the 13th of August, 1565: "As to the English marriage, I am almost of the same opinion as your Highness, as I have for my own part, for the present, put very little trust in it, *quia est mulier inconstantissima*."

Of the twelve daughters of the Emperor Ferdinand I., Elizabeth, one of the most beautiful princesses of her day, was married, in 1543, to King Sigismund Jagellon of Poland; she died in 1545, on which he married her sister Catherine, who, although not more than twenty, had already been left a widow by Duke Francis of Mantua; but she was sent back, as there was no prospect of her ever having any children. A third princess, Anna, became, in 1546, at the age of eighteen, the wife of Duke Albert V. of Bavaria. A fourth princess, Mary, was united in the same month to the Duke William V. of Juliers and Cleves, who had to cede Guelderland to Charles V., and who at first became Lutheran, then Catholic again, and at last went out of his mind altogether; after which she, the princess, underwent the same fate. With her son, the likewise demented John William, the possessions of Juliers and Cleves became vacant in 1609. A fifth daughter of the Emperor Ferdinand, Eleanor, married, in 1561, Duke William of Mantua, the brother of the above-mentioned Francis; and also the sixth and seventh daughters were wedded to Italian potentates—Barbara, in 1565, to Duke Alfonso II. of Ferrara, and Joanna to Duke Francis of Florence. Three daughters took the veil, and two died in infancy.

CHAPTER IV

MAXIMILIAN II.—(1564-1576).

1.—Personal notices of the Emperor.

MAXIMILIAN II. was the eldest son of Ferdinand I. He was born at Vienna in 1527, but was educated principally in Spain, under the direction of the Emperor Charles V., his uncle. He had for his tutors three distinguished scholars: Ursinus Velius, of Schweidnitz in Silesia, who had been secretary to the famous magnificent Bishop of Gurk, Mathew Lang von Wellenburg, and who, after having been nominated by Maximilian I. poet-laureate, and by Ferdinand I. councillor and orator in 1538, ended his career by drowning himself in the Danube—it is said from melancholy on account of his shrewish wife; secondly, the learned Bohemian John Horak von Hasenberg; and lastly, Wolfgang Schiefer, who had received his education at Wittenberg. His chief governor was John Gaudentius, Baron Madruzzi, an Italian; and his under-governor Don Piedro Lasso di Castiglia, a Spaniard. Navagiero, who saw the young Prince Maximilian at the Diet of 1547 and 1548, describes him thus: " Maximilian will be twenty-one on the 1st of August next. He is a youth of great promise, who has already fought at Landrecy in France, and in Swabia and Saxony (in the Smalcalde war). He is rather tall and spare, handsome, and of healthy looks; he has much more of the Emperor in his disposition than of his father, as he does not talk much, but is grave in his manner. He seems to aspire to great things, and, if he were brought up by energetic men, I think that high expectations might be entertained of him. Maximilian rides and also tilts well. He frequently practises with the arquebuse and the crossbow.

Besides German he speaks Bohemian and Latin, and also French, Spanish, and Italian—the latter languages not very fluently, only knowing them so far as to understand and to make himself understood. He has a strong disposition to command, and is very difficult to manage, which displeases the King."

Maximilian in his youth was indeed on very bad terms with his father. There is a Latin letter of Ferdinand's extant, written shortly before his departure for the war against the Elector of Saxony to his two sons Maximilian and Ferdinand. In it the father reproaches Maximilian that, notwithstanding his having received him once before, like the prodigal son, he nevertheless conducted himself very ill at the court of the Emperor; that he was given to drinking strong wines, as he did at the court of the Duke of Bavaria; and that the vice of drunkenness was the more dangerous to him as he was artful and hot-tempered (*callidus et iracundus*), so that in a state of intoxication he was liable to commit some serious crime. The father, moreover, reproaches Maximilian with being headstrong (*capitosus*), and averse to following the counsels of sensible men, deeming himself wiser than the rest of the world, whereas he had not yet seen or learned anything. Maximilian, his father says, associated only with loose people, and attended only to his bear and his musicians; but received grave men from the Emperor's court superciliously, and conversed very rarely and little with them. He urges him to beware of arrogance and conceit, and to remember the Italian adage: "*Quy asino è el cervo se crede al saltar del foso se vede.*" In conclusion, he says, "What has happened to you would not have happened if you had consulted serious men—*quodsi non possis abstinere luxuria, facias, ut dicitur, caute non scandalose, neque cum maritatis, et non vim vel injuriam in isto casu facias vel scandalizes.*"

This letter affords authentic proof of Maximilian's youth having been rather wild. Indeed, he was the Prince Hal of his dynasty; but he was the favourite of Charles V., who even gave him the daughter of his heart, Mary, the most pious woman of her day, as his wife. The wedding of Maximilian took place at Valladolid, 13th of September, 1548; and during the absence of Charles V. and Don Philip in Germany and the Netherlands, the son-in-law of the great Emperor held the vice-royalty of Spain. Charles bestowed upon him the highest praise for the manner in which he acquitted himself in this office. When, in 1551, he entertained the idea of causing his son Philip to be elected King of the Romans, it was part of his plan that Maximilian should become second Roman King, as it were second coadjutor. To assist in the negotiations concerning this affair, he came, in 1551, from Spain to the court of the Emperor, with whom he still was, during the last days at Innsbruck, in 1552. He afterwards was present at the negotiations of the Peace of Religion which his father, in the name of the Emperor, concluded at Passau with Maurice of Saxony; and in the same year he was appointed "*Gubernator*" of Hungary. He showed such decided leaning towards the Protestants that his father is said to have intended to cut him off from the succession, and even to divorce him from his wife. In 1562 only, Maximilian seems to have given a more satisfactory account of himself. In this year he became King of Bohemia and King of the Romans; and in 1563 he was crowned with the crown of St. Stephen of Hungary.

2.—*State of religion—The army—The Austrian nobility is made, by the matriculation of 1572, a close corporation.*

Maximilian was a merry and jovial sovereign, his humour keeping a happy medium between the undignified and exceedingly prolix garrulity of his father and the austere taciturnity of his uncle.

As soon as Maximilian, in the year 1564, had assumed the reins of government, he at once showed himself forbearing and tolerant on religious points; much more so than his father had been, or than was agreeable to many a Catholic prince of the Empire. In a letter to his brother-in-law, Duke Albert of Bavaria, dated the 30th of May, 1566, in which he alludes to this feeling of dissatisfaction, he lays down the maxim—
"*In religious matters one must not bend the bow until it breaks.*"

A Protestant divine, John Sebastian Pfauser, who had been left about Maximilian without any particular inquiry as to his tenets, remained for a long time his court preacher, and became his teacher in Protestant theology; and, after having been appointed dean at Lauingen, in the principality of Neuburg, he continued secretly to correspond with Maximilian, who was privately furnished by him with news and with books. Pfauser died in 1569, after the accession of Maximilian to the imperial crown.

Maximilian, moreover, lived in open and avowed friendship with the first Protestant princes of the German Empire. Among these were the Elector Augustus of Saxony and the Elector Palatine Frederic III., Landgrave Philip of Hesse, and the excellent Duke Christopher of Würtemberg. With the latter he had been intimate from boyhood, as Christopher, being kept in captivity after his father's discomfiture, was brought up at the court of King Ferdinand at Innsbruck. Letters are still extant of Maximilian, in which he writes to Christopher that he had read as many as two volumes of the Latin and five of the German writings of Luther, expressing a wish to possess all the works of Dr. Martinus, and likewise those of Melanchthon and Brentzius,[1] which he begs the duke to send to him.

Maximilian went far in his religious toleration. His motto was, "God alone rules the consciences of men, man only rules man." Carrying out this principle, he issued, in 1567, an edict for Bohemia, and, in 1568, one for Austria, in which to both these countries free exercise of their religion was granted. One of the first acts of his reign was to release John Augusta, the noble-hearted and learned bishop of the Moravian brethren, from his imprisonment, in which he had been kept by King Ferdinand for sixteen years.

As early as 1562 Maximilian had sent his Lord Steward, Adam von Dietrichstein, to Rome, to ask the Pope to sanction the administration of the Eucharist under both forms, and the abolition of the enforced celibacy of the priests. The

[1] A celebrated divine, who carried out the reformation in the Duchy of Würtemberg.—*Translator.*

Pope refused it; but Maximilian was not cowed by the threat of excommunication which Pius IV. repeatedly held out to him, and just as little by the opposition of his cousin, the Spanish Don Philip. Maximilian wrote from Vienna, dated 12th of February, 1574, to his beloved General Lazarus von Schwendi, the following letter, which acquires additional interest from the fact of the arch-Chancellor Kaunitz once having it fetched from the archives at Vienna and laid before the Empress Maria Theresa, as an example of toleration which she would do well to follow. After her death it was found in her escritoire, with the beginning of her reply written on it; "May stand over—after my death—the time will come for it."

"MY DEAR VON SCHWENDI,—I have received and read your letter in due time, and am particularly obliged for your kind Christian sympathy with my ailments. May the Almighty God in whose hands are all our affairs vouchsafe to deal with me according to his Divine Will; for unfortunately things are going on in this world in such a way as to give one very little joy or rest, but there is plenty of tribulation, faithlessness, and dishonesty everywhere.

"As to the foul deed which the French have tyrannically perpetrated against the admiral and his people (the Saint Bartholomew of 1578), I cannot commend it at all, and *I have heard, to my heartfelt grief, that my son-in-law* (Charles IX.) *has allowed himself to be persuaded to give his sanction to such an infamous slaughter;* but I know this much, that other people rule much more than he does. May God forgive those who are the cause of it! I wish to God he had consulted me; I would have advised him as a true father. It is true, as you very sensibly write, that *religious matters ought not to be settled by the sword.* No honest man who fears God and loves peace will say differently; nor did Christ and his apostles teach otherwise: for their sword was their tongue, their teaching God's word and their Christian life; and, moreover, those mad people might have seen in so many years that this tyrannical burning and beheading will never do. In short, I do not like it, nor will I ever praise it, unless God should make me foolish and mad, which I ever pray he will not do.

* * * * * *

"Let Spain and France do as they like; they will have to answer for it to God the just Judge. As to myself, I shall, if God wills, act honestly and sincerely like a true Christian; and, if I do so, I do not care for all this wicked and graceless world. With this I commend you to the mercy of God, who, in his heavenly wisdom may turn all things for the best, to ourselves and to all Christendom."

Maximilian II. was the last German Emperor who, *as such*, placed himself at the head of an army of the Empire and took the field in person. This happened in the year

1566, when Sultan Soleyman, who died in that campaign before Szigeth, had overrun Hungary. From that time until 1778, when Joseph II. took the field against the Turks *with Austrian troops*, no German Emperor took the command of any army at all in the old style of the Othos and the Swabian Emperors, as Maximilian I. and Charles V. had also done. Yet the circumstances attending the campaign were most deplorable; it was a state of transition between the old licentiousness of the soldiery and the modern system of military slavery.

The Emperor in disgust gave up the command, which devolved on Lazarus von Schwendi, who preserved Upper Hungary for the Emperor, and took, in 1567, the celebrated fortress of Munkatz from the Prince of Transylvania, the son of Zapolya. A truce for eight years was concluded with the successor of Soleyman, and the *status quo* was maintained.

Maximilian II. employed as his councillors learned doctors, just as his uncle, Charles V., did the Granvellas. Their names, Seld, Zasius, Sinkmoser, and Unverzagt, show at once that he took them from the *bourgeoisie;* and as Schwendi was the Emperor's most confidential adviser in military affairs, so Dr. Seld, the vice-chancellor of the Empire, was consulted by him on all affairs of civil government. The latter, unfortunately, was not destined to benefit him long by his counsels. Seld met with his death in 1565, at the early age of forty-nine. His horses having taken fright as he was returning with Dr. Zasius from an audience with the Emperor, he jumped out of the carriage, fell with his head against a stone, and died half an hour afterwards.

On the other hand, Maximilian II. gave permission to his nobility in Austria, by a general decree, dated the 10th of February, 1572, to constitute themselves as a close corporation. By virtue of this grant only matriculated members of the body of nobles could possess noble estates. This was called "The Privilege of Corporate Standing" (*Einstandsrecht*), according to which the corporation had the right to admit new members at pleasure. The Emperor confirmed the statute agreed upon, in 1572, by the three Upper Estates, the prelates, lords, and knights, for the preservation of the rights and honours of the ancient noble houses, "that in future no one but who was either the well-known proprietor of a seignorial manor of the country, or a person of ancient noble descent long settled in the country, should be matriculated and acknowledged as a member of their body, unless at the request of the honourable Estates, the prelates, lords, and knights."

In pursuance of this decree the rolls of matriculated lords and knights of the canton of Lower Austria were drawn up and completed about the year 1582. They were considerably altered under Ferdinand II. by numerous attainders and the admission of new houses; yet they continued to maintain their importance down to the times of Joseph II., who reduced them to a dead letter by depriving the provincial nobility of the privilege of corporate standing.

At the death of Maximilian II. the roll of matriculated nobles of Lower Austria contained only fifty-eight houses, fourteen of which—among others the still flourishing noble families of Harrach, Khevenhüller, Auersperg, Althann, and the Hungarian Palffys—had been admitted on the rolls under his reign.

There was not yet any permanently established court under Maximilian II., who resided at one time at Prague and at another at Vienna. His principal amusement and pleasure were the chase and Hungary wine. For the purpose of hunting he acquired the celebrated Prater (the Hyde Park of Vienna), which originally was a forest park with preserved game. Schönbrunn also, which he built in 1570, was in his time only a hunting-seat. In one of his letters to his brother-in-law Albert of Bavaria (dated 28th of September, 1568) he writes: "I have several times wished from all my heart that you were with us in the Prater, where lots of fine stags have shown themselves; and particularly on Tuesday last, when I had a boar-hunt there, at which I bagged thirty head of game," &c. The Hungary wine gave the Emperor the gout, which miserably tormented him ever since his accession, although at that period he had not yet exceeded the age of thirty-seven. In a letter (dated 29th of August, 1567) to the same correspondent, he says, with regard to his winebibbing, "I am much obliged to your Highness for your excellent advice concerning my gout; I will strictly follow it, and not fail to dilute my wine with water, as it is an excruciating malady. Yet it might still be borne, if only it did not grow worse."

But it grew worse and worse, and at last so bad, that Maximilian had recourse to hazardous cures. In the autumn of 1576 he attended the Diet of Ratisbon, where his son Rodolph was just being elected King of the Romans. Here Maximilian died suddenly on the 12th of October, 1576, in the fiftieth year of his life and the thirteenth of his reign. He was the last good ruler whom Austria had under the old Habsburg dynasty. A famous quack of Ulm, of the name of Magdalen Streicher, had given him an elixir of reported miraculous virtues; but, as John Crato, his body physician, foretold, he survived the effects of the nostrum only a few days.

A report, certainly quite unsubstantiated, was current, that the Jesuits had poisoned the Emperor for fear that he should at last yield too much in favour of the Protestants. According to the statement of the imperial postmaster-general, Hans Wollzogen, in a letter written immediately after the Emperor's death to the imperial ambassador at Constantinople, Baron Ungnad, Cardinal Christopher Madruzzi of Trent had administered the poison to Maximilian in "a Genoese soup," as far back as the time previous to the Smalcalde war, when Maximilian returned from Spain. At the opening of the body, a black substance as hard as stone was found in his heart. The physicians attributed to it the Emperor's suffering sometimes so violently from palpitation as to lie like dead for hours together.

The letter of Wollzogen to Baron Ungnad[1] contains the

---

[1] It is given *in extenso* in Stephen Gerlach's "Turkish Diary," published at Frankfort, 1674. Gerlach was almoner to the embassy at Constantinople at the time of Maximilian's death.

following remarkable details concerning the Emperor's death at Ratisbon:

"When his Majesty grew weaker and weaker, and fears were entertained for his life, the gentlemen and councillors of the court were not allowed to speak to him about his will and other things, because of their not being quite without blemish in the matter of religion. But the old Princess of Bavaria[1] ventured to remind his Majesty that, as life was uncertain, it might be advisable to make his will, to confess himself, and to receive the sacrament. He would not listen to her, but sent her away with unkind speech. Afterwards his son, the Archduke Matthias, entreated him to think of his salvation, and not to neglect himself; to whom he made answer, 'My son, all this is needless; I hope through the mercy of God and his merits to be saved as surely as you can be. I have confessed all my sins to Christ, and thrown them on his passion and death; and I am sure that they are forgiven, and I do not need anything else. Thereupon the Bishop of Neustadt, his almoner, earnestly pointed out to him the merit and atonement of Christ, asking him whether his Majesty would live and die on it, to which he answered, 'Yes, and not otherwise.'

"After his death he was dressed in his usual clothes, with the collar of the Golden Fleece round his neck. In this guise he was laid out on black velvet for three days with his face uncovered, and crowds of people were admitted to see him.

"The body, after being embalmed, was carried to the cathedral without any further ceremonies beyond a funeral sermon and singing a few psalms, the choir being hung with black cloth. A boat was prepared for the reception of the coffin, which was placed in it under the care of his chaplains. He was first conveyed to Linz, and from thence to Bohemia, the Austrians and Bohemians having disputed for the honour of having him buried among them. The Bohemians carried the day, and he was taken to Prague to the monastery of St. James."

3.—*The family of the Emperor Maximilian II.*

The Empress of Maximilian II., Mary, the pious daughter of Charles V., immediately after the burial of her royal husband, retired to Spain; she wished to die on pure Catholic ground. She survived Maximilian by twenty-seven years, dying, at the age of seventy-five, in 1603. She was the admiration and delight of the Jesuits; and a saying is recorded of Pope Pius V., the same who in 1567 issued the famous bull *In Cœna Domini* against the heretics, that "he had sufficient information concerning her to canonise her, if it were just and proper to do so during her lifetime." Her very considerable revenues in Spain were left to the Jesuits' college in Madrid.

Maximilian had by his wife not less than sixteen children, nine sons and seven daughters.

[1] Anne, daughter of Ferdinand I. and grandmother of Ferdinand II.

1, 2. The two archdukes, Rodolph II., born in 1552, and Matthias, born in 1557, succeeded to the imperial crown.

3. Archduke Ernest, born in 1553. He was for eight years with his brother Rodolph in Spain. Count Khevenhüller describes him as "taking after his father, gay and jovial." He was during Rodolph's reign governor of Austria, and from 1593 to 1595 regent of the Spanish Netherlands. He died in 1595, at Brussels, when just going to be married to Donna Isabella, the favourite daughter of King Philip II. of Spain.

4. Maximilian, born in 1558. His career was a very chequered one. He was twice elected King of Poland; first, in 1576, against Stephen Bathory, and again, after the death of this prince, in 1587. Both times he was unable to maintain the election. In 1588 the Poles even took him prisoner after having defeated him, and he was released only after a year's captivity. Since 1585 he was grand master of the Teutonic order, and in 1600 he was entrusted with the government of the Tyrol and of the Swabian provinces of Austria. He died, unmarried, in 1618; according to others, in 1620.

5. Albert, born in 1559. At the age of eleven he accompanied his sister Anne, who in 1570 was married to Philip II., to Spain, where he was educated, and became a favourite with his brother-in-law. In 1583 he was appointed viceroy of Portugal; in 1587 he became a cardinal, and in 1594 archbishop of Toledo and primate of Spain. Five years later, after having received a dispensation to quit holy orders, he married Donna Isabella, the princess who had been intended for his brother Ernest; at the same time he was appointed regent of the Netherlands. He died without any issue in 1621.

6. Wenceslaus, born in 1561. He was sent with Albert, in 1570, to Spain; but died, at the early age of seventeen, in 1578, as grand prior of the Maltese order in Castile.

7, 8, 9. The three other princes died in infancy.

None of the sons of Maximilian II. leaving any direct heirs, the elder line of the house of Habsburg ended with the Emperor Matthias.

Of the seven daughters of Maximilian II., two were

married to the most zealous Papist princes of those times—Anne, in 1570, at the age of twenty-one, to Philip II. of Spain; and in the same year, Elizabeth, aged sixteen, to Charles IX. of France. A third daughter, Margaret, died in a convent in Spain; the others in infancy.

Maximilian II. had, before marriage, a natural daughter, Helena Scharseg. Her mother, a Countess Anne of Ostfriesland, was lady of the bedchamber to his mother. The daughter is described as a pattern of beauty and sense. She was married to a Carinthian nobleman, Baron Andrew Everard von Rauber, who won her as his prize in a match against a gigantic Spaniard, whom, according to the terms of the contest, he put in a sack and thus deposited at the feet of the Emperor. The baron was likewise a giant in size and strength. His portrait, still extant in the Nuremberg Gallery, represents him with the remarkable appendage of a beard, carefully plaited, and reaching down to the ground, and from thence back to the girdle, with a legend stating its dimensions.

Ferdinand I. and Maximilian II. were the last Emperors who (the former from necessity, the latter by his own free will) followed a moderate and a tolerant policy with regard to religion and to the Reformation. Under Rodolph II. the counter-reformation already began.

CHAPTER V

Rodolph II.—(1576-1612).

1.—His court at Prague—His antiquarian, alchemical, and magic hobbies.

RODOLPH II., eldest son of Maximilian II., was born in 1552 at Vienna. Like his father, he was brought up in Spain at the court of Philip II., where he and his brother Ernest remained from 1563 to 1571, in which latter year they made room for their two younger brothers, Albert and Wenceslaus, who had arrived at Madrid the year before with their sister Anne. Philip at that time had no sons, the death of Don Carlos having taken place in 1568. Rodolph was in charge of Adam Dietrichstein, who, going as ambassador of Maximilian II. to the Spanish court, acted as chief governor of the prince. This nobleman was married to a Spanish lady, a duchess of Cordova. Colonel Wolf von Rumpf acted under him as governor of the prince. The plan of the two courts, which, however, was not realised, was to marry the princes Rodolph and Ernest to the two daughters of Philip, Donna Isabella and Donna Catharina. Rodolph stayed long enough in Spain to see the rise of the Escurial; the first outbreak of the revolution in the Netherlands also, and the death of the unfortunate Don Carlos, who was accused of having plotted against the life of his father, took place during his residence at the court of Philip. All these events and incidents left a deep impression in the soul of Rodolph. To judge from Dietrichstein's repeated and earnest representations, the long stay at that gloomy and ever-suspecting court had a decidedly baneful effect on Rodolph. Whereas formerly he had been gentle, good-natured, timid, but a lover of justice, he now was unmanageable, moody, gloomy, and at times breaking out into fits of the fiercest passion. In his twentieth year he came back to Germany, and in 1572 he was crowned as King of Hungary, and two years after as King of Bohemia and of the Romans. His father having died in 1576, Rodolph, like him, established his court at Prague.

Unmistakable symptoms of that deep melancholy which had twice before appeared in his family manifested themselves in Rodolph before he had completed his twenty-fifth year. Yet it was not the affecting sadness of Jane of Arragon, who could never turn her thoughts from that beloved husband whom she had murdered out of jealousy; nor was it the resigned tranquil greatness of Charles V., retiring from the vanity of all earthly things into the pious solitude of Yuste. In Rodolph's case it was rather a state of moody inanition and of hardened and perverse waywardness, sometimes even of downright insanity. His principal characteristic was indolence; in this respect he was the Emperor Frederic III. over again. As the latter idled away his days at Wienerisch Neustadt, so did Rodolph at Prague. With all the impatience of a silly and naughty child, he kicked against everything in the shape of public business; this deeply rooted aversion would, however, at once give way—for a while at least—as soon as he saw anyone else actively and zealously taking the affairs of government in hand. Rodolph was then sure to be seized with envy and the gnawing pangs of jealousy.

Rodolph thus for the greater part of his time lived completely unmindful of the affairs of his own States and of the Empire. He never held another Diet after the one of Ratisbon in 1594, which the breaking out of the Turkish war forced upon him. He never after his accession came to Hungary, nor even to Vienna, where his brother Ernest resided as governor. He shut himself up in his beautiful palace, the Hradschin in Prague, where he had established his museum of art and curiosities, his alchemical laboratory, and his magic kitchen. When the German princes sent ambassadors to him, he had them apprised that he was "just now very fairly engaged with loads of other business." In the same way the envoys of Hungary and of the Austrian Diet had to wait years and years for an audience in vain. The governors and generals were left without instructions, and had to make shift as well as they could. Curiosities of every description, and the fanciful pursuits of alchemy and magic, were the only objects he took any interest in; these hobbies took up all his time. He had great treasures, but carefully stowed them away and locked them up in his chests. It was a matter of the utmost indifference to him that the councillors and courtiers could not get their pay, that sometimes even actual want made itself felt at the imperial court; an example of which is recorded in a letter of the Bavarian resident minister, Boden, to the Duke Maximilian of Bavaria, his master (dated 19th of August, 1606): "To-day the chief people of the Emperor's household have not had enough to eat, there being no money to make purchases for the kitchen."

Rodolph was in Germany the first of those amateurs who have a mania for collecting all sorts of curiosities of all times from every part of the world, whereby many works of ancient art have been preserved, just as the Codices have been by the monks. After the peace of Westphalia this mania of collecting curiosities grew a fashion among the German princes, great and small; but what at first was a mere fancy and a pleasurable pastime, became afterwards an important agent in the promotion of art, literature, and science; people, after having so long hunted after the curiosities of bygone ages, began to feel an interest in the endeavours and productions of their own times.

Rodolph's collections comprised, besides the treasures of art, many rare specimens of natural history, minerals, exotic plants, foreign birds and animals, eagles, lions, and leopards; which he knew how to tame to such a degree that they would freely walk about with him in his rooms.[1] But his principal fancy was for Roman and Greek antiquities, which his agents

---

[1] The Welsers of Augsburg, who for 1,200,000 florins, lent by Bartholomew, the grandfather of the beautiful Philippina, to Charles V., had received from this Emperor a grant of land on the western coast of South America, and had founded the town of Valparaiso in Chili, used to send to Rodolph from thence many Indian curiosities, until the Spaniards took the country from them.

purchased for him in Italy. Most of the invaluable contents of the matchless imperial collection of coins, gems, and cameos at Vienna are owing to Rodolph. Among others, he acquired two of the most precious articles of classical *vertu* in the world: the magnificent sarcophagus with the battle of the Amazons, which he got from the Fuggers at Augsburg; and the even more valuable large tazza of onyx with the apotheosis of Augustus, for which he is said to have paid 15,000 ducats. The knights of the hospital of St. John at Jerusalem brought it during the Crusades from the East to Europe, where it owed its preservation in the nunnery of Poissy near Paris to the pious illusion that it represented the crucifixion of Christ. The so-called Rodolphine Treasury (museum) at Prague enjoyed a world-wide celebrity; unfortunately, it has, with most unpardonable carelessness, been scattered during the "enlightened" eighteenth century, at the time when Joseph II. put down the monasteries. Joseph had issued a decree which public indignation obliged him soon to revoke; the venerable old castle of the Hradschin in Prague was to be converted into barracks, for which purpose it was to be empty by a certain day. The statues were sold. A torso, finding no purchaser, was flung down through the window into the garden of the palace; an oculist at Vienna, of the name of Barth, at last bought it for six siebenzehner (about three shillings). It was no other than the celebrated Ilioneus, which is now in the Glyptotheca at Munich, and which the King, at that time Crown Prince Louis of Bavaria, bought at the congress of Vienna for 6,000 ducats. The ancient coins were sold by weight. In an inventory which was drawn up of the collections, and which was preserved at the Schönfeld Museum in Vienna, there is one lot, "a naked female, bitten by a mad goose." It is not very likely that anyone would recognise in this description the "Leda with the Swan," by Titian.

Rodolph possessed the first picture-gallery of any considerable extent in Germany; in which there were, among others, the noble Correggios now in Vienna and Berlin. They were a present from the first Duke Frederic Gonzaga of Mantua to the Emperor Charles V., through whose daughter Mary, the mother of Rodolph, they probably came to Prague. The two Correggios now at Berlin, Io and Leda, had a remarkable fate. They were, in the first instance, during the Thirty Years' War, taken from Prague as plunder by the Swedes; then went with Queen Christina to Rome; and from thence passed into the Orleans Gallery, at the dispersion of which they found their way to Berlin.

Heraldry, and what pertains to it in the art of engraving seals and cutting dies of coins and medals, appears to have been cultivated in the times of Rodolph II. with such remarkable proficiency as to justify the supposition that the Emperor himself took a particular interest in these matters. A great number of letters of nobility, and of heraldic diplomas, date from the reign of Rodolph II. The seals, especially those appended to the grants of princely fiefs and honours, are executed in the most ornamented Gothic style with such neatness and elegance as to remind one of the contemporaneous Elizabethan style of architecture in England. The Rodolphine coins, compared with those of the preceding and succeeding reigns, appear like an oasis in a desert. He must have employed the most distinguished masters to engrave his seals and to cut the dies of his coins.

Rodolph was called by his courtiers the second Solomon. He indeed was wise enough to do away with jesters at his court. In this he took the lead of all other potentates. Rodolph, the pupil of Philip II., was, like his royal tutor, possessed of a store of knowledge by no means common even among professional scholars. He spoke six languages: German and Bohemian, Spanish, Italian, French, and Latin. He was particularly well versed in mechanics and in all the mathematical and physical sciences, and more especially so in the occult lore of astrology, magic, and alchemy. This is fully proved by his letters published at Vienna in 1771. He was himself a very skilful practical mechanician. His taste with regard to the fine arts was of a very high order; he was not only a collector of pictures, but he painted remarkably well himself, especially portraits. He kept up an uninterrupted correspondence with all the learned people throughout the Holy Roman Empire. Many a scholar of all the four faculties was raised by him to the nobility of the Empire, or nominated *Comes Palatinus*, or poet-laureate. He even ennobled learned Lutheran divines, as, for instance, in 1590, the son-in-law of Lucas Cranach, Dr. Polycarpus Leyser, professor at Wittenberg, and afterwards first preacher at the court of Dresden.

But the people whom Rodolph prized above all others were those who ministered to his fancy for everything that was curious or wonderful. There were always living at his court a number of clock and instrument makers and painters, with whom he used to work; a host of astronomers and astrologers, who had to draw up horoscopes, to make prophetical almanacs, and to calculate astrological points for him. He kept up a constant intercourse with alchemists, Rosicrucians, and adepts of every sort, whose ranks, it is true, in several instances, comprised not a few impostors, quacks, and needy adventurers. These conjurors undertook to prophesy from magnetic mirrors or from boiling water; they promised to find for the Emperor the elixir of life and the philosopher's stone; and, even more than that, they gravely engaged in experiments to produce men, actual human beings, in the crucible, and to resuscitate mummies.

Dr. John Dee, the celebrated English alchemist and necromancer, was one of the most conspicuous characters among this motley crowd. Rodolph at one time had the very highest opinion of Dee. Each looked upon the other as a great magician, and they were not a little afraid of each other. Even a man like Count Khevenhüller fully believed that Rodolph saw in his magic mirror the remote future, and that he was able by means of his magnets to read the most hidden thoughts of persons living at a distance. When, in 1598, Count Adolphus Schwarzenberg had taken Raab from the Turks, and sent Colonel von Buchheim to convey the report to the Emperor, the colonel was not a little surprised at finding that his Majesty was already cognisant of it. "The Emperor," Count Khevenhüller writes, "told him that they had known it by means of an art, taught them by an

Englishman, of giving signals at a distance by moonlight with two mirrors and a magnet; and that Schwarzenberg had had a mirror thus prepared, and his Majesty another." Dee returned in 1590 to London, where Queen Elizabeth gave him a pension, As James I., being a despiser of the "art sublime," stopped the payment of the pittance, Dee prepared to leave his country a second time, when death prevented him. He died at Mortlake in 1608, at the age of eighty-two.

Edward Kelly, a friend and coadjutor of Dee, was less lucky with Rodolph. The Emperor at first created him a baron of Bohemia; but when afterwards the adept was either unwilling or unable to produce gold, he was in 1590, by the order of his imperial patron, imprisoned in a Bohemian castle, where he remained for six years. Queen Elizabeth, at the entreaties of Dee, interceded for him, but in vain. At last Kelly tried to gain his liberty by his own efforts, lowering himself from the castle by a rope; but he broke his leg in the attempt, and died soon after of the consequences of the fall.

Of itinerant adepts, who from time to time made their appearance at Rodolph's court, two famous Italians, living in the grandest style, are to be mentioned. These philosophers, who during the last half of the sixteenth century were the astonishment of the whole of Europe, bore the names of Marco Bragadino and Hieronymus Scotto. Marco Bragadino was a native of Famagusta in Cyprus, and made his appearance at several German courts, where he presented himself under the title of Count "*Illustrissimus.*" His proper name was Mamugna. He was of Greek extraction, but he represented himself as the son of Marco Antonio Bragadino, the Venetian governor of Famagusta, who at the fall of that place, in 1571, was made prisoner and killed by the Turks. On his first coming out as an adept in the East, he went by his real name of Mamugna. In 1578 he appeared as Conde Mamugnano in Italy, and showed himself with the greatest magnificence in the circles of the *nobili* at Venice, whom he greatly astonished by making gold at the Contarini and

Dandolo palaces. In 1588 he came as Conde Marco Bragadino to Germany, pretending to be persecuted by his family. Accompanied by two large black bulldogs, which were to convince people of his power over the spirits, he arrived at Prague. Here he was regarded as a second Paracelsus, as he treated gold like brass or quicksilver, giving away large lumps of it, and always keeping an open table. This Illustrissimus, however, came to a very ignominious end at Munich, whither he repaired from Prague. His deceptions having been found out, he died in the Bavarian capital on the gallows, in 1590.

Even a greater sensation was created by another Italian, Count Hieronymus Scotto, a native of Parma. Khevenhüller expressly states that the whole of Europe had resounded with the achievements of this man of wonders. He travelled in Germany from 1573, showed himself at Nuremberg, Cologne, and other places, and made gold. It was he who, in 1583, by the phantasmagoria of a magic mirror, made the Elector of Cologne, Gerard Truchsess, fall in love with the beautiful Countess Agnes of Mansfeld, for which that spiritual prince lost his see and his country. At a later period, in 1592, the handsome, clever, and insinuating adventurer earned little honour at Coburg, where he succeeded in ruining the Duchess Ann, the wife of the duke and daughter of the Elector Augustus of Saxony. The unhappy princess expiated her folly by a captivity of twenty years. This Hieronymus Scotto was a frequent and ever-welcome guest at the court of Prague.

Rodolph's physicians, Thaddäus von Hayek, Martin Ruhland, and Michael Mayer, were likewise celebrated alchemists. Michael Mayer, a native of Rendsburg in Holstein, acted besides as private secretary of the Emperor, and also was a Comes Palatinus and an Eques Auratus. He was Rodolph's favourite writer, recording the Emperor's own ideas and experiences; he was, moreover, a Rosicrucian and a very fertile author. His works, bearing the mysterious title "Chevalier Impérial," created an immense sensation. They were most of them published at Frankfort on the Maine, and some were translated into French. Having afterwards entered the service of the Landgrave Maurice of Hesse Cassel, Mayer died at Magdeburg in 1622. Rodolph's valets were chiefly engaged as assistants in his unceasing alchemical operations. One of them, Mordecai de Delle, a native of Vitri, in the duchy of Milan, acted the part of court poet, putting, for the amusement of his master, all the stories of adepts into German rhymes, which were exquisitely illustrated by some of the court painters. All itinerant alchemists were welcome at Rodolph's court; he always had some of them with him, and rewarded them most liberally if the experiments were to his satisfaction. Those who did not come of their own accord he sent for from all parts of the Holy Roman Empire. Thus he once ordered the magistrate of Strassburg to send to him, under an escort, Philip Jacob Güstenhöver; and, when the adept made his escape from Prague, Rodolph had him brought back by force. With alchemists of note in foreign countries the Emperor kept up an active correspondence, and he was generally called by the masters of the craft "the Prince of Alchemy," the German "*Hermes Trismegistus.*" It has been considered as a proof of his having really been an adept, that after his death there were found among his effects, besides an ash-grey tincture, eighty-four hundredweights of gold and sixty hundredweights of silver melted down into ingots of the form of bricks.

Yet there were some scholars of the highest celebrity and merit at Rodolph's court. Among these, three astronomers, the two Danes, Tycho de Brahe and Longomontanus, and the great Würtemberger, John Kepler, and the Bohemian historian, Wenceslaus Hagec, are to be mentioned. Kepler by himself is one of the greatest names of any time. He proclaimed to the world from Prague the discovery which has become the foundation of the whole system of modern astronomy, the discovery of the planets moving in elliptic orbits round the sun. The book "Nova Astronomia de Stella Martis," Kepler's most celebrated work, was published in 1609. He lived twelve years at Rodolph's court, having been appointed after the death of Tycho de Brahe, in 1601, as " His Imperial Majesty's Mathematician," with the modest salary of 1,500 florins, which was not always even regularly paid to him; so that, having afterwards entered the service of Wallenstein, he had to go and solicit for the payment of the arrears to Ratisbon, where the Emperor Ferdinand at that time resided with his court. And there the great man, as is well known, died of hunger in 1630. Kepler's principal work, written at Prague, was the celebrated Rodolphine Tables, thus called in honour of the Emperor. Besides this, he published, for the benefit of his patron, in 1601, the " Fundamenta Astrologiæ;" and in 1608, the " Explicit Report of the Comet of September, 1607, and its Bodings" (the celebrated one of Halley); to which is added, "A new, curious, but well-founded Discourse as to what Comets really are, and how far they are meant to instruct Mankind;" and in 1610, " Warning to some Divines, Physicians, and Philosophers, whilst justly rejecting Astrological Superstition, not to pluck out the Wheat with the Tares."

2.—The Italians at the imperial court—First beginnings of military rule—The first camarilla of clerks and valets.

Ever since the days of Charles V. and Ferdinand I., Spanish and Italian families had been transplanted to the Austrian court; as, for instance, the Spanish family De Hoyos, whose ancestor came, in 1520, with Ferdinand, and whose descendants are still among the high nobility of Austria; and the Italian Tyrolese Madruzzi, whose name is frequently mentioned as connected with the court intrigues of those times. But when, in 1593, after a truce of twenty-five years, subsequent to Soleyman's death before Szigeth, the Turkish war broke out again, a number of Spanish, Italian, and also Walloon adventurers and fortune-hunters entered the imperial army, which, owing to the Emperor's utter indifference to business, they soon got completely under their own control. This gave rise in Austria to that peculiar military rule which, after being more fully developed in the

Thirty Years' War, reached its fearful climax in the degenerate times of the Turkish and Hungarian campaigns under Leopold I. Among the military adventurers under Rodolph are to be mentioned the fierce, rapacious Italians Basta and Belgiojoso, the rough Venetian Count Rombaldo Collalto, the Spanish commander Don Balthazar Maradas, and the Walloon Dampierre. The three latter have every one of them played a conspicuous part in the Thirty Years' War. All these officers made their career, or at least began it, in Hungary.

Some Croat generals also began at that time to rise into eminence; among others the Kollonitch and the Isolanis. Baron John Mark Isolani, the father of the celebrated Croat general, descending from a family of the island of Cyprus, gained a victory over the Turks as early as 1596. The Kollonitch were in 1638 raised by the Emperor Ferdinand III. to the rank of counts, and under Leopold I., in 1676, all of them left the Lutheran for the Romish faith. One of them who, during the siege of Vienna by the Turks in 1683, was bishop of that see, wielded his pastoral power with such energy and heroism that the Grand Vizier threatened to have his head cut off if he could get hold of him.

But it was chiefly the Italians who, in the time of Rodolph, began to gain a firm footing at court and to form a strong and organised party. We find already a great number of Italians even among those who were nearest the Emperor. His master of the horse was Count Claudio Trivulzi; his gentlemen of the bedchamber the two Maltese knights, Ottavio Spinola, of a Genoese family, and Baron Colloredo. Of the latter family there were four in the imperial service, one of whom died in England in 1586 as imperial ambassador to Queen Elizabeth. Besides these we find belonging to the household of the Emperor, in different capacities, as cup-bearers, keepers of the privy purse, &c., the names of Gonzaga, Montecuculi, Trivulzi, Caretto, Millesimo, Malaspina, Strasoldo, Castaldo. These courtiers formed the nucleus of the Italian party which under Matthias, and especially under Ferdinand II., was swelled by a great many new arrivals.

Besides the Italians there was another sort of people at court, who, being always about the Emperor, enjoyed a great share of his favour, and thereby acquired great influence. These people were the lower personal attendants, part of whose business it was to assist him in his alchemical operations. Some of them, like Mordecai de Delle, were likewise Italians. Rodolph, for the very reason of his living in such complete retirement, wanted officious informers to supply him with news. This was done by his valets, to whom the Emperor, in his suspecting and ever mistrustful way, used to lend a willing ear. " From Rodolph," says Hormayr, "*dates the habit of the later Austrian Emperors of showing themselves mistrustful and taciturn towards their ministers and the higher aristocracy, and on the other hand familiar to their clerks and lacqueys.*"

The Habsburg rulers had, as it were, an instinctive perception of the necessity of keeping the proud and encroaching native aristocracy at bay; they therefore used mean-born foreign upstarts, clerks, and servants as a sort of barrier behind which the monarch might breathe more freely. Adventurers, recommended and pushed on by his Majesty's valets, ruled at the Hradschin in Prague, and carried orders from thence to Austria and Hungary. Even the grooms had an important standing at court, the stables being the Emperor's favourite haunt. Great influence was also possessed by the many artful courtesans, with whose tribe Rodolph, who never married, continued through life to carry on an ever alternating intercourse, the reign of his ephemeral sultanas frequently lasting even less than a week.

The cause of Rodolph remaining unmarried was a horoscope drawn for him by Tycho de Brahe. Its purport was "that he ought not to marry, as danger was threatening him from his nearest relation, his own son." It had been the intention of his father, and of Philip II., to marry him to Donna Isabella, the daughter of the latter, although the princess at the time of Rodolph leaving Spain had not yet completed her sixth year. The actual negotiations with reference to this marriage began, according to Khevenhüller, as early as in 1579, when the Infanta was not more than thirteen; but she reached the age of thirty-three before she was brought to the altar, Rodolph having put off his final decision for nearly twenty years. Philip, anxious to see his favourite daughter married before he was gathered to his ancestors, gave the Emperor a last respite of six months. Rodolph, however, came to no decision. The Infanta then married his younger brother Albert, with whom she went to the Netherlands, the regency of which she brought to her husband as her dowry. Her father did not live to see her marriage; he died in 1598, after having been nursed by her through the dreadful malady of which he died. Rodolph was very angry at this marriage of his brother; and just as angry was he when, in the following year, another lady, Mary of Medici, on whom he had likewise cast his eyes, was to his great surprise wedded to Henry IV. of France.

Besides these two matrimonial projects, Rodolph, who sent for the portraits of the most beautiful princesses from all the different courts, had entertained in succession five others: with two princesses of the Styrian branch of his own house, with another of the house of Lorrain, and even with a Russian and a Wallachian princess.

In 1600, after the failure of the marriage with Donna Isabella and of that with Mary of Medici, Matthias, Rodolph's brother, entreated the Emperor, if he himself would not marry, to secure the succession lawfully to him, as the eldest of the house after him. According to the authenticated statement published by Hammer, in his "Life of Cardinal Clesel," Barons Rumpf and Trautson, Rodolph's chief favourites, interceded for Matthias, which at once induced their ever suspicious master to banish both of them from his presence to their estates. Eight years after Rodolph was forced by Matthias to grant what he had refused to do voluntarily.

During this period, from 1600 to 1608, Rodolph's gloomy moodiness reached its highest pitch. Against Matthias he had conceived an unconquerable antipathy. Halley's comet, which made its appearance in 1607, strengthened his fear of murderous designs from his family, which the awful meteor seemed to him quite unmistakably to prognosticate. In vain the learned and sensible Kepler tried to turn him from these apprehensions. His mistrust grew to such a height that he listened to all the slanderous gossip and denunciations of his lowest menials. He went so far as to cause all those who approached him to be searched whether they had any arms concealed about their persons. Even his numerous mistresses had to submit to this regulation. Fear made him seclude himself in his castle at Prague. His bedroom was like a fortified place. He would often jump out of bed and order the governor of the palace to search, in the middle of night, every nook and corner of the imperial residence. Precautions were taken everywhere against the possibility of a surprise. Whilst attending mass, which he now only did on the highest festivals, he sat in a high, covered pew, the front of which was very closely latticed. For greater security during his promenades, he had long and spacious passages built on purpose, with narrow sloping apertures like loopholes, through which he need not fear to be shot at. These passages led to his magnificent stables, where he liked to be, and where, consequently, he passed much of his time. There he used to meet his mistresses; and there he kept his special pets, a number of the most splendid horses; but only for the pleasure of looking at them, as from fear for his life he never ventured out on horseback.

Daniel l'Hermite of Antwerp, who was attached to the Florentine embassy which the Duke Cosmo II., in 1609, sent to the German courts, has left in the account of his journey, which he published in German, a description of the Emperor's person and appearance. Rodolph was, when he saw him, in his fifty-eighth year. "The Emperor," he says, "is advanced in years, but his hair and beard have prematurely turned grey. He is of rather stately presence; his brow majestic; his mouth not unpleasing; his eyes sparkling, but nearly covered by his beetling eyebrows. He is of middle size, and he stoops a little, which is a peculiar feature of the princes of the house of Habsburg. But you may see at once that the Emperor is the Emperor. He still wears his clothes after the old fashion, deeming it requisite to his grandeur not to make any change in his costume. He is dressed in a short cloak trimmed with gold, and in a Spanish doublet over his girded trunk-hose. As we entered his cabinet he was standing in the background, leaning his hand on a table. Thus he received the embassy."

The people of Prague did not often know for months whether Rodolph was living or dead; only on particularly joyful occasions, as in 1603, after a victory over the Turks, he showed himself to his faithful lieges from the window of the palace. At last he was never seen by anyone. The people suspected that his favourites were concealing his death to appropriate his treasure. Then, after having allowed himself long to be entreated, and as at the same time a dangerous riot had broken out, he again presented himself at the window to pacify the assembled populace. He would sit for hours in moody silence, looking from his easy chair at the clockmakers and painters who were working under his eyes in his apartments; sometimes also he himself worked with them. But if anyone interrupted him during his meditations or his work, his Majesty, flying into a towering rage, assailed the unlucky intruder with a volley not only of abuse, but also of more dangerous missiles in the shape of tools, utensils, or anything that came first to hand. Such sudden fits of flinging even the most costly things about, and of smashing everything near him, would also happen when any annoying thought disturbed the monotonous listlessness of his pondering melancholy. In fact he was at times neither more nor less than a madman. As long as these fits lasted his servants and favourites were obliged to keep out of his way. He once even pointed his sword to the breast of his lord chamberlain. Now and then he had visits from some princes of the Empire. Duke Henry Julius of Brunswick especially, who, as president of the privy council, had frequent occasions to see him, was his faithful friend and boon companion, and would drink his old Hungarian wine with him. The Elector Christian II. of Saxony also applied himself with such zeal to the same generous beverage, that, on taking leave of the Emperor in

1610, he assured his royal host that he had been so hospitably entertained by his Majesty in Prague as scarcely to to have been sober for one hour during the whole time.

The Emperor repeatedly received ambassadors from the most remote countries. In 1597 an embassy arrived from the Shah of Persia to urge him to continue the Turkish war. The envoys were a couple of Armenians, father and son, from Djulfar on the Persian Gulf. Don Giacomo, the father, had been in Germany fourteen years before. Three other times, in 1601, 1604, and 1610, the ruler of Persia—no other than the great Shah Abbas—sent ambassadors to Rodolph. In 1601 Sin Ali Bey made his appearance, accompanied by that remarkable Briton, Anthony Sharley, who had eaten with Abbas from the same dish and drunk from the same cup. He and his brother, Robert Sharley, who came to Prague in 1610, were raised by Rodolph to the rank of counts of the Empire, Anthony having in the meanwhile entered the Spanish service. Robert Sharley,[1] as Khevenhüller states, " was dressed in black velvet, and wore on his head a Persian turban surmounted by a golden cross studded with precious stones, in token of his being a Christian and a faithful Roman Catholic. He visited all the churches in Rome, and also went from Rome to Spain." In 1595 and 1599 ambassadors arrived from the Grand Duke of Muscovy, and in 1600 a Turkish embassy. But it was generally very difficult for persons who had any business at court to get at the Emperor. Months might sometimes pass without their finding any chance of access to him. He was either shut up in his apartments or in his laboratories, or in his observatory, or in his menagerie; or in the gardens of the Hradschin, where trees, shrubs, and flowers from all parts of the world were growing round grottoes, with magic mirrors and water-works, from which the strains of sweet music were pouring forth.

Whoever wished to secure an interview with Rodolph—even ambassadors and persons of exalted rank—had to disguise themselves as grooms, as an audience could only be obtained of him in his magnificent stables. But even here

---

[1] No other than Sir Robert Shirley.—*Translator*.

it was dangerous to approach the eccentric, violent sovereign. Eva, the daughter of George Popel of Lobkowitz, who, in 1594, had fallen into disgrace, had, by means of a bribe, been admitted to that singular audience-hall, to entreat for the life and liberty of her father, when, fortunately, an honest groom kept her back, telling her that she would not be the first lady applying to his Majesty in affairs of importance, and falling there in the stable a victim to the lust of the royal madman. The ruin of Lobkowitz, who had formerly been all in all to Rodolph, was very likely brought about by the Jesuits, against whom he used very strong language at the Diet of Ratisbon in 1594. He died of grief in 1607, after a captivity of thirteen years. Rodolph then ordered his head to be cut off after his death, and from that time all the great lords of Bohemia turned against the Emperor.

Rodolph, with all his uncontrollable passions, was a strictly devout son of the Romish Church, joining the processions, even in the midst of winter, with uncovered head and with taper in hand.

3.—*Reformation and counter-reformation in Austria.*

Whilst Rodolph was idling away his time in Prague, the management of Austria Proper was left to the Jesuit councillors of the Emperor. In the fierce contest which thus arose between the Papist government and the zealously Protestant Estates of the archduchy the balance remained long undecided, until at last the Jesuits carried the day by the help of one of their greatest pupils, Ferdinand of Styria (Grätz), afterwards known as Emperor Ferdinand II.

The Reformation had found its way into Austria soon after Luther's first appearance. Charles V. tried to put down the new creed with fire and sword. In 1524 the burgher Caspar Tauber, of Vienna, became the first martyr of the new religious movement. In 1528 Balthazar Hubmayer, formerly a professor at the university of Ingolstadt, who had long been kept a prisoner at the Kärthner Thurm (the Carinthian Tower), was burnt near Erdberg, over against the Lower Prater, on the same spot where Richard Cœur de Lion was captured. But the new tenets soon gained ground and kept it. As early as in 1541, the Protestants in Austria felt themselves so strong already as to petition Ferdinand I., at that time in Prague, to grant them equal rights with the Papists in the exercise of their religion, —the inhabitants of Vienna being among the petitioners. Great numbers of young Austrian nobles went to study at Protestant universities, and several of them filled the honorary post of rector at Wittenberg and at Prague. After the peace of Passau, in 1552, the Reformation spread even more widely. In Austria, as elsewhere in Germany, the nobility were principally tempted by the spoil of the ecclesiastical estates. The heads of the movement were the Jörgers of Herrnals, especially the great champion of Protestantism Helmhard Jörger, president of the chamber of representatives of Lower Austria. With these Jörgers Luther exchanged a great many letters since 1525, when he sent them a preacher. Besides them, the Hagers of Alensteig, the Thonradls of Thernberg and Ebergassing, the Buchheims of Aspang, the Hoffmanns of Strechau, and many others, were zealous Protestants. Within the territories of these lords the monks and nuns were frequently expelled from their houses, the monasteries and churches ransacked and demolished, the statues and pictures of saints profaned, and the Roman Catholic livings left vacant for years, whilst the Protestant patrons appropriated the revenues. The movement spread from the nobility to the burghers and the peasantry. The abolition of the tithes was a bait for the people, as the clerical estates were for the nobility. Among these ranks of society also examples of a fanatical spirit of persecution were not wanting. The burghers made laws among themselves not to admit any Roman Catholic into the council, nor even to engage a Papist servant. The processions of Corpus Christi had to be discontinued, in order to prevent fights among the two religious parties in the streets. No priest dared read mass on week days, nor carry the sacrament to the dying without an escort. In 1549 a

Lutheran baker's boy in Vienna pushed into a procession, snatched the host from the hand of the priest, and flung it on the ground with imprecations against idolatrous abomination. He was burnt by a slow fire, after having his tongue and his hand cut off. Yet the only effect of these cruel punishments was to call forth so much the fiercer exasperation on the part of the followers of the new creed. All comedies, masquerades, and sledge-processions were full of abuse and ridicule of the Papists. In 1561 matters had gone so far that all these public popular amusements had to be prohibited. Ladies of Protestantised families were so conversant with gospel lore as to do duty as missionaries among the Catholics. Where gentle persuasion was of no avail, the Protestants had recourse to violence for the purpose of making converts. The followers of the old creed were not unfrequently pounced upon in the dead of night. It even happened, on the instigation of a pastor, Strohmeyer, that Nicholas Baron von Buchheim was treacherously murdered in the night at his own castle by the noble lord of Hofkirchen and Schönkirchen, who, under the pretext of a friendly visit, became his assassin. In fact, nothing could exceed the fanaticism and the bloodthirsty bigotry with which the Protestant preachers denounced their opponents from the pulpits. Their flocks only too readily took the cue from them; and the Lutherans were heard publicly to declare that they "would rather live in peace with the Turks than with the Roman Catholics." The introduction of the improved calendar, the necessity of which had so long made itself felt, was obstinately opposed in Vienna by the Protestants as the first letter in the Pope's alphabet, by which he only wanted to throw the noose over their horns, so that they might no longer be able to ward off his tyranny in the church of God. The prelates, provosts, abbots, and monks married and had families, after having divided the property of their chapters and conventual estates between them, which they sold, bartered, and mortgaged at their own pleasure, a proceeding for which they were publicly commended by the preachers from their pulpits.

The policy of Ferdinand I. with regard to the encroachments of the Protestants had been very forbearing, owing to the necessity of the times. Far from turning all the severity of the law against the new doctrine, he contented himself with keeping down the wild convulsions of fanatical party spirit until an imperial Diet or general council should have decided on the dispute. He merely issued a strict general edict that no one should dare to enter on any bargain with clerical personages concerning the alienation or mortgage of church property. During the first years of his reign he tried to induce the headstrong Pope Paul IV. to give his express sanction to the administration of the sacrament in both kinds, which the Pontiff until then had only connived at, and also to the marriage of the priests. The Emperor, moreover, protested against several disciplinary decisions of the Council of Trent; but that assembly, in its final session of 1563, pronounced for an entire and irrevocable rupture with the Protestant heretics.

The decrees of Trent, however, did not prevent Maximilian, the son and successor of Ferdinand I., from showing even greater toleration than his father had done. The Protestants already ventured publicly and freely to call him "a pillar of their doctrine." The Emperor, indeed, was enlightened enough to see in this religious antagonism the great evil of the age, for which he knew no other remedy but the open sufferance of the Protestants. He proclaimed accordingly in 1567 and 1568 free exercise of religion in Bohemia and Austria. The Protestant country gentlemen and noblemen in Austria were allowed perfect religious liberty at their châteaux and on their lands; they were, moreover, allowed to take their preachers to Vienna, and to admit anyone who wished to hear them to their places of worship. In 1574 the Protestants of Vienna were permitted to have regular religious service at the Laudhaus (the locality of the chamber of representatives), and afterwards also at the church of the Minorites.

It was the favourite plan of Maximilian II., at the head of a Christian army of Crusaders, and in alliance with Muscovy and Persia, to reconquer the countries taken from Hungary and to drive the Turks back to Asia. To pave the way for this vast plan he tried to gain the affection of the Protestant estates of Austria, and the assistance of the Protestant princes of the Empire. But in the last years of his life he found himself compelled to tighten the reins again, and to take repressive measures. The Reformation gained more and more ground, extending even to Bavaria. Here also great numbers of the people, and more especially of the nobles, embraced the new faith.

Under Rodolph, who never left Prague, the Austrian Protestants proceeded to open hostilities. The burghers of Vienna, joined by those of the country nobles who happened to be present in the capital, made an attempt to extort, by revolutionary means, perfect equality for the followers of the Reformed religion with the Roman Catholics. Upwards of 5,000 men appeared in arms at the imperial castle (the Hofburg) where Archduke Ernest, the Emperor's brother, resided. He promised to report about their case to his Majesty. Tranquillity was thus restored for the present, and after the lapse of about a year the ringleaders were brought to justice and condemned to death. Rodolph, however, mitigated the punishment to perpetual exile. In 1578 a Protestant of the name of John Schwartzenthaler was elected rector of the university of Vienna, in direct breach of the laws and of the oath prescribed by the statutes. This election was quashed by the Emperor; but the nobles now began, contrary to their pledge, to force the inhabitants of towns and boroughs, as well as their own vassals, to embrace the Protestant religion; in fact, nothing was left undone to wrest every day new concessions from the court. Whilst thus the prospects of the Protestants grew more and more promising, their cause received the first shock by the discords of their own preachers, who split on the Flacian controversy about original sin and grace. Dr. Opitz, the preacher at the Landhaus chapel at Vienna, gave himself up to the most outrageous Flacianism, for which the Emperor had him expelled not only from the town, but also from the Austrian dominions. In vain Dr. Lucas

Backmayster—sent, at the request of the Austrian representatives, by the celebrated Dean (superintendent) of Rostock, David Chyträus, to hold a visitation of the Protestant Church of Austria—exerted himself to restore order among the preachers. After having wasted his labour on them for nine months, he returned to Rostock, stoutly refusing to accept the post of "Superintendent" of the Austrian Protestant Church.

The last occasion for repelling violence by violence was at a riot of the peasants in the cantons above and below the confluence of the Erns, in 1595 and 1596. They had marched, 1,200 or 1,500 men strong, to the abbey of Lilienfeld, and had laid siege to St. Pölten. Heavy taxes, forced levies for the Turkish war, and persecution of the Protestant faith had exasperated them. Gotthard Starhemberg crushed them. On the plain of Steinfeld, near Wilhelmsburg, they were completely defeated by the imperial troops, and their ringleaders broken on the wheel and decapitated at Vienna.

As soon as the Jesuits became aware of the dissension in the Protestant camp they began in Austria the counter-reformation. The man who restored Popery in Austria, and very nearly made it triumph again throughout Germany, was Ferdinand of Grätz. His father, Archduke Charles, who died in 1590, had, ten years after Maximilian's having granted religious liberty to Austria, followed his example in his countries of Styria, Carniola, and Carinthia. When Charles afterwards attempted to introduce only two Roman Catholics into the town council of Grätz, he had the mortification to see his commissaries expelled and ill-treated. The Bishop of Gurk and the papal nuncio having been grossly insulted in a riot, Charles came in all haste from the watering-place of Mannersdorf, where he was staying for his health. The vexation at these annoying occurrences became the cause of his death. *When Ferdinand, in 1596, celebrated Easter in his capital of Grätz he was almost the only one who took the sacrament according to the Romish rite, there being not more than three Papists besides him in the town. In the whole of the archduchy of Austria there were, of all the noble houses, only five, in Carinthia seven, and in Styria not more than one,*[1] *that had remained Papists.* All the patronage, government of the provinces, administration of the revenue, besides the arsenals and the command of the mercenaries, were in the hands of Protestants. But Ferdinand said, "I too will be master in my country as the Electors of Saxony and the Palatinate are in theirs."

Ferdinand had been brought up at Ingolstadt by the Jesuits, together with his friend the Elector Maximilian of Bavaria, whose father, Duke William V., called by the Jesuits "the pious duke," was his uncle by the mother's side and afterwards his guardian. About the end of the year 1597 Ferdinand set out on a pilgrimage to Loretto, and afterwards to Rome. Here he took, at the feet of Pope Clement VIII., the vow to restore, even at the peril of his own life, the Roman Catholic religion. The reverend fathers of the Society of Jesus became his main supporters. At the age of not more than twenty he began under their guidance the great work of the counter-reformation.

First of all he issued, in September, 1598, a decree in virtue of which all the Lutheran preachers were to leave his countries of Styria, Carniola, and Carinthia. In 1599 the Protestant church in his capital, Grätz, the centre of Protestantism in his territories, was closed, and all Protestant worship prohibited under punishment of imprisonment and death. The Estates remonstrated against it; reminded him of the privileges which his father had granted, and *which he himself on his accession had sworn to respect*. They, moreover, refused to him their aid against the Turks, and Ehrenreich von Saurau, under-land marshal (lord-lieutenant) of Styria, said to him one day, that he should take care lest he "might fare as the King of Spain had done in the Netherlands." But Ferdinand remained immovable as a rock. He sent the commissaries charged with the counter-reformation, with a host of German soldiers, about the country; it was the prototype of the Dragonnade of Louis XIV. in France. The country people at their approach cried out in terror, "The reform is coming." Everywhere the Protestant churches

---

[1] The Herberstorfs, whose house became extinct in 1629.

were burnt down, blasted with powder, or otherwise demolished, and a gibbet and gallows erected on the spot where they had stood. The preachers were either exiled or imprisoned, *and thousands of Bibles and prayer-books burnt by the hands of the hangman.* The inhabitants who refused to return to the Romish faith were forced to emigrate, being at the same time mulcted of one-tenth of their property. One of those who at that time had to fly from Grätz was the celebrated astronomer Kepler, who had been appointed there by the Estates as professor, and who now went to Prague to the Emperor Rodolph. Ferdinand, with thorough-paced Papist zealotry, had even the churchyards of the Protestants dug up; an outrage which he afterwards repeated in Bohemia, where he disturbed the graves of the Hussites. For five years the commission of the counter-reformation thus raged in the country, where the inhabitants were as if completely stupefied. The country nobles of the three provinces under the sway of Ferdinand fled to Bohemia, and it was especially owing to these aristocratic refugees that the flame of rebellion afterwards blazed so fiercely in the kingdom. The Counts Thurn, the Tschernembls, Thonradls, Jörgers, Hagers, Hoffmanns, Auerspergs, Wurmbrands, Tiefenbachs, Pollheims, Wollzogens, and others, were none of them native Bohemians.

Ferdinand's example was followed in due time by Rodolph's councillors at Vienna. They were headed by the Cardinal Francis Dietrichstein, bishop of Olmütz, and by the Bishop of Vienna, Melchior Clesel.

Francis Dietrichstein was born in 1570 at Madrid. His father Adam was lord chamberlain to the Emperor Rodolph. Francis had in Rome by public controversies attracted the attention of the Holy Father and of the Sacred College. He became chamberlain to the Pope, canon of Olmütz and Breslau, and, at the age of twenty-eight, a cardinal and bishop of Olmütz. Diplomatic business led him to Naples, to Madrid, and to Brussels. After the fall of the Hungarian border fortress of Kanischa, in 1600, he obtained for the Emperor the aid of all the Italian courts, whereupon Rodolph, in acknowledgment of his services, appointed him governor of the archduchy of Austria, and afterwards president of the privy council.

Clesel, born in 1553, was, like Cardinal Wolsey, of very humble extraction, the son of a Lutheran baker at Vienna. Having been converted in early youth by the Jesuit Father Scherer, he in his turn converted his own parents. He received his education at Ingolstadt, then the headquarters of the order; after which he quickly made his way, being first nominated provost of the chapter of St. Stephen. Then, in rapid succession, chancellor of the university of Vienna, preacher to the court, and imperial councillor. In 1558, at the early age of thirty-five, he obtained the see of Neustadt; ten years later, that of Vienna.

Dietrichstein and Clesel sent round commissaries of the counter-reformation in the archduchy of Austria also; and here, too, the old Protestant preachers and schoolmasters had to leave the country. The Austrian Estates, on their side, leagued themselves against this reactionary aggression; and when Matthias, in 1608, was appointed Regent of Austria, they concluded an offensive and defensive alliance at the celebrated congress of Horn. They also joined the Evangelical Union entered into the same year by the princes of the Empire at Ahausen.

4.—*State of Hungary—The Bohemian "Royal Letter"—Rupture with Matthias—Deposition of Rodolph—Latter days and death of Rodolph II.*

In the midst of these stirring times, the Emperor Rodolph was forced to abdicate, or rather was deposed. The approximate cause of this event was the danger of a Turkish invasion and the insurrection of Stephen Botskay, the Prince of Transylvania, against Austria. Rodolph, who since his election as Emperor had never been to Hungary, contented himself with keeping garrisons of German mercenaries in the fortresses of that country. These troops were commanded by the generals George Basta and Count John Jacob Belgiojoso.[1] These two men, as governors and chief commanders, treated the unfortunate Hungarians worse even than the Turks did. Rodolph never checked them. Very rarely some imperial orders would arrive from Prague. The troops, being left without pay, indemnified themselves by plunder, arson, and murder. Ever since that time fierce mastiffs are called in Hungary Bastas. The Jesuits tried to crush the Protestants in Hungary also; the churches of Kaschau and Clausenburg in Transylvania were taken from them by force. In 1593 the Turks recommenced the war which had been in abeyance since the death of Soleyman in 1566. Just before this campaign, the famous Aulic Council of War (*Hofkriegsrath*) was instituted, which has since so often proved the bane of the Austrian arms. It did not then do much harm to the Turks, who, in 1594, took the important fortress of Raab, which fortunately was reconquered by surprise in 1598, by Adolph Schwarzenberg[2] and Nicolas Pallfy. The cruelty of Basta and Belgiojoso caused the Transylvanians to throw themselves into the arms of the Turks. In 1605 Stephen Botskay, who the year before had, with the consent of the Porte, been elected by the Transylvanians for their prince, rose against the power which was wielded under the name of Rodolph. Basta was driven back to Pressburg, and the Heyducks (Rascians) revolted and extended their forays to the very gates of Vienna. Yet Rodolph turned a deaf ear to every proposal of peace.

In this perilous conjuncture, at last all the archdukes agreed, at Vienna, upon the celebrated act of the 25th of April, 1606, in virtue of which Rodolph was forced to resign the government of Austria Proper and of Hungary. The

---

[1] Basta had risen from a drummer-boy to the rank of general-in-chief. His family came from Naples, whither it had immigrated from Epirus in Greece. Rodolph raised him, in 1605, to the rank of a count of the Empire. He died in Vienna in 1607, leaving one son; but the family now seems to be extinct. Belgiojoso was a scion of the Milanese house of Barbiano. He died in 1626 on his estates near Liége.

[2] It was on this occasion that the Schwarzenberg coat-of-arms was charged with a raven, the German word for which is *Rabe*, or *Rab*.

resignation was to be effected in favour of his much-hated brother Matthias, "as the senior of the house." The reason put forward in this act was that unfortunately it was too plain that his Roman Imperial Majesty, their (the archdukes') brother and cousin, owing to his dangerous fits of derangement, was neither equal to, nor fit for the conduct of the government of his countries.

The chief mover of this famous " Vienna Family Treaty " was Clesel, bishop of Vienna and Neustadt, who, however, acted with the perfect consent of the archdukes. Rodolph, being apprised of it, wanted to have him arrested at Prague; on which Clesel, to escape from the imperial anger, had to conceal himself, and to fly in disguise from Prague to Vienna. Yet even there Rodolph sought after his life. He had, as Khevenhüller states, an almost miraculous escape. One day, as he was going from Baden near Vienna to Neustadt, where some gentlemen had invited him to breakfast, the six horses of his coach growing restive just before the gate of Neustadt, he allowed the carriage to drive through the gate empty, and followed on foot; yet the vehicle had scarcely passed the gate when it was attacked by armed men. "On this," Khevenhüller adds, "Clesel became more active than ever in undermining the Emperor Rodolph."

As soon as the "Family Treaty of Vienna" was concluded, peace was made—likewise at Vienna—with the Hungarians on the 23rd of June, 1606, in which for the first time they succeeded in enforcing the concession of religious liberty to the Protestants.

Botskay, having no direct heirs, was confirmed in the possession of Transylvania and of Hungary; but he died a few months after. With the Turks a truce for twenty years was concluded at Comorn, on the 9th of November of the same year. Matthias at first obtained only the regency of Austria, as Rodolph delayed giving up Hungary. To force the latter kingdom from him, Matthias two years after marched with a host of 20,000 Heyducks to Moravia and before Prague. The helpless Rodolph had already formed a plan to escape to Dresden, but the Elector of Saxony had declined to receive him. Matthias intended to keep the Emperor quiet in a castle in the Tyrol; yet the Bohemians for the nonce protected Rodolph with their own army.

On the 17th of June, 1608, however, Rodolph was obliged entirely to yield the crown of Hungary and the countries of Austria and Moravia for a yearly pension; and on the 19th of November, 1608—Cardinal Dietrichstein having brought out from Prague into the camp of Matthias the Hungarian crown jewels, which until then had been in the keeping of Rodolph—Matthias was solemnly crowned under the canopy of heaven at Pressburg. The new king had to sign very hard conditions. Two Protestants, one after the other, received the dignity of Palatine of Hungary; in 1608 Stephen Illishascy, and in 1609 the great George Thurzo of Arva, lord of Bethlen-Falva, who died in 1616. The Estates of Austria leagued in the Union of Horn likewise refused to do homage until absolute religious liberty and equality should be granted. Matthias was forced to ensure it to them on the 19th of March, 1609. In virtue of this decree, which is called the "Capitulation Resolution," the right of a free exercise of religion was extended to the burghers and to the common people also. Immediately after Rodolph was compelled to grant to the Estates of Bohemia—who supported their by no means humble request by 3,000 men under the command of Count Henry Matthias von Thurn—the celebrated Royal Letter, called "Majestäts-brief," of the 11th of July and 20th of August, which secured to them absolute religious liberty and opened to the Protestants the university and the consistory of Prague, besides the schools and churches which they aleady possessed.

Rodolph was in a position similar to that of Charles V. when the German Protestants forced from him the Peace of Religion at Passau. As Charles was forced into this peace by his secret dissension with his brother Ferdinand, so Rodolph was forced by his public dissension with Matthias, and by it alone, into granting the Majestäts-brief—the "rag of waste paper," as the Emperor Ferdinand II. called it when he burnt it after the battle of the White Mountain.

Rodolph granted the Majestäts-brief with the utmost reluctance; the papal nuncio threatened him with excommunication. But even the Spanish family ambassador, Don Balthazar de Zuniga, advised the Emperor to yield for the present, in order not to jeopardise everything.

Zdenko Adalbert, Popel Lobkowitz, lord chancellor of Bohemia (afterwards the first prince of this family), could not be induced by any consideration to countersign this "waste paper." He declared that he would rather die than do anything contrary to his conscience. By command of the Emperor, the chief burgrave, Adam von Sternberg, signed in his stead.

One thing Rodolph thought to have secured to himself by granting the Royal Letter—that he would be allowed to die unmolested as King of Bohemia in his dearly beloved Prague. His ultimate view with regard to the succession was to obtain for the younger brother of Ferdinand of Grätz, Archduke Leopold,[1] bishop of Passau, not only the Bohemian crown, but also the imperial dignity.

Leopold being appointed by Rodolph as sequestrator of the countries of Juliers, which had fallen vacant in 1609, he enlisted for the occupation of that territory 16,000 men, who were called "Passau folk"; yet, instead of marching with these troops to the Rhine, he led them to Bohemia, and occupied with them the "Small Side" of Prague on Shrove Tuesday, 1611. At once the Bohemian Estates made an outcry against it. They believed, or pretended to believe, that these troops were intended to be employed for the purpose of repealing the concessions of the Majestäts-brief, of crushing the Protestant religion, and perhaps even of changing the old aristocratic constitution of the country into an absolute monarchy, after the pattern of that of Spain. Thus the helpless Rodolph was obliged to pay off the "Passau folk," and to send them out of the country. It caused some

---

[1] Leopold was for this purpose to get a dispensation from his clerical orders, which he afterwards (in 1626) actually did. He is the founder of the last side-branch of the Austrian house of Habsburg, the Tyrolese line, which became extinct in 1665. He was, in 1611, in his twenty-sixth year.

surprise that the Emperor, who until then had always complained of the extreme exhaustion of his finances, should find in his coffers the 300,000 florins which were required for this purpose.

After the departure of the "Passau folk" the Estates occupied the Hradschin. Making a show of assiduously paying their court to the Emperor, they guarded him so closely that he was not even allowed to take a breath of air in the grottoes of his fairy garden. In those times, when the proud Bohemian aristocracy had reached the summit of its power, from which it was so soon after to be hurled down into irretrievable ruin, it happened one day that as Rodolph was proceeding by a secret postern into the garden of the Hradschin, the sentry levelled his gun at him, and the Roman Emperor, without having had his walk, was forced to return to his apartments. Here he gave vent to his anger in a curse, which, opening the window, he pronounced on Prague: "O thou ungrateful Prague. By me thou hast been exalted, and now thou castest thy benefactor from thee. May the revenge of God fall upon thee, and his curse blight thee and the whole Bohemian country!"

The Electors of Mayence and Saxony having tried to intercede for the Emperor, who, they said, "was likewise their colleague in the Assembly of Electors," the Estates of Bohemia sneeringly answered to the Saxon and Mayence envoys that, if the Electors wished it, they would send to them the Roman Emperor and the Elector of Bohemia together in one sack.

In this emergency Matthias forced from his brother the Bohemian crown also. He appeared on the 24th of March, 1611, once more with an army of 18,000 men before Prague, and Archduke Leopold had to leave the city. Andrew Hanniwald, the privy councillor who during the later years of Rodolph's reign enjoyed the greatest share of the Emperor's confidence, was with two other councillors arrested as early as the 30th of March. He was threatened with torture in order to force from him a confession as to what Rodolph had intended with the Passau folk.

On the 11th of April, 1611, Rodolph was obliged to renounce the crown of Bohemia; and on the 26th of May Matthias was crowned by the Cardinal Francis Dietrichstein at Prague. Rodolph, by way of indemnification, received free residence at the Hradschin and an annual pension of 300,000 ducats, which were assigned on the revenue of the lordships of Budweis, Parduwiz, Lissa, and Rzedrow. When signing the document of resignation, Rodolph, in his anger at the ungrateful Bohemians who sided with Matthias, threw his hat on the floor, bit the pen with which he had signed his name, and flung it on the diploma; on which, as Hormayr states, "the blot of ink is seen to this day."

Matthias remained five months in Prague, where he took up his residence in the " Ring " (Circus) of the Altstadt; yet he never saw his brother the Emperor, who as usual was shut up in his apartments; they only exchanged messages through their lord chamberlains and privy councillors. On the 1st of September Matthias departed for the Lusatian countries and for Breslau.

The old monarch, who for several years past had been suffering from the gout, was quite childish and imbecile. Of all his crowns he had kept only that of the German Empire. The German princes, who had long held him in contempt, at last, in November, 1611, sent an embassy to Rodolph to compel him to cause a King of the Romans to be elected. Rodolph received the envoys standing, with his left hand leaning on a table. When the point concerning the election of a King of the Romans was mentioned, the blood rushed to his temples, his knees trembled, and he was obliged to sit down on a chair. After the embassy had withdrawn he thus expressed himself to his most intimate friend Duke Henry Julius of Brunswick: "Those who in my late troubles and calamities have lent me no help, and have never had a horse saddled in my service, have now held for me a sort of funeral oration; I dare say they have sat in council with the Almighty, and perhaps they know that I am to die this year, as they urge so very strenuously my appointing a successor in the Holy Roman Empire." The plan having already been mooted of electing another, and perhaps, for the first time, a Protestant Emperor, Rodolph was afraid lest he might be deposed also from the imperial dignity. In this apprehension he unexpectedly died—after having, on the evening before, appeared as usual at dinner—on the 20th of January, 1612, in the morning at seven o'clock, just as his valet was going to hand him a fresh shirt. He had not yet completed his sixtieth year, and so sudden was his death that there was no time for administering extreme unction. The death of his beautiful and faithful old lion, and of two eagles, which he had every day fed with his own hands, broke his heart. His death was kept secret for some time, even from his own household; for which purpose the table continued to be laid at the usual time, until his brother Matthias should be informed of the event. Mortification had seized his thigh. At the dissection, the heart and the other vital parts were found still sound and vigorous. The body was embalmed and placed in a coffin lined with red velvet, with a glass lid at the top, through which the corpse could be seen.

Matthias, after having received the news of the death of his brother, first sent Maximilian, Count Trautmannsdorf, as his commissary to Prague, where he himself arrived on the 30th of January.

5.—*Rodolph's natural children.*

Rodolph had by his numerous and ever-changed mistresses several natural children, of whom six, four sons and two daughters, have been known. After the example of Maximilian I., he allowed the four sons, whom he acknowledged as his own, to call themselves "Lords de Austria." They inherited the wild passions of their father.

1. Don Carlos de Austria served the Emperor Ferdinand II. in the Thirty Years' War; but having from mere wantonness, in one of the suburbs of Vienna, taken part in a riot caused by a woman of the town, he was killed without being known.

2. For the second son, Don Giulio de Austria, his father

bought the large Bohemian lordship of Krummau, which now belongs to Prince Schwartzenberg.

3. A third son of Rodolph, Don Matthias de Austria, as Khevenhüller states, "came in 1619 to Spain, to see the country and to try his fortune; but he was not allowed to come to Madrid; and, after his score had been paid for him, was sent back with 4,000 ducats to Germany, where he died in 1626.

4. A fourth of these illegitimate scions of the house of Habsburg was put to death by his father's orders. He was called Don Cesare. He had done violence to a young lady of noble birth and murdered her afterwards. Rodolph ordered him to die the death of Seneca, having his veins opened in a warm bath.

Of the two daughters, one, Donna Carlota, married a Spanish Count Cantacroy, of the Perrenot-Granvella family; and the other, Donna Dorothea, died in a convent.

CHAPTER VI

MATTHIAS—(1612-1619).

1.—*Personal notices of the Emperor.*

THE successor of Rodolph II. to the imperial dignity, as well as to the crowns—forcibly wrested from him—of Austria, Hungary, and Bohemia, was his brother Matthias, whose reign lasted not more than seven years (1612-1619).

Matthias was born, in 1557, at Vienna. His governors were Auger Gislain de Busbeck, of Comines in Flanders, and Colonel Ottavio Baron Cavriani, an Italian of Mantua. Busbeck was celebrated as a scholar, and had distinguished himself in the diplomatic career—especially as ambassador of Ferdinand I. at Constantinople, at the court of Soleyman (1555-1562). After the education of his princely pupil was finished, he was sent to the sister of Rodolph II. and Matthias, Elizabeth, the widow of Charles IX. of France, with whom he remained in the capacity of councillor until his death at St. Germain in 1592. Baron Cavriani, afterwards master of the horse to Matthias, was one of the most splendid and chivalrous cavaliers of his age, and, moreover, one of the most gallant men with the ladies. He died shortly before his pupil, in 1618.

Matthias profited much more from the cavalier than from the scholar and diplomatist. He was well formed, but small, and debilitated in body and mind. When not prostrate under the tortures of gout, which sorely tormented him, he knew no better employment for his time than court festivals, balls, jousting, pageants, and the chase. Dancing especially was most assiduously cultivated by him, which made Prince

Christian of Anhalt once say that his Majesty, if the right dance should once begin, was not likely to distinguish himself by his steps.

Rodolph's hatred had long rendered the life of Matthias cheerless. When in 1578 the Netherlanders, who had risen against Spain, called him in as their stadtholder, Rodolph as well as Philip II. were highly incensed against him; and yet he had only the title of a stadtholder, the real power resting with William of Orange. Being unable to maintain himself at his post at Antwerp after 1581, he resigned his office; but remained in that city nine months longer in poverty and retirement. In fact, he did not know whither to turn. The Emperor refused his consent to a marriage, yet, when on this he turned his eyes to clerical preferment, asking for the bishopric of Liège, the commissaries of his brother excluded him. After this he lived almost like a prisoner of state at Linz; he had not even the power of changing a servant. In vain he begged to be allowed to renounce all his hereditary claims on condition of the town and lordship of Steyer being settled on him. At the Polish election of a king in 1587 his younger brother Maximilian was supported in opposition to him. Afterwards Rodolph entrusted him with diplomatical commissions, in particular making him his proxy at the Diet of Ratisbon and appointing him to commands in Hungary; but refusing his imperial ratification to his decrees and the necessary means for making war. When the Emperor meditated, contrary to the family statutes, to deprive him of the succession in order to settle it upon Ferdinand and Leopold (the Bishop of Passau) of the Styrian line, Matthias had scarcely any other choice but to proceed to extremities. Thus then he forced, with arms in hand, the crown from his harsh brother.

A short time only before Rodolph's death Matthias was allowed to take a wife. The chosen lady was Ann, daughter of Ferdinand of Tyrol by the Princess of Mantua, whom that archduke had married after the death of his beloved Philippina Welser. Before that Matthias had lived with a mistress, Susan Wachter. Matthias, at the age of fifty-four, married the Princess Ann, who was then in her twenty-seventh year, on the 4th of December, 1611, just after his return from the Bohemian coronation to Vienna. Seven weeks after, Rodolph died; and on the 24th of June, 1612, Matthias was elected Emperor, in opposition to the far more able Duke Maximilian of Bavaria, whom Henry IV. of France, the wisest prince of his time, had suggested. Saxony, and the spiritual Electors, according to Khevenhüller, inclined rather to the Archduke Albert, governor of the Netherlands, the younger brother of Matthias, but they gave their votes to the latter. He was crowned at Frankfort with a magnificence scarcely ever witnessed before. He made his appearance on a brown Spanish stallion, with a retinue of 2,000 horses, more than 3,000 men, and a hundred coaches drawn by six horses each; the latter being a new fashion lately introduced from France to Germany. The Emperor, who lodged at the large mansion called the "Braunfels," remained from the 30th of May to the 23rd of June. All the Electors, except the one of Brandenburg, who sent his son as his proxy, and many other princes of the Empire, had appeared in person; "*it was*," as the historian says, "*as if people were to take leave of each other for ever*."

Matthias derived little joy from the crowns which he had wrested from his brother. Very nearly the same fate which he had himself prepared for Rodolph was prepared for him by his cousin Archduke Ferdinand; who was his tormentor, just as Matthias had been Rodolph's. In June, 1617, he was obliged, contrary to the most urgent remonstrance of Cardinal Clesel, to take Ferdinand to Prague to have him crowned as King of Bohemia; the Bohemians having consented to elect and crown the zealous Papist because he took his oath to them on the "Majestäts-brief." From Prague Matthias went with Ferdinand on a visit to his brother Maximilian, who since 1595 had been grand master of the Teutonic order; Cardinal Clesel repairing in the meanwhile to Dresden to gain over the Elector John George to the Austrian interest. The Emperor then went home with Ferdinand, intending to accompany him to Hungary, to have him crowned there with the crown of St. Stephen. Matthias, however, having fallen sick soon after his arrival in Austria, sent, as his commissaries to Ferdinand's coronation at Pressburg, Cardinal Clesel and Archduke Maximilian. Just as Ferdinand was proclaimed at Pressburg as King of Hungary, the great crash occurred in Bohemia which ushered in the Thirty Years' War.

2.—*The Thirty Years' War—"Defenestratio Pragensis"— Characteristics of the actors in it.*

Matthias had left behind, in Bohemia, a regency of seven Papist and three Protestant councillors. The Jesuits, who in 1617, at the coronation of their pupil Ferdinand, had made their entry into Prague in his train, were quietly at work among the councillors and the people. They had on that occasion caused a triumphal arch to be built for Ferdinand, on which, symbolically and significantly, the Bohemian lion was chained to the arms of Austria. The reverend fathers circulated a host of pamphlets, in which the means were discussed for bringing back the whole of Europe to the Church of Rome. An apostate Calvinist, Caspar Scioppius (Schoppe), a man full of wit and impassioned energy, in his "Alarm-drum of the Holy War," proclaimed in the plainest language that "the only way to reach that end *was a path of blood.*" As if a harbinger of the bloody events which were about to happen, a large comet was seen in the heavens every night of the year 1618. Men's passions were heated; the two parties faced each other in threatening attitude; the Protestants, conscious of theirs being the stronger one, were resolved to strike the blow as soon as any fitting opportunity should present itself. And an opportunity soon did present itself.

According to the clauses of the Royal Letter (the Majestäts-brief) of Rodolph II., free exercise of religion was only granted to the secular lords and knights (barons), and to the inhabitants of the royal towns and demesnes. When, therefore, it happened that the Protestants of two spiritual dominions of the territory of the Abbot of Braunau, and of the convent of Grab near Töplitz, were going to erect new churches, the Archbishop of Prague, in whose province those territories were situated, gave orders for the destruction of the commenced buildings. On this the Utraquists—which name the Bohemian dissidents had borne ever since the Hussite times—caused the assembly of their delegates, the so-called defensors, to be summoned. This was one of the privileges granted to them by the Royal Letter. They now applied to the Emperor at Vienna. His Majesty not only took no heed of their remonstrances, but an order was issued to dissolve the assembly. As the defensors thought themselves justified in supposing this order to have been concocted by the regents, they resolved upon the step of the 23rd of May, 1618—one of the most momentous in the history of the world.

The two most obnoxious of the Papist members of the regency were Barons Jaroslav Bortzita Martinitz and William Slawata.

Martinitz was born in 1582. He had enjoyed great favour with Rodolph II., whom, as a boy of fourteen, he had complimented in a Latin speech, for which the Emperor forthwith declared the little orator of age. At the age of sixteen he inherited the immense fortune of an uncle, from which he lent to the Emperor 100,000 florins for a war against the Turks. On a tour in Italy he was graciously received by the Holy Father, who made him a gift of some relics for his family chapel at Prague. Rodolph appointed him on his return lord-lieutenant of the circle of Schlan, in addition to which he was nominated, by the Emperor Matthias, Burgrave of Carlstein.

Slawata was born in 1568. Having for some time served under Rodolph II. as lord chamberlain, he was now lord chief justice and president of the chamber (lord treasurer) of Bohemia. He had gone over from the Protestant Church to that of Rome for the sake of his marriage with a rich heiress, and he now showed himself so intolerant against his former co-religionists that he is said to have driven his peasants with hounds to mass, and to have crammed the wafer down their throats by force.

On the 23rd of May, 1618, about noon, the Utraquist delegates, attended by a numerous train of servants, and nearly all of them armed, repaired to the Hradschin at Prague, proceeding straightway to the "Bohemian Chancellerie," the council-room where the regents were sitting. The Utraquists were headed by Count Henry Matthias Thurn,[1] with whom were William Lobkowitz, of the zealously Protestant Hassenstein line of that family; also Colonels Ulric Kinsky and Leonard Colonna von Fels, three Counts Schlick, Paul von Rzitschan, and a host of other Bohemian lords. They found in the council-room only four of the imperial councillors—Martinitz and Slawata, and besides them the old Burgrave Adam von Sternberg and Matthew Leopold Popel Lobkowitz, grand prior of the order of the knights of St. John in Bohemia. After a short altercation, Sternberg and Lobkowitz were with scorn and derision led out of the room; on the other two, Martinitz and Slawata, it was resolved there and then to execute, according to ancient Bohemian usage, the punishment of "defenestration," by flinging them, "as they were, in their Spanish costume, with cloaks and hats," from the window into the dry ditch of the castle. To complete the trio, the secretary Philip Fabricius was precipitated after them. They fell from a height of nearly sixty feet, but, owing to their cloaks filling with air and thereby breaking the fall, and to their alighting on a heap of waste paper and other rubbish, they all of them miraculously escaped with their lives. The very humble and very polite secretary, who was expedited last, is said to have had sufficient presence of mind, as he fell upon Baron Martinitz, most earnestly to beg his Excellency's pardon.

Martinitz, as Khevenhüller writes, fell in a sitting posture; Slawata with his head downwards, which he got so badly entangled in his cloak, that he would undoubtedly have been choked had not Martinitz assisted him to rise. Whilst

[1] Thurn was no native of Bohemia, but had inherited from his mother some, although not very considerable, estates in that country. He afterwards acquired there very extensive landed property to the value of half a million florins, which, combined with his eminent personal qualities, gained for him great influence in the Assembly of the Bohemian Estates.

Martinitz was still lying and rolling about, two shots were fired on him; one of which grazed his collar, and the other discoloured the flesh of his left hand.

Martinitz and Slawata took refuge in the adjoining house of the Chief Chancellor Adalbert Popel Lobkowitz, who at that time was at Vienna, which saved him from being involved in the catastrophe. His lady caused a ladder to be lowered to them from a window, and took the kindest care of them. Martinitz feigned to be dying, begged his confessor to give him absolution, and thus deceived his enemies. He then secretly had his beard taken off and his face stained, disguising himself as a groom. Thus attired he left the house of his heroic protectress at nightfall, went to his own house, and from thence to a light waggon which was waiting for him at the White Mountain, and in which he escaped to Munich. The secretary, Philip Fabricius, likewise was fortunate enough to get off at once and to reach Vienna, where he brought to the Emperor the first intelligence of the catastrophe. Ferdinand II. afterwards ennobled him under the very significant name of Baron von Hohenfall (Highfall), settling on him some fine estates from the confiscated property of the Bohemian rebels.

Slawata was detained for some time at Prague by his wounds. His wife having gone on her knees to the Countess Thurn, he received permission to remain as a prisoner in his own house, and then for some time at the springs of Töplitz. After having recovered his health, he was allowed to quit Bohemia likewise. Leaving all his property behind, he settled with the old Burgrave Sternberg at Passau, where they were joined by Martinitz, who was Sternberg's son-in-law. The Grand Prior Matthew Lobkowitz fled to Dresden.

All these lords returned to Bohemia after a short exile, and were loaded with favours by Ferdinand II. Martinitz was raised in 1621, as Jaroslav "Schmeissansky"[1] of Martinitz, to the rank of count in the Bohemian peerage, and in 1623

---

[1] Like the name "Hohenfall," this is an allusion to the throwing out of the window, "schmeissen" being an expression, now degenerated into a vulgarism, the meaning of which is "to fling."

in that of the Empire. He died in 1649 at the age of sixty-seven. His daughter married the outlawed Margrave of Brandenburg, the administrator of Magdeburg, whom Pappenheim made prisoner at the taking of that city. The male line of his house growing extinct in 1789, its name and estates passed through the heiress of the last count to the family of Clam-Martinitz.

Slawata likewise was created a count in 1623. He died at the advanced age of eighty, in 1652, at Vienna. Through his wife, Lucy von Neuhaus, he became possessed of the extensive estates of that noble family; but, as his own race became extinct in the male line as early as 1691, the Neuhaus property passed to the son-in-law of the last Count Slawata, Count Czernin of Chudenitz, whose descendants are still its owners.

The actual perpetrators of the defenestration were Thurn, William Lobkowitz-Hassenstein, Colonels Ulric Kinsky and Leonard Colonna von Fels, besides Albert John Smirczicky, one of the richest landed nobles, and a rich attorney, Martin Frühwein. Khevenhüller does not fail to point out that all the authors of this outrage came to an untimely end. Four of them died rather suddenly, and Frühwein especially. He was arrested in 1621, and, a short time before the day of bloody retribution in Prague, threw himself into the same ditch into which he had before helped to fling the imperial councillors; and, although the height from which he fell was much less than that from the council-room, he was killed on the spot.

Smirczicky, "a lord with a yearly income of 300,000 florins, and without any debts," was already dead six months after the defenestration. At the siege of Pilsen, a cannon-ball falling near him, and the loose soil flying into his face, he was so frightened that he fell into a high fever, of which he died, leaving his name and his property to his "laughing heirs."

Smirczicky's death took place in Prague, on the 18th of November, 1618. There was, however, a report alluded to by the "Rhenish Antiquary" (published by Baron Stramberg, Coblenz, 1844), that the "high fever" had had a very good reason, and by no means the futile one which we have given from Khevenhüller.

"*The laughing heirs*" *were the imperial treasury and the new Catholic "chain of nobles" of Austria.* After the battle of the White Mountain all the vast Smirczicky property was confiscated. Wallenstein, whose mother was a Smirczicky,[1] then acquired Gitschin, which now belongs to the Trautmannsdorfs. The surviving heiress, Baroness Slawata, was forced to emigrate, and went to live with the Landgravine Amalia of Cassel, who had formerly been engaged to her brother.

Colonel Ulric Kinsky also died a sudden death in 1619, during the Austrian campaign, and likewise Colonel Colonna von Fels in the Bohemian campaign of 1620. Henry Matthias Count Thurn got off with being exiled; as, after the battle of the White Mountain, he fled with Frederic, the Elector Palatine and the elected King of the Bohemians, to Holland, he lost all his estates. He passed through all the vicissitudes of the war, during which he served the Bohemian cause both as a soldier and as a diplomatist. In the latter capacity he went to Venice, to Constantinople, to Copenhagen, and to Stockholm. In 1630 he landed with Gustavus Adolphus in Germany; and in 1641 he died (having

[1] Smirczicky left two sisters, one of whom married Henry Slawata, who professed the Calvinist religion. This lady, Margaret Salome Smirczicky, had an elder sister, Elizabeth Catharine, whom her father had, for some suspicion or other, kept for twelve years imprisoned in a castle. Many considered her innocent, but her own sister had, from interested motives, most strongly opposed her being set at liberty. At the death of the brother Slawata came into possession of all the estates of the family, and also the guardianship of the imprisoned lady. The condition of the latter, however, had been changed in the meanwhile. A neighbouring Bohemian noble, Otto von Wartenberg, scaled the walls of the castle in which she was confined, and at once married her. Wartenberg was a Lutheran, which induced the tenants to acknowledge him, the husband of the elder heiress, as the rightful owner. A lawsuit ensued, in which Wartenberg, however, did not plead. In the meanwhile the Calvinist "Palatinate" King came to the country. As Wartenberg now surrendered, he was arrested, and the estates adjudged to the Calvinist Slawata. Wartenberg's wife was at that time at Gitschin, which afterwards belonged to Wallenstein. When Slawata, at the end of 1619, came thither, with the seven royal commissaries and a retinue of sixty persons, to take possession of the estates, *the heroic lady blew up the castle; whereby all her maids, the garrison of the castle, and the royal commissaries were killed on the spot. Her corpse was afterwards found, with the head and face burnt and all her bones broken.*

retired, after the battle of Nördlingen in 1634, to Sweden), at the age of seventy-three, at Pernau, in the Swedish province of Livonia. He came to Prague once more after the battle of Breitenfeld in 1631; but he found his wife gone, and never saw her again after his flight from Prague in 1620. His only son he lost in the Prussian war of 1628. His grandsons remained in Sweden. William Lobkowitz-Hassenstein, who had accepted from King Frederic the office of high steward (*Landhofmeister*), but who, after the taking of Prague, remained behind, and acted as mediator between the Bohemians and the Emperor's government, was included in the wholesale capital convictions of 1621, but escaped with imprisonment for life, his estates being given to Count Maximilian Trautmannsdorf.

The throwing out of the window, the *defenestratio Pragensis*, was the signal for the Thirty Years' War; the second and most sanguinary, which was waged under the pretence of religion, but in truth for very worldly, and even basely worldly, interests. The war of the Hussites was just as fanatical, but it was purer. Both wars began in Prague; the Thirty Years' War also ended there.

Immediately after the defenestration, Count Thurn rode through the streets of Prague, exhorting the people to be quiet. The castle was occupied by parliamentary troops; the public officers were sworn in, on the authority of the Estates; a committee of thirty directors was appointed for carrying on the government; and Count Thurn received his commission as lieutenant-general and commander-in-chief of the army to be raised. The first step of the Bohemians was the expulsion of the Jesuits. Three towns only remained true to the Emperor, Pilsen, Budweis, and Krummau.

3.—*Downfall of Cardinal Clesel—Death of Matthias.*

When the news of the catastrophe of Prague reached Vienna, the old, worn-out, gouty Emperor Matthias was for making concessions, in which opinion he was joined by Cardinal Clesel, who for the last six years had been his chief of the cabinet, all-powerful premier, and confessor. It was said that the Hussites had once made the whole of Germany and Hungary tremble, how should the Bohemians now be conquered, who were supported by the Union and by all their Protestant brethren in Europe? The Archduke Ferdinand (of Grätz) was so much the more determined in his opposition to leniency. He wrote to the Emperor that God himself had ordained the Bohemian troubles, in order that the chief pretext of the rebels, that they did everything for the sake of religion, might be defeated. Under this pretext they had hitherto only laboured to rob their sovereign of all his rights, revenues, and subjects. If authority was of God, then the conduct of these subjects must be of the devil; and he considered that nothing now remained but to let the matter be decided by the sword.

Ferdinand did not allow the irresolution of the Emperor to interfere with his levies for the army. On the contrary, he came to an understanding with the legate of the Pope, with the Spanish ambassador, Count Ognade, and with the court aristocracy, to remove, by a sudden and determined blow, the plebeian, the baker's son, Cardinal Clesel, from about the person of the Emperor. A rifle-shot which had been aimed at the cardinal's head at Pressburg during the Hungarian Diet had missed. King Ferdinand and Maximilian, the brother of the Emperor, were aware of Clesel's having said that "the archduke and Ferdinand were neither of them of any use at Vienna." They accordingly paid to the proud prelate—who, since he had been made a cardinal, claimed all the honours due to a crowned head—a visit, in order to oblige him, according to the existing rules of etiquette, to call on them in return. The old cardinal, lulled into security by Maximilian, had not the least foreboding of the storm which was gathering over his head. He came at two o'clock in the afternoon, on the 20th of July, 1618, with the apostolic nuncio, who, having just called on him, accompanied him to the imperial castle; and he went up with his suite to the apartments of Ferdinand, to whom he wished to pay his visit in return. On the staircase, he was received by the chamberlain Von Stein, who apologised in the name of the King; his Majesty, as he said, being prevented by slight indisposition from coming to meet the prelate. Ferdinand, however, was closeted in an inner room with Archduke Maximilian and the Spanish ambassador. When the cardinal entered the reception-room, he found the chamberlain Seyfried von Breuner, who, instead of announcing him, told him that the whole house of Austria, in agreement with his Holiness the Pope and his Catholic Majesty, had determined, on account of the cardinal's perverse government, and on account of the offences enumerated in a warrant herewith handed to him, not to allow him to remain any longer in Vienna. Wherefore he had to take off his cardinal's hat and cloak, put on the black hat and cloth mantle, in readiness for him, and to follow without delay the colonels then present, Count Dampierre, Rombald Collalto, and Ernst Montecuculi. A violent altercation ensued. Count Dampierre said to the cardinal, "You graceless, wicked knave! your evil doings can no longer be endured; if you will not yield quietly, we will teach you differently."

At last Clesel submitted to his fate. The colonels led the prelate through a long, narrow, secret passage out of the castle to the "Bastion;" and from thence through the fortifications, out by the Scotch Gate (Schotten Thor). There he was placed with Breuner and a Scotchman in a covered carriage drawn by six horses. Some way off two hundred cuirassiers of Dampierre were waiting, and relays of horses were in readiness at all the stages. Thus Clesel was carried through Styria to Archduke Maximilian's castle of Ambrass near Innsbruck, where, being every day sumptuously served on silver, he was waited upon as a prince, but at the same time kept in close confinement as a prisoner of state. After the death of Matthias only, he was allowed to reside at the Benedictine abbey of Georgenberg. In 1622 the Pope reclaimed him to be transferred to the castle of St. Angelo, where the Holy Father visited him in person; and in 1623 his innocence was acknowledged by the Emperor Ferdinand II., who the year after, through Prince Eggenberg, invited him to return to Austria. Clesel, however, did not at that time enter upon it, but wrote to Maximilian of Bavaria: "The journey to court is not advisable. I am not fit for such rule; I should relapse into the old offence. I cannot bear to hear of it, and still less wish to see it. I am so far from their ways that I do not understand their fundamental principles. I am too old to learn—*intelligenti pauca*." Three years later the old prelate after all came back from Rome. In January, 1627, he made his entry into Vienna among the ringing of all the bells. After his return to his see, he preached twice more. He died in his seventy-eighth year, at Neustadt, 8th of September, 1630, and was buried in the cathedral of St. Stephen at Vienna. Clesel, even after his restoration, pronounced against the harsh measures of Ferdinand, by which "the Protestant nobles, and even the richest of them, were driven to emigration, the money drawn from the country, trade and commerce ruined, and yet the Acatholics not made Catholics." He was for a middle course, —"not to allow the Protestant lords free exercise of religion and schools, but to keep them in the country; the children would then be obliged to become Catholics again." During the last three years of his stay at Vienna he was attached to that party in the court which was hostile to Wallenstein. He was indeed one of the principal enemies of the great general whose dismissal he still lived to see.

Immediately after the removal of the cardinal, the Dominican prior Hüttner, who was waiting for him in an outer room, was summoned before Ferdinand, and ordered to give up the keys of the chests where Clesel's papers and treasure were kept. There were found in the latter 400,000 ducats in ready cash alone, which strangely contrasted with the financial distress of the court. The cardinal's money was at once declared fair prize, and probably the desire of confiscation had not a little weight in deciding his fate.

When all was over the two archdukes appeared at the bedside of the invalid Emperor, telling him what had happened, and putting in his hands an information against "the man who had abused his confidence and whom they had been obliged to put out of the way of doing any more harm." Matthias, tormented by the gout, was quite flushed with amazement, pressed the coverlet of his bed to his mouth, but did not speak one word. He would fain have given orders for arresting Ferdinand and Maximilian, or at least their principal advisers, Eggenberg and Stadion; but he dared not do it, and he had no one with him in whom he might trust. He therefore submitted, increased his body-guard, and had his chamber more carefully bolted. As soon as he could say it, he declared that he felt much more hurt by Clesel's captivity than by the Bohemian outrage. He at once despatched a courier to the Pope; but the archdukes kept his messenger back until their own had got a start of him. Ferdinand resolutely declared that he would rather resign his two crowns of Hungary and Bohemia than allow the cardinal to be restored. He, however, offered "to throw himself at the feet of his Imperial Majesty, and to undertake in Clesel's place the presidency of the privy council, but to submit every matter before deciding on it to his Majesty's most gracious pleasure." The Empress, whom the archdukes apprised of the event through her chief chamberlain Maximilian Trautmannsdorf, was greatly agitated on hearing it, and bluntly declared to them that she saw very plainly that her husband and lord was living too long for them, and that they were already tired of waiting. She died some months after, on the 14th of December, 1618, at the age of thirty-two, and Matthias followed her on the 20th of March, 1619. His death, like that of his brother Rodolph, was quite sudden, overtaking him in the morning, at seven, in his bed, "whilst," as Khevenhüller writes, "he was just going to raise himself to take his usual cup of capon broth." They administered to him extreme unction, but he never was conscious again. A great sensation was caused by the fulfilment of Kepler's prognostic of seven M's, drawn for the year 1619: "*Magnus Monarcha Mundi Medio Mense Martio Morietur.*"

Matthias died almost under the same melancholy circumstances which he had himself brought about for his brother Rodolph—"deserted by everybody," as the Saxon resident stated, "there being very few in his antechamber at the ordinary hour of attendance, whereas in the King's (Ferdinand) apartments there is such a crowd that one can scarcely move." The Elector of Saxony had some time before proposed to the Elector-Archbishop of Cologne the question whether the Emperor could still be considered as *sui compos?*

About one month previous to Clesel's overthrow Ferdinand had been crowned with the crown of St. Stephen of Hungary. Very inauspicious omens happened on that occasion. The tower where the crown was kept having been struck by lightning, a link of the diadem got loose at the coronation, and the belt of the royal sword broke. Ferdinand took his oath on the Hungarian Capitulation which, in the point of religion, he as little intended to keep as he did the Bohemian. He was now master of all the Austrian lands of the house of Habsburg; and he soon made the world feel that he was so.

As he trusted no Austrian, the chief command of the army was given to two foreign officers, Boucquoy and Dampierre, commanders of Walloon regiments and pupils of the Spanish Spinola. Count Charles Longueval de Boucquoy, a native of Hainault, was called by his contemporaries the Netherlandish Hercules. Having been employed at the Archduke Albert's court in Brussels, he entered the service of the Emperor Matthias in 1614, and was, according to Khevenhüller, looked upon by the Bohemians with great jealousy. His second in command was Count Henry Duval de Dampierre, the same who arrested Clesel. Ferdinand sent for troops from the Netherlands, Spain, and Italy. The times of Charles V. came back again, when foreign soldiers were employed to crush the religious liberty of Germany.

CHAPTER VII.

FERDINAND II.—(1619-1637).

1.—Personal notices of the Emperor—The three steins (stones), the three bergs (mounts), and the dorf (thorp.)[1]

No Austrian ruler has entered upon the government of the hereditary possessions of his house under greater difficulties than did Ferdinand II. Whereas Charles V. on his birth found a world full of happiness and magnificence open before him, the career of Ferdinand II. lay through a world full of misery and danger. And yet he raised once more, and for the last time, the crown of the Cæsars to be the most dreaded in the world.

Ferdinand was born at Grätz in 1578. His father was Charles, the youngest son of the Emperor Ferdinand I. and founder of the Styrian line; a Tyrolese offshoot of which became extinct in 1665, whilst the main branch survived in the male line until 1740, and through the descendants of Maria Theresa, to the present day. Ferdinand's mother was Maria, daughter of the magnificent Duke Albert V. of Bavaria. There had been some negotiations on the subject of a marriage between his father and Queen Elizabeth of England; but Ferdinand I. would not allow his son to go to London, on which the Queen insisted as the prime condition of the possible, although not very probable, success of the affair. Her deeply rooted aversion to matrimony she expressed on that occasion in very strong terms to the envoy of Duke Christopher of Würtemberg, Ahasuerus Alinga, whom his master had sent (in 1564) to London to bring about

---

[1] This will be explained in the context.

"that marriage so desirable for an auspicious union of the two Churches." The very interesting conversations between Elizabeth and the envoy are given in the fourth volume of Spittler's "Historical Magazine," and are also reprinted in one of Hormayr's last annuals.

Ferdinand's first education was superintended by Catherine Countess Montfort, of the family of the Augsburg Fuggers, who had been mistress of the robes to his mother. His chief governor was Jacob Baron von Attems, "an experienced, godly, and fine cavalier," as Khevenhüller calls him. The family of Attems was of common origin compared with that of the Montforts. He was succeeded in this office by Balthazar Baron Schrattenbach, a Styrian. In 1590, at the age of twelve, Ferdinand entered the Jesuit university of Ingolstadt; in the same year he lost his father. At the age of seventeen he undertook the government of Styria; in 1598 he began to organise the movement of the counter-reformation, which he carried out with the most persevering tenacity. In 1600 he married Maria, daughter of the zealous Papist Duke William of Bavaria, the founder of the Jesuit college at Munich.

Ferdinand, on his accession in 1619, had already completed his forty-second year. He was corpulent, of low stature, but of a strong and excellent constitution. He was very temperate both in eating and drinking, and regularly went to bed at ten and rose at four. The prominent characteristic of his disposition was his devotion to the Roman Church, in whose most uncompromising spirit he had been nurtured from his early youth.

What Philip II. had been for Spain, Ferdinand II. wished to be for Germany. "*Better a desert than a country full of heretics*," he once said to Clesel, and the maxim remained his motto for life. He was the most faithful disciple of the Church of Rome, whose priests, especially the aristocratic Spaniards among them, were for him the mouthpiece of God. His own confessor, with due praise, states of him that Ferdinand had feared no one so much as he did the priests, whom he looked upon and venerated as something altogether superhuman. He is reported to have once said, in as many words, that if he met a priest and an angel at the same time, he would render honour to the priest first. This, however, only applied to the highly bred Spanish priests, who were ever ready to rage with fire and sword against the heretics; whereas, on the other hand, with all his Catholic zeal, he scrupled not to trample underfoot another more tolerant low-born priest, although that priest was a cardinal. It was to Ferdinand, and to him alone, that Clesel owed his downfall. From the terrible vow which Ferdinand, egged on by the reverend fathers his instructors, made in his youth to the Virgin of Loretto, he never swerved in the whole course of his life.

Ferdinand heard every day two masses in the imperial chapel, and on Sunday, besides a mass in church, a German and an Italian sermon, and vespers in the afternoon. He never missed kneeling before the crucifix at matins in Advent, and at vespers in Lent. He regularly, before and after Easter, attended all the processions and pilgrimages on foot and bareheaded. He would frequently take his meals at the monasteries of the Jesuits, Capuchins, Dominicans, and Carmelites; often also he would minister as an acolyte at mass, or toll the bell at the hermitage of Neustadt for vespers. He was the first to found, for the Church service, the celebrated Vienna chapel, which in his time consisted of eighty instrumental musicians and singers. From him dates the custom of the Emperors publicly joining in the Corpus Christi procession at Vienna, which was done originally to prevent, by the imperial presence, the fights which used to occur on that occasion between the two religious parties. And ever since 1628 the Emperors on that day have joined the procession, taper in hand. From him likewise dates the procession to Hernals, the estate of the Jörgers, "*where the Catholic doctrine had first been profaned by a Lutheran sermon.*" In 1632 the Capuchin convent was completed, which had been begun under Matthias, and where henceforth the Emperors were to be buried; his second wife, Eleonora of Mantua, having built in 1627 the Loretto chapel in the church of the Augustines, in which the hearts of the Emperors were to be entombed.

In 1622 Ferdinand received the Carmelites, and in 1626 the Barnabites; in 1630 the barefooted Augustines came to Vienna, and a new church was built for the Dominicans; in 1633, even from the distant Montserrat, Benedictines, the so-called "Black Spaniards," were sent for.

Ferdinand was a thoroughly monkish ruler. For the Jesuits he built a magnificent church and college, the church being consecrated in 1631. The Jesuits ruled him with absolute sway, constantly keeping near him, and never letting him out of their sight. "A couple of them," as the Saxon resident wrote as early as October, 1618, before Ferdinand's accession to the imperial throne, "were always to be met with in his antechamber; nay, they had such free access to him as to be admitted even at midnight to his bedside as often as they chose to send in their names." Fathers William Lamormain[1] and John Weingärtner had him completely in their power, and led him just as their order wished.

But Ferdinand was strong by his blind obstinacy, and by the very narrow-mindedness and fanatical impetuosity of his bigotry. His system—which he carried out with the most unbending pertinacity of a soul emancipated by religious zealotry from every scruple—was to bear adversity with the patience of a never-changing hatred against his heretical foes, and, whenever fortune favoured him, unmercifully and ruthlessly to let them feel his power. Every misfortune which befell Ferdinand—generally owing to his own fault, to his want of truth and faith—was in this system set down as a passing chastisement of the Lord, whose inscrutable and irresistible will was ever to be submitted to in humility and obedience. Ferdinand was the implacable enemy of the Protestants in Bohemia and Germany. The revenge on them being the task which he set to himself through life, he only abided the first glimmer of success and prosperity to try and annihilate the enemy, who, as the imperial disciple of the Jesuits conceived, was also the enemy of God. Ferdinand,

[1] William Lamormain, of the Society of Jesus, was a native of Luxemburg. He died at Vienna on the 22nd of February, 1648. He was said to have made upwards of 100,000 converts to the Roman Church.

in his petrified religious conviction, said once, in imitation of Luther, to Ehrenreich von Saurau, the speaker of the Protestant Assembly of Estates, "If my work is not of God, I shall not accomplish it. I will stake on it all earthly greatness, and life itself."

The rulers of the first Habsburg dynasty, from Maximilian I. down to Matthias—not even excepting Maximilian II., the best of the old line—had every one of them been given to all the excesses of illegitimate amours. The new Styrian dynasty began differently; debauchery having debilitated the stock, its usual consequence, devoteeism, made itself manifest in Ferdinand II.

Ferdinand was surrounded exclusively with ecclesiastics and women; the latter, however, belonging all to his own family. The allurements of gallantry were no temptation to him; he entirely lived for his own family and for his priests, who held sole possession of his ear and his heart. His mother and his wife, the two Marias of Bavaria, both of them most virtuous matrons and excellent mothers, were likewise only blind tools in the hands of the Jesuits.

Ferdinand, the imperial devotee, was engaged in war during the whole of the eighteen years of his reign. At first, it was forced upon him by the necessity of making head against his nobility—that Protestant "chain of nobles"—who were exasperated against him, not by mere religious, but much more strongly by political reasons. At a later period, after the battle of the White Mountain, and when Wallenstein and Tilly had crushed, with arms in hand, the sympathies which Germany had shown for the cause of the Austrians and Bohemians, that necessity existed no longer; but the second, the Papist "chain of nobles," pushed Ferdinand on, and he forbore making a fair peace with the conquered party.

Yet, although the whole of Ferdinand's reign was resounding with the clank of arms, he in his own person was anything but a warrior. Once only, in the Turkish war of 1600, he had allowed himself to be persuaded to present himself before the army in the camp near Kanischa in Hungary.

On that occasion, Ferdinand, a young man of not more than twenty-two, made his will before setting out in stately attire from Grätz to take the field. But a band of plundering Spahis, and the dust of a herd of bullocks and swine driven towards the camp, having spread a sudden panic, Ferdinand with the whole of his army ingloriously ran away; and it was not until he had crossed the river Mur into his own country of Styria that Adam Trautmannsdorf succeeded in stopping his flight. Since then Ferdinand contented himself with the trophies of the chase—which, besides music and religious exercises, formed his principal occupation—and with the deliberations and plots of the peaceful cabinet. It cannot be denied that Ferdinand, after his own fashion and in his own way of thinking, not only was a sagacious and clever sovereign, but that he also understood how to gather round him a circle of able and intelligent councillors.

Ferdinand spoke Latin and Italian very fluently. All the transactions of the high diplomacy were at that time still carried on in Latin, which was also the official language of the Hungarians. The Italian, French, and Spanish ambassadors at court were addressed in Italian. It was even used at the reception of the Turkish ambassadors, to whom an interpreter translated from it. Ferdinand did not speak either French or Spanish. His son Ferdinand III., however, was conversant with the latter language; he addressed the Infanta, when he went to meet her at Sömmering in 1631, in her own mother-tongue.

Of the councillors of Ferdinand there are to be mentioned in the foremost rank his six favourites, the "three noble (precious) stones" (steine), and the "three high mounts" (berge). The three "steins" were the Bohemian Wallenstein, and the two Moravians, Liechtenstein and Dietrichstein; the three "bergs," Eggenberg, a Styrian, and the *parvenus* Questenberg and Werdenberg, the former a Bohemian and the latter an Italian. Leichtenstein, Dietrichstein, Wallenstein, and Eggenberg were raised by Ferdinand to the rank of princes of the Empire.

Charles von Liechtenstein, formerly lord chamberlain and

privy councillor to the Emperor Rodolph II., was first raised by the Emperor Matthias when still King of Hungary, in 1608, to the rank of prince; in that country, in 1612, he was invested with the Silesian duchy of Troppau; in 1621, Ferdinand raised him to the rank of a prince of the Empire, and bestowed upon him in 1623 the Silesian duchy of Jägerndorf, confiscated from the Margrave of Brandenburg. Both those duchies are still in the possession of the family. Charles, the first prince, the Papist son of an ultra-zealous Protestant father, died in 1627 at Prague as one of the most strenuous patrons of the Jesuits.

The Eggenbergs were originally bankers like the Medicis, the Fuggers, and our own Rothschilds. Ulric and Balthazar Eggenberg were masters of the mint under the Emperor Frederic III., and used to negotiate his loans for him. But when Balthazar, after many unpaid old loans, refused further credit, Frederic sent him in chains to the keep of the castle of Grätz, and there extorted a new loan from him, for the easier repayment of which Eggenberg disappeared in his dungeon in 1493, and was never heard of again. One century later (in 1598) the family was ennobled by Rodolph II.

Hans Ulric Eggenberg, the minister of Ferdinand II., was born in 1568. He had been in Ferdinand's service ever since 1597, rising from one office to the other, until, in 1619, we find him accompanying his master to his election as Emperor at Frankfort. In the same year he received the Golden Fleece; and in 1621 he became director of the imperial privy council. It was he who in the following year fetched home Ferdinand's second wife, Eleonora Gonzaga of Mantua; acting as the Emperor's proxy at the marriage ceremony. A grant of Ferdinand, dated 6th of December, 1622, bestowed upon him the vast lordship of Krummau in Southern Bohemia, which, comprehending at that time no less than 311 towns and villages, was, in 1628, raised into a duchy, Eggenberg having been made a prince of the Empire by diploma, dated from Ratisbon, of the 31st of August, 1623.

As Wallenstein was all-powerful in the army, so was Eggenberg in the cabinet. The prince being nearly always confined to his bed by the gout and by disorders of the stomach, Ferdinand generally caused the privy council to be assembled at his favourite's house; to which, although situated at some distance, a secret passage led from the Hofburg.

Eggenberg's downfall happened in the same year as that of Wallenstein, whom he survived by only eight months, dying, at the age of sixty-six, at Laibach, 18th of October, 1634. His family grew extinct in 1717, when the duchy of Krummau passed to the Schwarzenbergs, forming the nucleus of the enormous landed property of that princely house.

The third favourite of Ferdinand, who rose highest to fall deepest of all, was the celebrated Wallenstein. He was raised to the rank of prince about the same time as his friend Eggenberg, by diploma, dated from Ratisbon, on the 7th of September, 1623.

The fourth of the favourites raised to the princely dignity was Francis von Dietrichstein, cardinal bishop of Olmütz, whose diploma is dated from Vienna on the 15th of February, 1624. He maintained himself in Ferdinand's favour and amassed vast landed property in Moravia and Bohemia, which, with the princely coronet, passed at his death, in 1636, to his nephew Maximilian, from whom the present family are descended.

The two other confidential advisers of Ferdinand had risen from the rank of clerks in the government offices, the one to that of baron, the other to that of count. Baron Gerard von Questenberg was the Emperor's factotum in the Aulic war office; Count John Baptist Werdenberg held the office of Aulic Chancellor of Austria. Both being friends of Wallenstein, were sent to him at Memmingen with the delicate commission of inducing him to lay down his command. Their families have long been extinct.

Besides the three "bergs" and the three "steins" we have to mention a "dorf" (thorp)—the honest Maximilian von Trautmannsdorf, who stood highest in Ferdinand's favour after Eggenberg.

Maximilian von Trautmannsdorf, the celebrated diplomatist of the peace of Westphalia, was, like Eggenberg, a Styrian, but from an old and distinguished family. As early as in the battle of the Marchfield against Ottocar of Bohemia, fourteen Trautmannsdorfs, and at Mühldorf, against the Emperor Louis of Bavaria, twenty of them, had fought and died for the house of Habsburg. Maximilian Trautmannsdorf first entered his public career under Rodolph II., in the the Imperial Aulic Council, the nursery of Austria's diplomatists; afterwards he was lord chamberlain to the empress of Matthias, and still under the reign of this Emperor a privy councillor. Ferdinand II. entrusted him with the most important diplomatic missions during the course of the Thirty Years' War. He was raised to the dignity of count in 1623; in 1635, he concluded the peace of Prague; and rose to be prime minister under Ferdinand III., in the account of whose reign we shall have occasion to say more of him.

2.—*Count Thurn before Vienna—"Nandy," Thonradl, and Dampierre's cuirassiers in the Hofburg—Election of Ferdinand as Emperor of the Romans, and of the Elector Palatine Frederic as King of Bohemia.*

Bohemia after the "Defenestratio Pragensis" was as good as lost to Ferdinand. Boucquoy and Dampierre, the generals who marched against Prague, were defeated by the malcontents. Pilsen, the first town after Prague which remained loyal, was, as early as the 21st of November, 1618, taken by the bastard Count Ernest of Mansfeld, who brought to the Bohemians a succour of 4,000 men. In December, Count Matthias Thurn, the head of the Bohemian malcontents, stood before Vienna. The Emperor Matthias was then still living. Zeidler, the resident minister of the Elector of Saxony at Vienna, reported about this time to his court that the Emperor had said: "I understand that my Bohemians now even walk into my country;" to which Ferdinand had replied: "They are getting rather too near us." Matthias perhaps was not at all sorry in his heart that the man who harassed him was now harassed in his turn.

The feeling at Vienna and throughout Austria, where by far the greater number of the people then professed the Protestant religion, was favourable to the Bohemians. Nevertheless, Thurn, without attacking the capital, marched off to Moravia. Here all the people declared for him. After having concluded at Brünn his union with the Moravian Estates, and thereby secured his retreat, he again appeared before Vienna in the spring of 1619. Both times he had advanced, scarcely meeting with any resistance, into the very heart of Austria. When being asked what he was coming for, he answered, "Wherever he met with any enrolled troops he disbanded them. There must in future be equality between Papists and Protestants; the Papists must not, as they had done until then, float on the top like a drop of oil on water." Whilst Thurn was for the second time standing before Vienna, the Emperor Matthias died, on the 20th of March, 1619.

Ferdinand II. stayed in the Hofburg at Vienna. He was without soldiers and without money. His councillors urged him to go to the Tyrol, where he would be nearer Bavaria. Even the Jesuits advised him to yield, or at least to temporise —"he who gained time gained life." But Ferdinand remained in Vienna and did not yield; on the contrary, he more signally than ever displayed all the peculiar tenacity of his inmost nature. His situation was terrible: the question was already mooted whether he ought not to be shut up in a monastery after the example of the Merovingian and Carolingian emperors, so that his children might be brought up in the *religion of the country—the Protestant faith.*

The Archduke Leopold of Tyrol, brother of Ferdinand II., was governor of Vienna. By way of precaution, and because a secret understanding between the citizens of Vienna and Count Thurn was apprehended, the archduke ordered all the townspeople to deliver up their arms.

The headquarters of Count Thurn were close before the city, in the suburb near the gate called Stubenthor, which opens on the road to Hungary; his cavalry was at Ebersdorf, his infantry at Herrnals. The Bohemian soldiers of the regiment of Tiefenbach, which at that time was commanded by Thurn, were to take the "New Gate" (Neuthor); a petard was fixed to it, but the plan of the surprise was betrayed. Thurn's batteries, pitched near the parish church of St. Ulric, poured their shot into the windows of the imperial residence, the Hofburg. It was the terrible night of the 6th of June, 1619. Ferdinand was obliged to retire from his own apartments. *He prayed against his enemies.* In the imperial Schatzkammer (museum of curiosities) at Vienna the crucifix is still preserved before which he was kneeling when, as he asserted, he heard the words called out to him, "*Ferdinande non te deseram.*" This passive tenacity and submission to an inevitable fate was what Ferdinand conceived to be trusting in God's providence.

That terrible night was soon followed by a terrible day—the 11th of June. Sixteen members of the Austrian Estates appeared before him in the desolate Hofburg.[1] Their leader was Andrew Thonradl, Lord of Ebergassing. They brought with them a document containing the articles of a union of the Austrian Estates with the Bohemians, to which Ferdinand was required to give his assent. Ferdinand refused to sign the paper. Then Andrew Thonradl, seizing him by the buttons of his doublet, called out to him, "Nandel [diminutive of Ferdinand], give in, thou *must* sign."

In this critical moment there happened one of those fortunate and almost miraculously opportune incidents, of which several examples are to be found in the history of Austria. Trumpets resounded in the courtyard. They announced the arrival of 500 Dampierre cuirassiers, whom Boucquoy had sent down the Danube from Krems to Vienna, and who, having just now entered the city by the unguarded "Watergate," were making their appearance at the Hofburg. These cuirassiers saved Ferdinand. Fear and their own evil conscience drove the craven Protestant lords from the Hofburg and from Vienna, to seek refuge in the Bohemian camp. On this the Papist citizens took courage again, and, together

---

[1] The noble names of Tschernembl, Hager, Jörger, Polheim, and others are mentioned.

with the students of the university, armed themselves for Ferdinand.

In Bohemia the fortune of war had in the meanwhile veered round a little. Boucquoy, having re-entered that kingdom from Krems, and at last defeated Mansfeld near Budweis, threatened Prague again. This induced Thurn to raise the siege of Vienna on the 12th of June, 1619.

Thurn had twice lost the opportunity of taking the Austrian capital by a sudden attack, and thereby speedily putting an end to the war. It was just as it had happened in the case of the League at Smalcalde and the Emperor Charles V.; the passive tenacity of the imperial family of Austria got the better of the sluggish, unwieldy, irresolute action of the malcontents. But no Elector Maurice now came to the rescue.

Thurn, however, appeared before Vienna a third time, having allied himself (2nd of November, 1619) with the great Prince Bethlen Gabor of Transylvania, who had taken possession of the Hungarian capital and of the sacred crown of St. Stephen. But the two allies mistrusted one another. Bethlen Gabor was not inaccessible to the bait held out to him by Austria, of a match with the Princess Maria Anna, Ferdinand's daughter, at that time in her eleventh year; who at a much later period (in 1635) was married to the old Elector Maximilian of Bavaria. Bethlen Gabor concluded a truce, and Thurn, after disposing his army in winter quarters, went to Prague to enjoy the gaieties of the carnival.

During the time intervening between Thurn's second hasty departure from before Vienna and his third campaign in conjunction with Bethlen Gabor, Ferdinand determined upon a bold and most resolute step. He went in all haste by Munich to Frankfort, to be elected Emperor of the Romans. He entered Frankfort, in his travelling carriage, on the 28th of July, 1619, just as a mutiny of a troop of horse was at its height; and four weeks after he was Emperor. It was not a little remarkable that all the six Electors, even the Protestant ones—not excepting the Elector Palatine—gave him their votes.

But, whilst Ferdinand was elected at Frankfort, he was deposed at Prague. The Bohemians, although they had elected and crowned Ferdinand in 1617, now ousted him " as the arch-enemy of the liberty of conscience, and as a slave of Spain and of the Jesuits;" he was charged with having obtained the Bohemian crown by fraudulent means, and with having betrayed the country to Spain by secret treaties. The Bohemian aristocracy were certainly never very sparing in their recriminations and calumnies, whereas they themselves revolved the most grasping and adventurous plans in their own proud hearts. Khevenhüller has recorded some such examples for the benefit of posterity. In May, 1619, Prince Christian of Anhalt, the general of the Evangelical Union, was sent by the Bohemians to the great Duke Emanuel of Savoy to offer to him the crown of Bohemia, and even the imperial crown; and from thence to the Signory of Venice. The Nobili advised the Bohemians "to make a stout defence, and, if it could not be done otherwise, to govern themselves *in formâ reipublicæ*, with the help of the Dutch and of Venice." The Venetians at the same time suggested the expedient of conquering the wealthy city of Genoa *(the rival of Venice)*, "to defray the expenses of the war." The Prince of Anhalt, whose papers after the battle of the White Mountain fell into the hands of Ferdinand, had spoken of his Majesty in the following terms: "*Qu'il seroit mieux de prendre plutost un Turc, avoir un diable à la succession de l'empire, que de la laisser venir au Ferdinand.*"

But the Bohemian aristocracy had no wish for a republic after the pattern of Holland or Venice. All that they wanted was a king; that is to say, a king of their own making, such as the Poles had.

And now the event happened which raised the exasperation between the three religious parties in Germany to its highest pitch—the election of the Calvinist Elector Palatine Frederic as King of Bohemia. Papists and Lutherans, however widely they might differ in other respects, agreed most cordially in their intense hatred of Calvinism; the Lutherans, in their blind fanatical zeal, were fond of quoting the saying of the bluff old Doctor of Wittenberg—*that the Calvinists were seven times worse than the Papists.*

The Elector Palatine Frederic was a prince of not more than twenty-three; a handsome and stately, and, as is proved by his own letters, jovial, gallant, and magnificent lord, who through all his life evinced a remarkable ease of mind and temper. His education had been a French one; he had passed his youth at Sedan at the house of one of his kinsmen, the great Huguenot chief, Duke of Bouillon; and afterwards resided with his maternal uncle Maurice of Orange, the son of the liberator of the Netherlands. At the death of his father he was not more than fourteen; and he was married before he had completed his seventeenth year to the Lady Elizabeth, daughter of James I. of England. The *fable convenue* of this princess having induced her husband to accept the perilous Bohemian crown by saying to him, " Rather starve under a kingly crown than revel under an Elector's cap," has been effectually refuted by the letters of her granddaughter, the well-known Duchess of Orleans (mother of the Regent). Elizabeth had not the slightest inkling of the election, and all her thoughts at that time turned only upon comedies, ballets, and novels. The principal adviser of Frederic in this momentous step was his uncle, the Prince of Orange, the arch-enemy of the house of Habsburg, especially of its Spanish branch. The ambitious and very influential court preacher of the Elector, Scultetus, may likewise have done his best in representing to Frederic that, in accepting the Bohemian crown, he was only fulfilling a duty of religion which he owed to his Calvinist brethren.

Frederic's election at Prague took place on the 26th of August, 1618, two days before that of Ferdinand as Emperor of the Romans. Frederic, on being informed of the deposition of Ferdinand by the Bohemians, exclaimed, " I should never have thought that this would come to pass. Heavens! if the Bohemians elected me, what should I do ? " He was at that time at Amberg in the Upper Palatinate, which is contiguous to Bohemia. There he received the news of his own election on the very day on which Ferdinand was elected at Frankfort. Frederic, surprised and confused, was long wavering whether he should accept or refuse the offer. Only when the Bohemians sent the third letter, in which they pressed for a categorical answer, he accepted the crown, which he knew very well how to wear with great stateliness, but not to maintain with honour. He said, in the canting style then in vogue, which Scultetus was most anxious to keep up at his court, "that he considered it an especial dispensation of the Almighty, and that therefore he would accept it."

Frederic had delayed so long that it was October before he set out for Bohemia. Seeing him depart, his mother, the clever Princess Juliana, of the House of Orange, said, with gloomy foreboding: "Alas! here goes the Palatinate to Bohemia!" But the easy king-elect was in high spirits. He relied on his uncle the Prince of Orange; on his father-in-law James I. of England; on the assistance promised by the Austrians; on the German cities which had engaged to supply him with money; on the Huguenots in France; on the Grisons, who had pledged themselves to stop the Spaniards on their march if they should advance by Switzerland from Milan and Naples; but most of all he relied, with his light youthful heart, on the chapter of accidents.

On the 31st of October, 1619, Frederic made his entrance into the ancient city of Prague with its hundred towers and steeples, which were so soon again to be surmounted by the double-barred papal cross. He was on horseback, splendidly attired, riding on a magnificent charger; the Electress followed in a gorgeous carriage with her eldest son, escorted by Prince Christian of Anhalt and his son, attended by Duke Magnus of Würtemberg, and by the Silesian Duke of Münsterberg and the other noble lieges of the crown of Bohemia. Before the gate a band of 400 Bohemians was drawn up wearing old armour from the times of Ziska, and on their standards the chalice; and, as a contemporary account relates, "when the Elector passed, they made such a noise and clatter with their Bohemian ear-picks (iron clubs), that he could not help laughing."

Four days after his entrance, Frederic and his English princess were crowned at Prague as King and Queen of Bohemia, 4th of November, 1619.

3.—Frederic's hopeless situation at Prague—The Bohemian aristocracy, and Calvinist outrages.

The new "Palatinal King" of Bohemia, as the Papists called him, was a lost man even before the battle of the White Mountain near Prague snatched the crown from his head. He was deserted and betrayed on all sides, even by his master of the mint, a partisan of Austria, who in coining the dollars of the new King had the D. of the D. G. in the legend reversed, which was considered as a very ominous sign that Frederic was not king by the "grace of God."

Frederic was the head of the "Evangelical Union" concluded in 1608 at the convent of Ahausen near the Odenwald —at that time belonging to Anspach—by the following Protestant princes: The Elector Palatine, the Duke of Palatine Neuburg, the Princes of Brandenburg-Anspach and Baireuth, the Duke of Würtemberg, and the Princes of Baden-Durlach and of Anhalt. In 1609 they were joined by the Elector of Brandenburg and by the Duke of Hesse-Cassel. Against this Evangelical Union the "Catholic League" was formed at Würzburg, in 1610, by the following Papist potentates: The Duke of Bavaria; the Bishops of Augsburg, Strassburg, Constance, Ratisbon, and Passau; the Provost of Elwangen; and the Abbot of Kempten. The three spiritual Electors of Mayence, Cologne, and Trèves joined it some time after. The life and soul of this Catholic league were the Duke Maximilian of Bavaria, an intimate friend of the Emperor's, and Lothair Metternich, Elector of Trèves, one of the greatest statesmen among the spiritual princes whom Germany has ever seen. Maximilian, Frederic's cousin, was therefore a most determined and bitter opponent of the Elector Palatine, and that not only from political and religious motives, but also for the very reason of his being his cousin, to whom he grudged more than to any other prince this accession of honour and power. On the other hand, the Elector of Saxony, John George, the head of the Lutherans, turned round upon the new King on account of his belonging to the much-hated body of the Calvinists; and thus the chiefs both of the Ultramontane and of the Lutheran parties worked for the Emperor, whose interest was not a little furthered by these splits among the princely aristocracy of Germany.

Frederic, immediately after his coronation, had hastened to Nuremberg to consult with the assembled princes of the Evangelical Union. Thither also Ferdinand sent his privy councillor Count Hans George of Hohenzollern-Hechingen to advocate the imperial interest. But the princes, pleading the clauses of the Royal Letter (Majestäts-brief) of the Emperor Rudolph II., in virtue of which Bohemia was included in the religious peace of the Holy Roman Empire, "treated the attack on the Bohemians as an infringement of the privileges of the Protestants as guaranteed by the constitution of the Empire, and declared that they on their side considered themselves justified in repelling it by force."

Yet this energetic resolution was not followed by energetic action. The upshot was that the members of the Union entered into a correspondence with Maximilian of Bavaria, the head of the Catholic League, and that many months were wasted in deliberations and negotiations. Maximilian having, in the beginning of the year 1620, received the Emperor's promise of the electoral palatinal dignity, took the field with his army of 32,000 men, very good troops, and encamped near Dillingen on the Danube. The army of the Union stood near Ulm. But, although the two hosts were thus only a few days' march distant from one another, no fighting ensued. King Louis XIII. of France, son-in-law of Philip III. of Spain, sent envoys, the Duke of Angoulême and MM. de Bethune and d'Aubespine, both to the Catholic League and to the Evangelical Union, in order to bring about a reconciliation between the two hostile parties. The result was that the Evangelical Union allowed themselves to be persuaded by these French envoys to "take unto itself the *salutare*," concluding at Ulm on the 3rd of July, 1620, a peace with the

"League" and disgracefully leaving the "Palatinal King" to his fate.

The peace of Ulm was scarcely concluded when enemies on all sides began to attack the King of Bohemia. Maximilian of Bavaria set out in the very month of July for Austria, which was in a state of insurrection against Ferdinand. It was the peasants who had risen again, and who even had slain Duke Ernst Louis of Saxe-Lauenburg, merely because, as he was hastening down the Danube to the assistance of the Emperor, he declared that they should be quite merry; they would soon have other guests. Maximilian speedily brought the peasants and the whole country to submission; having accomplished which, and having, on the 8th of September, joined Count Boucquoy, the imperial general, near Neupölla, in Lower Austria, he entered Bohemia. As early as in August 25,000 Spanish auxiliaries set out from the Low Countries, under the command of Marchese Ambrosio Spinola and Don Gonzalez Fernandez de Cordova. After passing the Rhine near Coblenz, they overran the Rhenish Palatinate, Frederic's hereditary country, which was guaranteed to him by the Evangelical Union, and the innocent Protestant inhabitants had cruelly to suffer for the delinquency of their absent lord. In addition to this, the Lutheran Elector of Saxony, Frederic's third enemy, allied himself, in March, with the two spiritual Electors of Mayence and Cologne against the Calvinist Elector Palatine and for the Emperor, and invaded, in September, with 15,000 men, Lusatia, at that time incorporated with Bohemia.

King James I. of England, Frederic's own father-in-law, turned from him like the rest. About Christmas, in 1619, Prince Rupert, who afterwards served in the army of Charles I. during the Civil War, was born. The courier whom Frederic sent to his father-in-law to announce this birth brought back some promises of money and men. But, as James at that time was negotiating with Spain about a marriage between the Prince of Wales and a Spanish Infanta, his own interest made him withdraw his help from Frederic, and truckle to the Emperor. The relations between James and the Bohemian King may be judged from the following letters of Frederic to his wife. On the 25th of February, 1620, he writes to her from Breslau: "Le roy s'amuse toujours à disputer de la justice de la cause, et semble qu'il voudroit bien être quitte du Baron Achatius,[1] et le laisser retourner à mains vuides"; and from Rockesan, shortly before the encounter with the Elector of Bavaria and Tilly, he writes (dated 10th of October, 1620): "Pour les ambassadeurs d'Angleterre j'ay fait commander qu'on les reçoive le plus honorablement qu'on pourra; mais que je suis nullement resolu de les defrayer, car les grandes depenses que j'ay, m'en peuvent bien excuser, et aussi le roy ne defraye pas le mien. Je m'etonne *s'ils me donneront le titre*, autrement je leur baise les mains de leur lettres."

But Frederic's worst enemy was himself. He did not understand the art of insinuating himself with the Bohemian aristocracy, who were offended by his bestowing his confidence exclusively on his German generals, ministers, and courtiers. Nor did he understand how to make himself respected, and the Bohemian lords soon got the better of him. These aristocrats, who, in speaking of their enemies, used to style the Emperor "the blind cur," the Elector Maximilian "the Bavarian hog," and John George of Saxony "the perjured, drunken clod," had but one thing at heart in their rebellion—the maintenance of their feudal rights, liberties, and privileges. They wanted, as a minister of Frederic expresses it, "a King, as it were, only for show, and one who would make their crooked things straight." This went so far that, when the King once summoned the Bohemian lords for a meeting of the council early in the morning, some of the principal men among them unceremoniously declared that they could not make their appearance as early as seven in the morning; a man must have his rest after having done his work, and the thing was contrary to their privileges. The towns, on the other hand, as the same minister states, were to be oppressed and made

---

[1] Frederic's envoy in London.

subservient to the nobles; besides which, they were to bear all the burdens. As to the officers of the army, Frederic had neither the energy nor the tact for keeping them in their place; they enriched themselves, whilst their King remained poor. About the latter end of September, 1620, the arrears due to the soldiery amounted to no less than four millions and a half of florins. The men therefore plundered and robbed to get their own, which caused great distress and many bitter complaints among the people. It was of no avail that Frederic and his wife, to court popularity, showed themselves exceedingly affable and polite, accompanying noble funerals on foot, and dancing at the balls of the citizens; they only lost respect by their condescension. Frederic also gave offence to the Bohemians by introducing the French language at court, and by displaying all the frivolity of French manners and fashions.

But the most serious stumbling-block was the religious point. "The church of the Jesuits,"[1] writes Khevenhüller, "was ceded to the Calvinist predicants, by whom it was spoliated; and in it sermons were preached in German, and in St. Wenceslaus Chapel in French. In preparing the church for Calvinistic service, they proceeded in the following manner. On St. Thomas's day afternoon, the beginning was made; the Lords Bohuslav, Berka, Ruppa, and Budowa, and many others of the same persuasion, were present, when all the altars, crucifixes, and statues were broken; nay, they themselves sometimes would take up the hatchet and pickaxe to help in the work of destruction. When the workmen were going to lower gently the large crucifix, which was above the entry of the choir, so that it might not break, they were ordered to throw it down, nor to spare anything; and it fell with a tremendous crash, as if the whole building was coming down. Whereupon the Lord Berbisdorf, kicking it with his foot, called out, 'Here thou liest, poor fellow! if thou be the Christ, save thyself.' All the wood carvings of the altars and the crucifixes and statues the Calvinist predicants had cut up, and used the pieces as firewood; and they would have

---

[1] The cathedral of St. Vitus on the Hradschin.

considered it a great sin to sell any of them to Roman Catholics."

By this most impolitic triumph of Calvinism, Frederic estranged from him not only the Roman Catholics in Bohemia, but also the numerous body of Lutherans in that kingdom, and, moreover, all the Lutherans in Germany. Egged on by his all-powerful chaplain Scultetus, he went so far as to allow sermons to be preached in St. Vitus's church against the Utraquists and Lutherans. On Christmas Day, 1609, he publicly celebrated the communion according to the Calvinist rite as a mere token of remembrance, not heeding that the Hussites, whose party was still very strong in the country, had carried on a war of seventeen years for the administration of the *sacrament* in both kinds. A contemporary writer relates: " A table with twelve chairs was placed in the choir for the Calvinist communion. The King broke the loaf for himself; to the others it was offered in bits on a salver, from which each took a morsel, ate it, and took a drink after it." Khevenhüller adds: " Many hundred persons of the congregation came to witness this extraordinary spectacle, and were greatly shocked at it, saying that they never in their lives had heard of such a Eucharist, and that they deeply regretted having chosen such a King for their head." A riot nearly broke out when the large stone crucifix on the bridge over the Moldau was, like the rest, to be pulled down. Count Thurn succeeded only with much difficulty in pacifying the great mass of the people. It was necessary to place a guard on the bridge with orders "to fling whosoever should lay hands on it, without any consideration of rank, from the parapet into the water." Khevenhüller expressly states that Count Thurn warned the King against the breaking of images, observing to him that his Majesty " would not be safe in his castle, as such things could not be done at Prague as easily as might be the case elsewhere."

The Lutherans, enraged against the Calvinists, left nothing undone completely to undermine Frederic. The Saxon court preacher, Hoë von Hoënegg, inveighing most violently in a pamphlet against the " The Calvinist Firebrand Foxes" (*Die calvinischen Brandfüchse*), exclaims, "Oh! what a shame and pity it is that so many noble countries should have been flung into the jaws of rank Calvinism! To break away from the Western Antichrist merely to exchange it for the Eastern is in truth very scant profit."

But the zealously puritan, yet withal very frivolously minded, Frederic did not shrink from the arch-enemy of Christendom, the Grand Turk. The Bohemians, immediately after the defenestration, had despatched the Silesian Baron Hans von Cölln as their envoy to the Sublime Porte. There was now sent in return Mehmed Aga, who made his solemn entry into Prague with Count Thurzo, the ambassador of Bethlen Gabor. The King received the Mussulman in public audience, and invited him to his table, where the King's own brother and the first dignitaries of the court drank the health of the new protector; but it made a very bad impression on the people that such an alliance should have been solicited. Upon this, Scultetus delivered, on the 15th of April, 1620, a sermon in St. Vitus' church, in which he undertook to prove *that in reality the Turks were also Christians.* It may easily be imagined that this sermon made even a worse impression. Yet the hopes of the court party were most sanguine—it was the pride before the fall.

Whilst they were befooling themselves at Prague with visions of succour from England, Venice, Savoy, and Italy, Maximilian and Tilly, the two fiercest of all their Papist enemies, had already set out to rescue the profaned capital of Bohemia from the grip of its Calvinist desecrators.

4.—*The expedition of Tilly and of the Duke of Bavaria to Bohemia—The battle of the White Mountain, and the executions in the Ring at Prague.*

Maximilian, after having been joined in Austria by Boucquoy, approached at the head of the united hosts of the Emperor and the Catholic League. The army of the Palatinal King of Bohemia, under the old Prince of Anhalt, whose headquarters had ever since February been at Egenburg in Austria, now retired by Budweis in Moravia to Neuhaus in Bohemia, and from thence to Thabor and Pilsen. Mansfeld and Thurn, who stood in his rear in Bohemia and Moravia, had as early as August fallen back farther into Bohemia for the protection of the country. Having crossed the Bohemian frontier on the 10th of September, Maximilian entered Budweis on the 22nd. He had for his second in command Field-marshal Count Tilly, the first of that succession of great captains who have earned their fame in the Thirty Years' War.

John Tserclas (Sir Nicholas) Count Tilly was a Walloon, born in the year 1559, of a very ancient noble family in the neighbourhood of Liège. Being a younger son, he had been intended for the Church, and received his education in the iron school of the Jesuits. Afterwards he entered the military career, rising from the ranks in the Spanish armies of the Duke of Alba, Don John of Austria, and Alexander Farnese. He also served in the auxiliary army which supported the Guises against Henry IV.

In the beginning of the seventeenth century he entered the Austrian service against the Turks in Hungary; and in 1609 that of the Duke of Bavaria and of the Catholic League. Tilly was long past the prime of life when he marched with Maximilian to Bohemia, but he was still very hale, having never been ill in his life. He was strong and muscular, although small and spare, and stiff in his movements. He was lantern-jawed, his complexion swarthy, his forehead arched, and usually contracted by deep thought; his sunken eyes, overshaded by beetling brows, were generally fixed on the ground, but when he raised them they were keen and piercing. Under his long, sharp nose he wore bristling moustaches; his hair cut short, and originally sandy, was now white; his chin pointed, and thickly covered with that description of beard which in these days would be called an "imperial." Tilly was naturally grave and taciturn, gloomy and stern; he was never seen to lose his temper. He was a thorough soldier, and just as thorough a churchman. Gustavus

Adolphus used to call him the "parsons' drudge"; but he was disinterested and modest, temperate and chaste, and very kind to children. Before the battle of Leipzig he could boast of never having drunk wine, of never having known woman, and of never having lost a battle. His appearance was very striking. He generally was mounted on a white pony, which he, although stooping, rode very fast. In his manner of speech and his movements he was exceedingly solemn, and there was much in him to remind people of his great master in the art of war, the Duke of Alba, only he was even more fanciful and ghostlike. He wore the costume of a Spanish captain—a bright green satin doublet, slashed in the sleeves; leather hose, large boots, a white scarf, a strong rapier, besides a dagger and a pair of pistols in his belt; to all of which must be added a very high-crowned hat surmounted by a red ostrich feather, which drooped down on his back. This attire was so uncommon that M. de Grammont[1] —who, after having fled his country for a duel, came to Tilly's camp, near Leipzig, to be initiated by him in the art of war— took him for a mountebank or a madman, and asked him what fashion this was. Tilly answered, "C'est à ma mode, et cela me suffit." But Grammont very soon found out that, as he says himself, he never had met with a more sensible, wise, and energetic commander. Tilly had in his army just as absolute power as, at a later period, his rival Wallenstein had in his. And now he was riding to his first great victory—the victory of Prague.

Tilly was accompanied in his ride by Pappenheim, his second in command, who afterwards became the most celebrated cavalry general of the great war. Godfrey Henry von Pappenheim was a descendant of the ancient Swabian house, which held the hereditary dignity of earl marshals of the Empire; and to which that Marshal von Pappenheim belonged who, in 1208, revenged the murder of the Hohenstaufen Emperor Philip on the assassin Otto von Wittelsbach. Godfrey Henry himself had, at Ferdinand's coronation in Prague

[1] Afterwards celebrated as Marshal Grammont.

(1617), as earl marshal, carried the golden orb. He was born in 1594, of Protestant parents. He entered this world, as it were, marked out for a soldier, with two large red seams like a couple of crossed swords on his forehead, which were at once considered to forebode a warlike career; and the prophecy certainly came true, as he became one of the greatest cavalry generals of the seventeenth century. Nothing could withstand the onslaught of his Pappenheimers, his iron cuirassiers, when, rushing on at their head like the wild huntsman, he swept the enemy's battalions from the field. In the doggerel ditties which were sung of him, he was commonly compared to the devil himself. Even Gustavus Adolphus acknowledged him, and him alone, as a true soldier, ranking far above the "parsons' drudge" Tilly, and above Wallenstein, whom his Swedish Majesty used to style a madman. Pappenheim, although having the artillery under his command, used to assault the fortresses without first breaching their walls. He had studied at the universities of Altdorf and Tübingen, then made the usual "grand tour," and rendered himself conversant with the French and Italian languages. In 1614 he turned Roman Catholic. At a later period he became one of the principal partisans of the Duke of Friedland. Ferdinand made him a count in 1628.

At the approach of the army of the League, the Bohemians, as has been stated before, retired on all sides. Near Budweis the Spanish Colonel Verdugo, with Walloon troops, joined the army of Maximilian, Boucquoy's division having been swelled before by Maradas, who brought Spanish infantry from Italy. The season was far advanced, and the weather began to be cold and rough. Boucquoy advised against proceeding by forced marches; Maximilian and Tilly were strongly for it. The latter, who, at the council of war, in his intense impatience, always used to tear something or to crumple it in his hands, called out at every turn of the debate, "Prague! Prague!" Near Pilsen, before which Maximilian encamped on the 13th of October, they at last fell in with Prince Christian of Anhalt and the new King of Bohemia himself.

Old Tilly incessantly pushed on, whilst Anhalt was retreating before him. The King himself fell back with Thurn on Prague. He was even at that early stage of the war so disheartened as to send the Crown Prince, a boy of seven years,[1] for safety's sake, to his sister (the mother of the "Great Elector") in Berlin.

Tilly rode on through a pelting rain from early morning to late at night, leading the van in person with drawn sword, and driving the enemy before him. He held to it, that a battle was the thing; Prague would then fall of itself, and the war be ended. In the Bohemian army confusion and terror reigned paramount. Eighteen Bavarian cuirassiers once put 250 Bohemian horse to flight.

On the 8th of November, 1620, at the dawn of morning, at last the three united armies of the Emperor, of the Duke of Bavaria, and of the League, arrived within somewhat less than a German mile of Prague. A thick fog lay on the country. It happened to be the Twenty-third (First) Sunday after Trinity, in the gospel of which day the passage occurs: "Render unto Cæsar the things which are Cæsar's." The army of the Bohemians, under the command of old Prince Christian of Anhalt, occupied a strong position on the White Mountain, celebrated by the heroic achievements of Ziska. Its numbers scarcely amounted to 21,000 men. The army of the allies was stronger by about 10,000 men; yet the Bohemians, although being aware of their own inferiority of numbers, weakened themselves even more by leaving seventeen half-battalions in the four different quarters of the city of Prague, where they likewise had sent all their artillery, with the exception of twelve large guns which they kept with them. Anhalt had drawn up the Bohemian army in two lines of battle. It consisted of Bohemians, Moravians, Silesians, troops from the Palatinate, 200 horse and 2,000 infantry under Duke William of Weimar, 500 Dutch horse under Count Styrum, and 8,000 Hungarian cavalry under the young Prince of Anhalt. It was a bitterly cold day, and

---

[1] The elder brother of the father of the Duchess of Orleans. He was afterwards drowned in Holland.

the ground was frozen hard. About midday the fog, in which until then they had scarcely been able to see five yards before them, dissolved in slight showers.

Single shots were already exchanging between the most advanced outposts of the two armies. The generals of the allies, Duke Maximilian, Tilly, and Boucquoy—the latter of whom had, on account of a slight contusion by a musket-ball, to be carried in a litter—formed a circle to consult. Boucquoy again opposed Tilly's advice, that they had better attack the enemy at once. Then the balance was turned by a Spanish Carmelite, Father Dominicus de Jesu Maria, who was held to be a saint and a worker of miracles, and had expressly come from Italy to the Duke of Bavaria. Dominicus got up and said to the generals: " What, ye sons of the Church, ye are fighting with empty words, now that the Lord of hosts has given the enemy into your hands? Look here, how they have treated his holy mother!" Saying this, he drew forth from his frock an image of the Virgin, which had been outrageously mutilated by the Bohemians, and held it up before them. The duke exclaimed, "Holy Mary!" and "Holy Mary" became the war-cry of the day.

It was just midday. The sun burst for a minute from the clouds. All went to their posts. The imperialists formed the right wing of the line of battle, the Bavarians the left. The imperial army comprised those German regiments which, newly levied at that time, afterwards fought in all the battles of the long war, and some of which still exist in the Austrian army, in particular the regiment of Rudolph Tiefenbach, to this day the oldest Austrian regiment of foot; with the Neapolitan infantry under Carolo Spinelli; and, most dreaded of all, the Spanish Walloon infantry, Boucquoy's musketeers. The imperial cavalry included the dragoons of Liechtenstein and Wallenstein's cuirassiers; the Spanish Walloon mounted arquebusiers of Don Balthazar Maradas and of Don Gulielmo Verdugo; the Milanese light horse of Montecuculi; and, most distinguished of all, the Walloon heavy cuirassiers of Boucquoy and St. Hilaire. The light horse of the fierce Croats, led now for the first time, besides the Polish lancers and Cossacks, by a German Emperor into the heart of Germany, were commanded by Colonel John Lewis Hector Isolani; the heavy cavalry of the League by Pappenheim. There was with Tilly's army an interesting volunteer, a young Frenchman of about twenty-four—no other than René Descartes, who afterwards earned a world-wide celebrity as the founder of Rationalism and of a complete system of philosophy.

Shortly after the hour of noon a dozen of heavy field-pieces, called the Twelve Apostles, from the arsenal of Munich gave the signal for the battle. The attack was headed by Tilly and Rudolph Tiefenbach, who led the troops up the declivity of the White Mountain. They had to defile by a single narrow bridge through a village commanded by the artillery of the Bohemians; but they reckoned on the confusion of the enemy, of which they were well aware. The advance was made in close squares of the infantry, the horse being placed in the intervals and on the flanks. They marched on with drums beating and with tremendous war-shouts.

The Bohemian artillery fired into the squares; the imperialists returned the fire. The cannonade lasted about half an hour. Now the young Prince of Anhalt made a successful attack with his Hungarian horse; the regiment of Tiefenbach turned to flight; another regiment was routed. Isolani's Croats also gave way. Only Don Verdugo, with his Walloons, withstood the attack of the Hungarians.

Maximilian and Boucquoy, who were in the rear, drove the fugitives with drawn swords back into the fray. Pappenheim then led his heavy Bavarian cuirassiers against the Hungarians. About the same time a Polish lancer stabbed the horse of the young Prince of Anhalt, who fell with it and was made prisoner. This incident decided the battle. The tide of fortune was now suddenly turned; the Hungarian cavalry fled, and involved the whole order of battle of the Bohemians in their wild confusion. The Neapolitans under Spinelli scaled the large entrenchment of the Bohemians, and took their battery, which had been firing until then, and had done great havoc among the enemy. The whole battle did not last more than an hour.

"And if Alexander the Great, and Julius Cæsar, and Charlemagne had been present," Prince Christian of Anhalt says, in his report, "they could not have induced these fellows to make a stand."

Only in the royal deer-park, at the so-called "Star," a picked body of young Bohemian nobles, with the son of Count Thurn, held out for some time, Duke William of Saxe-Weimar, with his two thousand infantry, particularly distinguishing himself: their defence was so heroic that, of all the two thousand men, twenty-six only escaped with their lives. It was on this spot that Pappenheim, covered with more than twenty cuts and stabs, in addition to innumerable bruises, remained lying for a whole night, buried under the corpses of men and horses. He had fallen whilst leading the attack, and been trampled under the hoofs of the horses of his own squadrons. Thus he lay unconscious all that long cold November night. On the next morning a Croat, prowling about for plunder, stumbled on him. The savage, being unable to draw a costly ring from his finger, tried to bite it off. The pain brought Pappenheim to life again. Wildly looking at the Croat, he roared out, "What do you want, fellow?" The Croat replied, "You have good clothes on you, you are to die." Pappenheim, although half dead, at once boxed his ears; but promised him a good reward if he would take care of him. The Croat now conducted the wounded general to the celebrated surgeon André, at Prague. Duke Maximilian, as soon as he was apprised of the news, sent to inquire whether Pappenheim was likely to get over it. André gave good hopes, "although," he said, "six of his wounds were fatal; only the general ought not to be so excessively impatient." Hearing this, Pappenheim bellowed forth from his bed, "But how in the world can one help losing all patience to be sewed and patched in this way?" André had prophesied true; his impatient patient recovered, having, as by a miracle, risen from the dead.

One hour had decided the fate of Bohemia for centuries.

Four thousand men of her troops covered the battlefield; the loss of the allied armies amounted to about the tenth part of that number. The conquerors took ten guns and about a hundred stand of colours; the number of prisoners, besides the young Prince of Anhalt, amounted only to about five hundred Bohemians.

Frederic had not been present at the battle. He was no hero in war, and had remained behind in Prague with his wife. That during the fight he had sat quietly down at the Hradschin to a banquet with his courtiers, and with the English ambassador, has never been proved, nor is it at all likely. People, be they ever so young and thoughtless, will not revel when a crown is at stake. The fact is that Frederic had remained in the town to superintend the supply of ammunition and provisions for the camp. But, with all that, there cannot be the least doubt of his want of courage, which completed the general confusion. In vain the young Count Thurn and others advised him to maintain Prague, which was strong enough, and which in winter could never be invested; where, moreover, besides those escaped from the battle, they had still seventeen half-battalions of fresh troops. It was quite evident that a hostile army could not hold out in Bohemia in winter time. Mansfeld stood near with upwards of twelve thousand men, occupying Pilsen and Thabor, and in a position to cut off the enemy from all their supplies and their communications in the rear and the flanks.

Frederic was timid, but instinctively shrewd; he was afraid, and justly so, of the Bohemian lords, who, to obtain better conditions of peace from the Emperor, might have given him up to Ferdinand. Such a policy was by no means unlikely to be adopted by the Bohemian aristocracy.

On the morning after the fatal day, the "Winter King" (king of a winter) fled from Prague, leaving behind, as he hurriedly entered his travelling carriage, his crown and jewels, even his George of the Order of the Garter, richly set in diamonds, a wedding present from his father-in-law— and, what was of greater importance, the archives of the kingdom, and his own secret papers, which were afterwards published in print by the imperialists under the title of "Anhalt's Chancellery" (*Anhaltische Kanzlei*). He was accompanied by his wife, who was in an advanced state of pregnancy; by his three younger children—the youngest, Prince Rupert, an infant of eleven months—by Count Solms, his German lord steward; by the old Prince of Anhalt; by Count Hohenlohe, and by old Thurn. They first went to Breslau, and from thence to Berlin, where Frederic arrived on the 3rd of January, 1621; then by Wolfenbüttel to Hamburg, and at last to the Hague. The Elector of Brandenburg, being afraid of the Emperor's anger, would scarcely allow his sister-in-law to lie in at Cüstrin. The melancholy and romantic queen followed her husband to Holland. There they held in that country a court at Rheenen, near Utrecht, where she hunted with her husband, conversed with the Dutch nobility, and cultivated flowers. The States-General allowed to the exiled Elector 150,000 Brabant guilders a year; the rest—and Frederic spent a great deal of money—was supplied by his father-in-law.

This was the battle of the White Mountain of Prague, "by whose thunder and roar," as Count Khevenhüller expresses it, "the stormy clouds which had hung for eighteen months over the house of Austria were dispersed and chased away." It was one of the most momentous in the history of the world. Bohemia, until then an independent European country, after having given the first impulse by its university of Prague to the spread of learned education in Germany, and by its example to the struggle for religious liberty all over the north and centre of Europe, became now, owing to the rottenness of its aristocracy, a mere province of Austria, which it has remained ever since.

At noon of the same day, 9th of November, 1620, in the early morning of which Frederic had fled, the Duke of Bavaria, with Tilly and Boucquoy, made his entrance at the Hradschin.

William Lobkowitz Hassenstein, the Bohemian lord steward of the "Winter King," undertook to negotiate between the conquerors and the rebels. On the 11th of

November the city, and on the 13th and 14th the Estates, made their submission. The Bohemian lords had at once become exceedingly obsequious towards the much-abused Emperor Ferdinand. On the 17th of November Maximilian left Prague, after having entrusted the regency to Prince Charles Liechtenstein, who had been appointed by the Emperor commissioner-general in Bohemia. Tilly marched to the Palatinate to occupy Frederic's hereditary country; Boucquoy went to Hungary to make war against Bethlen Gabor of Transylvania, and was killed in 1621 in a skirmish before the fortress of Neuhäusel; Dampierre had met with a soldier's death the year before at an attack against Pressburg.

Several of the Bohemian malcontents, imitating the example of William of Orange, had after the catastrophe discreetly fled the country; but most of the great lords, unwarned by the fate of the Counts of Egmont and Horn, stayed in Prague, as heretofore, in proud security. None of them had the least notion that the same might happen to themselves, otherwise they also would have gone.

The revenge of the Emperor was as complete as his victory had been; Ferdinand did the same thing at Prague which Alba had done at Brussels—he waited and went on temporising for seven months. His drift was to decoy the Bohemian lords, to reassure them, and to lure them into the trap; and he succeeded only too well.

Maximilian and Tilly on entering Prague had pledged themselves that an amnesty should be granted. It was Tilly's advice not to drive the Estates to desperate extremities; but the imperial commissioner knew very well that people who have a bad conscience are by no means prone to take desperate steps, but are rather glad to bow low. He seems to have expressed himself to that effect to Tilly, who, even as late as in February, 1621, dropped hints to several of the nobles to seek safety in flight; yet they were foolish enough to neglect the warning.

On the 28th of February, 1621, forty-eight of the leaders of the rebellion were arrested and placed in durance vile at the

Hradschin. Further proceedings were put off until Mansfeld should have left Bohemia; at last he was forced to fall back on the Upper Palatinate. Ferdinand was still vacillating as to whether the Bohemian rebels should or should not be dealt with in the Spanish fashion; but Father Lamormain, his Jesuit confessor, put an end to his scruples by declaring that he would take the whole responsibility on his own conscience; and Ferdinand, who saw in every priest a mouthpiece of the Divine will, gave in. On the following morning the dread messenger who was to carry to the governor, Prince Charles of Liechtenstein—the ancestor of the present princely house—the last order of the Emperor, was on his way to Prague.

And now followed the bloody day of judgment in the Altstadt Ring (Old City Circus) of Prague, the terrible 21st of June, 1621.

At four in the morning the heavy boom of a cannon was heard from the Hradschin—it was the signal for the executions. The prisoners, escorted by a squadron of cuirassiers and 200 musketeers, were driven in six or seven covered carriages to the Altstadt. The scaffold, covered with red cloth, was erected close before the town-hall in the Ring opposite the church called Theinkirche, which was surmounted by the large chalice with the sword, the emblem of the Hussites. The martyrs of the Bohemian cause stepped from the windows of the town-hall out on the scaffold, the top of which was on a level with the first story. Prince Liechtenstein was present in person, sitting on a raised platform under a daïs, with the other eleven commissioners appointed by the Emperor.

It happened with the Bohemian martyrs as with the magnanimous John Frederic of Saxony—they behaved like brave men in the hour of misfortune. They all died joyous in faith.

It was five before the executions began. A slight shower fell, and, to the no small comfort of the martyrs, a fine rainbow spanned the horizon.

The executioner began his task—he beheaded within four hours, from five to nine, twenty-four persons: three were hanged. The first to die was John Andrew Count Schlick, an intimate friend of Count Thurn. He had taken refuge in Saxony; but the Lutheran Elector John George delivered him up to the Emperor. Schlick stoutly refused to listen to the Papist priest who was appointed to attend him on the scaffold; but he prayed by himself before the crucifix which was stuck up there, after which he knelt down to receive the death-blow. After him followed his twenty-three fellow-prisoners, all of them Protestants, except one, Denis Czernin, an ancestor of the present family of Czernin and Chudenitz. This lord was beheaded, although a Papist, in order at least to make a slight show that this wholesale judicial slaughter had been a political necessity, not a mere act of religious persecution. There were good reasons for saving appearances for the present—another more important scheme was still kept in the background.

The decapitated lords were most of them very old; the aggregate age of ten among them was calculated to have been 700 years. One only, whilst already kneeling down, was reprieved, and had his punishment commuted into imprisonment for life—William Lobkowitz-Hassenstein.

During the execution, two squadrons of cavalry and three half-battalions of infantry were drawn up in the Ring. Troops were likewise placed in all the public squares of the city, and the streets scoured by mounted patrols of from six to nine cuirassiers. All the gates were locked.

It was very characteristic of Ferdinand, that, whilst the victims were meeting their doom, he prayed for them. He expressly made a pilgrimage on foot to the celebrated image of the Virgin at Mariazell in Styria, before which he prostrated himself, praying that the Bohemians might be enlightened in their last moments and led back, before their death, into the bosom of the only true and Catholic Church. It was an article of faith with Ferdinand "to work out salvation with fear and trembling;" he even boasted that he had his subjects tortured and executed only from Christian charity, so that their bodies might die, but their souls by forcible means of grace be blessed with everlasting salvation, and especially that unborn generations might not likewise be corrupted by heresy.

Eleven months after the executions in the Altstadt Ring, Ferdinand caused a general pardon to be proclaimed, 23rd of March, 1622. It was just the fourth anniversary of the "Defenestratio Pragensis." The proclamation called upon everyone who was conscious of being guilty to become his own accuser in order to obtain the Emperor's pardon. *And indeed the Bohemian aristocracy had not yet learned wisdom by experience; no less than 728 nobles were good-natured enough to inform against themselves*, for which they were rewarded by the confiscation, some of the whole, others of two-thirds, of half, and of one-third, of their property. *The main point in the Emperor's cabinet was the raising of money*. The confiscated estates not only furnished the Emperor with the means of binding the newly created nobles to the imperial interest, but also for continuing the war. This consideration evidently was paramount, being commanded by necessity; for Austria, as usual, had no money.

The sums raised from the estates which were thus confiscated from the pardoned Bohemian nobles amounted, about the period of Ferdinand's death, to 43,000,000 florins, an immense sum for those times, when money was still very scarce. The protocol of the confiscations formed a large folio. All the landed property of the country changed owners.

The innocent sons and grandsons of the condemned had to wear a red silk string round their neck, as a token "that the spawn of the rebels had likewise deserved the halter." The judges said, "If there be anyone among you without sin of his own, *yet there cleaves to him the hereditary crime of heresy and of being too wealthy.*"

Now followed the last act of the Bohemian tragedy—wholesale emigration. In those days, as Pelzel has averred from a manuscript of the then chief chancellor, William Slawata, no less than 185 noble houses of twelve, twenty, and even fifty persons each, and, besides, many thousand families of commoners and citizens, left their country for ever. The prophecy was then fulfilled, that "The time will come when a man's foes shall be they of his own household." Of the same house, sometimes one branch had its estates confiscated, whilst another branch was enriched by the confiscation. Many Bohemians went to Silesia, many to Saxony, and many to Nuremberg and Ratisbon; others to Brandenburg, to Holland, to Denmark, and to Poland. Among these emigrating noble houses who were thus stripped of their property, there were some very ancient and wealthy ones, as the families of Lobkowitz-Hassenstein, Sternberg, Schlick, Thurn, Kolowrat, Roggendorf, Czernin, Zierotin, Colonna-Fels, Wartenberg, Kinsky, Chotek, Berka, Bubna, and many others. The ranks of the rebels even comprised a scion of a family which now stands foremost among the loyal ones—Christopher Radetzky, who was mulcted in a third of his estates. From those days date the Bohemian congregations at Dresden and in other places. These Bohemian emigrants contrived withal to save considerable property; the congregation at Dresden, for instance, was very rich.

Yet, notwithstanding all this drain, there were, according to Rieger's "Materials for Bohemian Statistics," in the times of Joseph II., in 1787 and 1788, 45,000 Protestants, partly Lutherans and partly Calvinists, in Bohemia, most of them in the circles of Chrudim and Czaslau; in Prague itself not more than a hundred.

The chief burgrave, Adam von Waldstein, brought the celebrated Royal Letter, the Majestäts-brief of Rodolph II., and the other charters of the kingdom of Bohemia, to Vienna. Ferdinand received them with the notable words, "These, then, are the rags of waste paper which have given so much trouble to our predecessors." The Majestäts-brief he cut in pieces with his own hand, and threw it with the other "rags of waste paper" into the fire. Bohemia lost all her national liberties, the liberty of election and of religion, and the joint entail of the estates of the aristocracy. She also lost her language and literature. All the books written in Bohemian, the manuscripts and splendid codices from the flourishing times of Charles IV., George Podiebrad, and Rodolph II. were, as heretical abominations, publicly burnt under the gallows, and all the records of Bohemia's glorious past systematically destroyed.

The Roman mass was again celebrated in Prague on Maundy Thursday, 1622. The chalice and sword were taken down from the Theinkirche, and on the 6th of July, the anniversary of the death of John Huss, the churches shut up. Until then only the preachers of the Bohemian brethren had been banished the country, the Lutherans being spared out of consideration for the Elector of Saxony. Yet the time of forbearance was now past. In October all the Lutheran ministers were ordered to leave the country forthwith, after which the whole kingdom was overrun with Jesuits and Capuchins. Even the papal nuncio, Carlo Caraffa, expressed his fear lest this was going too much ahead; but Ferdinand, swayed by Lamormain, declared that his conscience urged him to annihilate all the heretics; and the Elector John George, whom his divines called "the Saxon David," but the Jesuits "the Merseburg Beer-Geordy," quietly put up with the expulsion of the Protestants. No Protestant was allowed any longer to entail his property; in all the towns the magistrates were changed, to the exclusion of everyone not a Papist. Those who refused to embrace Popery had the soldiers—Spaniards, Walloons, Croats, all sorts of ruthless and brutal cut-throats—quartered upon them, "to bring them to their senses by necessity," as Caraffa expressed it. Caraffa was quite amazed at the demure conduct of the citizens of Prague; every Sunday two or three thousand people were seen attending mass. At last, in 1627, all the Protestants were expelled from Bohemian soil. In the following year (25th of April, 1628) Ferdinand, as "Catholicæ fidei acerrimus defensor," founded, for the perpetual commemoration of the victory over the rebels, the church of St. Maria de Victoria on the White Mountain, the first stone of which was laid in presence of the imperial family by the Cardinal Archbishop of Prague, Ernest von Harrach.

The counter-reformation was enforced likewise in Moravia—where Count Thurn, after his flight from Prague, had in vain endeavoured to keep the insurrection alive—and also in Austria. In 1627 the Protestant citizens of Vienna and the noble landowners of Austria had a term of four months allowed them to declare whether they would turn Papists, or sell their property and estates and emigrate. The emigration then began; only a few old noble houses remained. New families, to whom these confiscated estates were granted, took the place of the emigrated. Many of the old family names, however, were propagated in Austria by apostate scions of the emigrated houses returning and abjuring Protestantism.

In Upper Austria alone a formidable opposition was offered. This province had been pledged by the Emperor to Maximilian of Bavaria for the payment of the expenses of the war. The duke appointed as his governor at Linz Count Adam Herberstorf, a very harsh man. The nobility had left the country. Easter day, 1626, being fixed as the last term by which every trace of heresy was to have vanished, the peasantry, the greater part of whom were Protestants, resolved upon staking their all in fighting for evangelical freedom. To the number of 80,000, part of them formed in regiments dressed all in black as mourning for the distress of the country, they appeared before Linz, under the command of Stephen Fadinger, a wealthy member of their own body, and of the so-called Unknown Student, whose name has never been revealed. Both these leaders met with their death in the contest. In November, 1626, Pappenheim, who was Herberstorf's stepson, succeeded in conquering the peasants; not, however, without having encountered the most resolute resistance on their side. He, who had long been familiar with all the horrors of war, states in a letter that he had never seen such wild fury of war as when the peasants, singing psalms, or with the terrible battle-cry of:

> "Since 'tis for our souls, for death or life,
> May God make us heroes in the strife.
> It must be, dear Brethren! It must be!"[1]

broke into the ranks of his troopers, tore them from their

---

[1] "Weil's gilt die Seel und auch das Blut,
So geb' uns Gott den Heldenmuth!
Es muss sein! Liebe Brüder! Es muss sein!"

horses, and stoutly attacked them with clubs, lances, and morning-stars (spike-clubs); and likewise he had lost many men by the galling fire from ditches and woods, and from behind bushes and hedges.

The principal ringleaders were executed at Linz; and the country, after being reduced by Pappenheim, was held in check by military occupation.

In this manner Bohemia, with Moravia and the whole of Austria, was brought back to Popery by force. We have Hormayr's authority for it, that throughout all the Austrian monarchy only about thirty old Roman Catholic noble families were left. Of the whole old Bohemian nobility there remained only about eighteen houses; among them the newly created Princes of Lobkowitz, and the newly created Counts of Martinitz and Slawata, the victims of the "Defenestratio Pragensis." Of the old nobility of Austria Proper not more than about thirteen houses remained; yet there were some converts, as, for instance, the Liechtensteins, the Althanns, and the Kuffsteins. Of the Bohemians, as has been stated before, many families emigrated to Silesia. Of the Austrian emigrants a great number settled in the Protestant cities of Nuremberg and Ratisbon; among them the Zinzendorfs, who, however, afterwards found a new home in Saxony, where the celebrated Bishop Zinzendorf formed the establishment of the Moravian brethren at Herrnhut. Many Bohemian and Austrian emigrants took service in the Swedish, French, Danish, Brunswick, Hessian armies; in that of the States-General, in Transylvania, in Poland, even in Turkey. Of the Austrians the greater part returned after some time to their own country, and became voluntary converts to the Roman Catholic faith.

The heart sickens at the horrors which attended the forced conversions. Shocking details of them are given, among others, by Hormayr, in his Annual of 1836. The things which happened then were much worse even than the atrocities of the Dragonnades under Louis XIV. All the brutal and barbarous religious fanaticism of the middle ages, aggravated and envenomed by Jesuit statecraft, found here a dreadful vent. To Frederic von Roggendorf the Emperor sent an offer of pardon if he would return. He declined the offer with the very pertinent remark, "What pardon? a Bohemian one? Head off! A Moravian? Imprisonment for life! An Austrian? Confiscation of every property!"

To Silesia better conditions were promised, because the inhabitants of this province had made their submission only on the express promise of the Elector of Saxony that their religious liberty should be secured to them. Yet, notwithstanding this imperial promise, the president of the chamber (lord treasurer), Count Charles Hannibal Dohna, with his ruthless bands of Liechtenstein dragoons, went from house to house throughout the whole country, accompanied by Jesuits and Capuchins, to convert the inhabitants by force. If threats, spoliation, torture, were of no avail, they snatched the children from the arms of their mothers and tormented them before the eyes of their parents. Two officers once took up a naked infant each by a leg, cleft it with the sword, and gave the two halves back to the parents with the brutal words, "*Here you have it sub utraque!*" This Dohna self-complacently called himself "the worker of salvation." The oppression of the Protestants in Silesia continued until Charles XII. of Sweden, on his expedition to Saxony in 1707, obliged the Emperor to fulfil the clauses of the compact; and even afterwards, until the conquest of Silesia in 1741 by Frederic II., whose advent was hailed there with delight.

Bethlen Gabor of Transylvania concluded, in 1622, his peace with the Emperor at Nicholsburg. Ferdinand left to him eight Hungarian counties, with the town of Kaschau, besides the two Silesian principalities of Ratibor and Oppeln.

The Elector of Saxony received, for the services which he had rendered to the Emperor, the two Lusatias as a redeemable pledge. The Elector of Brandenburg, *in reward of his inactive neutrality*, was invested as liege-lord of the fief of Prussia.

The Spaniards under Spinola and Cordova still overran the Rhenish, and Tilly reduced the Upper Palatinate.

5.—The new Catholic aristocracy of Austria, and the great creation of Counts and Princes.

The executions of the Protestants found a counterpart in the rewards of those who had remained faithful to the Emperor. It has always been the selfish policy of the house of Habsburg to purchase peace with foreign hostile powers by the sacrifice of territories not its own, but belonging to the German Empire; and likewise to reward its friends and servants with the honours and dignities, not of its own crown lands, but of those of the German peerage.

After the victory of the White Mountain, Ferdinand created new German princes and counts of the Empire "by dozens." A whole bevy of Italian, Spanish, Hungarian, Polish, and even Croatian recipients of the imperial favour were then foisted into the German aristocracy. From those times dates the difference between old and new princely houses. By the side of such families as the Guelphs, the Saxon Wettins, and the Holstein Gottorps, scions of which are now occupying the two first thrones in the world, the English and Russian, Ferdinand II. planted houses like the Liechtensteins, until then neither more nor less than simple gentlemen, small nobles, *viri nobiles*, not even *illustres*. These Liechtensteins have risen in the nineteenth century even to the rank of sovereign princes.

Among the newly created princes and counts, there were some whose merits and demerits the Duchess of Orleans set forth in very significant terms. She writes, in a letter dated the 12th of October, 1702, " Prince Taxis!" (created a prince by Austria in 1686); "well, that is a very odd principality. If you want to count that for a prince, you may find them by dozens!" And in a letter of the 18th of July, 1718, " Of the earldom of Wurmbrand" (created in 1701) "I have never heard before. I suppose it must be something upstart, or Austrian."

Besides Liechtenstein, there were Wallenstein, Eggenberg, the descendant of the Styrian banker, and Cardinal Francis Dietrichstein ; moreover, the Bohemian Lobkowitzes, the Swabian Hohenzollern,[1] and the Salms on the Rhine, created princes. Then, again, the princely dignity of the German Empire was bestowed on ten or fifteen Italian families; *e.g.*, those of Este, Gonzaga, Caraffa, Strozzi, and Aldobrandini; on the Spanish Count Cantacroy, the descendant of Nicholas Perrenot Granvella; on the two Transylvanian princes, Bethlen Gabor and George Ragoczy; and on the Polish noble family of Czartorisky.

The seventy or eighty, or more, families to which Ferdinand II., after the battle of the White Mountain, granted diplomas as counts of the German, or, to use the official title, of the Holy Roman Empire, were likewise not merely Germans, but Italians, Spaniards, Walloons, English, Scotch, and Irish, and also some Croats. Fourteen of them received the style of "*Illustrissimus*." The list comprised the names of Tilly (illustrissimus), Pappenheim (illustrissimus), Hatzfeld (illustrissimus), Terzky, and Illo; of the three upstarts, Aldringer, Götz, and Holk; of the Italians, Gallas and Colloredo; of the Spaniards, Maradas and Verdugo; of the Croats, Isolani and Kollonitsch. Besides these men of the sword, the dignity of count was bestowed on men of peace; among whom particular mention is due to the diplomatist of the peace of Westphalia, Trautmannsdorf (*justly* titled "*illustrissimus*"), and to the defenestrated Bohemians, Martinitz and Slawata.

This new aristocracy of the German Empire was body and soul given to Austria, or—as it was then called in the language of the court, and is still called in the language of Prince Metternich—"well disposed." These newly created princes and counts formed the nucleus of the *new Catholic chain of nobles* in Austria, which, having enriched itself with the spoils of the old one, succeeded in sharing with the Jesuits the helm of government. To obviate any attempt at a new rebellion, this oligarchy made use of the new Spanish expedients of "poisoning and stabbing." The Duchess of Orleans, in a letter of the 6th of December, 1721, says of

---

[1] Not to be confounded with the Brandenburg, the present royal, line of the house.—*Translator*.

them, " *Without the knowledge of the Emperor they send people into the other world!*" The first victims of this policy of crushing any obnoxious or too powerful, wealthy, and independent personage were Wallenstein and Bethlen Gabor.

6.—*The Protestant partisans, Mansfeld, Brunswick, &c.*

When the reigning Protestant princes abandoned the cause of their brethren in faith among the German people, it was taken up by partisans, who—like that Sforza who from *condottiere* rose to be a duke—placed themselves at the head of armed bands, in order to gain a principality at the point of the sword.

The first of these bold partisans who tried to make their fortune under the banner of Protestantism was Count Ernest Mansfeld, a bastard of the first Prince of Mansfeld, Peter Ernest, who died in 1604, as the Spanish captain-general of Luxemburg. The family had their estates in the Hartz mountains, but it is now extinct. Ernest was a man of very easy conscience, perfectly unscrupulous with regard to the means for obtaining his ends. He was a sort of brigand in grand style. He gave the first example of making war with soldiers who were fed by the war alone, and who, living by spoil, gave quarter only to those who were able to pay a ransom. It was he who imprinted on the Thirty Years' War the character of a bloody foray, in which robbery and murder were the main objects. Mansfeld had served Frederic, the "Winter King," in Bohemia; had taken Pilsen, and long kept it. For a considerable time after the battle of the White Mountain, he disputed Bohemia with the Emperor; who therefore repeatedly tried to gain him over by bribery. The last attempt of the kind was made through the Infanta Isabella from Brussels. In this instance, Mansfeld apparently came to a full agreement, so that nothing was wanting but his signature; after which he invited the imperial commissioners to his table, and at last introduced to them the King of the Bohemians, who had just then come from Holland by Paris to Germersheim, in his own Rhenish

Palatinate. When bribes proved of no avail, a prize of 300,000 crowns was set on the head of the obnoxious bastard, whom they would have so much liked to employ on the Papist side.

Mansfeld was small, fair, but hunchbacked, and besides disfigured by a hare-lip; yet he was endowed with a bold, enterprising, indomitable spirit. Even his enemies were obliged to acknowledge him to be a great general. He was the strangest compound of an indefatigable partisan and an ease-loving epicure, of a mercenary *condottiere* and an irresistible party-leader. Being the bastard of a prince, he considered himself as the equal of princes. In his letters of feud to the Bishop of Würtzburg he quite artlessly vowed that, as true as he was a cavalier of honour, he would rage against his lordship's country and people with fire and sword; and the man was as good as his word. After having quitted Bohemia, he appeared in the Upper Palatinate against Tilly, and in the Rhenish Palatinate against the Spaniards.

This first Protestant partisan was soon followed by another, Christian of Brunswick, administrator of Halberstadt, a younger brother of Frederic Ulric, the reigning Duke of Brunswick-Wolfenbüttel. Christian of Brunswick—whom the Papist historian Wassenberg, the author of the "German Florus," terms "a man born for the ruin of Germany," and "the worst pestilence which ever rose from the Dutch morass"—was certainly even worse, if possible, than Mansfeld. He was at that time in his twenty-second year, a most handsome man, of a vigorous frame, the most gallant of profligates, rapacious, but giving away his spoil with princely liberality; in short, he was one of the maddest adventurers among the most dashing "lions" of the seventeenth century. He began his soldier's career with 300 ducats in his purse, with 200 horse, and with a glove sticking in his hat. The glove was from the lady for whom he had drawn his sword, the romantic and melancholy Elizabeth Stuart, the exiled "Winter Queen." He had vowed to her, at her court at Rheenen in Holland, that he would return her this glove at Prague. Four months after his quitting Holland, he had collected a by no means despicable force. The device on his colours was, "Everything for God and for Her." He made his appearance in Lower (North-western) Germany and in Westphalia; and it was his plan to make his way through Hesse, to join Mansfeld in the Palatinate. He began by plundering the Lower Saxon and Westphalian cathedrals and chapters. When at Paderborn he found the statue of St. Liborius of pure gold, weighing eighty pounds; he embraced the worthy saint, thanking him for his civility of having waited for him. At Münster he found the Twelve Apostles of silver; and, reproving them for thus standing idle, called out to them to go forth and preach to the heathen—for which purpose he sent them to the mint. On the dollars which in 1622 were coined out of them, his bust is encircled by the legend, "God's friend and the parsons' enemy." On the reverse, there is a mailed *right* arm holding a sword; and the inscription, "*Tout avec Dieu.*" In the same year, he lost in the battle of Fleury his *left* arm—a circumstance which the Papists did not fail to herald forth as a punishment of the Lord. He had the limb amputated *in the presence of his whole army*, amidst the braying of trumpets and the roll of kettle-drums; and a medal was struck to commemorate the event, with the legend:

"Let me be maimed, let me be lame,
 I'll hate the parsons all the same."[1]

An "ingenious peasant from the banks of the Meuse" made an artificial iron arm for him—afterwards kept in the Wolfenbüttel Museum—which he was able to move like a natural one. He could grasp and hold with it, and it was riveted with gold.

To these two bold partisans a great number of reigning petty princes and of cadets of princely houses are to be added, who, under the banner of Protestantism, wished to gain or to recover lands. Their ranks comprised the Margrave John

---

[1] "Verlier' ich gleich Arm und Bein
   Will ich doch Pfaffenfeind sein."

George of Brandenburg-Jägerndorf, who had been outlawed by the Emperor, and his principality in Silesia given to Prince Charles of Liechtenstein;[1] the reigning Duke of Saxe-Weimar, William, who wanted to recover the electoral dignity for the Ernestine line; his brother John Ernest, who was killed in Hungary in 1626; the afterwards celebrated Duke Bernard of Weimar; Duke Magnus of Würtemberg, who was killed in the battle of Wimpfen in 1623; and, lastly, Margrave George Frederic of Baden-Durlach, who before the battle of Wimpfen resigned in favour of his son, and died in Geneva in 1638. All these princes carried on the war for the Protestant cause on their own account. Circumstances seemed favourable: shortly after the peace of Nicholsburg, in 1622, Bethlen Gabor had again broken with the Emperor, who thus was threatened in the rear: but the princes were not able to hold out against Tilly. It was of no avail that Frederic, in 1622, leaving the Hague under the disguise of a merchant, made his appearance in the Palatinate; nor did Mansfeld's victory over Tilly at Wisloch near Heidelberg do any good. Tilly defeated, in the same year, Brunswick near Höchst on the Maine; and utterly routed the Margrave of Baden in the battle of Wimpfen, near Heilbronn on the Neckar. These victories he crowned by the taking of the two principal fortresses of Heidelberg and Mannheim, which completed the conquest of the Palatinate. With delight did the papal nuncio see mass again performed at Heidelberg, the cradle of the celebrated Calvinist catechism. The magnificent library of the university Maximilian of Bavaria sent as a present to the Vatican, from whence it was recovered only in 1815.

Mansfeld, after having gone from Bohemia to the Upper Palatinate, had, since 1621, overrun Alsace to relieve Baden and Würtemberg. After the battle of Wimpfen, he went with Brunswick to the Netherlands, where the latter lost his arm in the battle of Fleury. Mansfeld paid two visits to England, where, in 1624, he was received with the same enthusiasm as were afterwards Prince Eugene, Blücher, and Kossuth. In 1625 Brunswick followed him to London. They returned

---

[1] He died in 1624, in Hungary, with Bethlen Gabor.

to the continent with English troops; but they were not able to do much, although they joined the King of Denmark, who, in 1624, had taken the war in his own hands. Mansfeld, having at last been driven from German soil by Wallenstein, went to Bethlen Gabor in Transylvania, and died near Zara in Illyria at the age of forty-six, as a true soldier, attired in his best uniform, and standing upright to the last moment. When death overtook him, he was on his way to Venice, where old Count Thurn was then staying, and where he intended to embark for the third time for England. Christian of Brunswick had died before him in the same year (1626), in the castle of his ancestors at Wolfenbüttel, at the age of twenty-seven. His malady was singular—the tapeworm.

The first act of the great war had closed in 1623, by the transferring of the electorate of the Elector Palatine to Bavaria, which was done at the Princes' Diet *(Fürstentag)* at Ratisbon, on the 6th of March. The Emperor Ferdinand, having run into debt with the Duke of Bavaria for war expenses to the amount of 13,000,000 florins, had mortgaged to him Upper Austria for that sum; now, however, he paid that *Austrian* debt by the cession of *German* territory, the Palatinate.

The despoiled Count Palatine justly complained of these proceedings of the Emperor. He especially referred to the case of Bethlen Gabor, which had been quite similar to his own, as that prince, likewise in opposition to the Emperor, had usurped the royal crown of Hungary, and yet been pardoned, and, besides, been invested with the dignity of a prince of the Empire, and with the principalities of Ratibor and Oppeln. Even the Spanish ambassador, Count Ognate, very strongly expressed his disapprobation of the measure; he did not even pay to the new Elector the customary visit, to congratulate him on his accession of dignity. The Spanish premier Olivarez had suggested a very different arrangement: " To give to the Count Palatine an appanage, such as Charles V. had granted to John Frederic of Saxony, but to confer on his son an eighth (newly created) electorate; to have him brought up in Vienna as a Roman Catholic, and to marry him to an imperial princess." To this a clause was added that a ninth electorate might be created in favour of Hesse-Cassel, nine (as an odd number) being preferable to eight.

The troops of the League under Tilly remained, as heretofore, stationed in Lower Germany, although Mansfeld and Brunswick had been driven out of Westphalia since 1623. This showed clearly the intention of the Emperor. The bishoprics of those provinces, which, having been secularised in the Reformation, were "administered" by Protestant princes, were now to be restored as Roman Catholic sees; and Lower Germany was to be treated as the southern provinces had been before. Bethlen Gabor had, in 1624, made his second peace at Vienna with the Emperor.

It was under these circumstances that Christian IV., king of Denmark—as Duke of Holstein, a prince of the Empire—placed himself at the head of the Protestants. Being captain-general of the circle of Lower Saxony, he united his forces with those of Mansfeld and Brunswick. Bethlen Gabor, in 1626, came to a third rupture with the Emperor. Christian likewise entered into an alliance with Holland and England, and also France promised subsidies. Cardinal Richelieu, having been placed at the helm of the government since 1624, returned to the old policy of Francis I. and Henry II., who, although persecuting the Protestants of their own country, leagued themselves with those of the Empire.

Until then the war in Germany had been conducted principally with the forces of the League. The Emperor could not wish that everything should be done by the house of Bavaria; but he wanted the means for equipping a large army. Then a new *condottiere* after the pattern of Mansfeld came forth, offering to carry on war on a grand scale, and to make it self-supporting. This was no other than Wallenstein. He became in the second period of the war what Tilly had been in the first.

7.—*Wallenstein and his plans for the establishment of the absolute sovereignty of the Emperor.*

Albert Wenceslaus Eusebius Baron Waldstein, or Wallenstein, was descended from an old Bohemian family, the ancestors of which may be traced as far back as the twelfth century. At the time of the Bohemian King Ottocar one of the ancestors of the Waldsteins presented himself with twenty-four doughty sons in knightly armour before the King, to accompany the monarch in his expedition against the pagan Prussians. This scene is represented in a well-known picture on a ceiling at the Waldstein castle of Dux, near Töplitz. The name of Waldstein, however, does not occur in the Bohemian public documents until the fourteenth century. A seal, appended to a roll of the year 1375, bears around it the legend, "Henricus de Valstein."

The celebrated General Wallenstein was born on the 15th of September, 1583, at Herrmanic on the Elbe, an estate of his father. His parents were Protestants, belonging to the community of the Bohemian brethren. The families also of his mother, Marusca Smirczicky, and of his grandmother, of the house of Slawata, were Utraquists. But Wallenstein lost his mother as early as 1593, and his father in 1595, when the boy, being in his thirteenth year, was placed by one of his uncles, Albert Slawata, a Protestant, in the school of the Bohemian brethren on his estate of Koschumberg. Afterwards, however, another uncle of his, John von Ricam, a Papist, who was a great friend of the Jesuits, had him educated at the college for young nobles which the reverend fathers kept at Olmütz; and there Father Pachta led him into the fold of the Church of Rome.

From early childhood the lofty and grasping spirit, as well as the harshness and stubbornness of Wallenstein's character, manifested themselves. One day when his mother chastised him, a boy of not more than seven years, he called out, "I wish I were a prince, that I might not be flogged!" At that tender age already, whilst playing at soldiers with other children of his age, he always chose for himself the part of general, and was fond of being waited upon like a grand lord. When his uncle, Adam von Waldstein, once rebuked him for it, remarking, "Well, cousin, you give yourself the airs of a prince!" the boy gave the ready answer, "That which is not may one day be." There were many anecdotes current about Wallenstein's haughty, ambitious spirit. Thus it was said that at the school of Goldberg he had once dreamed that teachers and pupils, and even the trees, had made obeisance to him, for which his preceptor Fechner had ridiculed him. At the University of Altdorf he had been once condemned to the black-hole, and as that place, newly built, was to be named after its first inmate, Wallenstein had pushed his poodle in before him, on which the black-hole had ever after been called Poodle.[1] And another time, when he was a page at the court of the Margrave of Burgau, the son of Ferdinand of Tyrol and the beautiful Philippina Welser, he had once in his ambitious day-dreams fallen from a window in the third story of the castle of Innsbruck, and escaped as by a miracle.[2]

But Palacky, the historian of Bohemia, has proved that Wallenstein never during his youth resided either at Goldberg or at Altdorf or at Innsbruck.

After leaving the college at Olmütz he went on his travels, by the advice of Father Pachta, his tutor, whom through life he remembered as a benefactor to whom he owed everything. He made the usual cavalier's tour in company with a wealthy young Moravian nobleman, Adam Leo Liceck of Riesenburg; and the two visited together southern and western Germany, and the principal cities of Holland, England, France, and Italy. They were attended by the learned mathematician and astrologer Verdungus, who first implanted in Wallenstein a taste for astrology. The latter

[1] The point of the joke is, that the beadle, among whose many offices is that of turnkey of the "Carcer" (the black-hole for recalcitrant undergraduates), is, in university parlance, called Poodle; so that the culprit, while saving his own name from being misapplied, turned the ridicule on his gaoler. This apocryphal anecdote is alluded to in "Wallenstein's Lager" of Schiller.—*Translator.*

[2] This anecdote also is alluded to by Schiller in "Wallenstein's Tod."—*Translator.*

also stayed for some time at Padua, to be initiated by Professor Argoli into the occult sciences, and into the mysteries of the Cabala. After his return, he entered the military career, serving first against the Turks, and afterwards, under Dampierre, against the Venetians. In the last-mentioned campaign, he was able to equip a regiment of dragoons, having married an elderly widow, Lucretia von Landeck, who had large estates in Moravia. This lady had nearly killed him by dosing him with a philtre; she herself died in 1614.

After the campaign against Venice, Wallenstein was, in 1617, created by the Emperor Matthias a baron of Bohemia, and appointed a colonel in the imperial army, a member of the Aulic council of war, and a chamberlain. At the outbreak of the disturbances, he was already so well known, and enjoyed such popularity, that the Bohemians wanted to nominate him their general. But he remained faithful to the Emperor, and was obliged to fly before Count Thurn from Olmütz to Vienna; he succeeded, however, in saving the war-chest, containing upwards of 90,000 crowns. Being now put under Boucquoy's command, he again raised a regiment of cuirassiers for the Bohemian war, in which he served as quartermaster-general. In the afternoon before the battle of the White Mountain, Tilly had sent him to cover a large foraging expedition, which kept him away till the battle was over. He then served against Bethlen Gabor. In 1620 he was raised by Ferdinand II. to the rank of a count of the Empire; and in 1622, after the peace of Nicholsburg, the Emperor granted to him Friedland, a lordship of nine towns and fifty-seven castles and villages in the north-eastern districts of Bohemia. Since then Wallenstein was generally styled the *Friedländer*. At last, in 1623, he was made a prince of the Empire. His wealth was vast enough to keep up his new dignity; by purchasing at a ridiculously low price the confiscated property of attainted nobles and the estates of emigrants, he had become the richest landed proprietor, after the Emperor, in Bohemia. The list communicated by the historian Rieger of the property which he had thus acquired, and which was afterwards confiscated, enumerates sixty-seven estates of a value of about 8,000,000 florins (£800,000 sterling); but they were bought by Wallenstein at a much lower figure. He carried on this traffic of buying and selling estates on the very largest scale; and his share in the spoil of the Bohemian rebels amounted to nearly a third part of the whole.

In the meanwhile he had formed a family connection of the highest importance for his interest at the court of Vienna, by his marriage with Isabella Countess Harrach, whose father, Count Charles Harrach, an imperial privy councillor and chamberlain, enjoyed very high favour with Ferdinand II.

In the spring of 1625 an order from the Emperor was issued to Wallenstein to raise for his Majesty an army of about 20,000 men by the side of that of Tilly. This he declined to do; but he offered to enrol one of 40,000 or 50,000 men, for, said he, an army of that strength would know how to feed itself. He thereupon received a commission from Vienna empowering him to raise that number; at the same time, he was nominated generalissimo of the Emperor, with absolute power in his army, in which he should have the right of appointing all the officers himself. On this he at once established his recruiting stations in Bohemia, Franconia, and Swabia, and before a few months were past, his army was formed, his name having attracted not only needy adventurers and starving people out of employ, of which certainly there was no lack in those hard times, but also men of the highest rank, who were glad to serve as officers under him. His headquarters were at Eger (Egra) in Bohemia, the same place where, nine years later, his career was doomed to come to a bloody end.

Wallenstein was born to be "a prince in war." He displayed the greatest splendour and magnificence, and commanded the homage of the world by his princely wealth, which he lavished on all sides most profusely; by his princely luxury, in which he allowed everyone about him to participate; and by a fanciful pomp, which dazzled all those who approached him.

Gustavus Adolphus, who did not at all consider him a great

general, was not far wrong in calling him a madman; but the fantastic, adventurous Friedländer knew how to bait the strongest passions of his people, and thereby to bind them to him even to the death. His officers, guests of his own table, led the most splendid life. He never rewarded but in a princely manner. He connived at all the excesses of his soldiers, under the sole condition of having the strictest discipline kept up on service. His camp was the most joyous and gay that a soldier could have wished. He allowed a train of servants, camp-followers, and waggoners; he allowed a train of women, of whom there are said to have been 15,000 in the camp of Nuremberg, but he allowed no parson. He admitted into his army freebooters of every political and religious creed. Light cavalry, troops of Croats, and Pulks of Cossacks were particularly welcome. His keen eye discerned at the first glance the most able, whom he would at once raise from the ranks: every private soldier had the way to the highest military honours open before him. On every occasion he praised the soldiers who distinguished themselves by their bravery; every daring achievement was on the spot rewarded by promotion and rich presents, the lowest sum which he gave being 100 crowns. He asked of the soldier but two things, intrepidity and the most implicit obedience. On the other hand, the severity of the punishment was just as excessive as the liberality of the rewards. Cowardice was inexorably punished by death; at the least breach of discipline, the general, whose word was in place of the sentence of a court-martial, briefly gave the order, "Let the brute be hanged!" He despised men, and accordingly treated them as mere tools of his plans. When, previous to the assault on his camp near Nuremberg, Gustavus Adolphus made him the proposition to give quarter in extreme cases, he sent back word, "The troops may fight or rot."

Even the appearance of the general struck the beholder with reverence and awe. A tall, thin, proud figure, with sallow countenance and stern features; a lofty, commanding forehead, with short bristling black hair; small, black, fiery and piercing eyes; dark, mistrustful looks; his chin and lips covered with a pointed beard and thick moustachios, the ends of which stood stiffly out; such was the man as we may still see him in his portraits. His usual dress consisted of a buff jerkin and a white doublet, scarlet mantle and hose, a broad Spanish ruff, boots of Cordova leather lined with fur on account of his gout; on his hat he wore, like Tilly, a long waving red plume.

Whilst in the camp the most riotous gaiety reigned paramount, the most profound stillness was enforced in his own immediate neighbourhood. He is said to have once caused a valet of his to be hanged for having awakened him without express orders, and an officer to be privately put to death for having startled him by the jingling of his spurs. He was always plunged in thought, occupied only with himself and his own plans and projects. He was indefatigable in mental exertion and practical labour; both in thought and deed he drew only from the resources of his own mind and his own will, in proud independence of every foreign influence. He even disliked being looked at whilst receiving reports or giving orders; and the soldiers were directed, when he walked through the rows of their tents, not to appear to take any notice of him. The men were struck with a strange awe when Wallenstein's tall thin figure glided along like a ghost; there was about all his being something mysterious, solemn, and unearthly. The soldiers were fully convinced that their general had a bond with the powers of darkness; that he read the future in the stars; that he could not bear to hear the barking of the dog nor the crowing of the cock; that he was proof against bullet as well as against cut and stab; and, above all, that he had charmed fortune to stand by his colours. Fortune, indeed, which was his deity, became that of the whole of his army.

Wallenstein was a man of the most fiery temper, but outwardly he always showed himself cool and collected. His orders were brief and terse. He was very chary with his words; but, although he spoke little, what he spoke was full of energy and to the purpose. Least of all he spoke about himself; yet the most ardent ambition burnt quietly and silently within him. To that passion he in cold blood sacrificed everything and everybody. George Zriny, ban of Croatia, one day brought to him the head of a Turk of high station which he had cut off himself. As the ban, in producing the ghastly trophy, made the remark, "This is the way in which one ought to pursue the Emperor's enemies," Wallenstein answered with icy coldness, "I have seen some heads cut off before, but I never cut off one myself"; and soon after, he treated the ban at a dinner to a poisoned radish of which Zriny died. This happened in 1626. Wallenstein was a perfect master of dissimulation; to which art, and to his rule of never in any case of importance committing himself in writing, he owed most of his influence and his successes. To ensure victory, he made ample use of the expedient which in later times Marlborough and Prince Eugene employed so felicitously—he kept on all sides a host of well-paid spies. Wallenstein was forty-two years old when he took the chief command of the troops raised for the Emperor.

It was in the autumn of 1625 that Wallenstein set out from his headquarters at Eger to march against the King of Denmark. He and Tilly carried on the war each independently of the other. Tilly attacked the King on the Weser in front, Wallenstein hurried along the Elbe to attack him in the rear. He wintered in 1625 at Halberstadt, Tilly at Hameln on the Weser. In the campaign of the following year, Wallenstein discomfited Count Mansfeld at the bridge of Dessau, and the defeated partisan was obliged to fly through Brandenburg and Silesia to Bethlen Gabor. When the latter had again come to a rupture with the Emperor, Wallenstein marched against him to Hungary, after which he took up his winter quarters at Prague. In the campaign of 1627 he recovered Silesia for the Emperor, and conquered all the Danish possessions on the continent, besides Pomerania and Mecklenburg, which afterwards became his own duchy. In these conquered countries, and in the marches of Brandenburg, he made his numerous and formidable army take up its winter quarters during the two years of 1627 and 1628. His own residence was at Güstrow in Mecklenburg.

In the year 1626, whilst Wallenstein was in Hungary, Tilly defeated the King of Denmark in a pitched battle at Lutter, near the Baremberg; and the conquered monarch had but a very narrow escape from being taken prisoner. In the same year, both allies of Christian IV., Mansfeld and Brunswick, were crushed; and Wallenstein obliged Bethlen Gabor to make his third peace with the Emperor at Leutschau. Tilly maintained his headquarters on the Weser, and in 1629 Christian was obliged to conclude peace at Lübeck. Things were now placed again on their old footing, and the Emperor once more was lord and master in the Empire.

Wallenstein in the Danish war had acted not only as the general, but also as the banker of the Emperor, who again showered rewards on his head. Ferdinand granted to him, on the 4th of January, 1627, the title of duke. In the same year he let him have the duchy of Sagan in Silesia and the lordship of Priebus for the nominal price of 125,000 crowns. In 1628 he met him at the castle of Brandeis in Bohemia, and bestowed on him, in payment of the 3,000,000 florins which he had expended in the war for his imperial master, the principality of Mecklenburg, an integral part of the German Empire, its dukes, as allies of the King of Denmark, having been attainted, whereby their territory became forfeited. Here, at Brandeis, whilst waiting on the Emperor during dinner, Wallenstein exercised the right of a prince of the Empire to appear with covered head before the Emperor.

On the 20th of April, 1628, Wallenstein was nominated "General of the Baltic and Oceanic Seas." Austria, deprived by the selfish dynastic predilections of Charles V. of her best coasts, those of the Netherlands, now thought of again becoming a maritime power, of creating a navy, and of giving a vigorous impulse to German commerce. Many were the plans to effect this purpose, but the result fell far short of the vastness of the conception. First of all, negotiations were set on foot with the Hanseatic towns for the supply of ships; the Danes were to be attacked in their isles, and the Emperor elected King of Denmark; an armed trading company was to be established, which was to have the monopoly of the traffic with Spain and Italy, to the exclusion of the newly risen maritime powers of Holland and England. Hamburg, which, although nominally neutral, had for several years privately supported Tilly, was to supplant Antwerp as the principal emporium of the commerce of the world. The imperial commissioner, Count George Lewis Schwartzenberg, publicly announced to the North German cities in a brilliant speech, which he delivered in 1627 at a meeting in Lübeck, the approaching revival of the old Hanseatic League. This bright hope remained unfulfilled. Not more than three years from that time the last Diet of that League was held.

It was one town, and not a very large one, of Northern Germany which then foiled the project of establishing the new maritime power of Austria, and prevented the General of the Baltic and Oceanic Seas from actually entering upon his office. That town was Stralsund. Wallenstein lay before it from February to August, 1628; but, as both the King of Denmark and Gustavus Adolphus of Sweden threw succour into the town from the side by the sea, Wallenstein was obliged to raise the siege, after having lost 12,000 men before it, and after having made the supercilious boast that he would take the town though it were riveted with chains to the heavens. The heroic defence of Stralsund caused the whole project of intimidating the North of Europe by an Austrian Catholic maritime power to end in smoke. The ascendency which Sweden soon after obtained in those seas made it impossible at a later period to revive the plan.

The discomfiture before Stralsund undermined Wallenstein's position, in which until then he had commanded the respect of friend and foe. The Emperor lost faith in his general's invincibility. The high aristocracy of princes now became loud in their remonstrances against the unmeasured pomp and magnificence of the upstart. The whole of Northern Germany resounded with grievances at the contributions which the general extorted from the countries where he had established himself. Up to that time all, as if stupefied by the amazing luck of the man, had remained silent; now, however, a universal outcry was raised against the tyrant who was wallowing in luxury at the cost of general misery. At a time when multitudes were pining from the distress superinduced by a war of twelve years' duration, when thousands literally died from starvation, Wallenstein revelled in princely profusion; and his commanders and officers, each in his degree, imitated his extravagant example. Whilst many citizens and peasants committed suicide to escape from the furious pangs of hunger, there was not in Pomerania a captain of dragoons belonging to Wallenstein's army who did not live in much more costly style than the former dukes of the country had done. In Silesia, where Wallenstein had seized all the crops and stores of corn, his soldiers lived in abundance, whilst the inhabitants were maddened by misery to such a pitch that cases occurred of people attacking their own brothers, and parents their own children, to kill them and feed on them. The damage caused to the electorate of Brandenburg by the quartering of Wallenstein's troops on the inhabitants and by the contributions levied by them, was calculated at 20,000,000 florins, that to Hesse-Cassel at 7,000,000 florins.

Of the manner in which Wallenstein's troops behaved in their quarters and on their march, we have a description by a member of the imperial family, Archduke Leopold of Tyrol, the brother of Ferdinand II. When, in 1629, the 20,000 picked troops which Wallenstein despatched to Italy for the war of the Mantuan succession approached, in the month of May, the territory of the Archduke, the latter wrote to the Emperor: "Your Majesty cannot imagine what the conduct of these people is during their marches. I have myself followed the military career for some years, and I assure your Majesty that I know quite well that excesses cannot always be prevented; but *arson, violence to women, murder, cutting off ears and noses, smashing windows and stoves, not to mention other tortures and outrages perpetrated against the wretched people*, that is quite possible for the officers to put down. Your Majesty may believe me, your faithful brother, that what I write is even below the mark; and you surely will give me as much credence as you will those *who have an interest to conceal the truth from you, and who have filled their purses from the sweat and blood of the poor people.* I could mention to your Majesty many high officers who, after having been in a very poor condition only a short while ago, are now possessed of 30,000 or 40,000 florins ready money, and who have not got it from the enemy, but most of it from the poor subjects of Catholic Electors and princes. May it please your Imperial Majesty only to imagine how these people will go on in Italy, where they now find all in plenty—and *most of the soldiers, even most of the officers, are Calvinists and Lutherans.* May God help the poor nunneries, of which there are great numbers everywhere. A good warning to the Duke of Friedland will not be amiss."

The whole of Northern Germany mutely obeyed Wallenstein's beck; he stood there like a dictator or an autocrat. The most unaccountable thing in this unaccountable man was, that the more the enemy dwindled, the more zealously he himself carried on his levies. The army, which originally mustered 40,000 or 50,000 men, was gradually increased to 100,000; and in 1629, the year before his dismissal, it amounted to 150,000. With such a force at his command, Ferdinand II. was much more formidable than Charles V. had been after the battle of Mühlberg.

This threatening supremacy of the imperial power in Germany now excited universal jealousy against Ferdinand, just as had been the case against Charles V. A secret opposition rose on all sides, comprising Maximilian of Bavaria, the leader of the League; the whole of the princely aristocracy, Papist as well as Lutheran, of the Empire; the Jesuits, and the Pope, who supported all the foes of Ferdinand with quite as much zeal and energy as his predecessor had evinced in abetting the plans of the Elector Maurice and King Ferdinand against Charles. The soul of all the plots directed against the threatening supremacy of the Emperor of Germany was Cardinal Richelieu, the prime minister of France. The war of the Mantuan succession having broken out in 1628, Richelieu's plan was to attack Austria in her most vulnerable spot —in Italy. He gained over Pope Urban VIII., of the house of Barberini, and made him enter into the strictest alliance with France for the carrying out of vast counter-plans, which certainly were conceived with masterly skill, and calculated to entrap the proud house of Austria, to undermine the ground under its feet, and to baffle its hopes of universal monarchy. Count Khevenhüller has recorded the views which Richelieu then set forth in support of his suggestions.

"Experience having shown that the house of Austria is a beast (*bestia*) of many heads, which, as soon as you cut them off, will always grow again, a new way ought to be struck out: decision by force of arms, for some time, no longer be thought of; and two other means employed to bring about the ruin of the whole house—*the Emperor's piety and his kindness of heart*.

"The Emperor's piety might be turned to his ruin by instigating him to reclaim all the Church property confiscated since the treaty of Passau in 1552, whereby the Protestant princes would be made his enemies for ever.

"His kindness of heart might be made available by touching his conscience, and exciting his compassion at the outrages committed by his soldiers. A great outcry especially ought to be raised against the rapacity of Wallenstein. If the Emperor, like a compassionate and kind lord as he was, attended to these complaints, Wallenstein's dismissal ought to be proposed.

"France then should proceed to extremities, and, when the Emperor had forfeited his popularity as well as his power, send a large army to Germany; use force where force was required, but where money and negotiations were more to the purpose, she should not neglect anything, nor make a sparing use of *promises of religious liberty*—FOR THE PRESENT.

"By supporting the malcontents, emigrants, and enemies of innovation, the French monarch might succeed in being elected King of the Romans; and then—*leaving to the Emperor, by that time a decrepit old lord, the Cæsarean title*—*assume the government of Germany*.

"Thus Austria would be lost, and what had not been obtained by force of arms would be gained by dexterity."

The Pope entered upon these proposals of Richelieu, and

the work of entrapping the Emperor began. The Holy Father, Cardinal Richelieu, and Father Lamormain, the Emperor's Jesuit confessor, suggested to Ferdinand that even the religious treaties of Passau and Augsburg were null and void, for the simple reason of their being concluded without the consent of the Pope. Upon this, the Emperor issued the famous Edict of Restitution (dated 6th of March, 1629), in virtue of which all that had become Protestant since 1552, that is to say, since the last seventy-seven years, should be made Catholic again. This ordinance affected the two North German archbishoprics of Magdeburg and Bremen, numberless monasteries and convents, and a great many towns and cities throughout the Empire. The only exception, evidently as a temporary concession, was made in favour of the most powerful of the Protestant princes, the Elector of Saxony, who was left in possession of the three bishoprics of Meissen, Merseburg, and Naumburg, which were inclosed in his territory. The edict was strictly enforced forthwith. The Protestants of Northern Germany indeed declared that they would rather cast off their laws and civilised existence, and reduce Germany again to the old savage state of forest life, than submit to the edict. The armies of Wallenstein and of the League compelled them to allow it to be carried out.

The Emperor, who had always been so lavish in reproaching the Protestant princes with their selfish spoliation of the bishoprics, now himself appropriated a good slice for the benefit of his family. Ferdinand's second son, Leopold William, had been made bishop of Strassburg and Passau. Immediately after the proclamation of the Edict of Restitution, he had the archsees of Magdeburg and Bremen and the see of Halberstadt conferred upon him, in addition to his having been before invested as bishop of Breslau and Olmütz, abbot of the rich Hessian monastery of Hersfeld, and grand master of the Teutonic order—an accumulation of not less than nine high dignities of the Church on the head of a youth of fifteen years!

The monasteries were just as arbitrarily dealt with as the

bishoprics. The Jesuits unscrupulously appropriated the religious houses for their own use, without heeding in the least that they had formerly belonged to the Benedictines or other orders.

In all the imperial towns the Emperor's soldiery enforced the restoration of the Popish worship, even in those where the Lutheran had been established long before the treaty of Passau. This was done especially at Augsburg, that obnoxious city where the Confession had been presented.

And, finally, the spoliation extended to the property of laymen. Whatsoever nobleman of the Empire had served the King of Bohemia, Mansfeld, Brunswick, or the Danish king had his estates confiscated.

Under the pretext of watching over the speedy carrying out of the edict, the troops of the Emperor and of the League remained still quartered in all the Protestant countries, with the exception of Saxony, and completely exhausted them by forced contributions. Every complaint was met by superciliousness, and even scorn. It was at that time that the harsh Habsburg speech was heard, "*The Emperor wishes the Germans rather to be beggars than rebels!*"

All the princes of Germany—even of the strongholds of the Protestants, Saxony, where the great Elector Maurice did not rise to life again, and Brandenburg, where the great Elector Frederic William had not yet risen—bowed before Ferdinand, and acknowledged the Edict of Restitution.

Magdeburg, as in the Smalcalde war, was again the only city in Germany which made head against the full weight of the Emperor's power. Wallenstein laid siege to it, but, after the lapse of twenty-eight weeks, he granted to it a capitulation, just as Maurice had done in his time.

The Emperor had for some time completely changed the old system of government in Germany, in a manner which was in perfect harmony with certain views and plans of Wallenstein, of which we shall speak more at large presently. Ferdinand altogether discontinued the old customary Diets for the despatch of the business of the Empire. The last

Imperial Diet (*Reichstag*) had been held under Matthias. *Ferdinand II. during the whole of his reign did not hold one.* As to the free imperial towns and cities, he no longer summoned them at all, transacting all the business of the Empire only at what were called Electors' Diets (*Kurfürstentage*), with the Electors and princes.

Now, however, arose the conflict between the old princes and the new duke.* Sixteen months after the issuing of the Edict of Restitution, the old princely aristocracy of Germany succeeded, at the celebrated Electors' Diet of Ratisbon, in carrying out that second *coup d'état* suggested by Richelieu, of inducing the Emperor to dismiss Wallenstein; that hateful upstart, in whom—and not of yesterday only—they, with very correct instinct, had recognised their worst enemy. Their leader was Maximilian of Bavaria, the head of the League, and Wallenstein's principal foe, and he acted in unison with France, the Pope, and the Jesuits.

Wallenstein, from the moment of his taking the chief command, had stamped upon the war a very different character from that with which it had been invested before. His plans aimed at an object quite distinct from the views entertained by the League. The latter, headed by Maximilian and Tilly, the tools of the Roman See and of the Jesuits, simply and steadfastly pursued the plan of driving back the mass of the German Protestants into the fold of the Church of Rome. The chiefs of this Papist alliance were fully aware that the Protestant zeal evinced by so many German princes was rooted much rather in their keen appetite for the property of the Church than in religious conviction; and that therefore that zeal must needs considerably cool down as soon as an insurmountable barrier was opposed to their covetousness. This barrier was now raised up by the Edict of Restitution, which repaired the losses sustained by the old Church. The most powerful Protestant princes, even those of Saxony and Brandenburg, had accepted the edict; and, if they should retain some lingering antipathy against the old Church, one might hope to overcome it by holding out to the younger sons of those Protestant potentates, who would allow themselves to be converted, the bait of investiture with the restored bishoprics.

But Wallenstein's plans were of a very different description; they were decidedly Ghibelline, diametrically opposed to those of the League. Wallenstein wanted to carry out what Charles V. had failed to accomplish. Like him, he aimed at the revival of the old policy of the Hohenstaufen Emperors. First of all, the Emperor was to be made absolute ruler of Germany, as the Kings of France and Spain were of their countries; and for this purpose the aristocratical constitution of the Empire, which for four hundred years had in a thousand ways trammelled the power of its head, was to be overthrown. Wallenstein intended to force the Papist as well as the Protestant powers of Germany into unconditional submission; and in so doing to restore indeed the old religion, but at the same time to reduce within reasonable limits the exorbitant mass of property possessed by the higher German clergy.

As soon as the peace of Lübeck was concluded with the King of Denmark, public opinion so decidedly sided with Wallenstein, that he could venture openly to give utterance to his thoughts: "*Electors and princes are no longer wanted. Now it is time to waive all ceremony with them ; as there is only one king in France and in Spain, thus also in Germany the Emperor alone shall be master.*" This language, which grated sorely on the ears of the princely aristocracy of Germany, was in perfect conformity with the idea of a new military nobility, which was to be invested with fiefs taken from the lands of the attainted German princes. Wallenstein himself had been made Duke of Mecklenburg, and Liechtenstein had received the confiscated principality of Jägerndorf. Recent researches in different archives have proved that in the same manner the other Protestant petty princes were also to have been driven from their countries, and their territories to be parcelled out among the officers of the Friedländer's army. *The Empire, thus remodelled, was to have been supported on this new military aristocracy;* just as Napoleon managed matters in later times. The lands which Wallenstein took from the Protestant princes he used as a bait for seducing the army of the League from its standard, and winning it over to that of the Emperor. Many officers of that army, among them even a couple of generals in command, Count Matthias Gallas and Count Anholt, had actually gone over to the imperial camp. Of the Guelphic possessions, three counties, which had formerly belonged to Christian, the administrator of Halberstadt, had been nominally sold to favourites of the Emperor; and, according to Wallenstein's plan, the dominions of Duke Frederic Ulric of Brunswick, who was without an heir, and had been an ally of the King of Denmark, were to be divided between Tilly and Pappenheim. Another plan was to make Archduke Leopold William Duke of Brunswick. Würtemberg was intended for the upstart Prince Eggenberg and Count Maximilian Trautmannsdorf; Baden for Count John Francis Trautson, a friend of Ferdinand III.; Saxony was to be bestowed on Duke Charles of Lorraine; and the Elector John George to be indemnified for the loss of his hereditary possessions by Jutland and Sleswick, parts of Denmark, which kingdom the Emperor would have taken for himself with a view to the naval supremacy in the Baltic. The newly acquired Lusatias, on the other hand, were to revert to Bohemia. Besides this transfer of secular property on a large scale, there was a question of secularising the spiritual principalities. A passage occurs in the diplomatic correspondence of that time between the courts of Vienna and Madrid, in which it is said that "*the German prince-bishops wore too long and too ample cloaks.*" Moreover, a plan had been mooted of making the imperial cities and the corporate nobility of the different circles defray the long-standing arrears of pay, which were due to the members of the Chancery of the Empire and to the imperial privy councillors.

It may easily be imagined that the court of Vienna was not much disposed to set aside a man who so far had worked with such wonderful success at the realisation of its proudest and most brilliant scheme—a universal monarchy, with the house of Habsburg for its head. Ferdinand was, however, in a desperate position at the Ratisbon Diet in June, 1630. All the princes there assembled joined to a man in the general outcry that the Emperor should grant peace to the Empire; that he should reduce his army, which had grown beyond all bounds; and, in fine, that he should dismiss from his military service the true author of the general misery, the enemy of the German constitution, "the insupportable dictator and oppressor of princes." They at the same time hinted, not very indirectly, that, if the Emperor would not yield, the Leaguers were determined to unite with the Protestants, or even with the King of France. It was very well known in Vienna at that time that an army of 40,000 French was stationed near the German frontier ready to take the field, and that King Louis XIII. had, through the Capuchin Friar Joseph, his envoy at Ratisbon, sent word to Maximilian of Bavaria that the duke needed only to despatch a courier, and the French army would immediately cross the Rhine for the protection of the (so-called) German liberty.

Wallenstein, on the other hand, proposed a remedy, but a terrible one. The Friedländer saw through all the intrigues of the League, and, to crush them with one blow, advised the Emperor to do neither more nor less than to surprise and destroy all the princes then present at Ratisbon. Other plans besides were at that time hovering before his bold and enterprising mind, if the Emperor could only have been persuaded to enter upon them. After having passed the winter of 1629 at Halberstadt, and then visited his Bohemian estates, Wallenstein took up a position in the south of Germany. The occasion for this step was the rupture of Austria with France in consequence of the war of the Mantuan succession, for which Wallenstein, as early as in May, 1629, had detached from his army a body of 20,000 men, whom Count Rombald Callalto, and under him Gallas, Aldringer, and Merode, had led to Italy. Wallenstein at first was against this Italian war; now, however, he went so far as even to offer the Emperor his help against the Pope. He apprised Ferdinand of his readiness to go to Italy, remarking, at the same time, "*It was a hundred years since Rome had been plundered, and its wealth must now be much greater than it was at that time.*" For the prosecution of all these plans—to which must be added another, *over and over again alluded to in his letters, the project of at last driving the Turks from Europe*—Wallenstein had marched, in the spring of 1630, about one hundred thousand men of his army to South-western Germany, and stationed them from the borders of the bishopric of Metz to the river Iller in such a manner that Alsace, Baden, the duchy of Würtemberg, and the towns on the Iller and Lech, were occupied by the Friedländer's troops. He had established his headquarters in the imperial city of Memmingen, in Swabia, where he remained from the 27th of June to the 2nd of October, 1630. The object for which Wallenstein took up this position in Swabia is self-evident; but, if there were any doubt about it, it would be completely dispelled by the evidence of the secret French State papers, and particularly by a report of the Venetian ambassador, present at Ratisbon, to his Signory. It was Wallenstein's plan to throw one-half of this large force into France, to rouse the princes of the blood, who were greatly exasperated against Richelieu, as also the Gallican party, to insurrection; and thus to kindle for the French, at their own hearth, a fire which would effectually have prevented them from meddling with German affairs. The other half were to be employed on German soil: 25,000 men were to pounce upon the capital of Wallenstein's principal enemy, Munich, which is distant from Memmingen only three days' march: with the last 25,000 men, Wallenstein intended in his own person to strike the chief blow; to surprise at Ratisbon—which likewise would be reached by a few days' march—the four Papist electors (of Mayence, Cologne, Trèves, and Bavaria), and the other princes there assembled, and to achieve one of those bold deeds of blood which were then deemed necessary for establishing absolute power against an over-weening aristocracy, and had been repeatedly perpetrated, in Germanic and Romanic states, since the latter end of the sixteenth century. The massacre of the Huguenot nobility on the night of St. Bartholomew, in 1572, was nothing else but such a stroke.

Wallenstein and his friends incessantly urged the Emperor to give—what alone was still wanting to make him the absolute ruler of Germany—his consent to the execution of these military measures.

But the party, which would not have shrunk from celebrating a German St. Bartholomew, nor from violence and outrage against the sacred head of the Church, did not carry the day. The victory fell to their rivals—to that party which, as Khevenhüller says, "tried completely to prostrate the house of Austria through the piety and kind-heartedness of the Emperor, by bringing about, at the hostile approach of the Kings of France and Sweden, the dismissal of the army and of the general." The Emperor did not give up the princes, as Wallenstein wanted him to do ; but he gave up Wallenstein, as the princes wanted him to do. He did so reluctantly, and contrary to his own conviction, "under protest of being held excused before God and the world for all the misfortune that might arise from the dismissal of the Duke of Friedland." These words of Khevenhüller plainly show who then ruled in Germany.

There is no doubt but that the Pope and the Jesuits saw through the Ghibelline plans of Wallenstein. They had formerly been his most zealous advocates, and now they joined in the general outcry against him. The papal nuncio, Rocci, at last succeeded at Ratisbon in gaining over the Emperor. In this task he was ably assisted by that greatest and most subtle of all the diplomatists of the seventeenth century, the famous Capuchin friar Joseph, whom Richelieu had sent to the Diet of Ratisbon, and of whom his own colleague in that mission, M. de Leon, said, "he had no soul, but only pools and shoals, on which every one must strand who entered into negotiations with him." On the 4th of July, 1630, Ferdinand signed the warrant for the dismissal of Wallenstein. With this act he, as it were, cut off his own right hand. Just at the most momentous crisis, when everything might have been gained, the Emperor gave up everything. Never at any time have the allied aristocratical and Papist parties in Germany celebrated a greater triumph.

Count Werdenberg and Baron Questenberg, two old friends of the generalissimo, were despatched from Ratisbon to take to Wallenstein the warrant of his dismissal. They found him at his headquarters at Memmingen, apparently buried in astrological studies; whereas, in reality, his mind was still pondering over the plan of surprising the princes at the Diet. He received and entertained the envoys in the most splendid style. The conversation for a long time turned only on trifling matters, whilst the envoys hesitated to come to the point with him, who was still all-powerful. But Wallenstein was well informed by his cousin and brother-in-law, Maximilian von Waldstein, of all the intrigues of the princes against him. He therefore broached the ticklish subject himself. Taking some papers from the table, he said, "These sheets contain the nativities of the Emperor and of the Elector of Bavaria. From them you may see yourself that I am acquainted with your commission. The stars show that the '*spiritus*' of the Elector domineers that of the Emperor, whom, therefore, I cannot blame for all this. I am grieved that his Majesty, by disbanding his troops, throws away the most precious jewel of his crown. I am grieved that his Majesty has so little taken my part; but I will obey." The imperial councillors now acquitted themselves of their commission, announcing to the general his dismissal. Wallenstein, in a letter to the Emperor, only asked his Majesty to protect him in his possessions; to which the Emperor, taking into consideration the request of the princes to restore the Dukes of Mecklenburg, replied that he would have the matter inquired into, and that until it was decided Wallenstein might betake himself to his estates in Bohemia. The senior Duke of Mecklenburg afterwards made his peace with the Emperor by paying to his exchequer 100,000 crowns, and to the Bishop of Vienna a sum which enabled the prelate to build a new palace, the Bischofs-hof (Bishop's Mansion), at Vienna. Wallenstein retired forthwith to his duchy of Friedland, of which he had made Gitschin the capital. Both his palaces there and at Prague, where he alternately resided, were got up with fairy-like magnificence. Wallenstein's departure from Memmingen took place on the 2nd of October, 1630.

A fortnight after the dismissal of Wallenstein, Mantua was

taken by assault by Collalto. By this conquest the Emperor became master in Italy, the same as he was in Germany. In the peace of Chierasco (1631) he obtained the right of keeping a garrison at Mantua, the most important military point of the whole of Lombardy. Hans von Kuffstein, who in 1628 had been sent as imperial ambassador to Constantinople, returned about the end of 1629 with the intelligence of Amurath IV. having gone to make war on Persia, and he brought back to the Emperor the letter of peace from the Sultan; moreover, Bethlen Gabor, the most dangerous enemy nearer home, died in 1629.

As soon as favourable news arrived from Italy, there were *not less than thirty regiments disbanded;* the rest joined the army of the League under Tilly. *The numbers which afterwards flocked to the colours of Gustavus Adolphus were for a great part composed of those disbanded troops of the Emperor.* At the Diet of Ratisbon, which continued sitting until November, 1630, the Protestant princes carried their point of having the Edict of Restitution suspended until a new compromise should be come to. On the other hand, the Emperor was not able even to procure the election of his son as King of the Romans.

The dismissal of Wallenstein and the suspension of the Edict of Restitution closed the second act of the Thirty Years' War. The Protestant cause, however, appeared still to be in the greatest danger; nay, it seemed doubtful, with the fanaticism of Ferdinand, who in his counter-reformation schemes had been so signally favoured by fortune, whether there would be in future any Protestant Church in Germany at all.

8.—Gustavus Adolphus of Sweden and the battles of Breitenfeld and Lützen—Wallenstein generalissimo " in absolutissimâ formâ."

On the very day that the Edict of Restitution was published, the army of Louis XIII. of France crossed the Alps near Susa. But, although the war of the Mantuan succession, and the plan which Urban VIII. and Richelieu had formed for expelling the house of Habsburg from Italy, had raised for a season the hopes of the Protestants, the taking of Mantua re-established Austria's ascendency. When thus the Protestant cause seemed with rapid strides approaching utter ruin, an avenger and deliverer arose in the person of the "Snow Majesty," as Gustavus Adolphus used to be called by gentlemen at Vienna, who had not then the least foreboding of the hot work which was in store for them from that "ice-king."

Gustavus Adolphus, the grandson of Gustavus Vasa, was thirty-six years of age when he determined to lead his Goths across the Baltic to the rescue of their German brethren in faith. Even before Denmark anticipated him, he had thought of placing himself at the head of the German Protestants. In the meanwhile he had made war on Poland, where a Papist king of his house was reigning who had been driven from the Swedish throne, which, according to the fundamental laws of the realm, could only be occupied by a Lutheran prince. This Polish war had matured the great military talent of Gustavus Adolphus. Although Sweden was a constitutional monarchy, he had with great energy and consummate prudence made himself all but absolute king, wielding almost unlimited power, with a standing army and permanent taxes; and indeed he knew how to keep the reins of the government with a very tight hand.

To occupy the King of Sweden in Poland, Ferdinand, in 1629, sent an army under Field-marshal Arnim to the help of King Sigismund; but, by Richelieu's mediation, Gustavus Adolphus concluded with Poland the truce of Altmark, in which he had Livonia and the coast of Prussia ceded to him. Now, therefore, his hands were unfettered for a war in Germany. His ambition was to become the champion and hero of Protestantism. In this aspiration he was supported by his unfeigned piety, which caused him to look with horror on the Jesuit thraldom with which his German brethren in the faith were threatened; yet he also wished to lead the Swedish nation to a wider field of action in the policy of Europe, and to secure for himself a prominent place in the world's history. His first and immediate care was to prevent the Emperor's plan of regaining Prussia and establishing in the Baltic a Catholic naval power to the terror of the North. He had therefore already hoisted his standard at Stralsund, which town he forced permanently to submit to his rule, and to take in a strong Swedish garrison. Here also Gustavus Adolphus showed himself as a born ruler, always using the most practical means for his end. He was by no means the ideal hero which modern historians have wished to represent him; Gförer has been the first to place his character in its true light.

Gustavus Adolphus—the Golden King, as the German Protestants called him, on account of his yellow hair and beard; the Lion of the North, as they more poetically styled him in the strength of their faith and their hope—was of unusually high stature and very powerful frame, but inclined to stoutness, or rather so corpulent that with growing years he felt it as an inconvenience, and only a very strong horse was able to carry him. His forehead was broad and high; his nose aquiline; his eyes large, of a bluish-grey colour, and of a good-tempered expression, but he was purblind; his carriage was proud and royal; his manners noble and commanding; his whole appearance bearing the stamp of self-reliance and frankness, whilst the rich, mellow tones of his voice called forth the confidence of his hearers. It was specially said in his praise, that his own people served him with the most devoted affection; and that, notwithstanding his strictness and earnestness, he won the hearts of everyone by the singular sweetness of his temper. Since Luther, no one had exercised greater power over the minds of men than Gustavus Adolphus, with whom we may perhaps in this respect couple Henry IV. of France. Eloquence was on his tongue. He spoke five languages, Latin, French, and Italian, besides German—the language of his mother, a Holstein princess—and Swedish; his conversation was full of elegance and affability. He cultivated the sciences: his favourite book was the work of Hugo Grotius "On War and Peace," which he had always with him, even in the camp. From his early youth, war alone had any charm for him; he was born to be a hero as well as a ruler. He had also that characteristic of a great man, that he understood how to gather around him a circle of eminent supporters in war and peace. We have stated before that he was sincerely pious, acting, however, on the maxim propounded by Spinoza and Grotius, that everyone is to be treated as of the right faith who obeys the laws. He used to say that "to prevent people from going to hell was the duty not of the prince but of the preacher." He therefore made no difference between Protestant and Papist.

But Gustavus Adolphus, if ever he was as harmless as the dove, was certainly also as wise as the serpent. His diplomacy went apace with his warlike prowess; he was as great a statesman as he was a general. His officials were very handsomely paid, and the Swedish cabinet was so remarkable for its impenetrable discretion that the French ambassadors constantly complained of never being able to find out the real intentions of the Swedish diplomacy. A whole network of Swedish ambassadors and spies was spread over all the European courts; there was an envoy of the King even at Constantinople. Gustavus Adolphus without the least scruple used the most effective expedient of diplomacy—bribes. Through Christina Munk, the mistress of the King of Denmark, the Swedish resident at Copenhagen was informed of everything. Gustavus Adolphus was extremely fond of over-reaching the foreign ministers and officers who came to his camp to negotiate by making them drunk, and then worming out of them their secrets, for which purpose he generally employed General Sir Patrick Ruthven, who was possessed of the rare gift of remaining cool-headed after having imbibed any given quantity of wine. Gustavus Adolphus also invited, indiscriminately, all the officers of his own army to his table, to study their character and disposition; and the petty trammels of etiquette were altogether proscribed from about him. He was always kind, ever ready to acknowledge merit wherever he found it, and averse to flattery under every form.

Such was the prince who crossed the Baltic for the defence of religious liberty in Germany. At the very time when Wallenstein's dismissal was urged at Ratisbon, on the 24th of June, O.S. (4th of July), 1630, the eve of the hundredth anniversary of the presentation of the Augsburg Confession, Gustavus Adolphus first stepped on German soil.

The King arrived with the Swedish fleet before the most westward of the three branches into which the Oder divides at its mouth, and disembarked, amid a violent thunderstorm, at the island of Usedom near the village of Peenemünde. Before landing, he had given orders to Colonel Alexander Leslie, a Scotsman who fought under his banner, to set out from Stralsund and drive the imperial garrison from the island of Rügen. Gustavus Adolphus had with him only 14,500 men, partly Swedes and Finlanders, partly English and Scotch, and partly Germans and Livonians; but they were a host of heroes, they were soldiers as it were from another world, quite different from the savage bands which Germany had until then seen with Mansfeld and Brunswick, and with Tilly and Wallenstein. Among the Swedes there was strict discipline and order; the King himself set the example of piety; there were prayers twice a day in the army, every battalion having its own clergyman. With this army were those officers who afterwards astonished the world by their achievements: Baner, Torstensohn, Wrangel, Count Niels Brahe, Gustavus Horn, Max Teufel, Dodo Kniphausen, Wolf Henry Baudissin; and of Germans, the Rhinegrave Otho Louis.

The imperial force under Tilly was at least twice as strong as that of the Swedes; besides which nearly all the towns of Northern Germany, except those of the electorate of Saxony, were garrisoned by the troops of the Emperor. Gustavus Adolphus, however, had the ranks of his own army swelled by the disbanded soldiers of Wallenstein; and, moreover, he forced the imperial garrisons of all those towns which he conquered to serve under him. Most of all, he relied on the sympathy of the German nation, which was manifested on all sides. Whenever he entered a place there was played from the steeples, with sackbuts and hautboys, the hymn "Behold the Saviour of mankind!" (*Nun kommt der Heiden Heiland*).

Gustavus Adolphus first tried to gain a firm footing in Pomerania and Mecklenburg. In Pomerania, where the old infirm Torquato Conti commanded, he took the capital of Stettin; the duke having no direct heir, he intended to combine the country with the Prussian coastland and Livonia, and thus establish a compact power on the Baltic. In Mecklenburg he called upon the people to abandon Wallenstein and to return to their allegiance to the old dukes. On the 13th of January (O.S.), 1631, he signed the treaty of alliance with the crown of France, concluded at Bärwalde in the New March. The negotiators were, on the French side, Charnace; on the Swedish, Horn and the brothers John and Charles Baner. Richelieu promised a yearly subsidy of 400,000 crowns towards the expenses of the war. As a security, the King asked for seven hostages, which were to be sent to Amsterdam. He likewise demanded hostages from the other powers which promised help; from England, Venice, and the Czar of Russia. The Dutch were the only power which he trusted. On the 3rd of April, 1631, Gustavus Adolphus took Frankfort on the Oder, which was defended by Tiefenbach. Horn was now despatched to Silesia, whither Tiefenbach had retired; the King himself turned to the Marches. It was his first care to secure the alliance of the Electors of Saxony and Brandenburg. Both, however, hesitated, and declined an alliance with Sweden against the Emperor, contenting themselves with making remonstrances against the Edict of Restitution. The only rulers immediately proffering a resolute adherence to the King who had come to save the cause of the Protestants from ruin, were the Landgravine-regent Amelia of Hesse, the Dukes William and Bernard of Saxe-Weimar, Duke George of Brunswick-Lüneburg, and the Dukes Francis and Francis Albert of Saxe-Lauenburg.

The irresolution of the two Electors of Saxony and of Brandenburg became the cause of one of the most terrible catastrophes of the terrible Thirty Years' War—the fall of Magdeburg, the bulwark of the Protestant cause in the north of Germany ever since the Smalcalde war. In compliance with the general outcry of the Papists, the devoted city was to be made an example of. Christian William, the brother of the Elector Sigismund of Brandenburg, had been "postulated," as early as 1598, as administrator of the archbishopric of Magdeburg; but the Emperor Ferdinand had outlawed him. The latter, after the passing of the Edict of Restitution, wanted to force upon the chapter his own son, Leopold William, and got the Pope to appoint him as archbishop. This the chapter opposed with might and main, and it was their obstinate resistance, for which the Emperor now wished to have his revenge. John George of Saxony, whose son Augustus had been postulated as archbishop in 1628, remained an inactive spectator.

Gustavus Adolphus had despatched to Magdeburg one of the commanders of his forty German companies, a Hessian nobleman, Dieterich von Falkenberg, whom the Landgrave Maurice of Hesse-Cassel had formerly sent as his envoy to Stockholm. Falkenberg, a very brave man, made his way into the city in the disguise of a sea-captain, through the ten thousand men of Pappenheim, who had been encamped before it ever since the winter of 1630. Scarcely had Falkenberg taken the command of the fortress, when Pappenheim, by the promise of a large sum, tried to bribe him to surrender the city; but he replied, "If Pappenheim (an apostate Lutheran) is in want of a rogue, he may seek him within his own bosom." On the 5th of April, 1631, Tilly arrived with thirty thousand men before Magdeburg, and took within four weeks all the outlying works—some of the forts were called "Dare Tilly," "Dare Pappenheim," and "The Succour"—and also the works on the islets of the Elbe. On the 18th of May, Tilly sent in a trumpeter, summoning the city to surrender; on the 19th, the cannonade was stopped, Tilly even causing the pieces from the Sudenburg battery to be withdrawn. He had been apprised that the King of Sweden was standing near Zerbst; the people of Magdeburg were likewise aware of this fact, and for this reason Falkenberg detained Tilly's trumpeter until the morning of the 20th. In the night of the 19th, Tilly held a council of war; he wished to raise the siege, but Pappenheim's advice prevailed, to take the city by a general

assault, although no breach had as yet been effected.
Pappenheim had ascertained that the citizens of Magdeburg
kept very good watch during the night, but that at five in the
morning they left their posts to go to sleep. Five o'clock
therefore was appointed as the hour at which the attack
should be attempted. Falkenberg had betaken himself to the
town hall as early as four in the morning, to despatch Tilly's
trumpeter; the magistracy were assembled, and against their
opposition he carried his own opinion, which was to reject
Tilly's proposal of a capitulation. Whilst the trumpeter with
his answer was leaving by the gate on one side, Pappenheim
had scaled the wall on the other. On his own responsibility,
without order from Tilly, who had again hesitated and once
more assembled his officers in a council of war, Pappenheim
had fired the alarm-gun, scaled the ramparts on the side of
the "New Town" (Neustadt) at the head of some dismounted
dragoons, and planted on the top the imperial banner.
Falkenberg, returning from the town hall, pulled it down
again; but he was laid low by a bullet. Now Pappenheim
was no longer to be stopped; he led four regiments in succession on the wall, and briskly attacked the administrator
of Magdeburg, Christian William, in the rear, taking him
prisoner with his own hand. The imperialists then entered
the city in close ranks; in vain the citizens made a desperate
defence in the streets and from the windows; at nine o'clock
already, the old cry of victory of the German lansquenets
"All won! All won!" resounded on all sides. It was
Pappenheim who lit the torch of the incendiary for the
destruction of the doomed city. From the very first, he set
fire to some houses in order to hunt out the enemy; a hurricane which suddenly rose fanned the flame into a general
conflagration; and then the imperial troops, angry at being
baulked by the fire of their plunder, killed all that came in
their way. At ten in the evening the whole city was burnt
down, with the exception of the cathedral, the Catholic convent of Our Lady, and some fishers' huts near the Elbe.
Tilly, greatly provoked by Pappenheim's arbitrary wilfulness,
did not enter the city until some time after ten. Some

officers of the League, revolted at the horrors committed by the furious bands of the Croats, Hungarians, and Walloons—who pounced upon the defenceless inhabitants like a pack of hell-hounds—implored the general that he would check the rapine and bloodshed, and have the soldiers called off by the sound of drums and trumpets. But Tilly, on his grey pony, sternly answered, "Three hours' plundering is the shortest rule of war. The soldier must have something for his toil and trouble. What would Pappenheim say? Come again in an hour and I'll see then what I can do." Pappenheim wrote to Munich on the 21st of May: "I think that more than 20,000 men have perished; and certainly, since the destruction of Jerusalem, no more awful work and judgment of the Lord has been seen. *All our soldiers have enriched themselves.*" In a later letter, written to Vienna, he says, with very questionable gallantry, "Nothing has been wanting to me and my brave companions in arms *but that your Majesty and your imperial ladies had been spectators of this wonderful victory.*"

The imperial soldiery called it the Magdeburg Wedding[1] and it certainly was a sort of German St. Bartholomew; of the 35,000 inhabitants of Magdeburg, about 5,000 only were preserved, 1,000 of them in the cathedral. To the latter, Tilly, at his solemn entry on the 24th, granted a pardon and fed them, after their having passed three days and two nights in continual fear of death. On the 25th of May mass was read and the Te Deum chanted in the cathedral. The imperial soldiery celebrated the victory in their own way by the doggerel:

> "O Magdeburg, with maiden pride,
> To the Emp'ror thou 'st the dance denied;
> With the lansquenet thou dancest to-night,
> Thou haughty maid, and serves thee right."[2]

From Magdeburg Tilly marched, in June, 1631, by the Harz Mountains—where the peasants killed a great number

---

[1] The St. Bartholomew is generally called in German "The bloody wedding of Paris."—*Translator.*

[2] "Magdeburg, du stolze Magd,
   Hast dem Kaiser den Tanz versagt;
   Jetzt tanze mit dem alten Knecht,
   Geschieht dir eben recht."

of his people—to Thuringia, against Saxe-Weimar; and from thence by Erfurt to Mühlhausen. He wanted to wreak his revenge on the Landgravine of Hesse-Cassel; but Gustavus Adolphus soon compelled him to return to the Elbe to the support of Pappenheim.

Gustavus Adolphus—who could not well undertake anything for the relief of Magdeburg before Saxony and Brandenburg had declared for him, and who in a special pamphlet had tried to cast all the blame on the two Electors—at last, after the fall of Magdeburg, took a decisive step against the irresolute Elector George William of Brandenburg. He advanced to Berlin, and before its gates, on the 11th of June, demanded a positive answer whether there should be peace or war between him and the Elector. George William was his brother-in-law, but allowed himself to be completely ruled by his minister Count Adam Schwartzenberg, a Roman Catholic, and a stout partisan of Austria, who besides was in the pay of the Jesuits. The Elector, afraid of the Emperor, and trembling at the very idea of losing his country, wished to remain neutral and to temporise. He had been heard to say, "*What is the common cause to me if I am to lose all my reputation, honour, and fortune? The Emperor has a son, and so have I; if the Emperor and his son remain Emperors, I and my son will remain Electors also.*" Now, however, he was obliged to come out to Köpenick to his brother-in-law, whom, in the greatest fright, he asked only for a short respite to consult with his councillors. In the meanwhile Gustavus conversed with the Brandenburg princesses. The Elector, at the instigation of Schwarzenberg, wished on his return to protest once more; but Gustavus simply left him the choice between signing the alliance or being treated as an enemy. Then at last George William signed, and immediately after drove back in all haste to Berlin. Gustavus amused himself with frightening him a little more by causing all the cannon to fire a *feu de joie* in celebration of the concluded alliance. The Swedes then occupied Berlin and the fortresses of Spandau and Cüstrin, which secured to the King a base of operations.

He was now in the heyday of his fortune; public opinion everywhere was in his favour. About this time the Marquis of Hamilton brought to him 7,000 Scots, who disembarked on the coast of Pomerania. He now crossed the Elbe near Tangermünde, and on the 1st of July pitched his camp in a position of extraordinary strength near Werben in the Altmark, where the Havel joins the Elbe. Tilly, who until then had had his headquarters at Mühlhausen, marched against him about the end of July, but was not able to induce him to accept battle. For want of provisions Tilly now led his army by Magdeburg to Eisleben; there he was joined by Count Egon of Fürstenberg with 25,000 imperialist veterans. His army now amounted to upwards of 50,000 men. Leaving part of it under John Aldringer near Erfurt, and under Otho Henry Count Fugger[1] in Hesse, he, *without any previous declaration of war*, entered the electorate of Saxony, and appeared on the 13th of September before the gates of Leipzig. This invasion of Saxony caused great annoyance in Vienna and Munich, as it had been the intention not to attack the Elector of Saxony. John George, after having so long wavered, now threw himself into the arms of the Swedes; concluding on the 11th of September, at Coswig, an alliance with Gustavus Adolphus, after having marched with his army of about 20,000 men to Torgau. Gustavus joined with the Elector on the 15th of September near Düben, between Torgau and Leipzig; and on the same day the latter city capitulated to Tilly.

On those fields in the heart of Germany, where her fate has at different times been decided in bloody combat, it was now to be shown whether old Tilly, who until then could scarcely be said to have been conquered, would be able to hold his own also against the young hero Gustavus Adolphus. The two armies were equal in numbers, each amounting to about 40,000 men. But Gustavus Adolphus, notwithstanding this numerical equality, was the stronger of the two. Tilly

---

[1] This nobleman is remarkable for having been the father, by one wife, of no less than eighteen children—nine sons and nine daughters—all of them born during the war, from 1622 to 1639, in successive eighteen years.

himself had three months before told Pappenheim in plain words that he was no longer at liberty to turn to the right or the left as he pleased, but was obliged to follow the movements of the enemy. Gustavus Adolphus had the superiority in strategy, but he likewise had it in tactics, which had been remodelled by him after a new system that gained him the victory. His Swedes, in their easy blue uniforms, without any cuirasses and armlets, moved much more rapidly than the imperial troops, who with their yellow dress wore armour, or at least cuirasses, greaves, and helmets; the Swedish pikemen carried weapons only eleven feet long, the imperialists much longer lances; the Swedish musketeers also fired much more briskly with their lighter matchlocks, which did not require to be supported on a fork like those of their enemies. On the same principle, Gustavus chiefly employed light cavalry—dragoons wearing hats and armed with carbines; moreover, his field artillery was of very light calibre: he had in the battle of Breitenfeld one hundred, Tilly not more than thirty guns.

The night preceding the battle of Breitenfeld[1] the King of Sweden passed at the village of Klein-Wölkau, three leagues to the north of Leipzig; not, however, under a roof, but in his carriage, attended by the generals of his staff, Baner, Horn, and Teufel. During a short slumber he dreamed that he had wrestled with Tilly, and at last got the better of him. Tilly had his headquarters that night at Leipzig, in a remote quarter of the town, and next morning became aware of its being the house of the gravedigger, decorated with ghastly pyramids of skulls and raw-bones. A gloomy foreboding then seized him, even Pappenheim stood with blanched cheek. At nine in the morning of the day of battle, 17th of September, 1631, Tilly sent Pappenheim with 2,000 cuirassiers against the Swedes and Saxons, merely to reconnoitre their positions. But the hot-brained, dashing cavalry leader at once engaged in a fight, and Tilly, to save him, had to send 2,000 cuirassiers after him, and was at last obliged to deploy

[1] The battle is called by both names, Breitenfeld and Leipzig; some old chronicles mention it as the battle of Badelwitz.—*Translator.*

the whole of his army, whereas his first intention had been to wait for the divisions of Aldringer and Fugger, and with them to take a position behind Leipzig, where he could never have been attacked. Tilly had been apprised of the junction of the Elector of Saxony with Gustavus Adolphus; Pappenheim, however, stoutly refused to believe in it, and urged Tilly "not to lose such an excellent opportunity, or he would never be able to answer for it before God, the Emperor, or the Elector of Bavaria." When Pappenheim sent to ask for the succour of 2,000 more cuirassiers, Tilly raised his clasped hands in despair, and called out, "That man will make me lose my honour and reputation, and the Emperor his country and his people."

To cover the retreat of that splendid body of cavalry, Tilly now arrayed his forces in order of battle between Breitenfeld and Seehausen, one league and a half to the north of Leipzig. His people wore white favours on their helmets and hats, and white badges round their right arm. Their battle-cry was "Jesu Maria;" that of the Swedes, "God with us!" Tilly, again, was decked out in a very strange costume, a green silk gown and a cap with variegated plumes; he was, as usual, mounted on his grey pony. Gustavus Adolphus wore a buff jerkin, a coat of bluish grey, and a white hat with a green plume. He knelt down, and, as was his custom, said a prayer. He then rode along the line of battle, addressed his soldiers, and despatched a trumpeter with a note to Tilly, according to old usage, to challenge him to combat. Tilly sent back word that he always felt honoured in meeting the King's wishes.

It was already midday when the imperialists and Swedes approached within range of fire of each other. The Imperialists opened with three shots the cannonade, which continued until two. Tilly's heavy artillery was pitched on a hill near Seehausen. The ranks of the imperialists being deeper than those of the Swedes, they suffered more from the fire of their enemy than the Swedes did from theirs. Gustavus Adolphus, to deprive the hostile army of the advantage of the hot sun of September, which shone full into the face of the Swedes, and of the wind, which drove the smoke and dust straight down upon them, wheeled more and more round towards the north. Then Pappenheim burst forth to ride over the right wing of the Swedes commanded by Baner; but the companies of musketeers placed between the squadrons of the Swedish cavalry repelled his attacks seven times in succession. Tilly tried to make a diversion in his favour by attacking the centre of the Swedes, where Teufel commanded; but he too was driven back by the galling fire of the Swedish light artillery. Teufel, on the other hand, paid for his success with his life. Thereupon Tilly gave orders to attack the left wing of the enemy, formed by the Saxon troops under Arnim, who was opposed by Count Fürstenberg. The Saxons did not make a stand. Their Elector himself fled from the field, pursued by the Croats. Remembering perhaps the terrible fate of his ancestor John Frederic after the battle of Mühlberg, he did not dare to stop and take breath until he reached Eulenburg, several leagues distant from the battlefield. Arnim had retired to Gustavus Adolphus.

The time had now arrived for the Swedish king to display all his military genius, and to give a brilliant proof of the superiority of his light infantry. He made front against the advancing columns of the imperialists; then, quickly turning with the head of his own column towards the hills where Tilly's artillery was placed, he took it, and directed the enemy's own guns against him. This manœuvre was decisive. It was now seven in the evening. The imperialist cavalry, driven from the field, left the infantry in the lurch. Only five regiments of Walloons, fighting in close ranks, and neither giving nor accepting quarter, cut their way through with great difficulty under cover of the night, carrying between their ranks "their old father Tilly," as they called him. Tilly himself was in the greatest danger. The Walloons pressed round him, defending him with their pikes. He gazed fixedly before him with his eyes full of tears. He had been grazed by three balls. The Swedes knew very well who he was, and they wished to take him prisoner. A captain of cuirassiers of the regiment of the Rhinegrave, called from his gigantic stature "Long Fritz," closed with him, seized him by the neck, and, knocking him with the butt-end of his carbine, called upon him to accept quarter, when Duke Rudolph of Saxe-Lauenburg at the right moment saved the old general by shooting Long Fritz through the head from ear to ear. Of 5,200 Walloons scarcely 900 escaped with their lives.

The imperialists retired to the Weser, to the bishopric of Paderborn. Here Tilly left a division under Count Gronsfeld behind him; Pappenheim went to Cologne, and Tilly proceeded to Hesse, where he was joined by Aldringer and Fugger.

The Swedes captured the whole imperial camp, which contained great wealth; so that every soldier of the King had at least ten ducats for his share. They, moreover, captured all the artillery, twenty-eight guns of heavy calibre, and nearly a hundred stand of colours. Tilly lost 7,000 dead, and 5,000 were taken prisoners. The King slept on the battlefield near a watch-fire. The battle of Breitenfeld gave to Sweden the ascendency in Germany for three years, until the battle of Nördlingen.

People at Vienna were at once changed as by magic. The court parasites, the ladies, the Jesuits and Capuchins, with Father Lamormain at their head, no longer bragged of driving "the new pretty little dear of an enemy" (*das neue Feinderl*) — as, in the genuine Vienna slang, they called Gustavus—with a birch-rod home over the Baltic; nor of their certain hope of seeing the Snow King melt as soon as he came further south. With the victory of Leipzig fortune at once turned completely in favour of the Protestants. "It's all correct about Leipzig," remained long after a popular phrase to express some unexpected and incredible thing. The Papist King Sigismund of Poland expressed his feelings on the event in the remark, "he could not understand how it was that the Lord of hosts had turned Lutheran." It was a crushing blow to the house of Habsburg; Austria was lost if Gustavus Adolphus had forthwith burst into Bohemia, taken possesion of Prague, and from thence advanced to the Danube, and knocked at the gates of the imperial castle in Vienna.

This bold plan Gustavus Adolphus did not carry out; very likely from a wish to draw nearer his ally, France. He left Bohemia and Silesia to the Electors of Saxony and Brandenburg. In the same year (1631) John George conquered Prague, whose defenceless condition was betrayed by Wallenstein to Arnim, who had formerly served in the Friedland army. Gustavus Adolphus marched by Erfurt and the Thuringian forest to Würzburg, took Hanau, and arrived on the 27th of November at Frankfort. Here he was joined by the exiled King of Bohemia; and by his own queen, Eleonora, who had followed him with his chancellor, the celebrated Oxenstierna. The latter greeted his sovereign with the words, "I had hoped to find your Majesty at Vienna." Mayence capitulated on the 23rd of December, and the whole Rhenish Palatinate, with the exception of Heidelberg, was cleared of the enemy. Gustavus now began to negotiate with Bavaria. But when the "old devil," as Gustavus called Tilly, had, under the cover of negotiations, surprised the Swedish general Horn at Bamberg, Gustavus, full of anger, proceeded in the the beginning of March, 1632, to the conquest of Maximilian's country.

In this campaign old Tilly fell mortally wounded, on the 15th of April, in the engagement on the Lech. A falconet ball had smashed his right thigh. He died on the 22nd at Ingolstadt. His last care was Ratisbon; his last words, as the priest held out the crucifix to him, "*In te, Domine, speravi, non confundar in æternum.*" Werner, his favourite nephew, a younger son of his brother, who died seven years before him, inherited the estates which the Emperor and Maximilian of Bavaria had granted to the general; the elder brother of Werner succeeded to his father as the heir of the family property in the Low Countries. The latter founded the Netherlandish, Werner the German line of the Tillys. Both lines are now extinct; the German in 1724, the Netherlandish in 1737. From some of the younger lines, which likewise branched off about 1630, there are descendants to this day in Belgium. One of the scions of them, Count Alexander Tilly, in his youthful days page of honour to the unfortunate Queen Marie Antoinette, blew out his brains at Brussels in 1816. He has acquired a very unenviable notoriety by his most scandalous and lascivious memoirs.

On the 18th of April Augsburg fell into the hands of Gustavus Adolphus, who created a great sensation by making the citizens swear allegiance to him. It appeared as if he intended to change that beautiful city into Augusta-Gustava, and make it his German capital. The Elector of Bavaria sent the French resident minister at Munich, St. Etienne, to the camp of Gustavus Adolphus before Ingolstadt, to treat with him. The Swedish sovereign spoke out in the following style: "What lie and deceit is this! Has not Tilly surprised my gullible Horn at Bamberg, under the cover of negotiations? A fortnight ago my people intercepted a courier, through whom Ferdinand in Vienna promised help to Duke Maximilian. Help by whom? By his old arch-enemy Friedland, who now comes forth again. I well know Maximilian and all the bevy of monks and priests who guide and lead him. He wears a double frock. At one time he turns the red outside, and at another the blue. No one is bound to keep faith with heretics—that's it, isn't it? May the devil trust you Papists! You just go to a priest and make him absolve you from all your oaths." St. Etienne wished to reply, but Gustavus Adolphus became even more incensed, and sharply rebuked the Frenchman: "You presume too far, sir. It is a King to whom you are speaking; do not forget that. Such a pert Frenchman has a very glib tongue, and will always sing some notes higher than is marked in the score. You want to intrude yourself as a mediator, and you have not even any special written credentials. The duke is defeated, and wants even now to treat with sword in hand on equal terms. He gives me credit for too much patience by far. I want Ingolstadt as a pledge. If he thinks to put me off by temporising until the Friedländer comes, my army shall go on in his country in a way which will make him feel what it is to have called down on his people, for the benefit of strangers, an angry enemy. The King of France," Gustavus Adolphus added, "needs not, however, give himself the trouble of sending an army into Germany. If he has an appetite for war, we will give him battle under the walls of his own capital."

The Elector of Bavaria had in the meanwhile possessed himself by stratagem of the important free city of Ratisbon. Nor did he surrender Ingolstadt. But Gustavus Adolphus, without stopping to lay siege to it, marched straightway to Munich. The court fled to Salzburg. Some of the magistracy, with the French minister, went to meet the King as far as Freising, bringing to him the keys of their city. On the 17th of May, 1632, Gustavus made his entry into Munich. He was accompanied by the ex-King of Bohemia, the Elector Palatine, who now with Gustavus took up his quarters at the palace of that same cousin who had driven him out of Prague. Gustavus celebrated Whitsuntide at Augsburg. An old chronicle relates: "On the 30th of May, being Whit-Monday, the King did not attend public service, but had his own chaplain, Dr. Fabricius, to preach before him, as well in the morning as in the afternoon, in his apartments. In the evening, at table, he suddenly felt a desire for a dance, whereupon immediately matters were arranged to have the young ladies of the patrician houses assembled, with whom the King and the other princely personages amused themselves for several hours in English and German dances." Gustavus Adolphus, in fact, was a great admirer of ladies. Once he tried to kiss one of the fair Augsburgers, Jacobina Lauber, with whom he was particularly pleased; but she in the struggle tore off the King's ruff.[1] From Augsburg Gustavus then marched to Franconia, where, on the 9th of June, he occupied Nuremberg. It was for the last decisive struggle against Wallenstein, on whom the Emperor, threatened in his own hereditary dominions, had actually again conferred the chief command, and who had united with Maximilian at Eger.

[1] It is still preserved, under glass, at Augsburg.—*Translator.*

Wallenstein had in the meantime lived in proud retirement, partly at Prague and partly at Gitschin, the little capital of his duchy of Friedland. At Prague he lived with almost royal pomp, but, as far as he himself was concerned, just as formerly at the camp, in the strictest seclusion. For the great palace which he built in the Bohemian capital one hundred houses had to be pulled down. All the streets which led to it were barred with chains; the entrance was by six gateways. In the courtyard a bodyguard of fifty gorgeously dressed halberdiers kept watch. His household comprised nearly 1,000 persons. At the head of his court, as lord chamberlain, stood Count Paul Liechtenstein, who, besides a monthly salary of 200 florins, had board for himself and forty-eight dependants, with forage for as many horses. His first steward was a Count Harrach, his chief equerry a Count Hardegg. The duke himself was waited upon by twenty-four chamberlains, who, like those of the Emperor, wore golden keys, and by sixty pages of honour of the first houses, all of them dressed in sky-blue velvet, laced and embroidered with gold. Many of the former officers of Wallenstein were living at his court, drawing pensions and receiving free board at his table, which was never served with less than a hundred dishes. His stables contained upwards of 1,000 saddle and carriage horses, which fed out of marble mangers. When he travelled, there were never less than fifty carriages, drawn by six horses, and fifty drawn by four. In a lofty vaulted banqueting-hall of his palace at Prague, he was depicted in a triumphal car, drawn by four horses of the sun, with a star over his laurel-crowned head. The long suites of rooms of this palace were filled with astrological, allegorical, and mythological figures. A secret staircase led from a small round saloon into a grotto of artificial stalactites, where there was a bath. Adjoining this grotto was a spacious portico, from which one entered the gardens, adorned with fountains, and with canals abounding with fish.

Wallenstein's fortune was colossal, even according to the standard of our own times. His yearly revenue was estimated at 6,000,000 florins (£600,000), derived partly from the large capital which he had placed in the banks of Amsterdam and Venice, and partly from his estates in Moravia and Bohemia, especially the duchy of Friedland and the principality of Sagan. Although no longer in the possession of the duchy of Mecklenburg, he continued until 1631 to coin ducats with the legend of his name, as Duke of Mecklenburg. On the obverse of these Wallenstein ducats, which are now very rare, his bust is seen with bare head and short-cropped hair, with the legend: "*Albertus D. G. Dux Megapol. Fridl.;*" and on the reverse a coat-of-arms, covered with the ducal crown, and surrounded with the collar and badge of the Golden Fleece, with the legend continued: "*Et Sagani Princeps Vand.*" As an indemnity for Mecklenburg, he had received the principality of Glogau. During the time of his retirement, he had been endeavouring to have this considerable estate created a new hereditary fief of the Empire, and, if possible, to add to it the two Lusatias. On the other hand, the Elector of Saxony was to be invested with Mecklenburg. With this potentate he concluded, on the 7th of January, 1631, an agreement mutually to respect each other's countries. He was untiring in making judicious arrangements for the management of his vast property; he tried to humour the Jesuits by rich donations; and he called into his service able men, like the celebrated Kepler. He had attached to his person the astrologer Seni, an Italian with whom he passed whole nights in astrological studies. Beyond this he conversed with very few persons, his only confidants being his brother-in-law Terzka, the husband of his wife's sister Maximiliana Harrach; and Terzka's mother, whom he particularly esteemed for her sound judgment. His health had been greatly impaired by over-exertion, the toils of war, and sleepless nights; he was obliged in walking to support himself on an Indian cane, and to live most abstemiously.

Wallenstein had kept up an uninterrupted correspondence with the Emperor, by whom he was constantly employed in diplomatic negotiations with the King of Denmark, to bring about an alliance with this sovereign against the "Swedish *canaglia*," as Wallenstein called the Swedes, whom he loathed to see in Germany. Wallenstein also, by command and in the interest of Ferdinand, negotiated through Arnim with the Elector of Saxony.

After the terrible blow of the battle of Leipzig, when it was requisite to win back a man whose credit among the soldiers was without its equal, Questenberg was despatched to Prague, to treat with Wallenstein about his resuming the chief command of the Emperor's army. Wallenstein, pleading the state of his health, declined every offer. Prague then surrendered without striking a blow to Arnim, Don Balthazar Maradas having withdrawn his troops and placed them in safety. Previous to doing so, he applied to Wallenstein for advice. The latter, however, answered that he should do as he pleased; he (Wallenstein) had no longer any command. Arnim, on his side, had given orders "not to harm even a chicken on the property of the Duke of Friedland." Wallenstein left Prague for Gitschin, after having sent his wife with his most valuable property, under the escort of his cousin Maximilian, to Vienna. Maximilian was now made the bearer of a pathetic note from Ferdinand to Wallenstein, in which the Emperor implored him "not to go out of the way in the present distress, and still less to abandon him." This letter had its effect. Wallenstein, in December, 1631, went to Znaym, in Moravia, from thence to continue his negotiations with the Emperor. Wallenstein at last was brought to a definitive decision by his friend Prince Eggenberg, whom Ferdinand sent to him to Znaym. He at first agreed to undertake the command again, but only for three months. Being pressed more and more earnestly he at last consented to take the chief command without any limitation of time, but "*in absolutissimâ formâ.*" The commission indeed conferred on the generalissimo such absolute power that neither the Emperor himself nor his son should have anything to say in the army, nor go to it in person, nor be allowed to claim the command. Articles 6 and 7 expressly stipulated that the duke should have unlimited power to seize the estates of rebellious members of the Empire; to pardon or to punish with confiscation whomsoever he thought guilty. It was moreover stated that neither the Supreme Aulic Council

(*Reichshofrath*) nor the imperial chamber, nor the Emperor himself, should have the least right to interfere in such matters. "For," it was said in the compact, "the Emperor was too kind-hearted, and granted his pardon to any guilty person who came to court; *thereby the means were cut off which were requisite to reward high and low officers.*"

These articles very plainly show Wallenstein's intention to take up again his old plan of crushing the existing high aristocracy of princes.

As an "ordinary recompense," Wallenstein demanded *the Emperor's securing to him one of the provinces of the hereditary Austrian dominions*, and, as an "extraordinary recompense," *to be made liege-lord of the conquered countries.*

The contract was concluded at Znaym, in April, 1632, after Tilly had been killed on the Lech. Its stipulations are so extraordinary as not perhaps to have their parallel in the whole history of the world. None but a man of such a strange fanciful turn of mind as Wallenstein could have blinded himself to the inherent danger of a situation, in which all the usual conditions of security between man and man were suspended, and the positions of sovereign and subject completely reversed.

No sooner did the recruiting begin in the name of the all-popular captain than crowds came in from all sides—Walloons from Flanders, Croats from Hungary, Pulks of Cossacks from Poland—to join his standard. Thus, after the lapse of only a few months, Wallenstein had collected a new army, consisting of 120 companies of foot, and 214 squadrons of horse; about 40,000 men in all, with 44 cannon. From the very first he used with the greatest profusion his old expedient of attaching to himself his officers by gifts of money and by promotion. Isolani, who had succeeded in bringing in a great number of men from Hungary, was appointed general-in-chief of the whole light cavalry; the four counts, Gallas, Aldringer, Mansfeld, Montecuculi, colonels of artillery.

The court and nobility, on their side, made the greatest exertions to supply money. The King of Hungary gave 300,000 crowns, Prince Eggenberg 100,000 Bohemian dollars, the Prince-Bishop of Vienna 80,000 crowns, and others in proportion. A heavy property-tax was laid on the clergy as well as laity. Every landed noble in Austria paid forty, the tradespeople of the court thirty, lawyers twelve, common tradespeople six, parish priests and chaplains four, the inhabitants of the suburbs of Vienna three, the country people two florins each. Even day-labourers and men and maid-servants had to pay a poll-tax of fifteen kreutzers.

After having, by the end of May, 1632, cleared Prague and the whole of Bohemia of the Saxons, who retired to Silesia, Wallenstein united, at Eger, with Maximilian of Bavaria, whose army amounted to about 20,000 men. The Elector, who formerly had been the principal author of Wallenstein's downfall, was now obliged to yield to him the chief command. The two princes, when meeting, each at the head of his army, embraced in sight of their troops, apparently reconciled and friendly. "But," Khevenhüller remarks, "the curious observers noticed that his Electoral Highness had learned better how to dissemble than the duke." Both now marched against the Swedish King, who was stationed at Nuremberg. Gustavus Adolphus thus entered the lists also against Wallenstein for the contest in which it was to be decided which of the two should be considered as the first general of the day.

On the 6th of July, 1632, the combined Wallenstein and Bavarian armies, after plundering and devastating with fire and sword all the countries through which they passed, appeared in the large plain before Nuremberg, in which city Gustavus Adolphus had entrenched himself with the help of the inhabitants. Wallenstein occupied the heights near what is still called Alte Veste (Old Fastness), two leagues from Nuremberg, and likewise fortified his camp, which spread over the slopes of those hillocks down into the plain. It was his plan not to give battle to the King, to whom he wished to show that he had it in his own power to fight or not to fight, just as he pleased. And there Wallenstein stood "as if frozen to the ground." Famine and misery began to spread all around. The King, whose army, originally amounting to

18,000, had been increased by the troops under Bernard of Weimar to the strength of 30,000, was obliged to fight or to retire. An assault, made on the 4th of September on Wallenstein's position, was repulsed with a great loss on the side of the Swedes. Gustavus Adolphus said, with assumed jocularity, " We have made a *tour de page*," but he never from that day recovered his old spirit.

A few days after this defeat, Gustavus Adolphus sent the imperialist Major Sparre, a native of Sweden, who had been made prisoner, to Wallenstein with proposals of peace. But, even without waiting for the arrival of the answer from Vienna, the King, on the 18th of September, marched his army off from Nuremberg. Passing by Wallenstein, who remained immovable within his lines, he led his troops to Ingolstadt, with the intention of again penetrating into the heart of Bavaria. With another division, Bernard of Weimar covered the Maine and Franconia. The Swedish chancellor, Oxenstierna, remained behind at Nuremberg. On the 23rd of the same month, Wallenstein also marched off in the direction of Franconia, giving, as a farewell to the desolate country around, the awfully magnificent spectacle of burning his camp, which was not less than one German league and a half (about seven miles English) in circumference, the train of his army alone numbering no less than 30,000 men and women, and as many horses.

The Elector of Bavaria followed Wallenstein as far as Coburg. Wallenstein, turning a deaf ear to Maximilian's urgent entreaties to protect his States, marched through Franconia to Saxony, forcibly to detach the Elector of the latter country from the Swedish alliance, and to interrupt the King's communication with Pomerania and Sweden. He also sent orders to Pappenheim to come and join him. The march of the imperialist army through the Erzgebirge and the Voigtland was, as usual, attended with the most wanton destruction and cruelty. Everywhere the cattle were carried off, the fruit-trees cut down, the villages and farm-houses set on fire. The Elector of Saxony, therefore, despatched messenger after messenger to Gustavus

Adolphus begging him to return to his assistance; and the King, in compliance with his request, left Bavaria by forced marches, and united, on the 2nd of November, near Arnstadt with Bernard of Weimar. At Erfurt he took, on the 9th, his last farewell of his beautiful Queen Eleonora. From thence he advanced to Naumburg on the Saale.

Here the King entered a fortified camp. He determined to wait for the arrival of the Saxon troops from Silesia, and of Duke George of Lüneburg from Westphalia. Wallenstein having on the 22nd of October taken Leipzig, and near Merseburg been joined by Pappenheim, looked upon the campaign as closed, and placed his army in winter quarters round Leipzig, firmly believing that Gustavus Adolphus would do the same. On the 14th, moreover, he sent off Pappenheim by Halle to the Rhine for the protection of Cologne. Hearing this Gustavus Adolphus marched on the 5th of November (O.S.) upon Leipzig, determined to give battle to Wallenstein.

Again, on the plains of Leipzig, not far from the spot where Tilly had been defeated, the two hostile armies met. Wallenstein in all haste wrote from Lützen, on the 5th of November (O.S.), to Pappenheim: "The enemy is marching down upon us. The general is to leave everything as it stands, and to set out immediately with all his troops and cannon, so that he may join us to-morrow morning early." The original of this order is still preserved in the archives of Vienna; it is stained with the blood of Pappenheim, who carried it about him on the day of the battle of Lützen, at which he was killed.

On the evening of that very day Wallenstein had his army called under arms by the usual signal of three cannon-shots; and Field-marshal Holk during the night placed the troops in order of battle. The Swedish army was stationed about one league from Lützen. Gustavus Adolphus passed the cold November night, as he had done at Breitenfeld, in his carriage, conversing with Bernard of Weimar and General Kniphausen. Scarcely had the morning dawned which was destined to be the last of his life, when the King appeared and made his dispositions for the battle. The tactical arrangement was as it had been near Breitenfeld—the army of about 20,000 men being drawn up in two lines of battle, divided into a centre and two wings. The cavalry again was mixed with platoons of infantry placed at intervals between it. The different divisions were arrayed in such a manner as not to impede each other's movements. The right wing was commanded by the King himself, the left by Duke Bernard; the first line of the centre by Count Niels-Brahe, the second by General Kniphausen. The centre was formed by eight brigades, before each of which five large field-pieces were drawn up, light pieces being distributed among the infantry regiments of the wings.

Wallenstein, like Tilly at Breitenfeld, had arrayed his army in large close square columns, likewise in two lines of battle, with the cavalry on the two wings, and with the canal of Lützen and the high road before him. That canal and the ditches along the high road were defended by his musketeers and artillery. In front of his right wing were windmills, which, as they commanded the whole plain, were occupied by fourteen pieces of heavy artillery. The right wing, which rested on Lützen, stood under the command of Holk, the left under that of General Götz. With the latter Pappenheim was expected to join, and then to take the command of it. On the morning of the 6th (16th) November Wallenstein sent for the generals and colonels to his carriage, which he was seldom able to quit as he continually suffered from the gout, owing to which he had sometimes even to be carried in a litter. After having given the necessary orders, he had his charger brought out, but the metal stirrups had to be wrapped in silk to prevent his aching feet from being roughly pressed upon. In this manner, keeping a firm seat on his horse, he rode through the ranks, encouraged the soldiers, and gave the battle-cry, which was again that of Breitenfeld, "Jesu Maria."

The whole field was covered by a dense fog, which completely intercepted the view. The King of Sweden likewise mounted his white charger, and addressed the Swedes, Finlanders, and Germans separately. He then caused to be sung, to the sound of trumpets and kettledrums, Luther's Hymn, "A strong fortress is our God," and his own favourite hymn, known as his "Field Song," composed by his chaplain Dr. Fabricius:

> "Do not despair, thou little band,
> E'en though the foe is near at hand,
> To bring thee to destruction." [1]

As a war-cry he too gave that of Breitenfeld, "God with us." He had not yet broken his fast, and again only wore his buff jerkin, with a coat of broadcloth over it, without any cuirass, as an old wound and his corpulency made it inconvenient for him to wear armour. On the morning of the battle he expressly declined it, saying, "God is my cuirass."

It was now nine o'clock. The King had approached Wallenstein's order of battle within range of cannon-shot. The artillery began to play, the cavalry to throw out skirmishers; but as the thick fog made it impossible to see anything, all was soon quiet again. Shortly after ten o'clock the fog began to disperse, and there was a little gleam of sunshine. The King was just staying with Duke Bernard opposite the windmills, in front of the right wing of Wallenstein; and he called out with a loud voice, "Now let us be at it! The Lord be with us! Lord Jesus, help! We fight to-day for the honour and glory of thy holy name!" Then drawing his sword, he charged with the word of command, "Forward," against the ditches of the high road, which were kept by Wallenstein's artillery and musketeers. It was his principal object to take the battery near the windmills, which was the key of Wallenstein's position. Behind the ditches he was received by a murderous fire; and only after three hours' hard fighting, three of the enemy's squares were broken by the Swedish infantry under Brahe. The King now descried the cuirassiers of Wallenstein's second line of battle, in their black cuirasses, and at their head, in glittering

---

[1] "Verzage nicht, du Häuflein klein,
Obschon die Feinde willens sein
Dich gänzlich zu zerstören."

armour, their colonel, Ottavio Piccolomini, the same who afterwards betrayed Wallenstein. Gustavus called out to Colonel Stalhantsch, who commanded the Finland regiment of horse, "Attack those black fellows!" But being at this moment apprised that the imperial cavalry in the centre had again driven back his previously successful infantry, he put himself at the head of the Smaland regiment, commanded by the wounded Colonel Steenbock, to hasten to the support of his own centre. Whilst he was thus riding on at full speed, few only could follow him. These were Duke Francis Albert of Saxe Lauenburg, with his equerry Luchau; the lord of the bedchamber, Von Truchsess; the page Augustus von Leubelfing, the son of a Nuremberg patrician house, a lad of only eighteen years; and, besides these gentlemen, two grooms. At once the King found himself in the midst of the enemy's horsemen, those "black fellows." His horse was wounded in the neck by a pistol-shot; after which he himself had his left arm shattered by another ball. His first words were, "It is nothing, follow me;" but the wound was so severe that the bones protruded through the sleeve. He now begged the Duke of Lauenburg to remove him from the fray, and turned round; but at the same moment he received from the imperialist Lieutenant-colonel Maurice von Falkenberg, the brother of that Swedish commandant who had been killed at the taking of Magdeburg, another pistol-shot in the back. Exclaiming with a sigh, "My God, my God!" he sank from the saddle; but his foot being fast in the stirrup, he was dragged on by his horse. The equerry Luchau now engaged Falkenberg; the Duke fled, and the page alone remained with the King. He was still alive, and the boy, who refused to tell that it was the King, was himself mortally wounded. The King, after being robbed of his golden chain, and stripped, at last called out, "I am the King of Sweden!" Upon which the black cuirassiers tried to carry him off with them; but at this moment Steenbock's regiment came up. The black cuirassiers took to flight, and, being unable to take the King with them, they shot him through the head, and stabbed him in several places through the body; after which they dropped him. The Swedish squadrons then rode over his corpse. This happened at two o'clock in the afternoon.

The King's wounded and blood-stained white charger, racing along the Swedish lines, was the first harbinger of the sad news. Von Truchsess carried the intelligence to Duke Bernard, whom Gustavus Adolphus had appointed as his successor in the chief command, if anything should happen to himself. General Kniphausen, who commanded the reserve, now voted for retreat; but Duke Bernard called out with great spirit, "There cannot be question now of retreat, but only of revenge. Either we win the battle or die!"

He now ordered the regiment of Steenbock to follow him; and on its lieutenant-colonel's refusing obedience, he ran him through the body before the front of his battalion.

The soldiers of three other regiments he encouraged to advance with him, calling out to them, "Whoever wishes to show that he has loved the King may do so now. Up, then, and boldly attack the enemy." After having said this, the duke, without minding that his hat was shot off his head, rushed a second time against the ditches to take the height on which the windmills stood. At that moment a powder-waggon blew up in the rear of the lines of the imperialists. This opportune accident decided the battle; the squares of the imperialists fell into confusion, and their ranks broke, as they were afraid of being attacked in the rear. Bernard now drove the imperialists from the ditches, and took the batteries. According to all appearances, the victory was his. Such was the state of things about three in the afternoon.

Then Pappenheim arrived from Halle with four regiments of cavalry, and joined the left wing of the imperialist army. He again retrieved the battle, and Bernard was forced back across the ditches; but Pappenheim also fell, pierced by two bullets, and had to be removed from the fight. Bernard now ordered up the reserve under General Kniphausen, and renewed the battle for the third time. All the Swedes advanced over the ditches; even those who were nearly worn out by the toil of the fight rallied once more; all called out,

"Up at them for another time." This last attack turned the scale. Wallenstein's luck waned before the rising star of Bernard of Weimar. Pappenheim's six infantry regiments only arrived after the order for retreat had been given, and were involved in the flight of the others.

Wallenstein, having ascertained the death of Gustavus Adolphus from a trumpeter of Holk's regiment who showed to him a spur of the King, now retired to Leipzig, and from thence through the Erzgebirge and the Voigtland to Bohemia, where he entered winter quarters at Prague. Here he caused several officers to be executed, the "imperialist arms," as he expressed it, "having through them suffered at Lützen a disgrace never to be blotted out again." Since then he was spoken of in the army as a tyrant. His own dark fate was to be fulfilled in Bohemia; the death on the field of honour, which his great foe had met with at Lützen, was not destined to fall to his lot. Pappenheim, at the early age of thirty-eight, died on the day after the battle, at the Pleissenburg in the city of Leipzig; the Golden Fleece, which was on its way for him, did not reach him alive. With his son, who died in a duel in 1647, his branch of the house of Pappenheim became extinct.

The Swedish army occupied all through the night the battlefield on which it had combated with almost superhuman exertions for eleven hours, from ten in the morning to nine at night. Their exhausted condition did not allow them to think of pursuing Wallenstein; his artillery alone became the booty of the conquerors.

On the following morning the Swedes sought among the many corpses which strewed the field for the dead body of their King. It was found stripped naked, scarcely to be recognised—so disfigured was it with blood and bruises from the hoofs of the horses—and covered with nine wounds; not far from the large stone which to this day is called the Swede's stone (*Schwedenstein*), near the little town of Lützen, a few yards off the high road leading from Leipzig to Naumburg. Duke Bernard caused the body to be taken to Weissenfels, where Queen Eleonora received it, and from thence conveyed the beloved remains herself by way of Berlin to Stockholm. The army swore to Duke Bernard, over the corpse of the King, that they would follow him to the end of the world.

The unexpected death of the King of Sweden, who had not yet completed his thirty-eighth year, caused the greatest sensation throughout Europe among Papists as well as Protestants. The Emperor had a Te Deum sung in all the churches as if he had gained the most glorious victory; but he wept at the sight of the blood-stained buff jerkin of Gustavus Adolphus with the holes made by the balls in the sleeve and in the back. At Madrid there were great rejoicings, and the death of the King was represented at the playhouse for the gratification of the faithful. The Pope, who in his heart had been not a little pleased that someone had risen to oppose the overwhelming supremacy of the Emperor, caused a low mass to be read for the soul of the fallen champion of the heretics. On the Protestants, on the other hand, the sudden disaster fell like a thunderbolt. The banished King of Bohemia was actually seized with paralysis on receiving the news at Mayence. He died at the age of thirty-six, leaving a family of thirteen young children, with whom his widow, for nearly thirty years, had to wander about the world without a home, and often without any means of subsistence, pursued by more than one romantic love and also by bloodthirsty hatred. Frederic had been mean and craven enough, after the peace of Lübeck in 1629, to offer to the Emperor to deliver up his children to the care of the Jesuits of Vienna for education. Under the condition of his family being restored, he would himself make amends in person on his knees, after which he would retire with a moderate pension as an exile to Holland or to England. Who could then have foreseen that he was to become the ancestor of the rulers of three of the greatest European realms? of the house of Hanover, which reigns in England; of the house of Orleans, which reigned in France; and of the house of Lorraine, which sits on the throne of Austria. The beautiful " Winter Queen " Elizabeth survived until

1662, when she died in the palace of her nephew Charles II. of England.

For Germany the death of Gustavus Adolphus was a decisive turning-point. His life was cut short in the midst of a brilliant career of victory, in which he had acquired by conquest considerable parts of the territories of the German Empire. Pomerania, Mecklenburg, the archbishopric of Magdeburg and the bishoprics of Halberstadt, Hildesheim, Bamberg, Würtzburg, Mayence, Spires, Worms, and Augsburg, the Palatinate, and part of Bavaria and Swabia, were in his hands. He had already conceived the idea of causing himself to be elected "King of the Romans." With this creation of a fresh, energetic Protestant head of the decrepit body of the German Empire, not only the Protestant cause would have been secured, but also the whole political life of the German nation would have taken a new and more vigorous start than it has afterwards had, and could only have had under the weak and phlegmatic rule of the Papist Austrian Emperors.[1] Germany was an elective Empire, not an hereditary demesne of the house of Habsburg; and it was the cherished plan of Gustavus Adolphus to marry his only child Christina to that son of the Elector of Brandenburg who afterwards earned the name of "The Great Elector." This son-in-law would, in all probability, have succeeded after Gustavus Adolphus to the imperial crown of Germany.

9.— Wallenstein's downfall—Rewards bestowed on his betrayers and murderers—Piccolomini, Aldringer, Colloredo, Butler, Leslie, &c.

After the death of Gustavus Adolphus, the Swedish chancellor Axel Oxenstierna was placed at the head of affairs. As the King had been one of the greatest captains, so the chancellor was one of the greatest statesmen. He forthwith applied to the Protestant Electors of Saxony and Brandenburg, engaging them to conclude with him a new and still closer alliance. On their refusal, he at last entered with the States of the four Southern Circles of the Empire, on the 13th of April, 1633, into the League of Heilbronn, in which a

---

[1] The reader will remember this work was written about 1852.

so-called *concilium formatum*, consisting of the councillors of the allied princes, was joined to him. Oxenstierna, moreover, secured the continuance of the French subsidies. The Swedish-German army was placed under the command of Duke Bernard of Weimar, who at once drove the Friedland garrisons from the electorate of Saxony, conquered Franconia, established himself in the Upper Rhine, and from thence harassed Bavaria. As a reward, the duchy of Franconia— the bishoprics of Würzburg and Bamberg—was given to him; and Erfurt with Eichsfeld to his brother William. At the same time, Gustavus Horn, Oxenstierna's son-in-law, together with Duke George of Lüneburg, swept the other imperialist troops from their scattered positions all over Germany; for which achievement Mergentheim, the principal seat of the Teutonic order, was given to the Swedish fieldmarshal; and George of Lüneburg appropriated as his prize the territory of the bishopric of Hildesheim.

Whilst all this was going on, Wallenstein remained quiet in his winter quarters in Bohemia, increasing his army again to the strength of 40,000 men. About the middle of May he set out again for Prague. His departure for the field was effected with his usual princely pomp, the procession consisting of fourteen carriages, each drawn by six horses. He was attended by forty cavaliers of his household; by twelve footmen dressed, like all his servants, in new scarlet and blue liveries; and by twelve trumpeters with silver-gilt trumpets. Wallenstein, first of all, reconquered Silesia for the Emperor; but, as early as the 7th of June, 1633, he concluded a truce for a fortnight with the Saxon field-marshal Arnim, with whom he entered into negotiations. It was evidently neither more nor less than his own well-considered interest, in conjunction with Saxony, to urge the Emperor to conclude a reasonable peace, which would have given him as strong a claim to be remunerated by Ferdinand as any successful military operation could have done. The Elector of Saxony himself began, in July, 1633, under the mediation of Denmark, to negotiate with the Emperor; but the transaction led to no result.

VOL. I 23

On the 12th (22nd) of August Wallenstein concluded a second truce with Arnim for four weeks. As late as in October the negotiations between Wallenstein and the two Electors of Saxony and Brandenburg were still in full operation. According to the Venetian Gualdo, a contemporary and eye-witness of all that then happened, it was the avowed plan of the two Electors and of Wallenstein to establish a third power in the Empire, as a medium between the Emperor and the Swedes. In October, 1633, at the camp near Schweidnitz, Wallenstein appears to have been perfectly in earnest with regard to the conclusion of an alliance for such a purpose, to which the Electors showed themselves not less inclined. Khevenhüller expressly states that Duke Francis Albert of Saxe-Lauenburg—who, after the battle of Lützen, entered the Saxon service, and through whom the negotiations in the camp of Schweidnitz were carried on—had asserted that Wallenstein had it there completely in his power to bring about a peace. A report, certainly an unwarranted one, was then current that all the exiles should receive back their estates, the Jesuits be expelled the Empire, and the Swedes should have their expenses of the war repaid to them, until which term they might keep possession of the fortresses which they occupied. Khevenhüller, indeed—but on the sole authority of a pamphlet of 1633, which he has embodied almost word for word in his " Annals "—states further that Wallenstein, in a secret additional clause, had claimed the crown of Bohemia, with Moravia, for himself. The Elector of Saxony, on the other hand, demanded in the same treaties the two Lusatias and one-half of Bohemia. According to the documents communicated by Helbig from the Dresden archives in his small pamphlet " Wallenstein and Arnim," Wallenstein demanded, in addition to Mecklenburg, the Rhenish Palatinate. Both parties seem to have bidden very high on purpose, in order that, although obliged to abate from their demands, they might still get as much as they really wanted. The Duke of Saxe-Lauenburg having asked Wallenstein in the camp of Schweidnitz, " What would become of the Swedes?" Wallenstein answered that they must "all join to kick the Swedes out of the country." The Electors, however, were afraid, and perhaps not without reason, of ulterior designs of Wallenstein, who, after having in conjunction with them driven out the Swedes, might turn his arms against themselves. However that may be, Arnim, who had been deep in Wallenstein's confidence, continued to maintain, even after the dictator's catastrophe, that Wallenstein had been in earnest, and that it was his real policy and intention, with the help of Saxony and Brandenburg, to induce the Emperor to conclude a fair peace.

Certain it is that Wallenstein, at the very same time, was also negotiating with France about the crown of Bohemia, and it is very probable that he was likewise in correspondence with the Bohemian exiles. Richelieu had gained a firm hold on the German affairs. On the 23rd of May, 1631, the Elector Maximilian of Bavaria concluded a defensive alliance with the crown of France for eight years. Ever since the 9th of July, 1632, a French garrison had been occupying Ehrenbreitstein, which was given up to them by the Elector of Trèves, the celebrated Philip Christopher Sötern, whom the house of Habsburg afterwards kept a prisoner for ten years. The negotiations with France—as Wallenstein generally used the precaution of not committing himself in writing—were carried on through Count William Kinsky, one of the exiled Bohemian Protestant lords, and brother-in-law of Wallenstein's brother-in-law Count Adam Erdmann Terzka. Kinsky treated in Dresden with the then resident French minister, the Marquis de Feuquières, a nephew of Father Joseph. Through Feuquières, who left Paris as ambassador-extraordinary on the 8th of February, 1633, and arrived on the 19th of May at Dresden, Cardinal Richelieu made to Wallenstein, who was then stationed at Breslau, the offer of 1,000,000 livres a year and the crown of Bohemia, if he would desert from the Emperor. On the 29th of September, 1633, the Elector of Trèves, as is stated by the "Rhenish Antiquary" (Baron Stramberg), was apprised of Wallenstein's impending desertion. But already at the end of that same year, Feuquières broke off the negotiations, *confessing himself to have been duped by Wallenstein, whose only object had been to set the enemies of the Emperor by the ears.*

Whilst the negotiations were going on with the two Electors of Saxony and Brandenburg and with France, Wallenstein entered into a correspondence also with the Swedes. At first it was Arnim who carried on the transactions with Oxenstierna, to whom he went, after the conclusion of the second truce in August, at Gelnhausen, near Frankfort, where he conferred with him on the 1st (11th) of September. Afterwards the negotiations went through the chief of the Bohemian refugees, Count Henry Matthias Thurn, whom Wallenstein had made prisoner, with a great number of other commanders, on the 11th of October of the preceding year, near Stenau on the Oder, in Silesia, but, to the great displeasure of the court of Vienna, had released as soon as they had surrendered the Silesian towns, until then occupied by them. Wallenstein, moreover, negotiated with Duke Bernard of Saxe-Weimar. To the Swedes he expressed himself thus: that he knew very sure means and ways to force the Emperor to conclude a fair peace. Oxenstierna, however, trusted him just as little as the two Electors and the French ambassador had done. On receiving the first intimation, the chancellor became, to use the words of the Swedish historian Chemnitz, "quite perplexed." He wrote, on the 28th of December, 1633, to the Elector of Saxony, "Although the last negotiations were more satisfactory in appearance, yet the offers were too great and extraordinary, so that I could not but suppose that there was some deceit lurking underneath."

It is quite possible that Wallenstein only played a Machiavellian game, if not with all the parties—not with Saxony and Brandenburg—yet with Sweden and France; and likewise he may possibly have diplomatised in reality only for the Emperor's interest, as long as he was sure that he was still favourably looked upon at the court of Vienna. But, having once entered into negotiations with the enemy, he availed himself of the connection with them when his own safety was at stake.

The actual disagreement between him and the imperial court came to a head when, contrary to the Emperor's wish, he did not march to the assistance of Bavaria against Duke Bernard. The latter had, in the autumn of the year 1633, taken the important city of Ratisbon, besides Straubing and other Bavarian towns. Duke Maximilian therefore entreated the Emperor to induce Wallenstein to lead his troops from Silesia to Bavaria. Instead of doing so, Wallenstein led the army from Silesia into winter quarters in Bohemia, merely sending from Pilsen to Vienna a letter, in which the opinion of his commanders was set forth, that the march to Ratisbon in winter time was a downright impossibility.

On this, Maximilian of Bavaria, at the head of Wallenstein's enemies, moved heaven and earth at the court of Vienna to bring about the downfall of the hateful adversary. And the moment for doing so was very well chosen.

The Emperor—especially since the death of Gustavus Adolphus seemed to have rid him of the greatest danger—felt the contract with Wallenstein more and more as an irksome burden. He openly complained that he had, as it were, a *co-rex*, a colleague in his kingly office; and that he could no longer freely act as he pleased in his own country.

The cabinet of Vienna first broke the contract with Wallenstein, under the pressure of the manifest necessity of having Duke Bernard of Weimar driven from Ratisbon and the Danube. Wallenstein having asserted his inability to effect this, they called from Italy the Duke of Feria, the Spanish viceroy of Milan, orders being despatched at the same time to John Aldringer, a general of Wallenstein's, and brother-in-law of Gallas, to join with his troops, which were stationed at Swabia, those of Feria, who was to advance from the Tyrol. To the Bavarian court, in whose behalf alone this succour had been summoned, the promise was also given, that Wallenstein should for the second time be dismissed from his command. Aldringer, who until then had been faithful to Wallenstein, at first hesitated; but, on the death of Feria, which took place before the year 1633 was quite past, he, true to his character of following that side which held out the greatest advantage to him, allowed himself to be gained over by the court. Wallenstein, furious at his conduct, summoned him to head-quarters to cashier him, but Aldringer refused obedience.

Wallenstein was at that time so severely tortured by the gout as to be obliged to pass one hour every day in the vapour bath; besides which he had to undergo the most painful operations in his legs. He now, in order not to be deposed a second time, resolved upon voluntarily resigning the chief command, but previously placing himself in a position in which he might enforce the fulfilment of the conditions granted to him in his contract. For this purpose he assembled in his camp at Pilsen all the generals and commanders of the troops stationed in Bohemia, Moravia, and Silesia. On the 12th of January, 1634, Field-marshal Illo gave them a banquet, at which, as a Bavarian agent wrote from Pilsen, the merriment was so riotous that the gentlemen, "after having had their fill of wine, began to smash the stoves, windows, chairs, and benches." In pursuance of a plan preconcerted with Wallenstein, Illo and Count Terzka set forth most emphatically that the commander-in-chief, on account of the injustice inflicted on him by the court, and on account of his miserable state of health, was resolved upon resigning the command. The officers stood aghast at this unexpected intelligence. The generals and colonels had raised their regiments at their own cost, and invested their fortunes therein, solely in reliance on Wallenstein's word, and in the hope of getting reimbursed through his interest; they therefore were afraid of being ruined themselves by the ruin of Wallenstein. A bond was now laid before them to be signed, for the duke's security and for their own, in which they pledged themselves to "stand by the duke to the shedding of their last drop of blood, and to persecute anyone who would separate from them, and to take revenge on his person or estates as a faithless and dishonoured traitor."

Forty generals and commanders, German as well as Italian, signed this very remarkable bond. Among the latter was the treacherous friend of Wallenstein, Piccolomini, who stood at the head of the Italian party at the imperial court. This party—now in conjunction with the Jesuits, who had become Wallenstein's bitterest enemies, and with the Spanish ambassador, Count Ognate—had gained the victory over the German party, which was headed by Prince Eggenberg. The latter, a friend of the dictator, zealously defended his interest to the last, and, although having ultimately abandoned him to the Emperor's anger, was himself involved in his downfall.

Ottavio Piccolomini was descended from a Siennese family which has become illustrious through Pope Æneas Sylvius Piccolomini, who, as Pius II., ascended the papal chair in 1458. Ottavio had come to Germany in 1615, as captain in a regiment raised by the Grand Duke of Florence for the Emperor Ferdinand. After the death of Dampierre, who commanded it, he became its colonel. Piccolomini enjoyed the most unbounded confidence of Wallenstein, who imagined he had read in the stars that he might place his full and entire reliance on him. Being, like Aldringer, shrewd enough to foresee that he would rise by Wallenstein's fall, he reported the substance of the bond signed at Illo's banquet to Vienna, and took good care to charge the duke with an actual dangerous conspiracy.

Ferdinand—as is manifest from the recently published [1] reports of the privy-councillor Bernard Richel, the Bavarian minister resident at Vienna—was regularly and fully informed of every step of Wallenstein. The Duke of Savoy especially had sent in to Vienna a full account of Wallenstein's transaction with the French court. The Emperor discussed the affair with his select council, which became the first nucleus of that confidential board which afterwards, under Leopold I., was formally organised under the name of the Conference Council. The persons let into the secret were Prince Eggenberg, Count Maximilian Trautmannsdorf, Bishop Antony

---

[1] They are contained in Buchner and Zierl, Neue Beiträge zur Vaterländischen Geschichte (New Materials for National History), 1832, vol. i.

Wolffrath of Vienna, the confessor Father Lamormain, the Spanish ambassador Count Ognate, Count Schlick, president of the Aulic Council of War, and Marchese Francis Antony Caretto di Grana, to whom besides we must add the Emperor's eldest son Ferdinand III. The most outrageous plans were imputed to the Friedländer. He was said to have expressed himself thus: " I do not care for God, and still less will I care for Ferdinand."

The Italian-Spanish-Jesuit party, which had long sworn the ruin of Wallenstein, egged the Emperor on. The Spanish ambassador called out, " Why hesitate ? A stab of a dagger or a pistol-shot will effectually settle the matter." Thus Ferdinand was induced not only to pronounce for the second time the dismissal of Wallenstein, but also to abandon him, who had been the saviour of the monarchy, to the revenge of the party which sought his ruin. How far those people—those Italian informers and envious detractors of Wallenstein—went in their infamous avarice and covetousness, which was the prime motive in bringing about such a speedy catastrophe, is sufficiently proved by the fact that, when the dismissal was yet a profound secret, they began to quarrel and even to fight duels about the division of the booty, the estates, houses, and gardens, even the carriages and horses, of Wallenstein ; nay, with the most brazen effrontery, they tried to make the court umpire of these quarrels.

The court proceeded against its dangerous adversary with consummate dexterity and astuteness. As early as on the 24th of January, 1634, Ferdinand announced by a memorandum to all the high and low commanders the dismissal of the commander-in-chief with the words, " that from most weighty and pressing reasons his Majesty had felt induced to make a change with regard to him." He released all the generals and commanders "from every obligation by which they had hitherto been bound to the Duke of Friedland ; " referring them, until further orders, to his beloved and trustworthy Lieutenant-general Count Matthias Gallas, and offering a full pardon and amnesty to all except Wallenstein and two other persons. In addition to this the Emperor promised favours and rewards to all those who would faithfully serve him, and assured the soldiers that he would take every care that they should want for nothing.

Even as late as one-and-twenty days after issuing this memorandum the Emperor corresponded about official matters with Wallenstein, calling him, as before, "Illustrious dear uncle and prince," and endorsing the letter, "To the Duke of Mecklenburg," &c.

The principal question at Vienna was how to win over the generals and commanders singly and with the greatest secrecy. The Italian, Spanish, and Walloon officers were the first applied to; the Germans, Bohemians, Moravians, and Silesians were too much attached to Wallenstein to be trusted with the secret. The imperial memorandum, therefore, only offered an amnesty to all except Illo and Terzka. To those commanders who were taken into the confidence, Prague was pointed out as the general rendezvous; and thither Wallenstein afterwards likewise gave orders to his regiments stationed in Silesia to march, both parties having an equally strong interest to secure the capital of Bohemia.

One month nearly passed away before the first imperial memorandum was followed by a second, the language of which was already much more explicit and severe, as in the meanwhile several more generals had been gained over. It was dated the 18th of February, 1634, and directed not only to the commanders, but also to all the private soldiers. The Emperor states in it that, according to most reliable information, Wallenstein had intended to drive him and his family from his hereditary kingdoms, and to appropriate his crown and sceptre to himself—nay, entirely to annihilate the Emperor and his imperial house; for which purpose he had tried to seduce his Majesty's faithful generals, commanders, and officers, to make them the tools of his wicked intentions, and thereby to rob them of their honour and their reputation. Ferdinand thereupon, "for the safety of himself and his house," refers the army, until the appointment of a new commander-in-chief, to the generals already gained over: to Gallas, as lieutenant-commander-in-chief; and, besides, to

Aldringer, Maradas, Piccolomini, and Colloredo. In conclusion, the Emperor assured the officers and soldiers that until then he had, for the benefit of his army, assigned many considerable sums of money to his former generalissimo; and that henceforth, also, it would be his care to find out ways and means how not only to maintain and remunerate them, but also, *ere long, to bestow on them imperial favours which would be sure to gladden their hearts.*

This last assurance was a very plain allusion to the estates which were intended to be confiscated from the rich victim, and which certainly again supplied the Emperor with means for maintaining and rewarding the army.

Wallenstein was only made aware of the true state of affairs when Gallas, Aldringer, Maradas, Piccolomini, and Colloredo, after the 13th of February, issued orders in which they forbade the colonels serving under them to obey in future any commands either of Wallenstein or of Illo and Terzka. The first of these orders was issued and signed by Gallas.

The commanders, as has been stated before, received orders to march upon Prague, to secure the capital of Bohemia to Ferdinand. Wallenstein now had, on the 20th of February, a solemn declaration prepared, to which he himself and twenty-nine generals put their signatures, setting forth that the former bond "*meant nothing whatever against the Emperor or against religion.*" He likewise ordered the troops to Prague, appointing the 24th of February as the day of their arrival on the White Mountain. As late as the 21st of February, he sent Colonels Mohrwald and Brenner to the Emperor, to whom he offered to retire to Hamburg or Dantzig, only stipulating "that he should be allowed to retain his duchies." But those duchies were the very thing which they also coveted at Vienna. On the 20th of February, Ferdinand had already issued to Gallas, Colloredo, and De Suys the warrants for the confiscation of the property and estates of Wallenstein, Terzka, and Illo, "*for the especial use and benefit of the army.*"

Wallenstein was fully aware of this; he therefore determined to guard against any emergency except the one which he did not and could not foresee, as it was beyond all calculation. Being himself placed in imminent peril, and forced to provide for his own safety, he now, and for the first time seriously, applied to the Duke Bernard of Weimar, who had his head-quarters at Ratisbon. He called upon him to advance as speedily as possible with his troops through the Upper Palatinate to the Bohemian frontier. The rendezvous should be at Eger, whither also Arnim, the Saxon general, who was posted at Zwickau and had likewise been summoned by Wallenstein, was to march his troops. Duke Bernard, however, remembering "how many a man the Friedländer had thrown overboard," could not make up his mind. He called out, "He who does not believe in God cannot be trusted by man." And yet there was not a moment to be lost. Wallenstein was apprised of the desertion of one general after the other. Aldringer sent from Frauenberg, excusing himself under the plea of illness; Gallas, his brother-in-law, who was with him, did not return either; and Colonel Diodati had absconded from Pilsen without leave from the generalissimo. Thirteen couriers hurried to Ratisbon and back. At last Duke Bernard got his troops in marching order, but with the greatest caution. The negotiations between the two parties were carried on by Duke Francis Albert of Saxe-Lauenburg, who, on the second day after the catastrophe, was going to return from Weiden to the Upper Palatinate, but was captured by a stratagem of the Croats, at Tirschenreit near Eger. The lieutenant who commanded them, pretended to be sent by Terzka to escort Duke Francis Albert to Eger, and the latter, falling into the snare, let out in the conversation with him, "*that Wallenstein, with Pilsen, Gross-Glogau, Frankfort on the Oder, and Landsberg, which would be left to him, might consider himself perfectly safe;* 6,000 *Swedes and* 4,000 *Saxons were marching on Eger.*"

Wallenstein's original plan, which, according to Khevenhüller, had been to betake himself to Prague, was baffled by the desertion of the generals; he was also obliged to give up another plan, of marching to Zittau, in order to be nearer to his Bohemian possessions and to Silesia. After these disappointments, he, as has been stated before, fixed upon Eger as the place for the Swedes to join him.

Wallenstein left Pilsen for Eger, a fortress on the Bohemian frontier, on the 22nd of February, 1634, about ten o'clock in the morning. The first night he slept at Mies, which belonged to his faithful field-marshal, Christian Illo.[1]

Wallenstein was accompanied by Field-marshal Illo and by his own brother-in-law, Adam Terzka. There were with them five troops of Terzka's cuirassiers; five troops of the Old Saxon regiment of horse, which deserted on the road and went to Prague; and 200 men of the Old Saxon foot regiment under Duke Julius Henry of Saxe-Lauenberg. William Kinsky, Terzka's brother-in-law, was likewise in his suite. From Pilsen, Wallenstein, on account of his gout, made the journey in a litter carried by two horses. Before reaching his first night-quarters, he was joined by the man who became his murderer, Colonel Walter Butler, with eight companies of dragoons.

Butler was a native of Ireland and a Papist. Wallenstein had sent to him from Pilsen to Kladrup, where the colonel was stationed, the order, under pain of death, to march with his regiment to Prague. This arrangement, which left the passes leading from the Upper Palatinate to Bohemia undefended, had roused Butler's suspicions. He therefore wrote to Gallas that if Arnim should approach Eger within two leagues, he (Butler) would either take prisoner or kill the traitor (Wallenstein). As, on his march from Kladrup to Prague, he fell in with Wallenstein before Mies, he received a new order to follow the generalissimo to Eger; and he had with his dragoons to march before Wallenstein's litter, together with Terzka's cuirassiers and the Old Saxons. At the first night-quarters at Mies, and at the second, on the 23rd of February, at Plan, Butler received orders, contrary to the usage of war, to remain with the colours and standards within the town, whilst the soldiers were encamped outside

---

[1] Illo, whose name is likewise spelled Ilow and also Illau, was a Brandenburger, and son-in-law to the president of the Aulic Council of the Empire, Count Vratislaw von Fürstenberg.

the walls. This precaution increased Butler's suspicions; he sent from Plan his chaplain, Patrick Taaffe, whose report is still extant, to Gallas or Piccolomini, "wherever they are to be found"; entrusting him with a few lines in English, written by his own hand, and with the verbal message that he marched with Wallenstein only from compulsion; but that perhaps he was forced on in this way by a special providence of God *to achieve some particular heroic deed*. Father Taaffe with this message went from Plan to Pilsen, where Piccolomini, immediately after Wallenstein's departure, had established himself by stratagem. Gallas, on the 22nd of February, stood at Linz. Maradas on that day was at Frauenberg, which belonged to him; but advanced from thence to Horasdiowitz, which Piccolomini had left. Maradas had secured Budweis and Tabor, and despatched Lieutenant-field-marshal Baron de Suys to Prague to maintain the troops there in the allegiance of the Emperor. Aldringer was at Vienna.

During the last day's march between Plan and Eger, Wallenstein sent for Butler to his litter, apologised for not having until then done more for him, and promised him two regiments, besides a present of 200,000 crowns. Wallenstein made his entry into Eger on the 24th of February in the afternoon, between four and five o'clock. Again was Butler quartered with the standards within the town, and his dragoons encamped outside in the open field. Wallenstein took up his quarters in the market-place, at the house of the burgomaster Pachhälbel;[1] Terzka and Kinsky, with their wives, put up at the outbuildings of the same house.

The post of commandant of Eger was held by John Gordon, a Scotch Calvinist and a lieutenant-colonel in Terzka's infantry regiment. To this officer, whom Wallenstein, after his arrival only, had promoted to the rank of colonel, Butler made the first overtures. The two then took into their confidence Walter Leslie, major in Terzka's regiment, whom Gordon had sent as far as Plan to meet the duke. Leslie, like Gordon, was a

---

[1] There are descendants of this Bohemian family still living in Prussia under the name of Pachelbl Gehag. One of them was, in 1850, ranger of one of the royal parks (*Hofjägermeister*) in Berlin.

Scotchman and a Calvinist; both of them turned Papists only after the catastrophe. These three islanders, Butler, Gordon, and Leslie, became the instruments of the vindictive plans which had been hatched by the Italians and Spaniards in the cabinet of Vienna. This energetic triumvirate, during the night of the 24th, pledged themselves at the citadel, the quarters of the commandant, by a formal oath taken on the drawn sword, "to make away with Wallenstein." It was arranged that Gordon should invite the generals for the following evening to a carnival banquet in the citadel, at which the deed should be perpetrated. Everything made it expedient to hasten, Illo having already triumphantly announced the news that, on the day after, the Swedes would enter the town of Eger.

On Saturday, the 25th of February, 1634, Count Terzka gave to the officers a banquet at noon. In the evening, at six o'clock, he drove in a coach with Kinsky, Illo, and Captain Neumann—the writer of the bond of Pilsen—to Gordon's carnival supper in the citadel. The guests sat down to table, and merrily enjoyed their meat and their wine. The banquet drawing to a close, the upper gate of the town was opened, as previously arranged by Gordon and Leslie; and a hundred men of Butler's Irish dragoons, and as many German soldiers, were admitted into the town to reinforce the guard-post in the citadel, which was now closed. In the meanwhile the dessert had been put on the table. Now a letter was brought to the Commandant Gordon. It was a forged despatch, pretended to be written by the Electoral Saxon cabinet, and to have been intercepted. It was stated in it that the Elector disapproved of Wallenstein's intention of deserting from the Emperor; and that he was resolved to give up Wallenstein to Ferdinand if he got him in his power. After having read the despatch, Gordon handed it to Illo, who, with the others, pooh-poohed it; a discussion arose, and, as if to be able to speak more freely, the servants were sent out of the hall to a distant room, where their supper was laid, and the door then locked upon them. Now the murderers were alone with their victims.

As soon as the servants were got rid of, there stepped from the two rooms adjoining the dining-hall the Italian Major Geraldino and the two Irish captains, Devereux and Macdonald, with thirty-six dragoons, most of them Irish, with not one German among them. Geraldino called aloud: "*Viva la casa d'Austria!*" Devereux: "*Wer ist gut Kaiserlich?*" (Who is the Emperor's friend?) To which Butler, Gordon, and Leslie quickly answered: "*Vivat Ferdinandus! Vivat Ferdinandus!*" and, seizing each his sword, and a candlestick from the table, they ranged themselves in a group on the side of the wall. The Irish now stepped up to the table and overturned it. Kinsky was despatched first, then, after a short resistance Illo. Terzka, who had succeeded in recovering his sword, placed himself in a corner, where he made a desperate defence. His buff jerkin warded off several thrusts and cuts, so that the dragoons thought him "frozen" (of charmed life); at last he too fell, stabbed by daggers in the face, and was then despatched with the butt-ends of the muskets. Captain Neumann had escaped wounded into the outer part of the house, and was stabbed there. The bodies of the victims were given up to the dragoons; who stripped them to the shirt.

It was about nine o'clock. Gordon caused the dining-hall to be locked, and remained with the guard in the citadel; Leslie went to the principal guard-post in the market-place; and Butler surrounded Wallenstein's quarters. It was a dark, boisterous night; the wind roared, and a drizzling rain pattered against the windows. Captain Walter Devereux, of Butler's regiment, with twelve of his men, now set out on his bloody errand to the duke. The sentinels, supposing he was coming to make a report, allowed him to pass. Wallenstein had taken a bath, and was going to lie down. In the anteroom Devereux met the valet, who had just carried in to his master his usual evening cup, a tankard of beer on a golden salver. The man requested Devereux not to make a noise, as the duke had retired to rest. A few minutes before his astrologer, Giovanni Battista Seni, had left him, who is said to have warned him by the stars even in the last moment.

According to Khevenhüller they could not agree in their calculations, the astrologer having found in his that the hour of danger had not yet arrived; and the duke, on the other hand, that it was past. The latter also prophesied that Seni would be imprisoned, which really came true. Wallenstein had been startled by the noise of the soldiers being drawn up in the market-place; and he had heard the shrieks of the Countesses Kinsky and Terzka in the outhouse, who had already been informed of their husbands' murder. This caused him to go to the window to inquire of the sentinel what all this meant. Devereux asked of the valet the key of the duke's room; on being refused, he forced the door, shouting, "Rebels! rebels!" and entered with his fellow-assassins. Wallenstein was standing in his shirt, leaning against a table. "You are to die, rogue!" Devereux called out to him. As Wallenstein turned towards the window to call for help, Devereux rushed up to him with a halberd; and then, without uttering a word, with outspread arms, the great man received the deadly weapon in his breast; "and," writes Wassenberg, the author of the German Florus, in his own quaint and graphic style, "his belly gave a crack, just as if a musket had been fired off; and, whilst thus breathing out his soul, he spouted from his mouth a great smoke, just as if he were all burning within. Such was the end of the German Catiline!"

Immediately after the murder, the papers of the Duke were locked up, Butler taking the keys with him. Wallenstein's master of the household, and his two chamberlains, who the day before had told Leslie that Wallenstein had proposed to them to give them their honourable discharge, lest they might get into trouble, received a guard for their security. The poor astrologer, Seni, on the other hand, was imprisoned, as his master had prophesied; nor did the soldiers release him until he had disgorged 4,000 crowns, given him by Wallenstein the day before his death.

The body of the Friedländer, wrapped up in a scarlet carpet, which had lain under his bed, was conveyed in Leslie's coach to the citadel. Here it lay, with the four other corpses, in the courtyard, during the whole of Sunday. On Monday they were all sent to Illo's castle at Mies, and there buried except Neumann; who, on account of his violent, abusive language at the last banquet, viz., that he "hoped soon to wash his hands in the blood of the house of Austria," was dug in under the gallows.

Wallenstein's coffin having been made too short, and the limbs having already stiffened, they were obliged to break his legs to get him into it. His widow, two years after, caused his remains to be transferred to the Carthusian convent of Walditz near Gitschin. There General Baner, in 1639, had his tomb opened, and his skull and his right arm taken off and sent as a trophy to Sweden. In 1785 Count Vincent of Waldstein received permission to remove the coffin of his illustrious ancestor to the family vault of the Wallensteins, at Münchengrätz, a market-town in the canton of Bunzlau, not far from Friedland.

Terzka's and Kinsky's widows were conveyed with the captive Duke Francis Albert of Saxe-Lauenburg from Eger by way of Pilsen to Wienerisch-Neustadt. The Countess Kinsky, Terzka's sister, was initiated in all the plans of the duke. Maximiliana Terzka, of the house of Harrach, had not been privy to anything, and was a loyal imperialist. The chequered career of the Duke of Lauenberg, who at first had been a field-marshal in the Swedish, and then in the Saxon, service, ended by his holding the same rank and commission in the army of the Emperor. He was killed in 1642, near Schweidnitz.

Everywhere the commandants reputed to be faithful to Wallenstein were imprisoned or executed. Thus Piccolomini put the commandant of Pilsen to death; and Colloredo arrested, at Ohlau, Hans Ulric Schafgotsch, the general commanding in Silesia, and had him conducted to Glatz, as the "Frankfort Relations"[1] have it, "in ignominious captivity, without sword, pistols, or spurs."

Wallenstein's downfall was the very counterpart of that

[1] One of the earliest German gazettes.

of the Guises in 1588. Just as they lorded it over Henry III., who was thrown into the shade by them, so Wallenstein did with regard to Ferdinand II. Apprehension for his own safety and avarice, but by no means a conscientious care for upholding the public law, prompted the Emperor to destroy the Friedländer.

Silent as he had been all his life, so also was he in taking leave of it. With the profoundest mystery, he locked up in his innermost heart the plans and designs of his ardent ambition; and an impenetrable veil remains spread over his life and his death. It probably will ever be doubtful how far Wallenstein was guilty or not. The controversy between Count Mailath in Vienna, who has taken the part of the Emperor, and Professor Förster in Berlin, who represents Wallenstein as completely guiltless, will most likely never be settled in a satisfactory manner. There is one fact favourable to the presumption of Wallenstein's innocence—that the court of Vienna took the trouble, by a special manifesto published in 1634, under the title of "*Alberti Friedlandi perduellionis chaos*," &c., to justify the murder before the world; but this very apology is completely refuted by other authentic documents. Even Count Mailath was obliged to allow that this apology was nearly in every point resting on *false statements*. Count Mailath and Baron von Aretin have, on the other hand, tried to prove that Ferdinand II. had only intended to depose Wallenstein and to drive him from Bohemia, but not to have him killed. This is completely disproved by what Eggenberg divulged to the Bavarian resident minister Richel; and likewise by the report of the Elector of Mayence from Vienna, which Förster has communicated in the third volume of Wallenstein's Letters. It is of the 23rd of February, *two days before his death*, and the following passage occurs in it: "Piccolomini, Gallas, and Isolani have orders to deliver up Wallenstein either living *or dead*, and the result is hourly expected." The document containing the *written* order to Gallas for apprehending Wallenstein, "*dead or alive*," was undoubtedly drawn up a considerable time after the deed, and dated back, to give, by this "*sententia post mortem*," to the Italian murderers protection from the revenge of the German party in the army; as immediately on the news of Wallenstein's death a terrible mutiny broke out at Prague. The Germans loudly maintained that Wallenstein was no traitor, but that he had fallen by the intrigues of the Italians. One duel after the other was fought; the German officers challenged the Italians, stabbed them or were stabbed. At last, whole battalions of Germans and Italians fought each other for the quarrel about Wallenstein's guilt or innocence; and order was only restored in the army by means of the most ruthless severity.

It certainly was most perfidious and undignified in the Emperor still to write to Wallenstein confidential letters, after having already issued the mandate which, insidiously driving him from the command, sealed his ruin. Wallenstein, whom the Emperor himself had voluntarily invested with unlimited power, was after all the man who had saved his monarchy for him. "*There is this to be said of the house of Austria, they have no gratitude,*" once wrote (27th of August, 1718) the shrewd Duchess of Orleans, the mother of the regent. "*The history of Austria is the history of ingratitude,*" says Hormayr; and no one ever knew it better, for he was for a quarter of a century director of the archives of Vienna, and was thoroughly aware of all the secret windings of Habsburg policy.

No evidence whatever of the treacherous plans imputed to Wallenstein was found in his papers; but, on the other hand, it is to be borne in mind that Gallas, on the 28th of February, 1634, wrote to the Emperor from Pilsen that Wallenstein *was said* to have burned, on the day before the catastrophe, 600 letters. The Marchese di Grana writes more distinctly from Pilsen (3rd of March, 1634): "The Lady Countess Terzka has in the last upset burned all the papers of her husband; as also others of Wallenstein and Kinsky have been destroyed in the same way." Some officers of the Austrian Etat Major discovered, in 1801, by mere chance, the papers of Wallenstein's field-chancellery in a garret of the town-hall of Budweis in Bohemia; where they had very likely been brought in the year 1634 for the purpose of the trial going on there against Wallenstein's partisans, and had in the course of time been forgotten and stowed away. These Wallensteiniana, published in the *Oestreichische Militairische Zeitschrift*, an Austrian military journal, throw a very doubtful light on the informers and murderers. But even more than this was brought to light. The Prussian Aulic Councillor Förster made the most important discovery of all. The papers and documents found by him, in September, 1828, in the archives of the War Office at Vienna afford the most undeniable evidence of Wallenstein having fallen the victim of Italian-Spanish-Jesuit intrigues, and of the imputations of Maximilian of Bavaria; a victim of ungrateful informers, most of whom the Friedländer had raised from the dust to honour and wealth. These documents were carefully kept secret for 200 years; Captain Aigner, the keeper of those archives, who had long known them, concealed them even from his junior colleagues, so that after his death they were completely forgotten. This very circumstance paved the way for their being discovered by a stranger. The whole state of the question may be summed up in a few words: *there is not one tittle of positive evidence against Wallenstein in all that has been found*, either at Vienna, or in the royal archives of Sweden; or in the papers of Arnim, which are kept at Boitzenburg, the family seat of the Arnims.

The estates of the murdered man were all confiscated. Wallenstein's landed property alone was estimated at 50,000,000 florins. Most of it fell to the Emperor, especially the duchies of Sagan and of Glogau. The former was sold, in 1646, by Ferdinand III.—it is true, for a mere nominal sum—to the Bohemian Prince Lobkowitz, from whose family it passed, in 1785, to the dukes of Biron-Courland. Glogau remained the property of the Emperor until the Silesian wars.

The generals Gallas, Piccolomini, Colloredo, Aldringer, Isolani, Tiefenbach, Morzin; and the imperial councillors Maximilian Trautmannsdorf, Count Henry Schlick, and Marchese Caretto di Grana; as also the three managers of the murder of Wallenstein and his friends, received a rich share of the booty.

Count Matthias Gallas had Wallenstein's lordships of Friedland and Reichenberg in Bohemia, of the value of 300,000 florins, besides Kinsky's house and garden at Prague, and several mines. The family of Gallas became extinct in 1757, and the estates are now in the possession of the Carinthian family Clam-Gallas.

Ottavio Piccolomini, Count of Arragon, next to Gallas the principal mover of Wallenstein's ruin, and the most perfidious of his betrayers, was one of the worst men of a most worthless set; and he had earned an infamous notoriety before. To him the richest prizes were awarded. The Emperor Ferdinand II. gave to this treacherous sneak, who had for his crest a tortoise, with the expressive motto "*Gradatim*," Terzka's lordship of Nachod in Bohemia, an estate of the value of not less than 600,000 florins. In 1654 he was raised by Ferdinand III. to the dignity of a prince of the Empire. Besides this, the crown of Spain restored to him the duchy of Amalfi in Naples, which his ancestors had possessed. Prince Piccolomini, Duke of Amalfi, died in Vienna, in 1656, at the age of fifty-seven, without any direct heir. The family honours passed to his brother Æneas, in whose line they descended. The German branch became extinct in the year 1757; after which the Italian branch of the Piccolominis sold the Bohemian estates. Nachod was, in 1792, acquired by the dukes of Biron-Courland, and from them it passed, in 1843, likewise by purchase, into the family of Schaumburg-Lippe.

Rudolph, Count of Colloredo, received the Friedland lordship of Opotschno in Bohemia. The Colloredos are descended from the Swabian house of the counts of Waldsee. A branch of them settled, in the beginning of the fourteenth century, in Friuli, and there built the castle of Colloredo—*in collo rigido*—on the bleak hill near Udine. They came first to the imperial court under Rodolph II. Opotschno is to this day in the possession of the princely line of the house.

Count John Aldringer received Kinsky's beautiful lordship

of Töplitz, at that time of the value of 195,000 florins. He was a native of Luxemburg; one of those bold upstarts of whom so many rose during the stormy times of the Thirty Years' War. His first start in life was as servant to some gentleman, with whom he went to Paris. Afterwards he was clerk to Colonel Madruzzi in Milan. From thence he entered the service of Cardinal Louis Madruzzi, bishop of Trent, in the same capacity; but, being ousted by some enemies, he left Trent for Innsbruck, with the resolution of taking anything that might happen to turn up. Meeting on the bridge of Innsbruck a soldier who was returning to Italy, he went with him and enlisted. His ready pen and his personal courage soon made him rise from the ranks to be a lieutenant. In 1622 Aldringer was already a colonel; and three years after he received from his patron, the Duke of Friedland, the important and most lucrative post of commissary-general of the army. In 1627 he was made a baron, and in 1632 a count. He became the brother-in-law of Gallas. His ruling passion, however, was avarice rather than ambition. He had contrived so well during the wars to enrich himself by plunder and forced contributions, that at last he had 800,000 crowns lying in the banks of Venice and Genoa. Like all low-minded upstarts, he was mercilessly harsh to those who were under him. He was killed in 1634, before the battle of Nördlingen, at the bridge of Landshut; and it was doubtful whether the ball which struck him was shot by the Swedes or by his own people. His property devolved on the family of the second husband of his sister, Jerome von Clary, whose descendants received, in 1666, the patent as Counts Clary-Aldringer; and, in 1767, the princely coronet. Töplitz is still in the possession of that family. Wallenstein's principal residence, Gitschin, was given to Count Maximilian Trautmannsdorf, in whose family it still is; other rich estates of the duke fell to Count Henry Schlick and to Count Sigismund Dietrichstein.

The murderers of Wallenstein were not less richly rewarded.

Colonel Butler, the principal manager of the tragedy of that night, went to Vienna; where the Emperor received him at the Hofburg, *shook hands with him*, and bestowed a golden chain of honour on him. He was raised to the dignity of a count of the Empire, was made an imperial chamberlain, and received Wallenstein's lordship of Hirschberg, besides several estates of Count Terzka's in Bohemia; not to reckon the very large plunder which he had already appropriated at Eger. Butler died childless, leaving his property to his grandnephew, from whom the present Counts Butler in Bavaria are descended. They sold Hirschberg, which now again belongs to the Wallensteins; and, having intermarried with the now extinct family of the Counts Haynhausen, they style themselves Counts Butler-Haynhausen.

The most successful of the British adversaries of Wallenstein was Walter Leslie, who held at the time of the catastrophe the rank of major only. Butler sent him, on the very night of the murder, with a written report to Gallas, who, in his turn, despatched him to Vienna. Thus Leslie was the first to bring the Emperor the news of the bloody deed; at which Ferdinand, as is well known, shed tears, just as at the death of Gustavus Adolphus, and ordered 3,000 masses to be said for the soul of his murdered general. Leslie was raised to the dignity of count of the Empire, and made an imperial chamberlain, captain of the imperial body-guard of halberdiers, and chief of a regiment. Besides this, he received the Friedland town of Neustadt on the Mettau, in Bohemia, of the value of 200,000 florins. He married the daughter of Prince Maximilian Dietrichstein, and thereby became brother-in-law to the celebrated Montecuculi. In 1650 he was appointed field-marshal-general, and received the government of Croatia, the richest one in the whole monarchy. In 1655 he was sworn a member of the privy council, and in 1665 he received the highest distinction of the Empire, the order of the Golden Fleece. He afterwards kept one of the most splendid houses in Vienna, was sent on an embassy to Constantinople, and died in 1672. The house of the Counts Leslie became extinct in 1802, when most of its estates devolved on the Princes Dietrichstein.

The third of the conspirators, Colonel Gordon, received

Wallenstein's lordship of Smidar—which now belongs to the Colloredos—besides some estates of Kinsky's in Bohemia. Captain Devereux, who had pierced Wallenstein's breast with a halberd, received a golden chain of honour, and likewise several confiscated estates in Bohemia. Major Geraldino was made a count. Butler, whilst still at Eger, had caused from the plunder 500 rix-dollars to be paid to each of the twelve soldiers who had struck the great blow with Devereux, and to all the other soldiers two ducats each.

On the other hand, all the partisans of Wallenstein were outlawed. Twenty-four colonels and captains—most of them Bohemians and Germans, like Mohrwald, Uhlefeld, Wildberger, and Hammerle—died by the hand of the hangman at Pilsen. General Hans Ulric Schafgotsch, of Kynast in Silesia, was beheaded at Ratisbon on the 23rd of July, 1635. To his last moment he protested his innocence; the torture forced from him some vague, unconnected statements; but it is expressly stated in the report to the Emperor that nothing had been extorted from him concerning the main point of the treasonable plot, and what pertained thereunto. His children were given to the Jesuits at Olmütz, to be brought up as Papists. The Emperor restored to them the confiscated estates of their father, with the exception of one lordship, Trachenberg, with which the faithful services of General Melchior, Count of Hatzfeld, were rewarded.

The widow of Wallenstein received the news of her husband's death at Prugg on the Leitha, in Lower Austria. "The lady," says Khevenhüller, "knew no end to her grief, and only begged for the body of her husband." The Bohemian lordship of Neuschloss was allowed her for her residence and jointure. Wallenstein left an only daughter, Maria Elizabeth. She married Count Rudolph Kaunitz, an ancestor of the celebrated Prince and Arch-chancellor Kaunitz. The only remainder of the colossal property of Wallenstein, which his heiress had for her dowry, consisted in the two lordships of Neuschloss and Lippa, which continued in the possession of the Kaunitz family until lately, when that house became extinct.

In his last will Wallenstein appointed his cousin, the imperial master of the horse, Count Maximilian of Waldstein, to succeed him in the entailed property. The descendants of that nobleman have still (1852) a lawsuit pending since 1841 for decision by the supreme tribunal at Prague, concerning the restoration of the entailed property withheld from them. Count Christian Waldstein-Wartenberg is the plaintiff in the cause. The principal evidence in favour of Wallenstein's heirs is a passage in the charter given by Ferdinand II., dated Vienna, 11th of May, 1627, in conferring on their ancestor the duchy of Friedland: "That in case some one or other of the Duke of Friedland's successors should be convicted of the crime of lese-majesty, he or they should not, as otherwise would be directed by law, be punished with confiscation of the duchy of Friedland or other estates, but should suffer capital punishment, and the duchy and the estates devolve on the next succeeding duke or prince of Friedland."

The death of Wallenstein was, under the circumstances, a most fortunate event for the house of Austria. Yet the year 1634 was marked by two other equally lucky occurrences—the taking of the important town of Ratisbon on the 26th of July, and the great victory gained by the imperial army on the 27th of August, near Nördlingen in Swabia. It was won by the King of Hungary, afterwards the Emperor Ferdinand III.—at that time in his twenty-seventh year—and by Lieutenant-general Gallas, over the Swedish Fieldmarshal Horn and Duke Bernard of Weimar. Horn's plan had been to wait for reinforcements under the Rhinegrave; but the reckless ardour of Duke Bernard carried him away. The King of Hungary, on the other hand, had been joined by the Cardinal Infant of Spain, Ferdinand, a brother of Philip IV., with 10,000 men of the old excellent Spanish infantry which the cardinal brought up from Milan. Thus the imperialists were 35,000 men strong, the Swedes only 23,000, among them 6,000 Würtemberg peasants gathered in a hurry. The object of the battle had been to save Würtemberg, and that duchy was lost with the battle. The feelings with which this event was looked upon by the Protestant princes may be gathered from a letter of the clever Electress of Saxony, a Brandenburg princess, to her by no means clever husband, John George I., when the Duchess-Dowager of Würtemberg *had applied to her for alms.* The letter is dated from Dresden, the 22nd of September, 1634. "It is," she writes, "a most melancholy and pitiful thing that it should have come to pass that the high potentates and princes of the Empire with their infant children are obliged to beg alms from their trusty friends. The Lord have mercy on us, but the Emperor has much to answer for before God, *and I do not believe that the Almighty can receive him into favour again; he has worked too much evil in his life.*"

One of the consequences of the victory of Nördlingen was that the Elector of Saxony concluded with the Emperor the peace of Prague in 1635, in which John George, for the cession of the Lusatias, gave up the cause of the Protestants, and allied himself with the Emperor against the Swedes. Puffendorf states that Hoë von Hoënegg, the electoral court chaplain, had been accused of having taken 10,000 crowns for inducing his master to sign that peace. Brandenburg and the other Protestant princes of Northern Germany, and in particular the Saxon dukes of the Ernestine line, and even Duke George of Lüneburg, joined in it; Hesse-Cassel, Würtemberg, and Baden-Durlach, on the other hand, remained true to Sweden. Hesse-Cassel succeeded in keeping out the imperialist army, by which Würtemberg and Baden, as also Alsace and the Palatinate, were occupied.

10.—*Duke Bernard of Weimar.*

The third act of the tragedy of the Thirty Years' War now began. In 1635 France declared war against Austria, and engaged as commander-in-chief the former generalissimo of the League of Heilbronn, Duke Bernard of Weimar, the great pupil of the King of Sweden.

Duke Bernard was the youngest of eleven sons whom the pious Princess Dorothy Maria of Köthen had, in as many successive years, borne to her husband Duke John of Weimar.

The father died in 1605, when Bernard was scarcely a year old, and the mother undertook the education of the infant prince. Frederic Hortleder, the author of the large work on the Smalcalde war, became his instructor in history. The prince went to the university of Jena; but before he had completed his eighteenth year he went to draw his sword for the cause of the Protestants. He at first served under his elder brother William, in South Germany, where he was present at the battle of Wimpfen; then under the Prince of Orange, in the Netherlands; then, from 1625 to 1628, as colonel under the King of Denmark, in Lower Saxony. Disgusted with the inglorious war under the Danish standard, he returned to the hereditary country of his family. But in 1631 he was one of the first German princes who joined Gustavus Adolphus, with whom he first met in his camp at Werben on the Elbe. The King appointed him colonel of his mounted regiment of guards. During the campaign, which resulted in the battle of Breitenfeld, he was charged with the protection of Hesse. He afterwards marched with the King to the Maine and the Rhine, to Swabia and Bavaria, commanding the vanguard of the Swedish army; his advance being only checked by the strongly fortified Ehrenberger Clause, the key of the Tyrol. He was present at the attack of the Alte Veste near Nüremberg; then went with the King to Saxony; and at Lützen decided the battle after Gustavus had fallen. The death of the King giving full scope to his ambition, he exerted himself to his utmost to get the lead in the affairs of Germany, causing thereby many a sleepless night to Oxenstierna. Having got Oxenstierna to give him the duchy of Franconia, he set out for the Bavarian campaign; conquered, in 1633, the free imperial town of Ratisbon; and was just negotiating with Wallenstein concerning a junction between them, when the latter was murdered at Eger in 1634. But in the same year Ratisbon was lost again, and Bernard with Horn was defeated at Nördlingen; the first and last time in his warlike career that he was beaten in a pitched battle. South-western Germany thus being lost to him, Bernard took up a position on the Middle Rhine near Frankfort and Mayence, whilst the

Swedish field-marshal Baner, who during the battle of Nördlingen had been stationed in Bohemia, covered North-western Germany. But in 1635 Duke Bernard was obliged to cross the Rhine, and to retire to the Meuse and the Moselle. On the 7th of December, 1635, Mayence, the last stronghold on the Rhine, capitulated. In the beginning of March, 1636, Duke Bernard made his appearance in Paris, and had, on the 10th of that month, an interview with Louis XIII. at St. Germain; and on the same day with Cardinal Richelieu at Rueil. After having stayed with the French for two months and a half, he returned to the headquarters of his troops at Vezelize in Lorraine. He now called himself "Generalissimo of the Crowns of Sweden and France, and of the Evangelical League." His first visit to Paris, in the spring of 1636, was followed by another in the beginning of 1637, when he stayed from the beginning of January to the end of May.

In the treaty concluded by Richelieu at St. Germain with Bernard's very clever agent at the French court, Tobias von Ponikow, as far back as on the 27th of October, 1635, 4,000,000 livres as long as the war lasted for the maintenance of 12,000 infantry, 6,000 cavalry, and an artillery, with 600 horse, and besides, by a subsequent order of the King of the 6th of November, the revenue of the landgraviate of Alsace had been promised to the duke. Alsace having already been partly wrested from the house of Habsburg, it was Richelieu's plan from thence to overrun the duchy of Lorraine; and, moreover, to conquer the Upper Burgundian provinces from the Spanish crown. These countries being once acquired, France would have had her ascendency secured over Germany, as they formed an uninterrupted chain from the Netherlands along the north-eastern frontier of France as far as Italy. Yet this plan of Richelieu's was wholly at variance with the views of Duke Bernard; whose aim, on the contrary, it was to establish Alsace as a principality for himself under the sovereignty of the German Empire, thus forming for the latter a bulwark on the Upper Rhine against France. This object he very nearly attained by his victory near Rheinfelden, on the 21st of February, 1638, where a great part of the imperial generals were made prisoners. He was brought even nearer the accomplishment of his purpose by the taking of the important fortress of Breisach (Brisac), which capitulated on the 7th of December, 1638, after Bernard had repulsed three attempts for its relief. Breisach being the key of the Upper Rhine, Bernard intended to make it the centre of his dominion. He hoped that, in league with England and the German Protestants, especially with Hesse-Cassel, he should be able to counteract the obnoxious tendencies of Richelieu's encroaching policy, and also to keep the Swedes in check. Austria lost with Breisach its advanced western provinces. The princes of Würtemberg and Baden-Durlach were enabled to return from their exile at Strassburg to their own countries. On the one hand, Breisach menaced the Spaniards in their Burgundian provinces, the Papist Duke of Lorraine in his own country, and the Catholic Swiss cantons; on the other, Duke Maximilian of Bavaria; and, moreover, it afforded a secure base for military operations to be carried on in Swabia, Franconia, and Bavaria.

Immediately after the taking of Breisach, still in December, 1638, Duke Bernard set out for a winter campaign to conquer the South Burgundian provinces. These he intended to cede to France, with the exception of the most important fortified places; all of which, like Alsace, he claimed for himself. By the middle of February, 1639, the best part of the country was in his power. About this time Duke Bernard conceived the plan of removing his headquarters from Pontarlier to the pleasant town of Joux. Previous to his departure a colonel gave in his honour a banquet. The duke went thither in perfect health, and was brought home ill. He was immediately taken to Joux, where he recovered in a few weeks. About the end of March, just as he was starting from Pontarlier to Alsace, a French envoy, De Lisle, came to him with despatches from Richelieu, whose paramount care was that Bernard should give up Breisach to the French. Bernard, however, gave a positive refusal, and the cardinal had to content himself with the duke's written promise that he would guard Breisach, as well as all the other conquered places, under the sovereignty of the King of France. After this compromise was concluded, Bernard, with the princes of Würtemberg and Baden-Durlach, and the Hessian and Palatine envoys, went to Alsace, where he kept his Easter at Breisach. He there behaved completely as the master of the country, issuing orders like a sovereign, as is proved by the still-existing documents.

The distressed courts of Vienna and Madrid, foreseeing the danger which threatened them from Bernard, immediately began to negotiate with him. As the price of reconciliation, they held out to him the promise of the hand of the daughter of Archduke Leopold of Tyrol; besides which, a German country was to be settled on him. But Duke Bernard did not enter upon it, nor would he agree to a plan which the celebrated Landgravine-regent Amelia of Hesse-Cassel proposed to him in the beginning of 1639, through the Netherlander Wicquefort, their joint agent at Amsterdam—to form with her the often mooted but never realised " third German party." Bernard wrote on this subject from Rheinfelden to Wicquefort (6th of June, 1639), "That the project was hatched by the Papists themselves, and was saddled with something even worse; for the foreign powers France and Sweden would be driven to desperate measures, and be forced to conclude a peace on their own account, *and divide Germany between friend and foe.* The experience of all treaties since the peace of Passau had shown that *no peace could be expected from Austria until one had forced it from her.*"

In the beginning of June Bernard had returned from Alsace to Upper Burgundy. At Pontarlier he was met by another French envoy, the Comte de Guébriant, whose mission again concerned the surrender of Breisach. Bernard repeated his former refusal, but remarked that he would never separate himself from France; and, though they might drive him out by one door, he would return by the other. Guébriant made two more attempts to induce the duke to give a more favourable answer. As he earnestly warned the duke of the possible consequences of his refusal, Bernard replied,

"Never fear, M. le Comte, I know the court. It is not the first time that unfair proposals have been made to me. Whenever I refused them the ministers complimented me, and excused themselves on the plea of duty; the cardinal himself once told me that this was the French fashion." Thus persisting in his first resolution, he handed, on the 23rd of June, to the count a written declaration, to be expedited to the French court.

This declaration caused the greatest sensation at St. Germain, and, as Richelieu saw through Bernard's plan of making himself independent, and forming a German border-country against France, the French cabinet determined by every means to oust Bernard from his conquests.

On the very same day that Bernard had delivered his written answer for the French court, he set out from Pontarlier to cross the Rhine for a new campaign. On the 3rd of July he arrived at the fortified town of Hüningen, where, on the 4th, he was suddenly seized with indisposition. He therefore went in a boat with the Swedish resident Mockel to Neuenburg, where his troops were just about to cross the Rhine. The illness daily increased. The doctors treated him for colic, whereas his disease was a malignant raging fever; and thus, on the 18th of July, 1639, at seven in the morning, this hero in the prime of his life breathed his last. "It was the most unfortunate day," says Hugo Grotius; "Germany lost her finest ornament and her last hope, almost her only prince who was worthy of the name." Bernard died in the thirty-fifth year of his age, unmarried. The King of Sweden had intended to give him his niece. His only love seems to have been the Princess of Rohan, the daughter of the Protestant Henry of Rohan, whose acquaintance he had made during his stay in Paris in 1636, and who was of such extraordinary beauty that Bernard is said to have trembled on first seeing her. The King of France, however, opposed such an alliance, for fear the Huguenots might thereby acquire too powerful a support. Another plan, mentioned by Baner, of a union with the Landgravine Amelia of Hesse, was meant —as Rommel very correctly observes—" for neither more nor less than a military alliance, in which Amelia, the mother of fourteen children, and the senior of Bernard by two years, would have brought him as dowry 20,000 men."

France, as well as Spain, was accused of having given poison to Bernard of Weimar in a plate of fish. Certain it is that letters from Switzerland, from Venice, and also from Milan warned the duke to beware of Spanish poison. On the other hand, the Swedish councillor, Müller of Hamburg, wrote, as far back as February, 1639, that the "duke's life was in great danger from the envy of the great French lords." Bernard's physician, Blandini, a Genevese, states, in his report of the opening of the body, that he had died of a malignant fever, whereas he was known to have treated the duke for colic. And this physician is said actually to have absconded some days after Bernard's death. The whole body of the duke was covered with blotches; also he himself on his sick bed gave it as his opinion that he was poisoned. Puffendorf says without disguise, "Because he could not be induced to dance to the tune of the French, they at last administered to him some of their little messes, upon which he died."

The duke was buried at Breisach, and it was only in 1655, seven years after the peace, that his body was removed to the town-church of Weimar. Bernard was a great man, on whom much rested, without however coming up to the standard of a first-rate statesman and general. Goethe, who had been commissioned to write a biography of the hero, very wisely got out of it, as he found a great many hitches in the way. Feuquières very likely had given a very correct opinion of the duke when he wrote, "*C'est un Prince d'un grand cœur et d'un esprit médiocre, fort vaillant, et d'une ambition sans bornes.*"

After the death of the duke, the French at once took his troops into their pay, and now occupied Breisach on the 19th of October, 1639. Bernard in his last will, which, one hour before his death, he dictated to his chancellor Rehlinger (of an Augsburg patrician family), had expressed a wish that "one of his brothers would take the conquered countries"; remarking at the same time, "The same can and should as much as possible insinuate himself with his Imperial Majesty and the crown of Sweden, in order that he may be so much the rather maintained in these countries. But if none of the princes, our brothers, should feel inclined to accept the countries, we consider it but fair that his Majesty of France should by all means have the next claim; so, however, that both his Majesty's garrisons and ours shall be kept in them, and whenever a general peace be concluded, *the countries shall be restored to the Empire.*" In the introduction already he had laid it down most distinctly, " We wish the countries to be maintained for the empire of the German nation."

11.—*Death of Ferdinand II.*—*His family.*

Two years before the death of Duke Bernard of Weimar, the Emperor Ferdinand II. had been gathered to his fathers. He died as he had lived, a devoted son of his Church, holding in his hand a consecrated burning taper which his confessor had offered to him. His death took place on the 15th of February, 1637, in the fifty-ninth year of his age.

Ferdinand II. had been married twice. The first time, he was wedded in 1600 at Grätz, when still an archduke, to Maria Anna, the sister of his friend Maximilian of Bavaria. She died in 1616. His second marriage, to Eleonora Gonzaga of Mantua, took place at Innsbruck in 1622, after his accession.

By his first wife he left two sons and two daughters. The sons were Ferdinand III., who succeeded him, and Leopold William. The latter, born in 1614, has become notorious as one of the richest ecclesiastical pluralists (having as a boy of fifteen accumulated no fewer than nine spiritual dignities, among which was that of grand master of the Teutonic order), and as the successor of Gallas, and most consistent loser of all the battles he fought. The tenth dignity with which he was invested was a secular one: he was for ten years, from 1646 to 1656, governor of the Spanish Netherlands, with residence at Brussels. The eleventh dignity which fell to him was that of guardian of his young nephew, the Emperor Leopold; in which capacity he greatly contributed to the rise of the house of Schwarzenberg.

Leopold William was a gay, easy-tempered prince, and a great patron of the fine arts; he collected in the Netherlands the nucleus of pictures which, combined with the gallery of Rodolph II., form the stock from which the present Imperial Gallery of Vienna has grown. He had for his court painter the celebrated Teniers, who purchased for his master many of the pictures from the gallery of Charles I. of England.

On account of the enfeebled state of his naturally delicate constitution, he retired, in 1656, from Brussels to Vienna, where, after the death of his brother Ferdinand III., he undertook the guardianship of the young Emperor Leopold I. Yet, notwithstanding his drinking asses' milk, and even bathing in it, he never recovered. He died 20th of November, 1662, of the gravel.

Of the two daughters of the Emperor Ferdinand II., the eldest, Maria Anna, born in 1610, was at first intended either to marry the great Prince of Transylvania, Bethlen Gabor, or the Prince of Wales; at last, instead of these two Protestants, she married the very Catholic Elector of Bavaria.

Bethlen Gabor married in 1626 the sister of the great Elector of Brandenburg, and died three years after. Suffering from dropsy, he put himself under the treatment of a physician who had been especially recommended to him from the court of Vienna. Six weeks after this great man, being not more than forty-eight years of age, was in his coffin, after having escaped unscathed from forty-two battles. The imperial camarilla removed that dangerous neighbour of the Habsburg dominions by one of those Spanish-Jesuit expedients, poison and the dagger, which, down to the assassination of the French ambassadors at the Congress of Rastadt, have so often been resorted to by Austrian policy.

Concerning the matrimonial project with the Prince of Wales, afterwards Charles I. of England, the reverend fathers of the Society of Jesus gave a very remarkable opinion, which is recorded in Khevenhüller. It is said in it: "*Connubium Esther cum Ahasvero pro recreando populo Christi qui tot annis in*

Anglia sub jugo servitutis Calvinisticæ gemuit, non solum judico licere, sed summe expedire." Also Prince Eggenberg, the premier of Ferdinand II., was favourable to the match, and wrote, in giving his opinion about it: " It is to be hoped that England would now rather be converted by Germany than by Spain; since, in times of yore, the greater part of Germany was brought to the Christian faith by missionaries from England."

These Austrian plans for converting England in the seventeenth century may be of particular interest now, inasmuch as *his Eminence Cardinal Wiseman, as has recently transpired, is on the most intimate terms with the cabinet of Vienna.*[1]

Maximilian of Bavaria, when he married Maria Anna, was already sixty-two years old, while she had but completed her twenty-fifth year. He had just lost his first wife, a princess of Lorraine, by whom he had no children. Maria Anna, who was his own niece, bore him Ferdinand Maria, the father of that Maximilian Emanuel who, in the war of the Spanish succession, was outlawed by Austria.

Cecilia, the younger daughter of Ferdinand II., was, after having attained her twenty-sixth year in 1637, married to King Vladislaus IV. of Poland, who was her senior by sixteen years. She died, without having borne him any children, in 1644.

[1] The reader is reminded that this part of the German original (vol. iv., p. 74) was printed as far back as 1852.

CHAPTER VIII

FERDINAND III.—(1637-1657).

1.—Personal notices of the Emperor—The premier Maximilian von Trautmannsdorf.

FERDINAND II. was succeeded by his son, Ferdinand III., born in 1608, at Grätz; crowned as King of Hungary in 1625; married, in 1631, to the Spanish Infanta Maria Anna, his senior by seventeen years; and, since 1636, Roman King-elect.

Ferdinand III. was of very delicate constitution. In the latter days of his life, which was cut short at the early age of forty-nine, he was so enfeebled by the gout that he could only be moved in a chair, and he died from fright at a fire which had broken out in the Hofburg of Vienna. As long as he was able, he now and then followed the chase. Although the miraculous luck of the house of Habsburg made him gain the victory of Nördlingen, yet he was even less warlike than his father. It was his most cherished wish to see the war brought to an end. He was endowed with many of those negative virtues which originate in the absence of strong passions and desires, and which are sometimes very respectable in a private man; but on the whole he was a monkish ruler, exactly as his father had been before him, and just as intolerant in what he allowed to be done by others in his name as Ferdinand II. had shown himself in his own acts. He was in particular one of the most zealous champions of the doctrine of the *Immaculata Conceptio Beatæ Mariæ Virginis*. He issued an order that no one should be made a doctor without taking the oath on the Immaculate Conception. When Torstensohn, in 1645, stood with his army before Vienna, the

Emperor made a vow to erect in the square, called "the Hof" (Yard), a monument in honour of that dogma. This monument, executed by him in marble, was replaced by his son Leopold, in 1667, by the one in marble and bronze, which has survived to this day.

The reign of Ferdinand III. fell in the most distressful time of the Thirty Years' War, the never-ending expenses of which compelled him to pledge the crown jewels, and to mortgage and sell one demesne after the other to his nobles, who by this means became wealthy and powerful.

Ferdinand possessed an honest minister in Count Maximilian Trautmannsdorf, who in his younger days had attended him at the victorious battle of Nördlingen, and afterwards concluded for Austria the peace of Prague. Trautmannsdorf had been well rewarded for his services. He had from the Wallenstein plunder received that fairy-like residence, Gitschin, and from the conquest in Würtemberg, Weinsberg and Neustadt on the Kocher. Gitschin, with fourteen other estates in Bohemia, is still in possession of the family; of Weinsberg and Neustadt they have retained the titles. On the accession of Ferdinand III. Trautmannsdorf remained lord steward, and in 1639 he became, besides, director of the privy council. Thus he was at the same time the first person in the court and in the council of the Emperor. Ferdinand II. had honoured him like a friend; Ferdinand III. honoured him like a father.

It was Trautmannsdorf who at last procured for his master the peace so long and so ardently wished for. He was the principal imperial commissioner at the conclusion of the peace of Westphalia. Trautmannsdorf was not only an honest, but also a very gentle and modest man. Early travels and repeated missions to different courts had given him knowledge of men and business experience; his tried integrity acquired for him the confidence and respect of friend and foe. As long as he lived, Ferdinand III. was well advised, and the government was carried on in a tolerant spirit. Trautmannsdorf was hated by the Jesuits, yet, in the teeth of their venomous antagonism, he over and over again carried the cause of rational toleration. In former days he had just as earnestly advised against Wallenstein's first dismissal as afterwards against his reappointment. His suggestions not being listened to, he had repeatedly left the court; but whenever he was called upon, he always returned to the service, undertaking with the same alacrity the most trifling as well as the most important commissions.

Trautmannsdorf died in 1650, two years after the conclusion of the peace of Westphalia. His wife, of the Palffy family, was the mother of fifteen children. He was succeeded in his office as lord steward by Prince Maximilian Dietrichstein, and as minister by the apostate Lutheran John Weichard von Auersperg, who, in 1653, was made a prince, and who, after Dietrichstein's resignation, became lord steward. The office of lord chamberlain at the Court of Ferdinand III. was held by Count Maximilian Wallenstein, a cousin of the Friedländer.

2.—*The last period of the Thirty Years' War, and the last Papist generals of the Emperor, Gallas and Piccolomini—The last Protestant generals of the Emperor, Holk, Götz, and Melander— Holzapfel—Austrian plans for seducing the Hessian and Bavarian armies—Baner's and Torstensohn's campaigns.*

The latter times of the Thirty Years' War were doomed to be its most terrible ones. The fury of the contest did not spend itself, until the general exhaustion separated the angry combatants. Awful as the rage had been with which the two German parties assailed each other in combat for life and death from the very beginning, the punishment now was just as awful which Germany had to submit to from the strangers who had so made the war their own that the Emperor had to wait for their pleasure to conclude peace. Sweden was not in a hurry, and still less was France.

Armies composed of nearly all the civilised and savage peoples of Europe were disporting themselves on German soil. On the side of the Protestants, there were first Hungarians, English, and Scotch; afterwards Swedes and Finlanders; and at last French. On the side of the Papists, Spaniards and Italians, Walloons, Irish, and likewise some English and Scotch; besides whole hosts of Croats, Poles, and Cossacks, who fought with Germans against Germans on German ground. Nearly every trace of the spirit of German nationality seemed to be extinguished by the religious quarrel, fanned in the first instance by the dogmatical fury of the theologians, and kept alive by the political lust of gain of the princes. The good-natured German people, quietly submitting to be kept in leading-strings by its spiritual and secular rulers, patiently allowed itself for years to be abused in fighting side by side with the most savage hordes of Europe, to drain the life-blood of its German brethren.

The manner in which Mansfeld, the Protestant partisan, carried on the war, has been described before. The Hungarians, who served as auxiliaries of the Bohemians, committed the most atrocious cruelties from the very beginning of the war. In the diary of Prince Anhalt, of the 3rd of September, 1620, when the Protestant army lay near Egenburg, it is said of them : "*Il y avoit un chastau auprès Fürnthal, que prirent les Hongrois (avec quelque peu de nos Mousquetaires) par feu, et puis sortis encore que les dits Mousq. leur vouloyent donner quartier si est ce, que les Hongrois ne voulurent pas et tuerent 60 personnes n'espargnans nul sexe, mesmes ils tuoyent de nos soldats qui avoyent du butin. C'est une nation très barbare.*" Nor was the Swedish army any longer composed of those pious men whom Gustavus Adolphus had brought with him across the Baltic, who had prayers twice a day, and who kept strict discipline. The fury of war had changed this godly and decorous host into a ferocious band, which carried on the soldier's trade with all the horrors and atrocities of exaction and cruelty. The "Swedish draught"[1] became at that time proverbial in Germany. Of Torstensohn alone it is recorded that he carried on the war in the most chivalrous manner, not only treating the imperial generals

---

[1] The victim of this cruelty was laid on the ground, and water poured down his throat, causing the most dreadful distension of the stomach, until the persons thus tortured consented to reveal the hiding-place of their property and treasure.—*Translator.*

and officers, his prisoners, with the greatest consideration, but also keeping such good discipline as in 1645, when his army stood before Vienna, to cause soldiers who had committed plunder and violence to run the gauntlet. In return for the considerate conduct of the general, one of his valets was allowed, with an imperial passport, to come from the Swedish headquarters to Vienna to make purchases there for his master.

The imperial soldiery, however, raged much worse in their own country than even the Swedes did. On the imperial side also the auxiliaries particularly distinguished themselves by their atrocities. The most dreadful scourges were, besides the Poles, the ferocious Walloons, and the still more ferocious Croats, who since the days of Tilly and Wallenstein became the terror of Germany. To them rapine and cruelty against the defenceless citizen—friend or foe, it mattered not—was a thing quite in the regular course of the profession of arms.

A real plague arose in the Cossacks, who at that period were for the first time called into the heart of Germany by a German Emperor. This savage nation, then under the sovereignty of Poland, made its first appearance in 1620 before Vienna, just at the time when the Estates of Austria refused to swear the oath of allegiance to the Emperor Ferdinand II. He brought his recalcitrant subjects to submission by taking at first 4,000 and then 2,000 more Cossacks into his pay. The first batch of these barbarians advanced in the middle of winter (January, 1620) as far as Moravia, where they laid hands on everything that came in their way. Among other atrocities, they once pounced upon a noble wedding-party at Meseritz, completely stripped naked all the gentlemen and ladies present at it, and afterwards publicly sold the plunder, both dresses and jewels, at Vienna. The Moravians went in pursuit and cut down about five hundred of them on the 10th of February, and drove them across the Danube into the neighbourhood of Vienna. Here the Emperor took them in his pay, *and formally let them loose against the Protestants.* Whoever could not repeat the "Ave Maria" was treated in the most outrageous way. Five hundred villages were then ransacked, the women and children making their escape to the islets in the Danube, where they perished miserably of hunger and distress. Neither friend nor foe was spared. A Baron von Grässwein, a Bohemian who had done good service to the house of Austria, and who showed an imperial safeguard for his protection, was murdered at his own castle merely because he was a Protestant. In July another horde of two thousand Cossacks arrived; at a later period, they offered themselves to the Emperor even in greater numbers than were wanted, and it was really difficult to keep them off. All these savage auxiliaries were procured in Poland by the agency of the Radziwill family, on which the Emperor Maximilian I., as far back as 1518, had bestowed the princely dignity of the Empire.

Wallenstein's murder—much as the Emperor gained by it, especially in estates and money for the continuation of the war—had, after all, been a desperate measure, suggested only by the pressure of the moment. Such a general as Wallenstein was not to be found again. Not one of his successors was at all to be compared to the man who had so well known how to fetter the goddess of fortune to his triumphal chariot. The imperial court was with difficulty able to keep its own against the united powers of the Swedes and French; especially as the former had the particular good fortune of having retained in Baner, Torstensohn, and Wrangel generals who were quite equal to Gustavus Adolphus and Bernard of Weimar; and at last the French also had Turenne.

Wallenstein was succeeded as generalissimo of the imperial troops by Count Matthias Gallas. This officer, a native of Trent, had served under Tilly in the Bavarian army, where he rose to the rank of colonel; but, having in 1629 passed into the Emperor's service, he went through the war of the Mantuan succession under Collalto; after whose death he held the chief command *ad interim*. Gallas had greatly enriched himself by the Mantuan booty. After having, on the 29th of June, 1631, concluded the peace of Chierasco, he was recalled. He next served under Wallenstein, but was not able to maintain Silesia, where he commanded. When Wallenstein's catastrophe was in preparation, it was to Gallas the Emperor referred the commanders of the regiments, who, as principal manager of the measures against the dictator, brought the affair to such a lucky issue. Yet, successful as he was as a diplomatist, he never, except at Nördlingen in 1635, was victorious in the field; besides which, like Piccolomini, he was a thorough profligate. His ill-luck in war was proverbial, and earned for him the nickname of "army spoiler." The Emperor, indeed, was at last obliged to transfer the chief command to Piccolomini. Gallas then retired to his estates near Trent; from whence he returned to Vienna, where, in 1647, he died at the age of fifty-nine.

Ferdinand II., the most religious Emperor of the house of Habsburg, had already in his time felt no scruple in raising to the highest commands of his army not only greedy converts, but also people who ever showed themselves obdurate heretics. Of the three bold upstarts who commanded his army, one only, John Aldringer, was a born Papist. The other two, Henry Holk and John Götz, were, the former a Lutheran, and the latter a convert to Popery.

Holk commanded the famous and much-dreaded mounted chasseurs, who were called after him. He was a native of Denmark, where counts of that name still flourish. He had lost one eye, and was, like Wallenstein, completely free from religious prejudices; and like him also he had the goddess of fortune embroidered on his standards. Having at first served his own King against the Emperor, and proved himself before Stralsund dangerous as an enemy, he passed, after the peace of Lübeck in 1629, into the service of Ferdinand; who received him with open arms and made him a count. Holk died in 1633, on his expedition to Saxony, at Adorf in the Vogtland, having caught the plague from his mistress, whom he visited at Zwickau. It had happened a short time before that the people of Zwickau, after having paid him a heavy sum of money, besought him that the soldiers of Wallenstein, who came after him, might not be billeted on them. Holk answered, "My good people, when the Lord comes, the apostles must hold their tongues." The corpse of this wild apostle of war was conveyed to Copenhagen.

John Götz was an upstart from Lüneburg. He commanded a regiment of mounted arquebusiers, who were not less dreaded than Holk's chasseurs. In the island of Rügen, Götz once with his Croats broke into a nunnery of noble ladies, where he made his men commit the most atrocious outrages before his eyes. He was such an abandoned drunkard that very often he was not even able to give out the parole. He survived Holk and Aldringer, turned Papist, and was made a count by Ferdinand II. in 1634, after the battle of Nördlingen. He was killed eleven years later in the battle of Jankau, in 1645, and buried at Prague.

The chief command, under Ferdinand III., during the latter years of the Long War, was held by a Calvinist, Peter Holzapfel, whose name was first changed into Melander, until, by the grace of the Emperor, he was created count of the Empire as Von Holzapfel. Melander, the son of a peasant in Hesse, a sandy-haired and very zealous Calvinist, had served his military apprenticeship under the Swiss and Venetians, from which he came forth a very able captain in war. Since 1632 he had commanded the brave Hessian army; but a box on the ear which he received from the Landgravine Amelia drove him into the service of the house of Habsburg. Having turned Papist, he first undertook, in 1645, a command in the service of the Elector of Cologne, then the command-in-chief of the imperial troops, and Ferdinand III. made him a field-marshal and a count of the Empire. It was certainly a thorn in the side of the lords of the old nobility to serve under such an upstart, against whose power they kicked not a little ; but he had sense and energy enough to keep his own. Count Holzapfel was killed in the last engagement of the Thirty Years' War, at Zusmershausen, near Augsburg, in 1648. His daughter and heiress married, in 1653, Prince Adolphus of Nassau-Dillenburg, and brought the county of Holzapfel-on-the-Lahn, and likewise the castle of Schaumburg, to the house of Nassau. From Nassau the possessions passed to the house of Anhalt-

Bernburg, and from the latter, by the *Felix Austria nube*, to Austria. Archduke Stephen is the present holder of them.

As early as 1637 Count Schlick, president of the Aulic Council of War, and the Elector of Cologne had tried to persuade Melander, by the promise of a yearly pension of 10,000 crowns and promotion to the dignity of count, to enter the Emperor's service, *bringing over with him the whole of the Hessian army*. The "Catholic policy" of the house of Habsburg-Austria did not shrink even from such expedients. But Melander was not able to carry out the scheme, as he was not sure of his officers and soldiers, and besides, he well knew the court of Vienna, where there was but rarely any money for the new counts, especially for those who were not either Austrians or Italians. He thus expressed himself about that time: "The court of Vienna has since the last ten years created six-and-twenty of its upstart counts of the Empire; yet these are mere empty titles, sullied with the blood of robbed populations, and yielding all of them together not more than 26,000 crowns. *Twenty-eight generals are still waiting for the dotations promised them by the Emperor;* they being once satisfied, nothing will remain for me."

The Swedes were, during the latter years of the war, much more fortunate in their generals than the Emperor. They still had three great captains from the school of their great King—John Baner, Leonard Torstensohn, and Gustavus Wrangel.

Baner was one of the greatest heroes of the Thirty Years' War. It was said in his praise that he had destroyed more than 80,000 enemies, had conquered more than 800 stand of colours, and had not once lost an action. To the imperial court he became a most formidable foe—so formidable that at last attempts were made to bribe him, even so far as to offer him the princely dignity in the Empire. But Baner refused every offer, and there was a report that he had at last been poisoned, like Bethlen Gabor. The poison was said to have been administered at the great convention at Hildesheim.

Baner opened his great career of victory at Wittstock in Brandenburg, on the 24th of September, 1636, where he routed the Saxons, at that time the allies of the Emperor. After this victory the north of Germany breathed freely again. Baner from thence advanced as far as Erfurt; then, turning back again, he entered the camp on the Elbe near Torgau. There he remained stationary for four months. At last he was obliged by want, just as his King had once been near Nuremberg, to retire before the imperial Field-marshal Count Hatzfeld to Stettin, where he arrived on the 19th of June, 1637. Having at Stettin been joined by reinforcements from Sweden, he opened the campaign of 1638, driving Gallas before him as far as Bohemia. In the campaign of 1639 he was obliged to retire before the superior forces of Piccolomini as far as Erfurt in Thuringia. Piccolomini stood in a fortified camp near Saalfeld, where Baner was not able to force him to accept battle. In 1640 Baner joined with the French commander the Duc de Longueville on the Fulda in Hesse. Baner's camp was at Wildungen, where likewise he was unable to force Piccolomini to accept battle, who now started for the Weser, Baner following close on his heels to protect the Guelphic countries. In the winter of 1640 Piccolomini went with the Emperor to Ratisbon, who had come thither to hold a Diet, the first for twenty-seven years. In January, 1641, Baner undertook his bold march from Westphalia to scare the Emperor and the Diet from Ratisbon. Having joined with the French marshal Guébriant, he set out from the Weser to the Danube, where he made his appearance before Ratisbon with 20,000 men. He bombarded the town. The Emperor might see his enemies from his windows. But a thaw setting in, the well-planned expedition had to be abandoned. Guébriant now separated from Baner; the French entering winter quarters near Bamberg, and Baner remaining stationed in Bavaria at a short distance from Ratisbon. Here Piccolomini was at him again; but Baner succeeded in executing just as perilous a retreat as he had four years before. He escaped as by a miracle through the narrow defiles of the Bohemian forests and of the Erzgebirge to the fortress of Zwickau. For not less than eleven days the imperialists had ridden in pursuit of him, without once unsaddling their horses. In the Vogtland he was again joined by Guébriant; he then passed the Saale near Weissenfels, and thence reached Halberstadt. Here his glorious career ended; he died on the 10th of May, 1641. His death needs not to be attributed to any other cause but to the wild excesses to which this seemingly sedate and taciturn man, but who harboured the strongest passions in his bosom, used to give himself up. He wâs often drunk four days running with Hungary wine. On the 28th of May, 1640, in the camp of Saalfeldt, he lost his fondly loved first wife, a Countess of Erbach, who had accompanied him all through the fierce war, and who once during these peregrinations had even given birth to a child in her travelling carriage. He buried her at Erfurt. At her funeral he was smitten with the granddaughter of Margrave George Frederic of Baden-Durlach, and already on the 16th of September, 1640, the hoary general celebrated his second marriage at Arolsen, where the young princess, at that time in her eighteenth year, was staying with some relations. But he enjoyed his newly found happiness only eight months.

Baner was succeeded by Torstensohn, formerly one of the pages of Gustavus Adolphus. Torstensohn, protected by the truce with Brandenburg which the Great Elector had concluded, left in the spring of 1642 the Guelphic countries again, to closely press the Emperor. Passing the Elbe, he marched through Silesia and Moravia as far as Olmütz: his outposts arrived within six leagues of Vienna. He then returned through Silesia into Saxony, where, on the 2nd of November, 1642, he defeated in another battle, on the fields of Breitenfeld, Piccolomini and the Archduke Bishop Leopold William, the brother of the Emperor Ferdinand III. In consequence of this victory Torstensohn advanced for a second time to Moravia, and Wrangel, who was sent in advance, again stood in the beginning of July with 3,000 horse near Vienna. The plan was in conjunction with George Ragoczy, the new Prince of Transylvania, to dictate a peace to the Emperor.

Then, by a masterpiece of Austrian policy, a new enemy was raised in the rear of these tormentors. Ferdinand having induced Denmark to declare war against the Swedes, Torstensohn was obliged to turn against this new enemy, and executed in 1643, with the greatest secresy, an exceedingly bold march, as if it were only a promenade, from Moravia across the whole Empire, suddenly making his appearance in Holstein. In the campaign of 1644 he conquered Jutland; after which he drove Gallas from the Baltic to the Elbe, and from the Elbe into Bohemia, where the Emperor was trying to collect a new army at Prague. Torstensohn with only 16,000 men gained the last grand battle of the Great War on the 5th of March, 1645, near Jankau, seven leagues south of Prague. The victory was so decisive that the whole Imperial-Leaguist army was completely scattered, or rather annihilated. The generals of that army, the imperialist Count Hatzfeld and those of the League, Jean de Werth and John Götz, had disagreed among themselves, which was the principal cause of the loss of the battle. It had been a standing complaint in the imperial army that there were too many commanders. Hatzfeld with 4,000 men was made prisoner; Götz with 4,000 more was killed on the spot; Jean de Werth, twice captured by the Swedes, escaped with the cavalry into the Upper Palatinate; thirty-six cannon and all the ammunition waggons were lost; Torstensohn had seventy-seven stand of colours to send to Stockholm. The three imperial regiments of Piccolomini, Pompejo, and Bassompierre consisted together of not more than 450 men; and somewhat later 400 men marched out from Prague to Vienna, who, as Puffendorf writes, called themselves twenty regiments, and carried 120 colours before them. No imperial regiment of cavalry had more than sixty men left. It was necessary to create a new army altogether.

The Emperor, who was still staying at Prague, set out on the 8th of March for Vienna, where he arrived on the 19th, accompanied by his household and 200 musketeers; the imperial party having been obliged to take the circuitous road by Pilsen and Ratisbon, and from thence down the Danube by Linz. Four weeks after the victory of Jankau Torstensohn made his appearance for the third time in the heart of Austria, and on the 9th of April the Swedish army arrived before Vienna. The outworks on the right side of the Danube being soon taken, the river remained still the only barrier between the enemy and the capital. Ferdinand III. now trembled in his Hofburg, just as his father had done before him. The imperial family, the whole court, the treasure, the archives, were in a thousand carriages and waggons conveyed for safety to Grätz; many of the nobility and clergy fled as far as Salzburg and Venice. It was the same state of things over again as when, twenty-six years before, Count Thurn stood before Vienna. Ferdinand alone stayed behind in the capital. Torstensohn's headquarters were at Hammersdorf; Ragoczy was already at Pressburg. The Archduke Bishop Leopold William, the Emperor's generalissimo, was with a few troops encamped in the Brigittenau (Bridget-fields). A romantic but unauthenticated legend relates that on the 30th of May, the feast of St. Brigitta (Bridget), a Swedish cannon-ball had fallen at his feet in his tent, and that the archduke had then made the vow, afterwards accomplished, to found the chapel dedicated to that saint; round which now every year, on the anniversary of its consecration, the gay crowds of the merry Viennese celebrate one of their most joyous popular festivals. The priestly generalissimo had no authority over his soldiers, who infested all the roads, committing robberies on all sides; plundering even the court carriages on their way to Grätz— nay, the Empress herself, as she was travelling to a watering-place. The most terrible punishments were inflicted on the perpetrators of these outrages: officers by dozens were quartered and impaled in the principal squares of Vienna and before the gates, whole regiments decimated, and the ringleaders buried up to their heads, which were then played at with heavy balls as at nine-pins.

Torstensohn remained for eight months, until October, 1645, in the centre of the monarchy. His headquarters at Stammersdorf he, however, had left after four days. On the 4th of April, which happened to be Good Friday, he set out for Moravia, to be nearer Ragoczy, with whom he had afterwards, on the 17th of August, a meeting at Eisgrub. The capital of Austria was saved once more by the tardiness of Ragoczy and by the obstinate resistance of Brünn in Moravia, where Louis Rattuit (Radewich), Count de Souches, another upstart and convert, held the command. This officer became the saviour of the monarchy. De Souches was by birth a Frenchman, a native of La Rochelle, and formerly one of the most zealous Huguenots. He had once stoutly defended his native town against Cardinal Richelieu; afterwards he emigrated and took service with the Swedes; offended by them he passed over to the imperialists, and, partly from revenge, partly from avarice, turned Papist. When Torstensohn summoned him to surrender Brünn, or else he would give him no quarter, De Souches replied that he neither required nor gave quarter. Torstensohn, owing to the spirited defence of De Souches, was at last obliged, after a siege of sixteen weeks, to march off, on the 23rd of August, 1645. He went once more to Austria, and from thence back into winter quarters in Bohemia, after having left behind garrisons in the conquered places, particularly at Kornneuburg and Krems. These garrisons maintained their posts until August, 1646. At that time, the last public Lutheran service in Austria, until the days of Joseph II., was held at Krems; within the short space of two months, 10,000 country people took the sacrament in both kinds.

De Souches was richly rewarded by the Emperor with honours, dignities, and estates. He was made a count of the Empire, a field-marshal-general, and a privy councillor; and he was appointed commandant, first of Comorn, and afterwards of Vienna, where, as late as 1683, during the great siege by the Turks, he was still alive, and able to be of good service to Starhemberg, the heroic defender of the imperial city.

Yet, although Vienna was saved, the consequences of the battle of Jankau continued to be very disastrous to the imperial court. On the 13th of August, 1645, Denmark concluded a peace, and a fortnight later Saxony a truce, with Sweden; at last, on the 14th of March, 1647, their example was followed by Bavaria. On the other hand, the monarchy was protected from Ragoczy by the peace of Linz: it is true, at the price of the Emperor's securing religious liberty to the Protestants of Hungary.

The truce with Bavaria was wrested from the Elector by the last Swedish commander-in-chief of the Thirty Years' War, Gustavus Wrangel. Torstensohn, to the great joy of his enemies, who thought him equivalent to 10,000 men, had, on account of the sad state of his health, given up the command. He was suffering so acutely from the gout that he had to be carried in a litter to the battlefields where he won his victories. He returned to Stockholm, where he died in 1651.

Gustavus Wrangel abandoned Torstensohn's plan of penetrating through Moravia into the heart of Austria; instead of which, he came back to that of Gustavus Adolphus, of assailing it from Southern Germany through Bavaria. Wrangel, in conjunction with the afterwards celebrated French marshal Turenne, again added to the old glory of the Swedish arms in Southern Germany, overrunning Bavaria with terrible plunder and devastation as far as Bregenz, on the confines of Switzerland. At the same time Gallas was in the Upper Palatinate, where he likewise mercilessly plundered the country of his Emperor's ally. The Elector of Bavaria was therefore in a desperate plight, and now the most singular complication of affairs followed.

Maximilian was negotiating with Wrangel. This very likely was known to the cabinet of Vienna, and on that account Gallas conducted himself with the same hostility in the Upper Palatinate as Tilly had done in Saxony, just before the battle of Leipzig. A few days before the negotiations with Wrangel were brought to a conclusion, Maximilian wrote to Gallas: "My dear Count,—It almost seems as if people were looking out for a pretext to break with me. If I only know it, I may act accordingly, and throw the responsibility upon him who is the cause of all this. I cannot allow everybody to be master in my country."

Then followed the conclusion of the truce between Bavaria on the one hand, and Sweden, France, and Hesse-Cassel on the other. In accordance with its stipulations, the Swedes and French evacuated the whole of Bavaria and the Upper Palatinate. Wrangel led part of his army to Franconia, and part to Bohemia. In the latter country he took the important fortress of Eger; and there, on the 20th of July, 1647, the Emperor Ferdinand III., who was in person with the army, had a very narrow escape from being captured by the Swedes. With the earliest dawn a party of the Swedes attacked the imperial outposts, and, after having overpowered them, penetrated to the quarters of the Emperor. Two Swedes were already in the Emperor's room, when assistance arrived just in time; the imperial soldiers killed one man, took the other prisoner, and dispersed the rest.

Before the miraculous good fortune of Austria was once more proved in this case, an undertaking of the imperial cabinet had miscarried, which most plainly shows in what light those who wielded the power in Austria looked upon the princes of the German Empire, and how little they shrank from any expedient that might further their own objects.

The Emperor's councillors were afraid lest the truce concluded by Maximilian, *which now, for the first time in the whole war, reduced the Emperor's power in the field to his own army*, should lead to a separate peace, or, even worse than that, to the Elector throwing himself into the arms of France, with whom he, indeed, was already negotiating, and had gone so far that, even at a later period, when he was again allied with Austria, he still kept up a secret correspondence with the French cabinet. Austria therefore determined to provide for her own security in any emergency. The expedient by which this was to be effected was neither more nor less than *to seduce the whole of the Bavarian army*, to lead it over to the Emperor, and even to carry away the Elector and his obnoxious councillors as hostages to Vienna. If this plan succeeded the Elector would not only have lost his army, but his country, in its defenceless state, would have been laid open to the full revenge of the Swedes, who, of course, would never have believed but that the going over of the Bavarian army to the Emperor had been a mere preconcerted game on the side of the Elector. And if

26—2

they succeeded in getting the Elector to Vienna, he was irretrievably lost. Neither of these two plans, however, succeeded; Bavaria was this time saved by her own good fortune, and by the penetrating sagacity of her Elector.

As soon as the conclusion of the truce by Bavaria was known at Vienna, the imperial cabinet issued a declaration *that there was no such thing as a Bavarian army; that the troops of Bavaria were only part of the general army of the Empire, commanded*, UNDER THE EMPEROR, *by the Elector*. Orders were accordingly sent to the Bavarian generals to bring in their men to the imperial army. Jean de Werth[1] was especially applied to; and this general, as wily as he was brave, allowed himself to be bribed by the supreme head of the Empire.

The affair was managed most cunningly. De Werth was especially fitted for covering such unheard-of treachery with consummate dissimulation, and for carrying it out with an energy calculated to overcome every difficulty. To excite no suspicion against himself, he sent in all the orders which the generals had received from the Emperor to Munich, whither he went himself. As soon as he had made his appearance at court, Maximilian caused him to be put to the test in several ways, and by different trustworthy persons; but De Werth eluded them all, and knew so well how to manage all his conduct, gestures, and speeches that no one could have doubted his fidelity. The Elector alone, who was even more cunning than his general, instinctively clung to his suspicion, and determined at all events beforehand to break the thread of the web which possibly might be spun round him. He sent orders to Jean de Werth to summon for a certain day all the officers of his army to Landshut, where the pleasure of the Elector would be communicated to them by the commissioners of his Highness.

[1] Jean de Werth was a Walloon, and had risen from the ranks. He was, after Pappenheim, the greatest cavalry general of the century. Having, in 1638, been made prisoner near Rheinfelden by Bernard of Weimar, he remained confined four years in the donjon of Vincennes, where he was a great "lion" of the ladies of Paris, and astonished the world by his feats in the eating and drinking line. He was, in 1642, exchanged for the Swedish field-marshal Horn, who had been made prisoner in the battle of Nördlingen.

Jean de Werth now speedily made arrangements for having the plan carried out before the arrival of these commissioners. He ordered all the cavalry under his command to set out immediately from their garrisons and to assemble at Vilshofen on the Danube, near Passau, quite in the vicinity of the Bohemian frontier. Hither the foot regiments were directed to march, the quarter-master-general Holz being forced by threats to sign the orders to the different colonels. Whilst the regiments were on their march, Jean de Werth placed a detachment on the road from Munich to Landshut, with orders to arrest the commissioners; who in this manner would have been prevented from communicating to the officers who had been summoned to that town the pleasure of the Elector.

A mere lucky chance saved Maximilian—one of the commissioners having proposed to his colleagues the more pleasant journey by water down the Isar to Landshut; the detachment lying in ambush for them on the high road waited in vain for their intended victims. The commissioners arrived on the 2nd of July, 1647, at Landshut; but Jean de Werth and his generals, among whom was the afterwards famous Count Spork, were already on their way to Vilshofen.

Hundreds of messengers were now at once sent off by the commissioners to convey to the troops orders for stopping their march. Some regiments returned without delay; others, whose colonels refused obedience, continued on their way to Vilshofen. Here Jean de Werth led them across the Danube; and all was going on quite smoothly, when at the last moment a public proclamation of the Elector to his army arrived, and all the superior officers received special letters to warn them. A price of 10,000 florins was set on Jean de Werth's head, whether dead or alive; and 1,500 on that of every one of those officers who had intended to desert. Jean de Werth now hoped to win over his troops by granting them liberty of plunder; but they rose against him. The regiments tried to make out each other's intentions by one watching the demeanour of the other, and at last they came to an agreement. Spork's cuirassiers at once rode off. The other troops, after having first whispered to each other, gradually spoke out their minds louder and louder; and at last broke into a threatening outcry, that no one should venture to lead them over to the Emperor. Jean de Werth and Spork had now not a moment to lose. They hastily mounted their horses and galloped off to the Bohemian frontier, both being obliged to leave behind their baggage, and Spork even his wife. The Emperor received them with great honour. Jean de Werth was appointed to the chief command over the whole of the imperial cavalry; he died only four years after the peace, at the noble estate of Benatek in Bohemia, which had been granted to him by the Emperor, and where Tycho de Brahe had once had his observatory. Spork, a very remarkable rough old campaigner, became field-marshal-lieutenant, and died as general of the cavalry. The Elector of Bavaria caused a month's pay to be given to his whole army; the officers receiving, moreover, his written and verbal thanks, besides more substantial tokens of his certainly very just gratitude for having saved him from the most imminent danger.

Austria nevertheless attained her object of frightening the Elector; who, being harassed now by the Swedes, because they no longer trusted him, gave them warning to break off the truce on the 14th of September, 1647. Count Maximilian Gronsfeld, however, the new commander-in-chief of the Bavarian troops, was secretly instructed never to fight against the French.

In the last campaign of the Thirty Years' War, in 1648, Wrangel advanced repeatedly into Swabia; and, after having again joined with Turenne, forced in June the passage through Bavaria into Austria. From March to May, the hostile troops stood facing each other on the Danube and on the Lech, both parties plundering and robbing. The imperialists had thirty, and the Bavarians—now allied with them—twenty troops of horse; the number of infantry was the same in both armies. The whole strength of combatants of the allied Austro-Bavarian army amounted to 40,000 men; to which, however, were added 140,000 camp followers of both sexes. No wonder that, notwithstanding the strictest orders of the Elector against marauding, plundering, and robbing, the country was completely exhausted. The Swedes had forty-eight troops of horse, the French twenty-two; both together twenty more than the Austro-Bavarians, to whom they were likewise superior in artillery. The imperialists were commanded by Count Holzapfel, who was posted with Gronsfeld near Günzburg, on the Danube. In the engagement of Zusmershausen on the western side of the Lech, not far from Augsburg—the last general action of the Thirty Years' War—Holzapfel was killed, on the 17th of May, 1648; after which the army retreated across the Lech.

When the Swedes encamped near Thierhaupten on the Lech, on the same spot where, sixteen years before, their great king had burst into Bavaria, Gronsfeld's council of war determined upon retreating with their army into the interior of Bavaria. This retreat, however, degenerated into a real flight. The army dispersed and Gronsfeld himself was, on the 4th of June, 1648, arrested by order of the Elector and conveyed to Munich, and from thence to Ingolstadt; yet he was afterwards released, having succeeded in completely justifying his own conduct.

The Swedes and French now entirely overran Bavaria. When the escort of Holzapfel's corpse marched down into Austria they found all the inns of the Bavarian country on the Danube quite deserted; so that they were able to help themselves to their heart's content from the kitchens and cellars. All the people now fled from the open country into the woods; the Elector Maximilian to Salzburg. Amidst columns of smoke from burning castles, villages, and hamlets, Wrangel and Turenne marched through the whole of Bavaria, and on the 15th of June, 1648, arrived before Wasserburg on the Inn, the intended goal of their march being Austria. Once more, and for the last time, Piccolomini was entrusted with the chief command to protect Austria; Jean de Werth commanded the cavalry under him. The latter appointment was contrary to an express promise given by the Emperor to Maximilian, but the Elector had to put up with it, and also with Piccolomini doing nothing at all for some time to protect Bavaria. At last Piccolomini advanced to Munich, and two days later—on the 4th of October—Jean de Werth surprised Wrangel and Turenne out hunting near Dachau, and both these generals, from fear of being cut off from the Lech, retreated, on the 12th of October, to the other side of the river. In the meanwhile, the Swedish partisan, Hans Christopher von Königsmark,[1] sent by Wrangel from Swabia to Bohemia, had, on the 26th of July, 1648, by a bold surprise, conquered the "Small Side" (Kleinseite) of Prague. This event became the proximate cause of peace being concluded, and thus the long war ended on the same spot on which it had commenced.

3.—*The peace of Westphalia and the new position of the imperial court with regard to the German princes and to the aristocracy in the Austrian dominions.*

The peace of Westphalia was concluded, on the 24th of October, 1648, with the Swedes at Osnabrück, and on the same day with the French at Münster. It was one of the most ardently wished for which has ever been negotiated. The negotiations had been opened as far back as seven years before, at Hamburg, but it had taken all this time to adjust the balance, the greediness of the foreigner and the obstinacy of the Austrian cabinet over and over again delaying the final settlement. It was the first barter of German lands which Austria carried on with the foreigner, but it was repeated once more, a century and a half later, when, after the French revolutionary wars, it again took about seven years, from the opening of the congress of Rastadt, to come to an agreement as to how much should be taken away from Germany. In both instances the defeated rulers of Austria availed themselves of their position as elected Emperors of Germany to pay the losses of their dynasty with lands not of their own, but of the German Empire.

[1] The grandfather of the celebrated Aurora, the mother of Marshal de Saxe.

The imperial ambassador at the Westphalian congress was Count Maximilian Trautmannsdorf, the premier and favourite of the Emperor Ferdinand III. He was the soul of all the negotiations, which, after a great deal of opposition, he at last succeeded in bringing to a conclusion, conformably to the secret instruction of his master. He met the overbearing exactions of the victorious Swedes and the insolence of the French with imperturbable equanimity; with his phlegmatic temper he always soothed down the susceptibilities which the conquerors excited by their pretensions, and, whilst they were forced to acknowledge his incorruptible integrity, he at last succeeded in obtaining for his conquered dynasty very tolerable terms. Trautmannsdorf was modest enough to allow an equal share in what was but the merit of his own exertions to the co-operation of his learned colleagues. These were the hot-tempered Tyrolese chancellor, Dr. Isaac Volmar—whom the Emperor, in reward for his services, created Freiherr (Viscount) von Riedern, and who died in 1662, at the age of nearly eighty—and the imperial Aulic Councillor Krane.

The Swedish ambassadors at Osnabrück were John Oxenstierna and Salvius. The former was the son of the celebrated chancellor, whose modest doubts concerning his own fitness for a diplomatic commission his father met with the well-known words, "*Veni, mi fili, et vide quantula cum sapientia regatur mundus.*"

The French ambassadors at Münster were Count d'Avaux, generally called " his wicked Excellency," and Servien.

Spain and the Netherlands had each sent eight plenipotentiaries. The German electors and princes (down to the most petty ones), the counts of the Empire, and the free cities were likewise represented at the congress. The Elector of Saxony had sent the Aulic Councillor von Pistoris and Dr. Leuber; Brandenburg, Count John von Wittgenstein and three privy councillors, Von Löben, Von der Heiden, and Peter Fritz, the latter of whom was afterwards replaced by Matthew Wesenbeck. Bavaria was represented by Baron von Haslang, Brunswick by Lampadius, and Würtemberg by the very able Chancellor Löffler.

The mediators in the negotiations of peace were the papal nuncio Fabio Chigi, who in 1655 became Pope as Alexander VII., and the Venetian ambassador Contarini. The Pope, however, refused to confirm the peace.

The principal and, on all sides, most eagerly sought for point of negotiation of that peace, which was to put an end to the great so-called "Religious War," was disgusting in the extreme. All the parties, the foreign as well the German powers, and amongst these Protestants as well as Papists, agreed only in one point—all wanted to be indemnified by cession of territories. Nor were the intermediate petty squabbles about points of etiquette, which played such a great part there, less odious. Those ridiculous and trifling questions of precedence; of the right of reception at the top, the bottom, or the middle of the staircase; the honour of the first greeting, or of taking the right-hand side, were treated as the most serious matters, and then raised to the imaginary importance which they maintained down to the period of the French Revolution. Even the improved Gregorian calendar, which the Protestants were required to adopt, gave rise to the most envenomed debates, as they saw in it nothing but a snare of Popish insidious treachery; and German Protestant Christendom actually accepted it only in the year 1700.

The great barter of German territories which was ultimately settled in the peace of Westphalia, yielded a profitable result to three of the powers only—viz., Sweden, France, and Brandenburg.

Sweden gained most. It received that part of Pomerania which is west of the Oder (Vorpommern), and the important port of Stettin, besides the duchy of Bremen at the mouth of the Weser. In these two provinces the German Empire again lost two coastlands, important for her commerce, in addition to that most important one which the unpatriotic policy of Charles V. had already torn from the German Empire and made over to the crown of Spain. Bremen especially was of such consequence, in a commercial point of view, that, not more than eight years afterwards, Cromwell, who coveted it, formed the intention of snatching it from Sweden, which, however, maintained its prey for seventy-one years, the duchy of Bremen passing to Hanover-England only in the peace of Stockholm in 1720.

The French, after having proffered by "his wicked Excellency" the most extravagant demands, at last contented themselves with Alsace, in which their power settled as an incubus on South Germany; Strassburg, the principal stronghold of the province, was not yet given up to them; but they received the Rhenish fortress of Breisach.

Brandenburg was also very richly endowed. The Great Elector obtained, with the archbishopric and city of Magdeburg, the command of the Middle Elbe, and the strongest fortress of the whole of North Germany, which, during all the vicissitudes of the perilous Seven Years' War, Frederic the Great maintained as the principal point of support of his military power. Besides Magdeburg, the Elector received the rich Westphalian bishoprics of Halberstadt and Minden; of the Pomeranian inheritance, on the other hand—the whole of which was to have fallen to the lot of the house of Brandenburg after the death of its dukes, who had died during the war—he only obtained the part east of the Oder (Hinterpommern) with the abbey of Camin. Pomerania thenceforth supplied to Brandenburg its best soldiers. Stettin, the possession of which the Great Elector had so earnestly coveted—he called it the gate of the Empire—was only acquired at the peace of Stockholm in 1720. The Silesian duchy of Jägerndorf, which had been taken from the outlawed margrave, and given to the house of Liechtenstein, remained lost to Brandenburg until Frederic the Great put forward his claims to it with that well-known success which gained for him the whole of Silesia.

By the energetic intercession of Brandenburg, the Calvinists obtained the same religious liberty which the Lutherans enjoyed, whose jealousy had until then kept them out of it.

The object of the most violent contest was the settlement of the disputed territorial claims between Protestants and Catholics. The former insisted upon having the *status quo* of 1618 restored; the Catholics, upon having the question settled on the basis laid down in 1630, after the issuing of the Edict of Restitution. On the proposition of the electoral Saxon minister to meet halfway, the *status quo* of the year 1624 was at last adopted as the rule. The Protestants, although having conquered Austria in the field, thus lost a considerable part of what they held. They retained the two archbishoprics and the twelve bishoprics[1] of Northern Germany, which had been secularised since the treaties of Passau and of Augsburg. On the other hand, the Catholics retained all those territories in which, during the four years following the battle of the White Mountain, Austria had forcibly restored the old religion. To this category belonged, in particular, the whole of the hereditary Austrian dominions, Bohemia included; and the three Westphalian bishoprics of Münster, Hildesheim, and Paderborn.

The Brunswick Guelphs thus did not receive Hildesheim, which they had so long coveted, nor Halberstadt and Minden, which fell to Brandenburg; and Hanover had to share the bishopric of Osnabrück with the Papists; so that, by a very extraordinary arrangement, the see was to be held alternately by a prince of the house of Brunswick and by a Roman Catholic bishop. Hesse-Cassel, which had so energetically defended the Protestant cause, had to content itself with the princely abbey of Hersfeld.

The powerful Protestant house of Saxony also made no acquisition beyond being confirmed in the possession of the two Lusatias.

Bavaria retained the electorate, besides the Upper Palatinate (Amberg and Sulzbach), which was taken from the Elector Palatine.

The outlawed Elector Palatine, and the likewise outlawed Dukes of Mecklenburg, were restored.

Two of the most momentous stipulations of the Westphalian peace, moreover, concerned the definitive acknowledgment of the republics of Switzerland and Holland as

---

[1] They were the archbishoprics of Magdeburg and Bremen, with the bishoprics of Halberstadt, Osnabrück, Verden, Minden, Brandenburg, Havelberg, Naumburg, Merseburg, Meissen, Lübeck, Schwerin, and Ratzeburg.—*Translator.*

sovereign powers. *Holland even obtained the right of shutting up the navigation of the Scheldt and the Rhine, and thereby completed the ruin of German commerce.*

The plan which Ferdinand II. had entertained of changing the German Empire into an absolute monarchy was completely frustrated by the Westphalian peace, just as in the case of Charles V. by the march of the Elector Maurice to Innsbruck. The Empire was formally constituted as an aristocracy of princes, with oligarchic rule; the different members of the German body having the right expressly granted them of forming alliances with foreign princes, except against the Empire. The Emperor was confined to the dynastic power in his hereditary dominions. "The princes," as the Duchess of Orleans once expressed it, "made a point of being considered as depending on God alone, and not having the Emperor for their master." Only when Austria's miraculous fortune had given her the victories against the Turks, and the conquest of Hungary, the ascendency of the house of Habsburg was again felt in Germany. The petty princes had to bow; but the great ones, especially Brandenburg, gradually emancipated themselves. The house of Austria, as far as the imperial dignity was concerned, had to be content with the *prestige* of still retaining the uncontested precedency over all the European princely houses. *The true supremacy of power in Europe, however, now rested for some time with France.* As co-guarantee of Sweden, in the Westphalian peace, the crown of the fleur-de-lis thenceforth obtained an ever-ready opportunity of meddling with the affairs of Germany.

When the heralds flew from Westphalia to all parts of the German Empire to announce by sound of trumpet to the warring princes, to the beleaguered towns, and to the famished and sorrow-stricken people the conclusion of peace which it had not enjoyed for nearly a whole generation, Germany was a very different country from what it had been thirty years before. Its fields lay waste; its population was gone. This was true also of Austria, and especially of Bohemia. The Tyrol only, protected by its mountains, had kept off the enemy. In Bohemia, instead of flourishing, populous, industrious towns and cheerful, thriving villages, the eye, as far as it reached, was met only by heaps of smouldering ruins and by newly dug graves: where formerly golden crops waved, there were now bogs and a wilderness of brushwood and bramble; and the men whom the long savage war had left among the living had, from hunger and despair, formed themselves into bands of robbers and murderers, driven from house and home, and vying with the active and disbanded soldiery in outrage and rapine. From that time dates the harassing system of passports, which was then adopted on account of those brigands.

The principal burden lay now, as usual, on the peasants. They had suffered most in the war; but even in peace not only their harsh seigneurs, but likewise the selfish citizens and townspeople did their utmost to keep them down. This is proved, among other things, by a remarkable decree of the Bohemian Diet which Ferdinand III. held in 1656 at Prague. "It being well known that the poor peasants, on account of the low price of agricultural produce, can scarcely maintain themselves, it has been decreed, *lest they should be obliged to part with the corn, the raising of which has cost them so much, for a ridiculously low price, or half give it away, that a fair tariff of all sorts of grain shall be established*, below which no one, either in the country, or especially in the towns, shall buy or sell under forfeiture of the same."

Whilst the Emperor did not succeed in his plan of breaking the power of the German princely aristocracy and changing Germany into an absolute monarchy, he carried out his object, at least to a certain extent, in his hereditary dominions. The principal gain which the house of Habsburg derived from the bloody Thirty Years' War was that the *ascendency of the imperial court over the Austrian aristocracy was established on a new and solid basis*. The old dynasts and lords of Austria and Bohemia—who in their proud castles had been the true masters of the country, endowed with "*autonomy*," as the court expressly designated it, and who, *especially since the time of their turning Protestant*, had been very little dependent so the crown—had nearly all of them been outlawed and exiled. They were now broken down, those strong castles, donjons, and mansions of the old nobility of Bohemia, Austria, and Styria, in the courtyards of some of which a moderate-sized village might have stood, whose fountains and cisterns might in many instances be compared to the grand works of the Romans, and whose kitchens, galleries, and halls, as Hormayr says, " even in their majestic ruins, exhibit a much grander character than the palaces of modern times." The old mediæval systematic opposition of the nobles against the crown was thereby shaken to its centre. The new aristocracy had been only created by the court, and been made rich and powerful with the confiscated estates of the defeated old Protestant nobility. Whatever, therefore, might be their services, and to however great rewards these new men thought themselves entitled, yet they could not forget the origin of their fortune, nor repudiate the duty of gratitude to the court which had founded it. The new Catholic aristocracy consisted of very heterogeneous elements ; besides a nucleus of a few old houses, like the Liechtensteins, Dietrichsteins, and others, who had remained faithful to the crown, it was composed of a mass of new military nobility, most of whom were foreigners, Italians, Spaniards, Walloons, &c., or mere upstarts raised by the fortune of war. Such a body could never be so closely and intimately connected in the opposition against the Catholic court as the old Protestant " chain of nobles " had been.

At the end of the war there were still a considerable number of Protestant Austrian noble houses holding estates in Austria below the confluence of the Enns, for from Austria above the Enns, from Styria, Carinthia, Carniola, Bohemia, and Moravia, all the Protestant noble houses had been exiled. A list published by Von Meiern enumerates forty-two houses of counts and barons of Austria below the Enns, and twenty-nine houses belonging to the immatriculated nobility of the same province, which at the time of the peace of Westphalia publicly professed the Protestant religion—without mentioning the secret Protestants and the Protestant nobility in Silesia. When in the session of the congress at

Osnabrück the Swedish ambassador, on the 27th of February, 1647, publicly read the petition in which these Protestant nobles urged their claims, Trautmannsdorf three times rose uneasily, and Salvius was scarcely able to induce him to hear the petition to the end. Their demands were restitution of all the churches, schools, hospitals, orphan-houses, with the revenues pertaining thereto, as granted by the dearly paid for[1] royal letters and patents. The imperial chief commissioner at last emphatically declared that "*his Imperial Majesty would rather lay down his sceptre, crown, and life, and even see his own sons slain before his eyes, than allow worship after the Augsburg Confession, or the autonomy* [of the nobles], *in his kingdoms and hereditary dominions.*" Salvius drily replied that such a thing might really come to pass. The negotiations for peace very nearly split on this point. Yet the Swedes at last gave in, merely reserving to themselves the right, as new members of the Empire, to urge their representations in favour of those petitioners on a further occasion.

The fault of the Swedes not succeeding in their remonstrances lay with the Austrian Protestant lords themselves, and with the manner in which the Protestant Church had used the privileges acquired by its first founders. No sooner had the Emperor Maximilian II., in 1568, granted religious liberty in Austria, than the Protestant cause began to be most glaringly compromised and disgraced by the mad fanaticism and the wanton lust of controversy of its divines, who were abetted and supported by the noble houses.

The first families of the country were the zealous patrons of the fanatical and quarrelsome Flacian[2] preachers, who

[1] The Majestäts-brief of the Emperor Maximilian II. had cost forty-two "tuns of gold" (£400,000 sterling). See Raupach, "Evangelisches Oestreich," iii., 124, note.

[2] The Flacian sect carried the Lutheran doctrine of original sin to such lengths as to teach that man was not only sinful, but sin itself. A subdivision of them, calling themselves Magdeburgians, from Joachim of Magdeburg, held the doctrine that man was sin itself, even in the grave and to the last judgment. Others, the Spangenbergians, from Cyriacus Spangenberg, believed man to be sin itself only before regeneration, after which he was a deadened sin. The two sects assailed each other with the most odious abuse, the latter calling the former Cadaverists and Gravesinners, and they in return calling the others Corpse-praisers, &c.

gave the spectacle of the most scandalous controversies. But, with all this fanatical zeal, the Protestant nobles showed in their lives how very little they cared for anything beyond the dead letter of the dogma. The Protestant physician Florian Crucius writes, on the 13th of August, 1619—even before the battle of the White Mountain—a letter which contains the following remarkable passage concerning those Protestant lords: " In the midst of the general distress they give vent to their tyranny against the peasants. And there are among them great numbers of traitors who, under the cloak of the gospel, are mere downright Epicureans, not caring for any religion but for that which panders to their palates and to their lusts."

Thus the Protestant nobility had for the most part deserved their fate, and they merely earned the punishment of their own sins. Most of them soon became converts to Popery, and, as is usually the case, the most fanatical champions of the religion which their houses had been the foremost to assail as long as there was anything to be gained by their opposition.

4.—*Diet of Ratisbon—Death of Ferdinand III.—His family.*

Ferdinand III. summoned an Imperial Diet, the last but one as long as the Holy Roman Empire lasted, to Ratisbon in 1653, for the purpose of having his son Archduke Ferdinand elected King of the Romans. The latter, born in 1633, was, at the age of thirteen, elected King of Bohemia, and the year after, King of Hungary, under the name of Ferdinand IV. At the age of twenty, he became King-elect of the Romans; but he died the year after of the smallpox, on the 9th of July, 1654.

After the death of Ferdinand IV., Leopold, the second son of Ferdinand III., hitherto intended for the Church, was elected King of Hungary, at the age of fifteen, in 1655, and King of Bohemia the year after. Before his election as King of the Romans could be accomplished, the Emperor Ferdinand III. died suddenly, on Easter Day, April 2, 1657, at the early age of fifty-seven. The debilitated monarch died from the effects of a fright. A fire broke out in the night, between eleven and twelve, in the imperial palace, in the very apartment where the Emperor lay sick. A halberdier of the guard, who wished to save the youngest imperial prince, an infant only two months old, fell with the cradle, which broke, without hurting the child, who, however, died the year after; but the father had been so much frightened by the accident that three hours afterwards he breathed his last.

Ferdinand III. had had three wives. The first, Maria Anna, the mature daughter of King Philip III. of Spain, whom he married in 1631, died suddenly in childbed at Linz, in 1646: a female child—who, however, died soon after—was taken by surgical means from the mother after her death. He then married, in 1648, Maria Leopoldina, the daughter of his uncle Leopold of Tyrol; she died in 1649, at the age of seventeen, twelve days after the birth of a son. His third wife, to whom he was united in 1651, and who survived him nearly thirty years, was an Italian princess, Eleonora Gonzaga of Mantua, the niece of his stepmother, and at the time of the marriage twenty-four years of age. In her person mystic devotion and worldly vanity were blended in a most remarkable manner. In 1662 she founded an order of the "Female Slaves of Virtue"; in 1668 the order of the Star of the Cross, for Roman Catholic ladies, in honour of a crucifix which had remained uninjured during several fires which broke out in the Hofburg in 1667; and she every week lay prostrate at the feet of her Jesuit confessor, craving his absolution. But she was exceedingly ambitious and domineering, and retained to the day of her death the greatest influence over her stepson Leopold I., of whose court she was the centre and the ruling spirit. She inhabited the garden-palace called the Old Favorita, which was destroyed, even in her lifetime, during the great siege of the Turks in 1684, and on the site of which the Emperor Joseph I. afterwards caused the present Augarten to be laid out. There Eleonora Gonzaga kept her own most magnificent court, which to the last days of her life she knew how to make most pleasant and brilliant by comedies, ballets, lotteries, and other Italian amusements, which she first introduced in Vienna. She died in 1686, at the age of fifty-nine, after an illness of three weeks.

By these three wives Ferdinand III. left two sons and three daughters. By the first marriage he had Leopold I., his successor, and Maria Anna, who was first betrothed to the Spanish Crown Prince Balthazar; but who, after the death of that youth at the age of seventeen, in 1646, was married in 1649, when only fifteen, to his father, King Philip IV.

By his second wife Ferdinand III. had a son, Charles Joseph, who at the age of thirteen became Bishop of Passau and grand master of the Teutonic order, but died two years after, in 1664.

His third wife bore him the two princesses—Eleonora Maria, who in 1670 married, at the age of seventeen, King Michael of Poland, and after his death, in 1678, Duke Charles of Lorraine, the grandfather of the husband of Maria Theresa; and also Maria Anna Josepha, who in 1678, at the age of twenty-four, married the first Papist Elector Palatine John William.

CHAPTER IX

Leopold I.—(1657-1705).

1.—The election of the Emperor at Frankfort.

The reign of Leopold I. was one of the longest and most warlike in the history of Austria. It comprised three great wars with France, extending altogether over twenty-two years, and two severe wars with the Turks, extending over twenty-one, besides three serious insurrections of the Hungarians. Leopold, although called by the Jesuits " the Great," was one of the weakest rulers on record; but if ever at any period the extraordinary fortune of Austria was manifest, it was in his reign. She came off victorious out of the last war with France, and likewise out of the Turkish campaign; and Hungary also, after being wrested from the Turks, was reduced to obedience. Even as it has ever been proved in the history of the world, that war is one of the most effective means for the promotion of despotism, thus also the house of Habsburg derived from these wars a considerable increase of its ascendency in the Empire; and the German princes, after having gained much ground in the peace of Westphalia, were only too soon to feel the supremacy of the imperial power again, and might have felt it even more strongly, had it not been for Austria's new rival, Prussia.

Leopold was born in 1640, and, being a younger son, he had been intended for the Church. His instructor was the Jesuit Neidhard, or, in the Italian version of his name, Everard Nitardi, who afterwards, as the confessor of the Queen of Spain, Leopold's sister, became cardinal and grand inquisitor, having, it is said, insinuated himself into the distinguished favour of that royal lady by secretly furnishing her every morning before mass with a small flask of wine.

Neidhard had given his pupil a genuine Spanish, bigoted, and gloomy education; the childish play of Leopold consisted in decorating images of saints and little altars. On the death of his elder brother, Ferdinand IV., in 1654, Leopold became heir-presumptive of Austria; in 1665 his father had him crowned King of Hungary, and in 1666 King of Bohemia. But the old Emperor died before he was able to have his son elected King of the Romans.

It remained long doubtful whether the house of Habsburg would retain the imperial crown of Germany; the interregnum lasted more than fifteen months, as, notwithstanding the opposition of Dr. Volmar, Leopold's ambassador at Frankfort, a French embassy had been admitted there. It consisted of the celebrated Marshal Antony, Duc de Grammont, and of M. de Lionne, Marquis de Fresne.[1] These two ambassadors made a magnificent entry into Frankfort, attended by their cavaliers, equerries, and pages, with a train of halberdiers and running footmen, cooks and grooms, trumpeters and kettledrummers, with their gilt and varnished carriages, splendidly caparisoned horses and mules; besides which a long file of baggage-waggons had preceded them.

France had gained over by enormous bribes the Elector-Archbishop John Philip of Mayence (no other than the celebrated Count Schönborn, who in 1658 formed the Confederation of the Rhine of that century) and the good-natured Elector Maximilian Henry of Cologne, a prince of the house of Bavaria; also the shrewd Elector Palatine, the son of the " Winter King " of Bohemia; and lastly, the ambassadors of the Great Elector of Brandenburg, who was just then absent in Prussia, over which he had succeeded in acquiring the sovereign power. These ambassadors were Prince Maurice

---

[1] The titles of the two ambassadors figured as follows: Grammont as " Duc, Pair, et Maréchal de France, Ministre d'Estat, Souverain de Bidache, Gouverneur et Lieutenant-general en Navarre et Béarn, de la Citadelle de S. Jean de pied, Port de la Ville et Château de Bayonne et Pays de Labourt, Maistre de Camp du Regiment des Gardes du Roy Très Chrestien, Ambassadeur Extraordinaire et Plenipotentiaire de Sa Maj. en toute l'estendue de l'Empire et Royaumes du Nord "; and Lionne as "Conseilleur du Roy Très Chrestien en touts ses Conseils et Commandeur de ses Ordres, Amb. Extr. et Plenip. de S. M., en toute l'estendue de l'Empire et Royaumes du Nord."

of Nassau-Siegen, the conqueror of Brazil, and the privy councillors Raban von Canstein and Jena. On the two latter personages the French lavished their money in profusion; and it was, as Grammont states in his Memoirs, "more eloquent at Frankfort than Cicero at Rome or Demosthenes at Athens."

The intention of the French was neither more nor less than to exclude the house of Habsburg altogether; in its stead the Elector Ferdinand Maria of Bavaria was to be elected Emperor. The negotiations were protracted for several months, as the weak-minded Elector was unable to form a resolution, notwithstanding the earnest admonitions of his wife Adelaide of Savoy, who was as beautiful as she was energetic and ambitious. When at last Grammont, in the spring of 1658, went himself to Munich to push the affair, or at least to find out the real state of things, he very soon convinced himself that nothing was to be done with the poor-spirited prince. The project therefore was abandoned, and the French embassy, which had put forth, as the ostensible pretext of its appearance in Frankfort, some complaints of the house of Habsburg having transgressed the clauses of the peace of Westphalia, had now to content itself with bringing about a very strict capitulation, to be signed by the new Habsburg Emperor, who had made his entry into Frankfort on the 19th of March. Leopold actually signed it, although his partisans had long declared in their writings that he would never put his name to a compact so humiliating to him, and that he would rather leave Frankfort than accept the imperial crown under such conditions. After having signed it on the 18th of July, 1658, he was definitively elected and crowned on the 22nd. The ceremony being over, the Elector of Cologne, who had placed the crown on his head, said to him: "Your Majesty has had a tedious time of it here, and has waited long; but it would have been worse if you had not signed the capitulation unchanged, just as we laid it before you— for in that case you would not have become Emperor at all." His imperial Majesty being at a loss what to reply to this short and significant speech, only opened his large mouth and said nothing. Thus Leopold, with his court, and his two regiments of cuirassiers, who had accompanied him to the election and coronation, returned home to Vienna.

The "Memoirs of Grammont" contain a very piquant description of the Habsburg candidate for the imperial throne, who was at that time in his eighteenth year.

"There have been," says the marshal, "so many descriptions of Leopold's person, that it is superfluous to add a new one. As to the qualities of his mind, I have heard it said that he is naturally of a kind and gentle disposition, but his knowledge of languages and sciences is very limited; for he only understands German and Italian, which, however, he speaks very well. On the other hand, he does not know one word of Spanish, which is very odd, for more than one reason.[1] He is fond of music, and understands it so far that he composes very correctly most doleful melodies. His answers are always very laconic; yet he is considered to possess much judgment and firmness. Up to the time of his coming to Frankfort he had never spoken to any woman but the Empress, his stepmother, and he had given great proofs of continence, a virtue which is the more estimable as it is so rarely to be found in princes of his age and rank.

"He seldom stirs from his house. After dinner he plays with his uncle a simple game called prime (with four cards), but it is a very dull affair, as neither of them speaks a word. He drives only rarely into the country to get a breath of fresh air, but he goes *incognito* in a coach to the gardens of the Spanish ambassador, where he most heartily enjoys the noble game of nine-pins, a pastime undoubtedly most worthy of a young prince who is in daily expectation of being elected Emperor.

"Having an unusually large mouth, which he always keeps open, he, one day, whilst playing at nine-pins with Prince Portia, complained, as it began to rain, that the drops fell into his mouth. The Prince of Portia, his favourite, then taxed his ingenious brain, and, after having pondered for some time, advised his royal master to shut his mouth. The King of Hungary forthwith did so, and found himself considerably the better for it.

[1] The Emperor afterwards learned Spanish from his first wife.

"The King of Hungary (Leopold) has been visited by all the Electors. His manner of receiving them is rather strange: he waits for them standing at the top of the staircase. As soon as he sees them below, he descends three steps, but, in ascending with them again, he takes precedence and the right-hand side. The Elector of Mayence, paying his visit to him, observed that the King had only descended two steps; he therefore stopped at the bottom of the staircase until the King of Hungary had been told that he had to descend another step—so punctilious is this nation, and so averse to allowing any innovations in the existing etiquette."

Marshal de Grammont, anxious to outdo in splendour the festivities which the German lords had given, regaled the partisans of his King with extraordinary magnificence. Speaking of himself in the third person, he describes it in the following manner:

"The marshal caused, in the garden adjoining his hotel, a large hall to be erected, in which he gave a dinner to the Electors and to several princes and counts of the Empire, all of them belonging to the French party. He had also a stage prepared, which was not seen from the dining-hall. During the banquet the curtain rose, and a ballet was danced, with music between the acts. The feast was most sumptuous and in the best taste, and the Germans were exceedingly pleased with it. It lasted from midday until ten o'clock in the evening.

"The house of the marshal was at the same time thrown open to all the citizens of Frankfort. All the servants of the King of Hungary and of the Spanish ambassador, notwithstanding the order of their masters to the contrary, were likewise there; in fact, the whole of Frankfort was present. Great wine casks were placed here and there, with people beside them to draw for anyone who pleased, and the whole went off with great merriment and to the satisfaction of everybody. There were trumpets and kettledrums on all sides, and people shouting at the top of their voices, 'Long live the King of France! and his ambassador, who treats us with such magnificence! We shall not leave here and go to the others, with whom there is no pleasure, no liberality, no thanks to be got.' Such language was used only forty yards from the residence of the King of Hungary and of the archduke, his uncle, which appeared particularly surprising in a city where, six months before, the French were so much hated that people would gladly have burned them."

2.—*Leopold's ministers: Portia, Auersperg, Lobkowitz, Montecuculi, Sinzendorf, Lamberg, Schwartzenberg, Hocher, &c.*

Next to the Jesuits, of whose order the young Emperor was a lay associate, and whose influence during the whole of his long reign was rampant at court, Count John Ferdinand Portia, his lord steward, had the principal management of affairs. This Italian was descended from a noble house which was possessed of landed property in Friuli. He had been, in his earlier years, a friend of Ferdinand III., who made him chief governor of his son Leopold. After having, in conjunction with the domineering Empress Eleonora Gonzaga, ruled Leopold in his youth, he became, on the accession of his pupil, his first minister. The accident of his having been the Emperor's chief governor could alone have raised him to the position of minister, his knowledge of every sort of business being, as Grammont states, " the most scanty in the world."

Notwithstanding these insufficient qualifications, Portia acquired great wealth and honour. Leopold even raised him, in 1662, to the dignity of a prince of the Empire; the Golden Fleece of Spain Portia had obtained before. Being naturally a man of the most ordinary capacity, he made it his constant study—especially when the effects of old age began to impair the little ability which he had—to gloss over the shortcomings of his intellectual and physical powers by a display of phlegmatic stolidity and stiff, strutting Spanish gravity. His policy in the greatest affairs of the state was *to let things take their own course and work their own way.* His wretched system of timid procrastination, of tacking and trimming, threw him altogether into the hands of the shrewd Spanish ambassador, who completely swayed him—so much so, that the latter once said to the Swedish ambassador, Esaias Puffendorf, the brother of the celebrated philosopher,

"I am obliged to lead Portia like a little boy, lest he should stumble." Marshal Grammont mentions, besides, as a proof of the forgetfulness of Portia, that the people who had to deal with him were often obliged to lay before him the same memorandum seven or eight times, even in cases which the prince was himself most anxious to settle.

Prince Portia died in 1665, and the helm of government fell to Prince John Weichard Auersperg, who had been principal minister under Ferdinand III., and who had since then held the second place in the councils of Leopold. With the latter, Auersperg enjoyed little favour, having neglected him at the time when, as a younger prince, he had no likely prospect of becoming Emperor. The young Empress, the Spanish Margareta Theresa, was likewise against him, because, as a partisan of France, he allowed the Emperor to remain a quiet spectator when France, in 1667, enforced by arms her reversionary claims[1] on the Spanish Netherlands; and when, in 1668, at the peace of Aix-la-Chapelle, Louis XIV. helped himself to Lille, Tournay, and Southern Flanders. Auersperg remained in the privy council until, in 1669, Prince Lobkowitz, who had succeeded Portia as lord steward, brought about his downfall. Auersperg, having lost his wife, entreated the Emperor to propose him for a cardinal; but, by the contrivance of Lobkowitz, the imperial recommendation was given to the Prince Abbot of Fulda, the Margrave Bernard Gustavus of Baden-Durlach. Auersperg, after a violent scene with Lobkowitz, then applied to the French ambassador, M. de Gremonville, who promised him the interest of Louis XIV. Pope Clement IX., however, sent the letter which he had received from the French King to the Emperor at Vienna, and Lobkowitz found it not difficult to persuade Leopold that this connection with France had been the sole reason for which Auersperg advised against any effectual aid being given to Spain. Auersperg was put on his trial and condemned to death. Leopold granted a reprieve, but sent him orders by the Aulic Chancellor Hocher

---

[1] Louis XIV. claimed a large portion of the Netherlands by the "right of devolution," according to which the daughters of the first marriage were entitled to succeed in preference to the sons of the second. His queen was daughter of Philip IV. by his first wife.

to leave Vienna within twenty-four hours and to retire to his estates. This happened in 1670, and in 1677 Auersperg died at Seisenberg in Carniola, at the age of sixty-two.

Prince Wenceslaus Eusebius Lobkowitz succeeded him. The Lobkowitzes were an ancient race of Bohemian dynasts. The wealthy line of the house, the Lobkowitz-Hassensteins, had embraced the cause of the Reformation, and had been involved in the general ruin. Prince Wenceslaus belonged to the junior line of Lobkowitz-Popel, which in the person of Zdenko Adalbert Lobkowitz was, in 1624, raised to the princely dignity. His mother was that heroic lady who lent the first help to the defenestrated councillors Slawata and Martinitz.

Prince Wenceslaus Eusebius, born in 1608, followed three careers at once—the court as chamberlain, the civil service as Aulic councillor of war, and the army as colonel, and afterwards major-general. He then became lord steward, and having at last succeeded Auersperg as premier, he was the first man in the state as well as at court.

He married in 1653, as his second wife, a sister of the Count Palatine Christian Augustus of Sulzbach, who turned Papist in 1655, and who became the ancestor of the last Elector of Bavaria of the elder line. Lobkowitz was very wealthy. His fortune in 1674, the year of his downfall, was estimated at 12,000,000 ducats, besides which Leopold I. had conferred on him the place of lord-lieutenant (*Landhauptmann*) of Silesia, which was worth 200,000 dollars.

Lobkowitz, a man of stately presence and fond of magnificence and display, was of exceedingly agreeable and obliging manners, always good-humoured, generous, and open-handed. He was, like Prince Kaunitz after him, a partisan of the French alliance, and succeeded in actually bringing about, in 1671, a secret treaty with France. But he was opposed by the compact phalanx of the whole Spanish-Austrian party, headed by the generals, especially Montecuculi. Lobkowitz wished to introduce the language and manners of France into Austria. He very justly calculated that "as they did not know how to make head against the great captains of Louis XIV., one ought at least to understand how to keep the peace with them." This same opinion was about that very time set forth by the celebrated Leibnitz in his " German Patriotic Alliance " (*Deutschgesinnte Allianz*), in which he endeavours to show that " the best means of keeping France within bounds was that the people about the Rhine, her nearest neighbours, should maintain friendship with her." This was the fundamental idea of the " Rhenish Alliance"—the Confederation of the Rhine of the seventeenth century—which the Elector of Mayence, Count John Philip Schönborn, then established. Leibnitz, who, before going to Hanover, had been in the service of that spiritual potentate, saw very clearly the danger *which even at that time began to threaten from the opposite quarter—from Russia*. Endowed with the keenest penetration, which made him equally distinguished as a politician and as a philosopher, Leibnitz—in the celebrated pamphlet which, after the resignation of the last King of Poland of the house of Vasa, he published in 1668, under the pseudonym of Georgius Ulicofius Litthuanus —laid his warning finger on that most important point, which to this day is fraught with the greatest danger to Austria.

Spanish haughtiness and Spanish oppression and obscurantism were alike repugnant to the spirit and temper of Lobkowitz. He was fond of pleasure, and a master of the art of enjoying it such as Vienna had never seen before; but unfortunately he was also a slave fettered by those chains of roses which he forged for himself—women and money-brokers were said to have had the key to all his secrets. Lobkowitz possessed neither virtue nor greatness; but he possessed much gentleness of disposition and a refined taste, which gave him the superiority over all his countrymen. His jovial, easy humour imparted to his conversation a singularly fascinating charm; the Emperor, who, notwithstanding his own gravity and pompousness, was particularly fond of the society of merry people and merry ministers, was never happy without him. He was full of animal spirits and liveliness, teeming with wit, and always ready with some pretty *bon-mot* or other. A happy knack of intrigue, by means of which he understood how " to push affairs," served him instead of a confirmed habit of business and industry. His keen wit turned everything and everybody into ridicule, not even sparing the Emperor, of whom, with a frankness bordering on the most thoughtless indiscretion, he one day said to the Marquis de Gremonville, the French ambassador, "The Emperor is not like your king, who does everything himself, but like a statue which is carried about and placed or moved at convenience." This jaunty recklessness of Lobkowitz made the clever Samuel Puffendorf say of him that there had been in his conduct "*aliquid ab insania parum abiens.*"

As long as Leopold's first Empress, the Spanish Margareta Theresa, lived, Lobkowitz was all-powerful. But when, half a year after her death, the Emperor married the Tyrolese Princess Claudia (15th of October, 1673), a formidable adversary arose for the premier. Being a woman of most energetic and lively spirit, Claudia soon gained an extraordinary influence over her husband, which she made the world feel in a manner that could not be mistaken. Her contemporaries describe her as an heroic lady of great intellect, conversant with many languages, religious, liberal, compassionate to the poor, and "of most gentle speech and expression of face." Had not death carried her off at the early age of twenty-two, after a married life of only two years and a half, great things might have been expected of her. Lobkowitz had incurred her personal dislike by the opinion which he gave the Emperor on her portrait when Leopold was about to make his choice of a second wife. Lobkowitz would have given the preference to the Princess Eleonora of Neuburg, the same whom Leopold afterwards married as his third wife. Auersperg, the old enemy of Lobkowitz, had informed the Empress Claudia of that circumstance. Lobkowitz was also accused of having indiscreetly divulged the slight doubts which the Emperor in strictest confidence had hinted concerning Claudia's chastity before marriage; and especially of having made some most offensive remarks, alluding to the love of Claudia in her youth for Count Ferraris of Innsbruck.

This new enemy leagued herself with Lobkowitz's old adversaries the Jesuits. All the artillery of the keen wit of the prince was directed against the reverend fathers of the Society of Jesus, whom he most unmercifully lashed, not only in all kinds of scurrilous pamphlets, but also in caricatures. The Emperor's treasury was constantly at the very lowest ebb; but whilst the troops, kept for months without their pay, often plundered their own master's provinces, Leopold lavished his bounties on the Jesuits with unsparing hand. Lobkowitz in several instances prevented these foolish gifts, and even had the courage to annul one of the most important by tearing in shreds the title deed which would have conferred on the order the whole of the rich county of Glatz in Silesia. When the Jesuits came to Lobkowitz to fetch the deed, he pointed to a crucifix, and interpreted to them the usual legend on the label at the top, J. N. R. J. (Jesus Nazarenus, Rex Judæorum), in the following manner, *Jam nihil reportabunt Jesuitæ*.[1] Even his last will, which was executed in all legal form and publicly read, bore witness to the sarcastic humour with which he loved to lash the "Spanish priests." The introduction was couched in terms of the most piteous and humble contrition. After which he proceeded to bestow on the reverend fathers, as a token of the love which he always bore to them, and for the gladdening of their hearts, 80,000 ———. Here the page ended. When the reader turned the leaf he found, " board-nails for a new building."

Lobkowitz, the magnificent, liberal, eloquent, and everjovial minister, was always a great favourite with the people; even with the Hungarians, who were generally so ready to grumble. Yet he was like one walking in his sleep on the brink of a precipice; and misfortune suddenly broke in upon him. Just one year after the second marriage of the Emperor, on the 17th of October, 1674, Lobkowitz was driving at his usual hour, ten o'clock in the morning, to his audience with the Emperor, when he was arrested by General Prince Pio, the captain of the bodyguard of halberdiers. Pio announced to him at once that it was by special order of the Emperor. Lobkowitz found himself unceremoniously deprived of all his dignities and honours. When, with very natural astonishment, he demanded the cause of this extraordinary treatment, his question was met by the strict command of the Emperor

[1] Now the Jesuits shall carry back nothing.

under pain of death not to inquire. On the very evening before this piece of Oriental justice was enacted, Lobkowitz had been at court and been received with every mark of favour. From the minutes of Prince Schwartzenberg's diary on this affair, which, according to the historian Count Mailath, is still extant in the Schwartzenberg archives at Vienna, the crimes imputed to Lobkowitz were " disclosure of secrets, the alienating of the princes from the Emperor, and the thwarting of imperial decrees," and that " for the exalting of France and lowering of the Emperor."

The affair created an immense sensation, not only in Germany, but also at all the European courts. The imperial order was to the effect " that Lobkowitz, being *dismissed* from his offices and honours, should leave, within three days, the court and the imperial capital, and betake himself to his estate of Raudnitz in Bohemia, where he was to remain in exile without ever absenting himself or corresponding with anyone. The cause of all this he should never ask to know; if he dared to disobey, he should forfeit his life and all his property."

After having received this order, Lobkowitz went to his familiar friend Emeric Sinelli, the father guardian of the Capuchins,[1] with whom he took a solitary dinner. At the expiration of the three days he was, early in the morning, conducted from Vienna across the bridge of the Danube in an open carriage, under the escort of three troops of dragoons, as a spectacle to the astonished crowd. He was conveyed to his castle of Raudnitz. Count Martinitz, the chief burgrave, received strict orders to make arrangements for his being closely watched, and not to allow any letter or book or visitor to reach him. Yet the fallen minister was soon after forgotten altogether. Even in the midst of this sudden reverse of fortune, the jovial spirits of Lobkowitz never failed him. He had, at Raudnitz, a hall erected, one half with princely splendour, and the other half as a miserable hovel. In one half he lived and occupied himself as behoved his former splendid station, in the other as was suited to his deep fall; and on all the walls he wrote ridiculous or scandalous

---

[1] Sinelli was a Hungarian, and became, in 1680, Bishop of Vienna; in 1682 a privy councillor of the " Conference Council." He died in 1685.

anecdotes of the lives of his enemies. He died on the 22nd of April, 1677, at the age of sixty-nine, having received, after the death of the Empress Claudia, for his solace, some marks of favour from the Emperor, and the assurance that he had not deserved any punishment. His two private secretaries, the German one as well as the crafty Italian Mattioli,[1] a Florentine, were likewise arrested, as it was intended to force from them some confession concerning the correspondence of the Prince with France, and the money received from thence. Mattioli afterwards fled from the fortress of Raab to France, and became one of the most active emissaries of Louis XIV. with the Signory of Venice and with the Sublime Porte. The wife of Lobkowitz, a princess of Sulzbach, survived him by five years, and died in 1682 at Nuremberg.

In the same year that Lobkowitz fell into disgrace (1674), the Spanish party, and in its train the Jesuits, were again placed at the helm of affairs. The first war of Austria with France had already broken out, contrary to all that Lobkowitz wished and intended. For a period of eighty years, from the time of the downfall of Prince Lobkowitz until the times of Prince Kaunitz, no premier in Austria was able to rule with absolute power. Nor was the post of prime minister ever again combined with that of lord steward, as had been the case under Lobkowitz, and under his three predecessors, Auersperg, Portia, and Trautmannsdorf. The great families of the aristocracy thenceforth shared the power among themselves, with the aid of some bourgeois "red-tapists," upstarts, and converts.

A short time before the dismissal of Prince Auersperg, in 1670, the Emperor Leopold, after the example of Ferdinand II., had established the so-called "Conference Council." It consisted of a few confidential persons, with whom the most secret affairs of state were discussed and settled.

The first man at the court of Vienna, after the fall of Lobkowitz, was the Italian Count Raimondo Montecuculi, who, after a long interval, had gained the first victory over the Turks. The Emperor raised him, in 1662, to the dignity of a prince of the Empire. Montecuculi, born in 1608, was a

---

[1] Mailath calls him Perri

native of Modena. He was called from Italy by his cousin Ernest Montecuculi, a general-field-marshal in the Austrian service. He had, however, laid an excellent foundation of scientific military knowledge in Italy, and continued his studies when the Swedes, under Baner, kept him for two years a prisoner at Stettin. After the death of Prince Ottavio Piccolomini in 1656, he was appointed colonel of his regiment of cuirassiers; he rose, in 1664, to the rank of general-field-marshal and governor of Raab, and in 1668 became generalissimo of the imperial armies and president of the Aulic Council of War. In the last year he also received the order of the Golden Fleece. According to the statement of the Italian tourist Abbé Pacichelli, he had a yearly revenue of sixty thousand florins; and each campaign, the abbé adds, might yield him one hundred and fifty thousand florins. In 1664, with the aid of a body of auxiliaries of Louis XIV., he utterly routed the Turks near St. Gotthardt which was the first glimmer of success for the Christian arms for a period of two hundred years, since the days of the great Hungarian king, Matthias Corvinus. After this a truce was concluded at Vasvar for twenty years, the end of which, marked by the great siege of Vienna by the Turks, Montecuculi did not live to see. He died on the 16th of October, 1680, at Linz, whither he had accompanied the Emperor on account of the plague. Twice before, in the same town, he had had a narrow escape from death. Once he was all but drowned; and another time, riding by the Emperor's side under the gateway of the castle, he was very nearly crushed by some falling timber.

Montecuculi was of a cold and thoroughly unsympathising character, unaccommodating, censorious, and always grumbling, full of intrigue, and utterly unscrupulous, but of very keen penetration, and of a well-disciplined intellect, and such a cautious, circumspect, deliberate general that he was called "*Centum Oculi*"—a master of marches and castrametation. Deeply versed in military science, he has earned fame also as an author by his " Memorie della Guerra," in which he bitterly complains of his enemies Gonzaga and Portia, especially of the latter, without however mentioning him by name. Montecuculi was of middle stature and of a spare figure; his complexion and the expression of his features markedly Italian; the fire of his dark eyes was toned down by the blandness and sedateness of his manner. His mode of life was very simple. He was alike averse to riotous amusements and to etiquette. His temperament was decidedly melancholy. In his old age he suffered severely from *hæmorrhoidal complaints. Montecuculi, however, was not only a hero in war, and a thoroughly scientific military commander, but likewise a very well-read theologian, philosopher, naturalist, and jurist; in fact, a statesman of universal genius. Pacichelli, during his stay at Vienna, often saw him at his library, where he had many an argument with him. He states that the generalissimo had always about him the great work on theology by P. Gonet, a professor of Bordeaux; the mystic theological writings of the celebrated Englishman, Robert Flood, physician, alchemist, and Rosicrucian, he was able to recite word for word. He was president of the Society of Natural Philosophers. His power of oratory was of the highest order, and supported by his extraordinary memory. He made verses; several sonnets of his have been preserved. He possessed at Vienna an extensive library; his picture gallery, which contained the finest pieces, served at the same time as his domestic chapel; and he had a beautiful garden near his palace. In 1658, at the age of fifty, he married the beautiful sister of Prince Dietrichstein, at that time in her twenty-first year, who bore to him a son and three daughters. The son became privy councillor, a field-marshal, and captain of the guard of halberdiers. The daughters, according to Pacichelli, were the most lively and eccentric persons of the whole court of Vienna. From one of them the still flourishing princely house of Rosenberg is descended. The Princess Montecuculi died of small-pox in 1676, two years before her husband.

The first man in the Emperor's council was, after Montecuculi, Count George Louis von Sinzendorf. He was a scion of the younger branch of that house to which the well-known bishop of the Moravian brethren belonged.[1] He began his

[1] The branch of the Bishop of Herrnhut spelled their name Zinzendorf. Both branches became extinct in the beginning of the present century.

career as chamberlain to Ferdinand III. and as a councillor of the Aulic chamber. In 1653 Sinzendorf, who had been steadily progressing on the way to offices and honours, became a convert to Popery. At the accession of Leopold, in 1657, he was raised to the important post of president of the Aulic chamber (lord treasurer); besides which the Emperor conferred upon him the government of the Tyrol, which in 1666 reverted to the crown.

When Sinzendorf, a younger son of a younger branch, was appointed president, his private fortune amounted to not more than 20,000 rix-thalers, but afterwards it increased so vastly that he is said to have paid 60,000 thalers for a set of pearls for his second wife, who, it is true, was of princely birth. Duchess Dorothea Elizabeth of Holstein-Sonderburg-Wiesenburg sprang from an ancient house, which was, however, much impoverished by the division of the family property. She was likewise a convert to Popery, and became, at the age of sixteen, in 1671, the second wife of the president; his first wife having been a Protestant of the zealously Lutheran family of the Jörgers.

According to old custom, Sinzendorf, through whose hands all the revenue of the State passed, *enjoyed the privilege of rendering no account of the public expenditure.* "The Austrian lords," Esaias von Puffendorf says, "have long since deluded their sovereigns into the belief that the care of the financial concerns *was derogatory to their imperial dignity and grandeur, and, besides, was very harassing and burdensome; and that, therefore, the sovereign should leave these affairs completely and absolutely to those whose business they were; that, in short, in these matters they ought to see with the eyes of others.*" Protected by this most exceptional of all privileges, Sinzendorf took good care, whilst working for the imperial finances, to work at the same time for himself: he bought estates and lordships one after the other. Yet this was only one of his ways of accumulating wealth. At one of his estates at Neuburg he openly and unblushingly carried on the nefarious trade of manufacturing counterfeit money. Buying good Bavarian groats by thousands, he re-issued them as bad five-groat pieces. It was of no avail that the Bavarian government complained, Sinzendorf went on with his precious trade just the same. Nay, the president went so far in his effrontery as to set up before his mint of counterfeit coin at Neuburg the stone statue of the Virgin, which, before exchanging it for a bronze one, the Jesuits had had in front of the college of their order at Vienna. There was in fact no kind of industrial speculation in which the president would not engage; and in all of them he either cheated and then persecuted his partners, or allowed them for their benefit and his to cheat the shareholders and the public. He was on particularly good terms with the Jews, who, since the days of Ferdinand II., had become the favourite money-brokers of the house of Austria, and yet, in 1670, in consequence of some riots of the populace against them, had been removed from Vienna. The president soon relaxed this prohibition, and in 1675 some rich Israelites from Amsterdam came to Vienna, and remained several days concealed in Sinzendorf's garden. They were said to have offered, as the price of their re-admission, to raise ten regiments of horse and foot, and also to maintain them for a certain time.

Of all these fraudulent practices of the president, the Emperor Leopold neither saw nor heard anything; and Sinzendorf continued to enjoy the highest favour with his Majesty. Things went on smoothly and brilliantly until 1679, the year of the peace of Nimeguen. This peace, as is well known, was concluded in spite of the protest of the Emperor's faithful ally, Brandenburg, which the court of Vienna then, for the first time, perfidiously left in the lurch; and the sole reason of its being hurried on in such an extraordinary manner was that the gentlemen in Vienna wished the public money to be tied up no longer by the expenses of the war. This was especially manifest when, immediately after the conclusion of the peace, the army was reduced to such an extent that, as the "Frankfort Relations" expresses it, "many persons learned in war (Montecuculi, &c.) were greatly astonished at it." The old practised veterans were discharged, and the consequences were most signal; war being then threatened by the Turks, and also by Brandenburg, on account of its claims to the Silesian principalities. France, moreover, annexed in 1680, one year after that untoward peace, the whole of Alsace; and in 1681 even took Strassburg, the key of Southern Germany. The discontent, which now became too loud, at last led to Sinzendorf's downfall.

The crash which, however recklessly he was going on, he had so long warded off, came from Bohemia. A former attempt to bring him to account for his dealings as president of the chamber (treasury) of that country had been foiled by Lobkowitz, who at that time was still prime minister. Sinzendorf had suggested to Lobkowitz the way in which he might revive an old claim of his family to a sum of not less than 200,000 florins. Lobkowitz entered into it, took the steps which were pointed out, and the treasury paid the money over to him. This happened in 1672. In 1679 the imperial court had fled, on account of the plague, from Vienna to Pesth, and Sinzendorf was staying there with the Emperor, when suddenly he was suspended. A commission for his trial was appointed, before which, notwithstanding his pleading the privilege of not having to render any account, he was arraigned and condemned. Sentence was passed on the 19th of June, 1680, and published on the 9th of October at nine in the morning, in the presence of a great mass of people admitted for the purpose, at the house of Count Nostitz, the chairman of the commission: he was condemned to perpetual imprisonment and to the confiscation of all his estates.

The evidence against Sinzendorf proved a defalcation amounting to nearly twenty tuns of gold. The crimes laid to his charge comprised perjury, theft, and fraud. His wife, the duchess, having three times implored mercy for him on her knees before the Emperor, some of his estates were restored, in order that he might live in retirement in one of his châteaux, in a manner suitable to his rank. Yet scarcely a year had passed after his conviction, ere he succeeded in procuring an imperial "*absolutorium*," by virtue of which he was relieved from all further claims of the treasury against him, and *fully acquitted*. A residuary claim of 1,940,000 florins was remitted him, and he was allowed to take up his residence where he liked in the imperial hereditary possessions, even in the capital itself. There he died on the 14th of December, 1681, having nearly completed his sixty-sixth year. He is said to have left in his will, to his wife 400,000 florins, and to each of his children (a son and two daughters), 100,000 florins.

Four years previous to the downfall of Lobkowitz, in 1670, the privy councillor Count John Adolphus Schwartzenberg had been raised to the post of president of the Imperial Aulic Council. His father Count Adam Schwartzenberg was that minister of the Elector of Brandenburg who in the Thirty Years' War did the Emperor such signal service. Count John Adolphus, owing to the liberality of that Archduke Leopold William who held so many church benefices, had, during the minority of Leopold II., become one of the richest noblemen at the Austrian court. The archduke had given him, in particular, from the Bohemian crown domains, the large estate of Wittingau, near Budweis, whose celebrated fish-ponds, which furnish the market of Vienna with that noted dainty, Bohemian carp, have been a rich source of revenue to the Princes Schwartzenberg. He had in 1644 married a Countess Starhemberg, and had been the archduke's lord steward ever since 1646. After the death of the Emperor Ferdinand III., Schwartzenberg had suggested to the archduke to become a rival candidate of his nephew Leopold for the imperial crown of Germany, and, moreover, to throw up the government of the Netherlands—for which reason he was neither popular with Leopold nor with the Spaniards. Yet, notwithstanding this unfavourable disposition against him, he maintained himself in a brilliant, although not the very first position at court. He was a thorough Austrian aristocrat, one of the very best specimens of his class; and Leopold, who was forced to respect him, even raised him in 1671 to the rank of a prince of the Empire.

Schwartzenberg kept one of the best houses in Vienna; but he was such a good manager as to be able, regularly every year, to lay by part of his revenue. With these savings he purchased a number of estates, especially in Bohemia, from which country his family originally came.

Their real name was Czernahora; and only as late as during the Hussite wars they had emigrated to Franconia, where they purchased the countship of Schwartzenberg.

Prince John Adolphus was a gentleman of very stately presence and of good address, and moreover a man of great resolution and courage. In the year of the plague (1679), when so many cavaliers fled from Vienna, he remained and exerted himself in a most praiseworthy manner for the people. But he was very difficult to deal with in the way of business. Puffendorf states that people use to call him "doctorem perplexiatum et dubitatorem perpetuum." He died suddenly in 1683, at the age of sixty-eight, whilst paying a visit to Father Sauter, the confessor of the Empress, at Laxenburg; having just before attended a sitting of the privy council.

Besides these noble lords, an upstart "red-tapist," John Paul Baron Hocher, the first Aulic chancellor—a man who had risen from the rank of a common lawyer to that of minister—exercised the greatest influence at court. He was one of the most unblushing tools of that absolutism which, having been first hatched during the Thirty Years' War, has been established principally by him on a quasi-lawful basis, after the pattern of the sophistry which served in lieu of law at the court of the Byzantine rulers. Being a faithful ally of the Jesuits, and consequently a friend of the Spaniards, and being moreover deep in the confidence of the Empress Claudia, he became one of the principal agents in the ruin of Lobkowitz. A most obscene and scurrilous epigram, casting on the Empress the imputations alluded to before, and which was said to have been found among the papers of the fallen premier, was very likely manufactured by Hocher himself.

Hocher, this "hard-boiled" minister, died in his sixty-seventh year at Vienna, on the 1st of March, 1683. He left a fortune of more than 1,000,000 florins, a sum quite fabulous for those times and for a man of his extraction and position. He had no male heir.

Among the most influential men of the last period of Leopold's reign, we must not omit the Jesuit Father Wolff. His real name was Baron von Lüdingshausen. He was a native of Westphalia, actual privy councillor, and employed in many secret diplomatic commissions in war and peace. To the Emperor he was particularly welcome, owing to his most agreeable conversation. He was, with Prince Eugene, the principal adviser of the war of the Spanish succession, and he it was *who procured the royal dignity for Prussia*. In the interest of his order he tried to win the favour not only of the new Prussian King, but also of the Russian Czar Peter the Great, when the latter câme on a visit to Vienna.

3.—Wedding festivities at the marriage of Leopold I. with the Spanish Infanta, 1666—The great equestrian ballet during the carnival of 1667.

In 1666 Leopold I. celebrated his marriage with his first wife, the Spanish Infanta, the negotiations concerning which had been carried on for some time. He was at that time in his twenty-seventh year; the Infanta Margareta Theresa had not yet completed her sixteenth.

The Infanta, having embarked at Barcelona, landed at Finale, near Genoa, on the 20th of August, 1666. She was accompanied by her lord steward, the Duke of Albuquerque, and by Cardinal Colonna. Here she was received by the governor of Milan, Don Vincent Gonzaga; and by Count Montecuculi, who had been sent by the imperial court to meet her, and who presented to her a jewel from the Emperor. The journey from thence to Vienna was performed with the greatest ease; it lasted more than three months. The Infanta proceeded by Milan, where she arrived on the 11th of September; and by Brescia—where the republic of Venice complimented her by an envoy-extraordinary, and caused her to be entertained in the most costly manner two days—along the Adige, to Roveredo. At this place she was to change her household; her new lord steward being Prince Ferdinand of Dietrichstein. The Duke of Albuquerque kissed hands on taking leave, on the 19th of October, and had on the same evening to return with the whole of the Spanish suite to the next village. The young Count Lamberg, as newly appointed chamberlain of the Infanta, states, among other things, that at the exchange the Duke of Albuquerque had, according to custom, received from the plate of the imperial bride "several small silver chairs and tables, forty dozen dishes, seventy dozen plates, and all her other table service."[1] Lamberg, at the next fête of the Emperor, on the 15th of November, brought to the Emperor, as a present from the future Empress, a diamond ring, valued at 150,000 florins, and a chess-board and men of gold studded with diamonds, of the value of 6,000 ducats. The Emperor, on the 26th of November, surprised the Infanta at Schottwien, where he at once made his appearance, and made himself known, whilst the cavaliers were admitted to the princess to kiss hands. When he took leave, his royal bride presented him with a band for his hat, with a precious jewel appended worth upwards of 12,000 rix-thalers; "but, as it had not been properly fixed, and his Majesty had ridden back in great haste to Neustadt and repeatedly doffed his hat, it was lost on the road, but found again by a butcher, and returned, with, however, three stones missing, to his Majesty on the following day, when he came back to Vienna; at which recovery his Imperial Majesty was not a little rejoiced."

The entry of the Infanta into Vienna took place on the 5th of December with a pomp which afforded to the court historians of the time a most fruitful theme for gorgeous details. In an old woodcut, Leopold appears in a Spanish mantle and plumed hat, wearing a flowing wig *à la Fontange*, with collar and frill of point lace *à la Van Dyke*, and moustache and beard on the chin *à la Henry IV*. His Roman Imperial Majesty is riding under a canopy carried by some of the principal burghers of Vienna.

Her Imperial Majesty the bride rode "in a golden carriage made in the most costly and cunning fashion." It cost nearly 100,000 rix-thalers (about £15,000 sterling), and, like all the state carriages of that period, was very long, and covered with a roof similar to a pavilion. It was drawn by six horses; the Infanta sitting far back, and opposite to her, in front, her first lady of the bedchamber. The horses deserve particular notice; they were six cream-coloured steeds, with long white

---

[1] The Duke, being afterwards sent as viceroy to Sicily, lost in a storm two plate-chests containing from seven to eight hundredweight of silver.

manes—a present from Count Antony of Oldenburg, whose stud of more than 1,500 horses was celebrated all over Europe.

This magnificent procession took three hours in passing through the illuminated city to the church of the Augustines; there the bridal pair alighted, and, after praying in the chapel of St. Maria of Loretto, they went to the high altar, where Cardinal Count Harrach, the papal nuncio, attended by all the prelates present in the city, pronounced the nuptial benediction, the ceremony having been previously performed by proxy at Madrid. The imperial bride and bridegroom then sat down, at nine o'clock in the evening, to supper, with the empress-dowager and the two imperial princesses, in the large hall of the imperial palace; remaining until one o'clock, when all retired to rest.

Of the festivities in honour of the wedding, particular mention is due to some magnificent fireworks, accompanied by a grand mythologico-symbolic representation on the Bastion (*Bastei*), near the imperial palace, the Hofburg. The programme of this most remarkable pageant is given in the "Frankfort Relations." On the large flat plain where the exhibition took place, two artificial mountains sixty feet high were raised; on the left, Etna, the forge of Vulcan, the artificer of the weapons of war; on the right, Parnassus, with the nine Muses, all of them in flowing wigs and hoop petticoats, with the winged Pegasus at the summit. Between these two mountains, Etna and Parnassus, was the scaffolding for the fireworks; in the background a temple surmounted by the imperial eagle.

"Introduction. Scene 1.—Enter Mercury, with the nuptial torch, to announce to the world the blaze of triumph kindled on Mount Olympus at the wedding of the Emperor of the Romans. The Emperor himself from a window of the palace lights this nuptial torch; whereupon five hundred rising fires symbolically represent 'the universal blaze of triumph of the whole world.'

"Scene 2.—In token of the whole world's really being one blaze of triumph, thirty guns of large and small calibre are fired from the nearest bastions, and the trumpets and kettledrums sound from all the orchestras." These thirty salutes were the signal for the beginning of the actual fireworks, which had three acts of three scenes each.

"Act I. Scene 1.—Mount Etna is kindling. One sees the threefold hell of Vulcan, who, with his assistants, is forging arms.

"Scene 2.—Cupid flies through the air into the forge, expels its inmates, breaks the weapons, and then hammers out the golden wedding-ring. Having finished his task, he carries it through the air to heaven, there to deposit it in the treasury of perpetual bliss.

"Scene 3.—The double-peaked Mount Parnassus appears blazing in flames of joy. The nine goddesses make sweet music to attest their approval of the act performed by Cupid. The whole mountain is then lit up with bonfires amidst the sound of trumpets and kettledrums.

"Act II. Scene 1.—On the space between the two mountains two gateways are seen, each surmounted by a heart with the letters L. and M. (Leopold and Margareta). The god Hymen lights them in pure white flames.

"Scene 2.—Centaurs with burning torches come from Mount Etna; Hercules, at the command of Jupiter, makes head against them, and drives them in brave pursuit from the field.

"Scene 3.—On the right is seen the archducal house of Austria as a strong tower; on the left the Spanish castle, in allusion to the arms of Spain. From each of these large towers, surmounted by the letters V. A., V. H. (*Vivat Austria, vivat Hispania*), a thousand rockets rise; and on each side a hundred salutes are fired from small mortars. The fire-balls shot from the mortars explode in the air with several thousand reports, after which the letters V. L., V. M. (*Vivat Leopoldus, vivat Margareta*) are seen. Flourish of trumpets and roll of kettledrums.

"Act III. Scene 1.—In the background of the large space is seen the Temple of Hymen with twenty-seven pillars, and on the roof thirty-nine statues, with thirty-three pyramids of dazzling fire. Jupiter sends his eagle from the clouds to light on the altar of the temple the flames of joy.

"Scene 2.—The Phœnix, consuming himself from love for his young, appears in flames above the temple." As the flames of joy were meant to represent the flames of the most humble offering of submission on the side of the faithful and obedient subjects on the altar of patriotism, so the miraculous bird was to appear as a symbol of the provident care and affection of his Imperial Majesty for his most humble and obedient vassals and subjects.

"Scene 3.—From all the pillars, statues, and pyramids of the Hymeneal Temple there rise 73,000 lights, with at least 300 rockets, each charged with three pounds of powder. The letters A. E. I. O. U. (*Austria erit in omne Ultimum*) float in the air. From the mortars ten large triumphal balls are shot." Some of them had the calibre of 200, and the others of 300 pounds, and made themselves heard in the air with several thousand explosions. Moreover, thirty great rockets rose in the air—ten of the weight of 50 pounds, ten of 100, and ten of 150.

Thirty shots from guns of large calibre marked the conclusion of these most ingenious and costly fireworks; the author of which is said to be Bartholomew Peissker, master of the arsenal of the fortress of Glatz.

The whole winter passed in festivities. The crown of all was the equestrian ballet, which after several rehearsals, was performed, on the 24th of January, 1667, in a wooden building as high as a tower, which had been erected for the purpose in the large space before the Hofburg. The performance lasted from one o'clock to five in the afternoon, and was repeated with some omissions on the 31st of that month. In the first representation the Emperor himself took a part. Thirty cannon-shots, as at the fireworks, were the signal for commencing. The two Empresses witnessed the spectacle from one window, and the two princesses from another in the apartments of the Empress, the windows being surmounted by a canopy of gold brocade, and pieces of gold cloth spread over the sills, and hanging down in front.

The pageant was opened by the Goddess of Fame, dressed in white, standing, with a trumpet in her hand, on the poop of a ship. The vessel was a large Turkish galley, painted red and gilded profusely, with a crew dressed in red with gold lace, in the costume of Turkish galley-slaves. The masts, rigging, and flags were likewise red. A band of music was playing on the deck, and the ship was surrounded by forty Tritons. The Goddess of Fame addressed the Empress in a speech. The ship resting on a kind of truck was drawn for some time round the arena; but the burden being too heavy, the wheels broke, so that at the repetition on the 31st of January, the galley was found to be disabled.

After a flourish of trumpets, the prelude to the equestrian ballet now began. It was a mythologico-symbolic representation, purposing to exhibit the contest of the four Elements "as to which of the four had a better claim to produce *pearls;*" an ingenious allusion to the name of the imperial bride Margareta. The four Elements were represented by four troops, companies, or squadrons, each consisting of a considerable number of persons. There were upwards of a thousand performers engaged in it. The author of the programme received from his grateful Emperor, " for well-devised invention," 20,000 florins, as a reward for his trouble; also a yearly pension of 1,000 florins; besides which he was raised to the rank of a baron.

1. The first company was *the company of Water*, commanded by the Count Palatine of Sulzbach. The persons composing it were dressed in blue and silver, and wore fish-scales and shells on their clothes.

2. The second was *the company of Earth*, commanded by the master of the horse, Dietrichstein. Their clothes of green and silver were sprinkled with roses and other flowers.

3. The third, *the company of Air*, commanded by the Duke of Lorraine, had clothes of gold brocade shaded with "the colour of Aurora," and trimmed with those of the rainbow.

4. *The company of Fire* was to have been commanded by Montecuculi; but, owing to his being indisposed, his place was taken by some one else. The persons belonging to it wore dresses of red and silver, decorated with flames.

The procession was headed by the horsemen of the Water Squadron; behind them, on a huge car, was a colossal whale, spouting a considerable volume of the watery element from his mouth and nostrils. On his back rode Neptune with his trident. He was surrounded by all kinds of marine monsters holding fireworks in their hands, together with tridents, and a chorus of thirty persons personating the " Winds," who, like Neptune, held tridents.

Then followed the squadron of Earth, and behind it, on another large car, two huge elephants carrying on their backs castles on which the Earth rested. The car itself represented a garden in which the sylvan god Pan was sitting with his herdsmen, who carried on their shoulders large clubs, which were afterwards to be burned to illuminate the vast building. Besides a host of those mythical characters which are said to dwell in the earth, there was on the car a singer, who for some time sang in Italian the praises of the Empress.

After this followed the cavalcade of the squadron of Air, and behind them, on a car, the Air riding on a terrible dragon, and surrounded by a flock of all sorts of birds and by thirty griffins which, being covered with gold cloth, carried in their paws burning fires. Over the car there was a rainbow, on which sat another singer, likewise singing in Italian the praises of the Empress.

The rear was brought up by the cavalcade of the Fire squadron, with silver hammers, escorting a machine with a colossal flame of fire, and in the midst of it the imperishable salamander, from the mouth of which the prettiest fireworks were issuing. This squadron was joined by the car of Etna, spouting fire, and on it the god Vulcan, likewise with a silver hammer, and dressed in a flesh-coloured and black suit. There were walking by his side thirty Cyclops with silver hammers, and a bevy of small Cupids.

The different divisions having carried on a smart dispute, another tremendous flourish of trumpets with kettledrums resounded, and the challenge was given. The theatre then changed into a ship in which the Argonauts sat, with a golden fleece by the side of an imperial crown; and, whilst a brisk contest was being carried on for this rich prize, the sky was illuminated, and a small cloud arose which gradually expanded in the horizon.

As soon as the cloud had separated there appeared in sight

a large star-spangled globe, and over it Immortality sitting on a rainbow as an emblem of peace. The genius bade the cavaliers not to fight, intimating to them that there was no need to wrest from the elements the two guerdons of the Fleece and of the Crown, as they had from the beginning of time been destined for the house of Austria. The globe then opened and displayed the Temple of Immortality, with the figures of the fifteen deceased Emperors of the house of Austria, all of them mounted on stately horses and arrayed in gorgeous robes. These figures approached the temple preceding the car of Glory, which was in the shape of a silver shell, with a magnificent colossal pearl lying in it. The shell besides exhibited the portrait of the Empress, and carried the figure of the Emperor Leopold as the sixteenth Cæsar of the house of Austria. This car was followed by three others with captive Indians, Tartars, and Moors.

The stage being cleared of all the cars, the equestrian ballet began. It was likewise divided into four troops, consisting each of eight cavaliers riding together in pairs; between every two pairs a file of twelve attendant squires. The cavaliers of all the four troops had boots of silvered leather; those of the Emperor alone were gilt. They now began the contest, each for his element, with pistols and swords.

The scene then changed again into a sky of clouds over a triumphal arch. High in the air an angel sang a sweet song; six cavaliers came forth in wide-flowing robes trimmed with silver point-lace and diamonds, and carrying silver arrows in their hands. They were followed by the Emperor himself, surrounded by a host of pages clothed in gold stuffs. The Emperor was dressed like those six cavaliers, only that he wore on his dress deeper point-lace and a larger crown on his helmet. Twelve cavaliers dressed in suits of white point-lace followed behind the Emperor. Then came a triumphal car, which was drawn by eight snow-white horses, and on which seven singers were sitting in robes studded all over with precious stones. Having made the round once the car stopped before the Empress, and the singers performed most delightful music.

The triumphal car being removed in its turn, the Emperor concluded the ballet. From the cautious expressions of the courtly accounts, it seems likely that a little accident happened to his Majesty; in fact, that he fell from his horse. The conclusion was again marked by the discharge of thirty guns.

The expenses of this pageant were said to have amounted to 90,000 florins; an enormous sum for those times. To the items of the expenditure for the gaieties of the carnival may be added, that at the different festivities plate was purloined to the value of 9,000 florins.

The Jews of Vienna showed their loyalty by presenting the Empress with a beautiful piece of plate with a pretty silver infant on it, the whole weighing about fourteen pounds. This silver baby became the happy omen of an auspicious event, which happened on the 28th of September, 1667; on which day, in the morning between seven and eight, the Empress was delivered of a son. Count Lamberg, the lord chamberlain, brought the first news of it to the Emperor, who rewarded the messenger with 15,000 florins. On the following day, the Feast of St. Michael, the christening was performed in the hall of the new Hofburg. The prince received the names Ferdinand Wenceslaus Leopold Joseph Michael Elzearius; the sponsors being the King of Spain and the Empress Dowager, the Emperor himself standing proxy for the king. The royal infant, however, was not destined to enjoy a long life. He died on the 3rd of January, 1668.

END OF VOL. I

www.ingramcontent.com/pod-product-compliance
Lightning Source LLC
Chambersburg PA
CBHW022111300426
44117CB00007B/670